Notable British Trials Series No. 89

TRIAL OF

# HENRY HUNT AND OTHERS

## THE PETERLOO MASSACRE

EDITED BY

Caitlin Kitchener

First edition published 2020

Copyright © Caitlin Kitchener, 2020

The right of Caitlin Kitchener to be identified as the author of this work has been asserted in accordance with the Copyright, Designs & Patents Act 1988.

All rights reserved. No part of this book may be reprinted or reproduced or utilised in any form or by any electronic, mechanical or other means, now known or hereafter invented, including photocopying and recording, or in any information storage or retrieval system, without the prior permission in writing of the publishers.

ISBN: 978-1-911273-98-1 (hardback)
ISBN: 978-1-914277-14-6 (softcover)

Notable British Trials imprint ©William Hodge & Company (Holdings) Ltd
Used with kind permission.

General Editors:
David Green - M.W. Oldridge - Adam Wood

Published by Mango Books
www.MangoBooks.co.uk
18 Soho Square
London W1D 3QL

Notable British Trials Series No. 89

TRIAL OF

# HENRY HUNT AND OTHERS
## THE PETERLOO MASSACRE

EDITED BY

Caitlin Kitchener

Henry Hunt

# CONTENTS.

Preface by Clive Bloom . . . . . . . . . . . . . . . . . . . . . . . . . . . . . . . . . . . . . . . . . . . .i
Introduction . . . . . . . . . . . . . . . . . . . . . . . . . . . . . . . . . . . . . . . . . . . . . . . . . . . 1
Leading Dates. . . . . . . . . . . . . . . . . . . . . . . . . . . . . . . . . . . . . . . . . . . . . . . . 43

THE TRIAL —

    FIRST DAY — THURSDAY 16 MARCH 1820.

| | |
|---|---|
| Opening Speech for the Prosecution. . . . . . . 48 | James Standering . . . . . . . . . . . . . . . . . . . . . 70 |
| Thomas Fidler. . . . . . . . . . . . . . . . . . . . . . . 61 | John Chadwick. . . . . . . . . . . . . . . . . . . . . . . 70 |
| Henry Lomas . . . . . . . . . . . . . . . . . . . . . . . 62 | James Murray. . . . . . . . . . . . . . . . . . . . . . . . 74 |
| Michael Bentley . . . . . . . . . . . . . . . . . . . . . 65 | John Shawcross . . . . . . . . . . . . . . . . . . . . . . 77 |
| Mary Cadman. . . . . . . . . . . . . . . . . . . . . . . 66 | John Heywood . . . . . . . . . . . . . . . . . . . . . . .78 |
| Samuel Morton. . . . . . . . . . . . . . . . . . . . . . 67 | |

    SECOND DAY — FRIDAY 17 MARCH 1820.

| | |
|---|---|
| William Morris. . . . . . . . . . . . . . . . . . . . . . .75 | Roger Entwistle . . . . . . . . . . . . . . . . . . . . . . 90 |
| John Eaton . . . . . . . . . . . . . . . . . . . . . . . . . 83 | Francis Philips . . . . . . . . . . . . . . . . . . . . . . . 93 |
| Joseph Travis . . . . . . . . . . . . . . . . . . . . . . . 84 | Rev. Dr Jeremiah Smith . . . . . . . . . . . . . . . 97 |
| John Ashworth . . . . . . . . . . . . . . . . . . . . . . 86 | John Barlow . . . . . . . . . . . . . . . . . . . . . . . . .99 |
| William Standring. . . . . . . . . . . . . . . . . . . . 86 | Thomas Styan. . . . . . . . . . . . . . . . . . . . . . . .99 |
| Jeremiah Fielding . . . . . . . . . . . . . . . . . . . . 87 | Edmond Simpson . . . . . . . . . . . . . . . . . . . 100 |
| James Heath . . . . . . . . . . . . . . . . . . . . . . . 88 | Matthew Cowper . . . . . . . . . . . . . . . . . . . 100 |
| James Duncough. . . . . . . . . . . . . . . . . . . . 88 | |

    THIRD DAY — SATURDAY 18 MARCH 1820.

| | |
|---|---|
| Joseph Mills . . . . . . . . . . . . . . . . . . . . . . . 106 | Joseph Green . . . . . . . . . . . . . . . . . . . . . . 123 |
| Henry Horton . . . . . . . . . . . . . . . . . . . . . . 109 | John Ellis . . . . . . . . . . . . . . . . . . . . . . . . . 125 |
| Jonathan Andrew . . . . . . . . . . . . . . . . . . 119 | William Hulton. . . . . . . . . . . . . . . . . . . . . 126 |
| Thomas Hardman . . . . . . . . . . . . . . . . . . . 121 | |

    FOURTH DAY — MONDAY 20 MARCH 1820.

| | |
|---|---|
| John Walker . . . . . . . . . . . . . . . . . . . . . . . 137 | John Shawcross (recalled) . . . . . . . . . . . . 147 |
| John Willie . . . . . . . . . . . . . . . . . . . . . . . . 143 | Michael Fitzpatrick. . . . . . . . . . . . . . . . . . 148 |
| Joseph Slater. . . . . . . . . . . . . . . . . . . . . . . 145 | |

Opening Speeches for the Defence
Mr Barrow for Moorhouse and Jones ....150
Mr Holt for Saxton....................156
Samuel Bamford......................159

George Swift........................162
Joseph Healey.......................162
Joseph Johnson......................164

## FIFTH DAY — TUESDAY 21 MARCH 1820.

Opening Speeches for the Defence (continued)
Henry Hunt..........................167

Evidence for the Defence
Edmund Grundy.......................195
James Dyson.........................196
John Barlow.........................199

William Kendall.....................201
James Frankland.....................201
John Turner.........................202
Mary Lees...........................202
Elizabeth Sheppard..................203
Mary Yates..........................203

## SIXTH DAY — WEDNESDAY 22 MARCH 1820.

William Elson.......................205
Edmund Newton.......................206
Jacob Dakin.........................207
Lucy Morville.......................208
John Hampshire......................209

John Smith..........................209
James Stott.........................214
John Hampshire (recalled)...........215
John Shuttleworth...................216
John Tyas...........................221

## SEVENTH DAY — THURSDAY 23 MARCH 1820.

John Brettargh......................229
Henry Andrews.......................231
Edward Baines.......................233
Thomas Scofield.....................238
Robert Harrop.......................239
William Nicholson...................240
John Hulley.........................241
Nancy Prestwich.....................242

Robert Wood.........................244
John Rockliffe......................245
Mary Jones..........................246
John Lees...........................246
John Fell...........................247
Mary Bryan..........................247
Joseph Watson.......................248

### EIGHTH DAY — FRIDAY 24 MARCH 1820.

| | | | |
|---|---|---|---|
| Robert Wrgiht | 251 | James Scholefield | 269 |
| Sidney Walker | 254 | Thomas Brooks | 272 |
| William Thelwall | 255 | William Brooks | 273 |
| Robert Grundy | 256 | John Hobson | 273 |
| Thomas Rothwell | 264 | Joseph Barrett | 273 |
| Joseph Schofield | 265 | Jonathan Hobson | 274 |
| Samuel Slack | 265 | William Burns | 275 |
| John Molineux | 266 | John Smith | 275 |
| Isaac Wood | 268 | Thomas William Sanderson | 276 |

### NINTH DAY — SATURDAY 25 MARCH 1820.

| | | | |
|---|---|---|---|
| Edmund Darley | 279 | Rev. Mr. Robert Hindmarsh | 280 |
| William Phillips | 279 | John Robinson | 283 |
| Rev. John Gough Roberts | 280 | Prosecutor's Reply | 284 |
| Michael Heaviside | 280 | Judge's Charge | 304 |

### TENTH DAY — MONDAY 27 MARCH 1820.

| | | | |
|---|---|---|---|
| Judge's Charge (continued) | 313 | The Verdict | 321 |

Appendix I . . . . . . . . . . . . . . . . . . . . . . . . . . . . . . . . . . . . . . . . . . . . . . . . . . 327
Index . . . . . . . . . . . . . . . . . . . . . . . . . . . . . . . . . . . . . . . . . . . . . . . . . . . . . . 331
Notable British Trials Series . . . . . . . . . . . . . . . . . . . . . . . . . . . . . . . . . . . . 341

# PREFACE

CLIVE BLOOM
Professor Emeritus of English and American Studies,
Middlesex University

Any Englishman in the mid-eighteenth century who might have boasted that the British constitution made him the freest individual in the world would hardly have been recognised by the agitators of the early nineteenth century. They were worlds apart, worlds which had been divided by the tide of industrialisation both in factories and on farms, the build-up of new urban populations, the mass vagrancy and unemployment of soldiers returning from the Napoleonic Wars, and a series of poor harvests, as well as the growing belief in the power of entrepreneurial capitalism and the significance of money. The old relationships, between farm tenant and labourer, between independent craftsman and factory hand, were now irreparably eroded as new social groups began to emerge and as an awakened political sense pervaded the life of ordinary working folk now pushed to the margins. The main radical force within the towns was those self-educated craftsmen who were both economically threatened and politically aware. What they knew they needed for economic wellbeing was parliamentary representation and reform: to have their voices heard and acknowledged. They had the will, but they did not yet have the leaders.

They knew they were not free, nor had ever been free, but were oppressed by those above whose blindness to the conditions of the poorer classes could no longer be ignored. A veil had been rent, first by the American Revolution, whose impact could already be felt in the Gordon Riots of 1780, and then by the political agitation that so exercised the minds of the land-owning squirearchy and self-made factory owners after the French Revolution.

From the 1770s to the 1820s, a new breed of disgruntled individual appeared whose own personal disappointments and failures led to a universal understanding of collective need and collective action. Liberty had to be balanced with brotherhood and equality, a fair distribution of wealth and a share in the organisation and running of national affairs. This new breed of political agitator looked back to the theories of seventeenth century radicals such as John Lilburne and forward to the collective and 'scientific' theories of Karl Marx. At the same time, they were usually able only to articulate their frustration at a system they perceived as unfair and incapable of freeing the masses into the world enjoyed by their superiors; taking direct action was more difficult.

These new agitators, brought up in the glow of French patriotism, knew

## Hunt and Others.

what they wanted: the revolutionary conditions of the French Revolution, almost, but not quite, brought to the shores of Britain. They were, however, for the most part neither Jacobinical nor revolutionary. What they wanted was radical reform, full representation, reasonable working hours, food on the table and respect. They waited in vain. And so the long road to enfranchisement began with meetings of respectable men, educated to read, write and argue, who took it upon themselves to debate the state of the country at assignations in rooms above inns, secretly hired on behalf of societies or associations that were themselves proscribed by law. Such knots of men, conversing over their pipes and beer, were also rallying on lonely moors, called to muster by word of mouth, secret sign or chalk marks on walls, and drilling with old weapons, farm instruments or sticks. Would change come through talk or violence?

I have said that Englishmen felt free in the eighteenth century, but the feeling of oppression did not cross borders. The French example had rallied the Irish in 1798 and the Scottish radicals as early as 1794. War in Ireland was matched by dissent at home. Such dissent, in the poisoned atmosphere of the time, was accounted sedition or treason, and it was a brave man indeed who toyed with those accusations. Against those who were brave enough to speak out for liberty and equality was the full weight of a growingly authoritarian and organised alliance of powers, not yet centralised in the 'state' but quite powerful enough to crush opposition. There was the local magistracy, made up of the vested interests of town or country, men whose families had regulated life for generations, themselves backed by the pomp of perambulating court sessions and the majesty of bewigged judges. Such men, however, were impotent without the instruments of rudimentary police forces such as existed in Manchester, where a group of local bully boys were commanded by a famous thug, Joseph Nadin; or, if no constables could be called, the local yeomanry under the command of a landowner to whom they owed their livelihoods, could be mustered and sent to quell the 'mob'. As a last resort, the regular army might be called from barracks as the frustration of the magistrates grew and the information from paid spies became more exaggerated and more earnest. This was, in the North of England, the state of 'war' from 1816 to 1820.

A prelude: since the authorities had been unable to catch Tom Paine, the world's first professional revolutionary, they had been on the lookout for any deviation from traditional views. First the Scots suffered with a series of treason trials around the likes of Thomas Muir, where Lord Justice Clerk Braxfield had intoned from the bench, 'The British Constitution is the best the ever wis since the creation o the warld, and it's no possible tae mak it better.' Such sentiments were no doubt believed by the judges presiding over the trials of Thomas Hardy

# Preface.

and John Horne Tooke. The civil war in Ireland confirmed that no one could be trusted, and Theobald Wolf Tone and Lord Edward Fitzgerald were duly captured, but died before they could stand trial for treason. And so it goes on until the English crisis years leading towards 1820, when debate gave way to conspiracy and Arthur Thistlewood and his little gang were brought to the gallows after their failed assassination attempt on the cabinet. The Cato Street conspirators close the period with their deaths and more temperate men take up the challenge of reform.

Henry Hunt, whose trial is the subject of this book, stands at the centre of this extra-parliamentary world of political demands. His platform was new and reasonable. The authorities would be forced to listen to plain speaking. Secrecy was out and open debate had to replace Jacobinical conspiracy. There was a difficulty, nevertheless. On the one hand, Hunt believed in the power of advocacy; on the other, he saw no clear path to success. He was a populist and a speaker of much conviction who would suffer for his audacity, but he couldn't see that his audacity was not going to be successful.

He had no real theory of radical change, but he had a voice, and, at six foot four, a commanding presence. He would, like so many of his kind, have a meteoric rise, but like those whose fame is at its zenith while alive, leave merely a name behind him, overtaken in fame as the path to reform takes a distinctly different turn and as he himself, losing his nerve through incarceration, turned to less dangerous pre-occupations.

Unlike Robert Owen, he had few followers; unlike William Cobbett, he left no legacy except an autobiography, now sadly neglected; and unlike Feargus O'Connor or Bronterre O'Brien or Daniel O'Connor, he led no organised party of reform. Nevertheless, Hunt's life, work and trial are of lasting interest and historical importance as the exemplar of the political mood of the period.

Hunt was born in Upavon, Wiltshire, in 1777, and took to farming. Nevertheless, he was drawn to radicalism and the belief that there might be another politics not yet espoused by either Whig or Tory. He was part of a rare but growing group of disgruntled independents of the sort unheard of since the English Civil War. His personal concerns were, like those of Paine before and Thistlewood later, universalised as he recognised that his concerns were not merely personal but part of society's malaise, and so projected into politics. It was this same itch that motivated Cobbett and made of Hunt a follower of Francis Burdett.

When he was invited by the Patriotic Union Society of Manchester to address the crowds at St Peter's Field, he already was at the height of his fame and influence. He arrived as a hero in a fine coach, as a country gentleman with

# Hunt and Others.

a slight westcountry accent, and as a man who may have had little understanding of the volatility of the situation into which he had entered and of which he alone would be the central attraction.

After addressing a meeting in London's Spa Fields in 1816, his opponents (perhaps Robert Southey) nicknamed him 'Orator' Hunt and the name stuck as a badge of honour. He was already a darling of the crowd who called him 'Henry the Ninth'. It was he who was the main target of the magistrates, and when he stood to speak he was grabbed by Joseph Nadin. Nadin was six foot two, but yielded two inches to Hunt on his cart. It availed Hunt only momentary respite, as he was unceremoniously hauled off. His trial led to thirty months inside Ilchester prison where he spent his time writing.

Things were moving on. Politics had turned. At the same time, the Great Northern Union was founded and men like Elijah Dixon, who had been at 'Peterloo' (the defining political demonstration of a generation), took political agitation towards greater collectivism and slowly but ultimately towards Owenism and Chartism. Although Hunt participated in these new movements, he was not the great speaker he had been, and he now modified his radicalism and speeches accordingly.

Broke and unanchored, the gentleman reasserted itself in entrepreneurial activity. Hunt tried his hand at producing breakfast 'powder' (a type of hot drink), shoe blacking and even synthetic coal. Hunt was, after all, a product of the capitalist entrepreneurial system he had tried to open up to all with political reform. The difference was, of course, vital, as he only had the opportunity to fail in a system without parliamentary representation. And fail, to a large extent he did. Prison had damaged Hunt psychologically and frightened him politically. He posted political slogans on his packets of cereal, but only disappointed colleagues who had once been allies. He refused to back an armed uprising. He refused to back the Reform Bill as well. Nevertheless, there is heroism in defeat, and Hunt was feted when he returned to Manchester on 19 August 1830. A statue was later erected, but it deteriorated so much that it had to be demolished. It was not rebuilt. His star had now waned and, defeated in the Preston election of 1833 after he had been previously elected, he went back to Whitchurch in Hampshire to live out his last years as a country gentleman. He died of a stroke on 15 February 1835.

This book is the record of the trial which stands as affirmation of his defeat by authorities so scared by what was occurring that they brought in the most draconian civil order acts ever put on the British statute book in a time of peace. This is, perhaps, ironically Hunt's greatest political triumph, for he represented the monster the government and the ruling elite couldn't quite slay.

# HENRY HUNT et al.

## INTRODUCTION.

### I.

On a fine August day in 1819, several groups of reformers from various Lancastrian industrial towns marched towards St Peter's Field, Manchester, to petition for parliamentary reform and suffrage. It was a colourful display of solidarity, with those gathered proudly holding aloft banners proclaiming their political message. Many in the crowded meeting space eagerly awaited the arrival of the famous political orator, Henry Hunt, who had travelled north to chair this meeting of 60,000 people. As he arrived, the crowd cheered heartily; Hunt bowed to them, and waved his trademark white top hat.

After about ten minutes, the Manchester Yeomanry approached the hustings. They had been sent by the on-looking local magistrates to apprehend those who had organised the meeting, as well as those who were expected to speak. Hunt asked the crowd to give the yeomanry three cheers as a friendly gesture – but the crowd's peaceful nature was ignored. The yeomanry arrested all on the hustings, and then charged into the crowd, using their sabres on terrified reformers. These violent actions resulted in a tragedy: eighteen dead and at least seven hundred injured, the first victim being a two year old child, William Fildes.[1] It was not lost on those present that the military had gone from victory at Waterloo to violence at 'Peterloo'.

The Peterloo Massacre is an important moment in the democratic and political history of Britain. It has received academic attention that has cemented it into the narrative of the fight for popular suffrage. However, although some legal historians have considered it,[2] the trial of those arrested at Peterloo tends not to receive the same coverage: this omission is a kind of secondary injustice against the five men who were convicted of conducting a 'seditious' meeting. The trial is important for other reasons, too. It enables us to revisit the events of Peterloo through witnesses' testimony, and it showcases the tensions that existed between reformers and authorities. The following transcript is therefore a vital document by which to supplement our holistic understanding of Peterloo, as well as contemporary views on the reform movement; and it serves as a commemoration of reformers' efforts to win the right to vote.

---

1  See Bush (2005).
2  See Lobban; Tilly and Tilly (eds.).

## Hunt and Others.

This introduction seeks to situate the transcript of the trial within its context. It will provide an overview of the political radicalism of Regency Britain, the fear of revolution and insurrection prevalent in the middle and upper classes, the idea of sedition, and the call for the suspension of *habeas corpus*.[3] As the trial took place in York rather than Lancaster, some of these examples will be drawn from Yorkshire. Several of the important figures within the trial – Henry Hunt, Samuel Bamford, Joseph Healey, Joseph Johnson, and John Knight – will be given their own short biographies. We will examine the courtroom, the judicial landscape and the introductory remarks of the prosecution counsel at the trial. We will consider the activities of Hunt and his fellow defendants prior to the trial in York, as well as a sympathetic march by reformers from Manchester to York.

But the trial should also be placed into the context of what happened afterwards – not just what precipitated it, but what it precipitated. This section will cover the imprisonment of those defendants who were convicted at the trial, Hunt's attempts at prison reform, and radical attempts at rhetoric, propaganda, and print. It will also revisit political radicalism more generally, tracking the course of the reform movement to the 1832 Reform Act and Chartism. In conclusion, we will reflect on the importance of the trial, identifying interesting aspects and themes which arose as it progressed, and noting its connections with other trials.

## II. Regency Radicalism

The political landscape of early nineteenth century Britain was overshadowed by the wars with Napoleon. While the Battle of Waterloo brought an end to the continental conflict, the cost of war was far-reaching, and is arguably identifiable in the cocktail of factors which influenced the flare-up of radicalism after 1815. The Tory government under Robert Jenkinson would discover, as subsequent governments would discover, that it is rarely tenable to ask people to leave their communities and to risk their lives in international wars unless they are repaid with a greater stake in, and greater influence over, the peacetime affairs of the country.

The years of 1815 and 1816 were beset by grave economic problems: the demobilisation of the army strained resources at home, and 1816 was the 'Year

---

3    The writ of *habeas corpus* is a legal protection which entitles an individual to report his imprisonment to a court, where it will be determined whether his detention is lawful. The suspension of habeas corpus results in this right being stripped, and, without its provisions, individuals can be detained without evidence or justification.

# Introduction.

without a Summer', during which severe food shortages were experienced across Britain.[4] In this period of economic and agricultural crisis, the government attempted to stabilise the economy by introducing the much-hated Corn Laws and coinage acts.[5] The Corn Laws were particularly despised by the emerging working and industrial classes because, in their attempts to protect British agriculture and restrict imports, they inflated the price of grain for bread. The bad feeling had not subsided by 1819: banners at Peterloo proclaimed 'No Corn Laws',[6] and the anti-Corn Law movement gathered pace in the late 1830s and 1840s with the formation of the Anti-Corn Law League.[7]

During the years of war, several important developments in radical politics had occurred. Hampden Clubs[8] were formed to assist in the organisation of political campaigns, and also to act as venues for conversation and debate. The first was formed in London in 1812, probably by the prominent radical John Cartwright, who was also known to his contemporaries as 'Major Cartwright' and 'The Father of Reform'.[9] Petitioning was a key part of their activism: the Birmingham Hampden Club, for example, petitioned their objection to a riot which had taken place, aiming by this gesture to distance reform politics from violence.[10] The clubs thereby acted in a manner similar to that of the London Corresponding Society, a forum for radical political activity in the early 1790s. Cartwright himself promoted the idea of franchises in the north-west of England; the first (formed in Royton) was shortly followed by one in Middleton, founded by the poet and Peterloo-ist Samuel Bamford. Conversation and the establishment of social networks were important aspects of life within radical communities, and the radical tradition of political oratory can be heard in the speeches given – particularly by Hunt – in the transcript of the trial.

In late 1816, the Spa Fields Riots occurred, and the impact of the resulting suspension of *habeas corpus* reached into the new year. On 15 November and

---

4    Food shortages occurred across the world after the eruption of Mount Tambora in 1815; disjecta from the volcano clouded the atmosphere, and the colder and darker conditions caused crops to fail. See Wood.
5    The 1846 repeal of the Corn Laws is seen as an important moment in Britain's move towards a free trade economy. See Marrison.
6    See Pickering; Tyrrell.
7    See Miller, H.; Turner.
8    Hampden Clubs were named after the English parliamentarian John Hampden, who was one of the 'Five Members' of the House of Commons to have incurred the wrath of King Charles I [NBT 43] (see Muddiman, 14). The Hampden Clubs were popular with the working classes, but following a national convention in 1817 the clubs were suppressed by the government. See Cannon.
9    See Miller, N. C., on Cartwright's role in the establishment of Hampden Clubs. Cartwright also founded the Society for Constitutional Information, which actively circulated reform ideas (see TNA: PRO TS 11/1133).
10    The petition stated 'That no Benefit ever has arisen, nor ever can arise, from such wanton Violations of the Laws ... That for the redress of Grievances, the Constitution has provided a legitimate Mode of Complaint – PETITION'. (TNA: PRO HO 40/9/145.)

# Hunt and Others.

2 December 1816, in Spa Fields, Islington, reformers gathered to petition for relief from distresses caused by poverty, and to demand electoral reform. The first meeting occurred without any violent or riotous behaviour. Henry Hunt gave a speech to the multitude – 10,000 strong – and was elected, along with the Radical MP Sir Francis Burdett,[11] to deliver the petition to the authorities. Hunt was denied access to the Prince Regent, however, and a second meeting was therefore called. This meeting was co-opted by a group of radical Spenceans, so called as they were followers of the radical thinker Thomas Spence.[12] In a letter sent to prisoners at the notorious Marshalsea Prison,[13] a Spencean claimed that on 'the 2nd December 1816 ... by Firmness and Intrepidity the English Nation will be brought back to its former Glorious Condition ... demanding the Restoration of our Liberties – as our Native Birth Right'.[14] During Hunt's speech, the Spenceans begun to agitate for disorder, and headed to the Tower of London, robbing a gun shop on the way. Upon reaching the Royal Exchange, however, the protestors were dispersed or arrested.

Like other events of the period, proceedings were tainted by the actions and influence of a government spy or informer. John Castle was working as an informer and arguably as an *agent provocateur*. During the trial of James Watson, one of the Spencean leaders, Castle's character was no match for the defendant's reason and wit; Watson was acquitted, and the charges against the other defendants were dropped. It is worth remembering that the Spa Fields Riots were deemed to be 'riots' by conservative commentators and reporters. A violent minority faction was, of course, present; but it is important to recognise that emotive and prejudicial language – including words such as 'mob' and 'riot' – was often utilised to depict reformers as a violent *majority*. Eric Hobsbawm labels the Regency as the 'hysterical 1810s' due to the authorities' intense fear of revolution and insurrection.[15] These competing understandings of reform and

---

11 Sir Francis Burdett was a radical MP for various constituencies. In his early parliamentary career, he was particularly involved in demanding an inquiry into the inhuman and squalid conditions which prevailed at the infamous Coldbath Fields Prison. Throughout the early 1800s, Burdett attempted to secure parliamentary reform and an end to the legal and civil restrictions imposed on Roman Catholics. His writings on Peterloo provoked official displeasure and, at the Leicester Assizes in 1820, Burdett was found guilty of writing and publishing seditious material and imprisoned for three months.

12 Spence was a famous radical of the late eighteenth and early nineteenth centuries. He developed a plan for the common ownership of land and utilised the idea of Utopia (through the fictional state of Spensonia) to imagine and conceive of his ideas for political and social change. Spence's Plan was frequently discussed in radical literature; its six main points included the abolition of aristocracy and landlords, universal suffrage (that is, for men and women), and an early idea of welfare or benefits through a 'social guarantee'.

13 Marshalsea Prison was located in Southwark and was especially associated with housing debtors, although several prisoners were imprisoned there on charges of sedition.

14 TNA: PRO TS 11/200.

15 See Hobsbawm.

# Introduction.

radicalism will be revisited when we analyse the anxieties which existed at the time, with the possibility of revolution – perhaps – on the horizon.

1817 was a busy year for radical efforts. It saw two major events: the Blanketeers' March, and the Pentrich Rising. The former was a demonstration led by Lancashire weavers to petition the Prince Regent for urgent support for the textile industry in Lancashire, but also to protest the suspension of *habeas corpus*. The aim was to march from St Peter's Field, Manchester, to London: around 5000 weavers agreed to participate, each with a knapsack of food and a blanket (hence the name). The participants were divided into groups of ten, and each group carried a petition containing twenty names. However, before the march had left Manchester, the gathering was dispersed by a force of dragoons, and the organisers were arrested. Three hundred marchers made it to Stockport, where they were instructed to turn back. There were reports that other Blanketeers got onto the road to Derby, but none was successful in reaching the Prince Regent.[16] The leaders of the march – John Bagguley, John Johnston and Samuel Drummond – were imprisoned.[17]

The Pentrich Rising, by contrast, was an attempt at insurrection. Beginning in Pentrich, Derbyshire, a few hundred men were to march to Nottingham to join other insurrectionists. They were led by Jeremiah Brandreth, known as 'The Nottingham Captain', an unemployed stocking worker who had possibly been involved in Luddite activity in 1811. In some ways, the rising was a prequel to the Cato Street Conspiracy of 1820,[18] and – just as at Cato Street – it is arguable that government subterfuge encouraged Brandreth and his fellow conspirators

---

16  See Poole, R. (2009), who highlights that there was more coherence to the 1817 reform movement than is usually acknowledged, noting the use of mass petitioning on regional and national scales in particular. The main players looked to English history (the Magna Carta and the English rebellion of 1381) first, rather than the French Revolution.

17  Bagguley, Johnston and Drummond were radicals based in Manchester. At a reform meeting at Stockport on 28 June 1819, a letter was read from Bagguley, who was at that time imprisoned in Chester Castle, arguing that 'the Deity created man for happiness, and a sufficiency of good things to make all men happy; but that the majority of that meeting being miserable in the highest degree, the intentions of the Deity had been frustrated by their rulers: that when a government was guilty of destroying or diminishing the happiness of the people, such government acted in direct opposition to the will of heaven, and rebellion against it was an imperative duty!' (*Newcastle Courant*, 10 July 1819.)

18  The Cato Street Conspiracy was a plan to assassinate the cabinet. Led by Arthur Thistlewood, who was involved in the Spa Fields Riots, the aim was to ambush and execute the Tory MPs and Prime Minister at a cabinet dinner. Following this, they would establish a 'Committee of Public Safety' in the vein of the French Revolution. The information that a dinner was occurring was provided by the second-in-command, George Edwards, who was also a police spy. Thistlewood was seen by the government as a prime target upon whom to spy and to attempt to manipulate: 'Thistlewood is the boy for us; he's the one to do our work: he will very soon be out of Horsham Gaol' (see Gardner (2002)). The conspirators were caught in their rented meeting place on Cato Street. Thirteen were arrested, resulting in the execution of five conspirators for high treason and the transportation of five others to Australia.

to take a violent course of action.

Brandreth met William J. Oliver (also called 'Oliver the Spy') in May 1817. Oliver was a police informer who had been instructed to root out sedition and revolutionary activity. He toured the North and the Midlands, pretending to be a reformer who was co-ordinating an attack on the Tower of London, with up to 70,000 reformers being involved. In June 1817, Oliver was exposed as a spy and, upon entering Nottingham, he underwent a thorough examination administered by the Nottingham reformers. This information arrived too late for Brandreth and the Pentrich conspirators. They marched to Nottingham on 8 June and found no insurrection; they were soon dispersed by the Hussars.[19] Brandreth was arrested and subsequently executed, as were two of his associates, William Turner and Isaac Ludlam; thirty other conspirators were transported.[20] Edward Baines, the editor and proprietor of the *Leeds Mercury* (a newspaper which was supportive of reform and dissent) and the father of the reporter Edward Baines who was present at Peterloo, argued in several powerful articles that Oliver the Spy was the main instigator of the attempted rising, and that Brandreth would not have taken his eventual course of action without Oliver's input. Debates about Oliver's level of involvement have continued since June 1817, and still occur in historical and scholarly discussion.[21]

A general election was held in August 1818 and resulted in the Tories, led by the Earl of Liverpool, winning a clear majority of ninety-five seats over the Whigs, led by Earl Grey. A Tory government had been in power since 1812, and had pushed through the repressive 1817 Seditious Meetings Act. Arguably, the reaction to Peterloo might have been different had a Whig government been elected, but the pressure on radical factions was now increasing. Arthur Thistlewood – a notable radical of the time, a veteran of the Spa Fields Riots, and one of those at the centre of the Cato Street affair – was imprisoned for breaching the peace after challenging Lord Sidmouth to a duel over confiscated property.[22] In the summer and early autumn of 1818, male and female weavers across Manchester, Stockport, and Ashton-under-Lyne went on strike.[23] They held huge meetings which were addressed by Bagguley, Drummond and Johnston of the Blanketeers, and they undertook long marches between the industrial towns with banners and bands. Bagguley, Drummond and Johnston

19  *Derby Mercury*, 19 June 1817.
20  High treason was still punishable by hanging, drawing and quartering, although in later executions the quartering was often commuted.
21  See Plowright; Thompson.
22  Henry Addington, 1st Viscount Sidmouth, was Home Secretary between 1812 and 1822.
23  *Morning Chronicle*, 4 August 1818; *Caledonian Mercury*, 7 September 1818.

# Introduction.

were promptly confined at Chester Castle for making seditious speeches.[24] The rumblings of dissent and discontent continued.

And then the year of Peterloo – 1819. Reformers were actively pushing their agenda: numerous mass platform meetings were held across the country, with the Smithfield meetings in London being particularly notable for their size, and for having attracted speakers from far and wide. Henry Hunt, the chairman of the meetings, spoke at great length, and numerous letters were read, and speeches heard, on the subjects of liberty and universal suffrage. The crowd dispersed peacefully. Alongside these meetings, the first female reform societies were founded.[25] The Blackburn Female Reform Society was formed in July – the first of its kind. At their first meeting, the chairwoman, Mrs Alice Kitchen, presented a splendidly-made liberty cap to the elected chairman, Mr John Knight.[26] Both Kitchen and Knight were later present at Peterloo.[27] Female reform societies were also created in Stockport and Manchester, and many more were founded in response to the shocking and bloody events of St Peter's Field.[28]

Who were the activists, the protesters, the radicals? Reform was, often groundlessly, associated by its critics with atheism and anti-church beliefs,[29] but Christianity featured strongly within the radical value set. Dissenting Christianity was particularly connected to political reform[30] and it has even been suggested that religious beliefs were more important than socio-economic factors in influencing voting behaviour and political beliefs.[31] Henry Hunt was Christian, often borrowing biblical or clerical language in his radical orations. The female reformers wrote in a letter to the *Manchester Observer* that Jesus Christ 'was the greatest reformer of them all',[32] and Mr Joseph Brayshaw of

---

24  *Black Dwarf*, 4 March 1818.
25  The female reform societies were mainly active in 1819 and predominantly in the north of England. Led by working women, these were spaces for women to actively debate and contribute to the reform movement. These societies did not escape scorn or criticism, however; they were mocked in the George Cruikshank print The Belle Alliance and their members deemed 'women well known to be of the most abandoned of their sex' (*Exeter Flying Post*, 15 July 1819).
26  *Morning Chronicle*, 13 July 1819
27  The presence of female reformers at Peterloo and other meetings was greeted with 'repugnance' (*Leeds Intelligencer*, 12 July 1819) in some quarters of the press. Women who were active in their support for reform were considered to be transgressing the boundaries of expected behaviour.
28  The idea of forming a female reform society was also an exciting one for the women involved. At a meeting in Huddersfield, the idea of forming a society was suggested, 'at which', said one reporter, 'the countenances of the women assembled, lighted up to amiable fervour, and their small shrill voices gave enthusiastic applause' (*Leeds Intelligencer*, 9 August 1819).
29  Thomas Paine is perhaps the classic example of this. Despite being a deist, Paine was accused of harbouring atheistic beliefs.
30  See Waterman.
31  See O'Gorman; Phillips.
32  The *Manchester Observer* was a lively and energetic radical newspaper published and printed in Manchester

## Hunt and Others.

the Freethinking Christians proclaimed, 'I am a firm believer in Christianity; Jesus, the founder of our system, was one of the greatest reformers that ever appeared on earth!'[33] Again, there is evidence of a clash of readings: how the reformers perceived themselves was not necessarily how they were perceived or characterised by others.

Alongside Christian beliefs, reformers articulated the idea of there being ancient British liberties. Historical legitimacy was used as a central argument for defending the right to meet publicly, and for advancing suffrage rights. Connections were made to the Anglo-Saxons, the Magna Carta and the Bill of Rights. A long tradition of mass mobilisation was conceptualised. Despite the diversity of the radical movement,[34] historians have demonstrated how radical activity of the post-Napoleonic years tied itself to an understanding of Englishness which saw protest and petitioning as an ancient right, and which drew parallels between the Peasants' Revolt of 1381 and the Glorious Revolution of 1688.[35] Many examples exist in the radical speeches and prints of the period: Mr Russell, at a Glasgow reform meeting on 5 November 1816, stated, 'At the revolution in 1688, the prerogatives of the Crown were defined, and the privileges of the people restored and guaranteed by the Bill of Rights'.[36] Banners and flags at reform meetings would often refer to these ancient liberties too. For instance, meetings in Halifax and York following Peterloo had banners proclaiming the slogans 'Magna Carta' and 'Bill of Rights' – reminders to the authorities of their obligations to the people.[37]

The colourful prints and engravings of the time were also used to communicate the idea that freedoms were under threat from government action and state suppression. Fears surrounding censorship of the press and the Stamp Act can be seen in *Poor John Bull: The Free-Born Englishman Deprived of His Seven Senses by the Six New Acts?*.[38] There were nascent expressions of support for women's rights. S. Ferrand Waddington deplored the 'strange

---

between 1818 and 1820. John Knight and Joseph Johnson, two of the defendants at the Peterloo trial, were regular contributors. The only editor was James Wroe, who was also involved in the Patriotic Union Society. Wroe was sentenced to twelve months in prison for his writing and publication of the fourteen-part pamphlet series, *The Peterloo Massacre: A Faithful Narrative of the Events*. The *Manchester Observer* was forced to close in February 1820 due to government fines. It was briefly revived, but finally came to an end in 1821, shortly after the *Manchester Guardian* (now the *Guardian*) was founded.

33  *Manchester Observer*, 31 July 1819; *Exeter Flying Post*, 22 July 1819.
34  See Burgess and Festenstein; McElligott.
35  See Crick; Hewitt.
36  *York Herald*, 9 November 1816.
37  *Manchester Observer*, 2 October 1819.
38  Similar themes of fear of press suppression grew up in the 1790s, following the Two Acts (of which more later). See *A Free Born Englishman!* (1795) for a print which deploys tropes similar to those found in the work of Cruikshank.

# Introduction.

inconsistency in allowing women to wield the sceptre, without being entitled to hold any subordinate situation', and the image evoked was of the Anglo-Saxon woman and the powerful female monarchs of the past.[39] As described by Robert Poole,[40] it is possible to see in post-war radicalism the seeds of the future radical movements of Chartism and trade unionism, making these tumultuous years of struggle, poverty, and inequality fundamental to the history of political rights and suffrage.

## III. Anxieties and Fears

One of the prevalent fears of the post-Napoleonic period was that Britain was close to revolution. Anxieties abounded that seditious and revolutionary radicals were planning insurrections, and that they sought more than just parliamentary reform. As we have already seen, these fears translated into – to name just one example – the maintenance of a spy and informant network. It is also debatable to what extent violent actions would have been undertaken without the provocation of government informants: the spies, justifying their existence, perhaps made violence into a self-fulfilling prophecy. Conservatives created a 'phantom terror' and exploited the police and spy networks as a way of suppressing civil liberties and resistance.[41] Conspiracy was a popular buzzword. Michael Taylor's work shows that, in a section of conservative thought, the Illuminati[42] were seen to be undermining the establishment and working towards its dismantlement.[43] Of course, some factions of radicals and reformers – albeit not all factions – did discuss the idea of adopting violent modes of achieving change.

The idea of the public meeting, whether this was held to refer to a mass platform event or to the more contained gathering of a more formal society, induced fear in the upper and middle classes. The aforementioned Hampden Clubs were purposely stifled by the authorities because they were viewed suspiciously and considered to excite radicalism.[44] Following the efforts of Oliver the Spy and the Blanketeers, a crackdown on radical activity occurred in

---

39    S. Ferrand Waddington writing in *The Republican*, a radical journal, 1819.
40    See Poole, R.
41    See Zamoyski.
42    In contemporary discourse, the idea of the existence of the 'Illuminati' has taken on its own identity. However, in the nineteenth century, the term was derived from the Bavarian Illuminati, a secret society founded in 1776. There were ideas that, following the French Revolution, such secret societies had survived and were part of an international conspiracy. The idea of shadowy elites controlling the world as puppeteers can be traced back beyond the internet age to the end of the 1790s.
43    See Taylor, M.
44    See Belchem (1978).

## Hunt and Others.

Manchester, with local leaders imprisoned. Samuel Bamford was one reformer on the receiving end of this maltreatment, and he wrote a pamphlet documenting it. On his first night in the cell, he wrote a poem, 'To Liberty':

> O Liberty! Dear to my heart
> Are the blessings which thou canst bestow;
> But dear as I love them, I from them must part,
> And all thy enjoyments forego [sic].[45]

The heavy-handed suppression of Hampden Clubs resulted in Manchester reformers founding a new society, the Manchester Patriotic Union: this was the union which invited Hunt to speak at the meeting it organised in August 1819. Contemporary political and social commentators recognised the power and ability of the crowd, which had come to be characterised as something comprehensible and rational: an entity in the singular, rather than the plural; the group, collective, or complex visualised as something individualised, homogeneous and manageable.[46] The French Revolution's example of the potential of the crowd (or the 'mob', as it was commonly described in contemporary reports) was projected onto British radical and reform crowds, and, to this manner of thinking, meeting in large numbers was tantamount to conducting revolutionary violence.[47] These understandings of the crowd were depicted through political satire and caricatures across the late eighteenth and early nineteenth centuries. James Gillray's prints frequently used grotesquery and violence to denote the rampant and menacing nature of the 'mob'. Alongside Gillray, other conservative caricaturists were instrumental in developing counter-figures to the revolutionary crowd, carefully deploying Britannia and John Bull (amongst others) in counterpoint to the radicals' preferred symbolic precedents. These figureheads reinforced British identity in terms of stability, tradition, and defending the constitution. Even the moderate reformer and caricaturist George Cruikshank was fearful of the power of the crowd. Cruikshank often used the skeleton or the emaciated body in depicting radical groups – the link between radicalism and death being very clear.[48]

It is possible to encapsulate the establishment's fears of the body politic in a single item of material culture: the liberty cap. Originally a Roman symbol of the freed slave, the liberty cap underwent complex interpretations throughout the early modern period before the French Revolution secured its status as a

---

45  Bamford (1817), 5.
46  See Harrison.
47  See Lodge.
48  See his prints Death or Liberty! and A Radical Reformer for examples of this.

# Introduction.

radical object. Its links to freedom also include Brutus' adoption of it on coinage to symbolise Rome's liberation from the tyranny of Julius Caesar.[49] In early modern Lancashire, the liberty cap was adopted as a multi-faceted item, with different groups able to appropriate it in different ways.[50] The tumult in France, however, made even recent uses of the liberty cap – those created shortly before its meaning became fixed – instantly obsolete. Britannia was often depicted with a cap on the end of her pole from the mid-eighteenth century onwards, and the location of the trial of Henry Hunt – the York Assize Court, constructed in the 1770s, on the point of the French Revolution – had a liberty cap carved into its façade. By the time of Peterloo, the presence of a liberty cap at a meeting invariably signalled to conservative or loyalist outsiders that revolutionary thought was being fermented. Claims that the Peterloo meeting was seditious often relied upon the evidence that liberty caps were present, but this did little to deter its adopters. Following Peterloo, reformers sang:

> With Henry Hunt we'll go, my boys,
> With Henry Hunt we'll go;
> We'll mount the cap of liberty
> In Spite of Nadin Jo.[51]

## IV. Sedition and Legislation

With the national climate of fear and suspicion reaching critical mass, the idea that reform was really a euphemism for revolution prevailed, and 'sedition' became an accusation commonly made against leading radicals: indeed, the initial charges brought against the defendants in the trial presented in this volume included sedition and high treason for their actions at Peterloo. This fear of sedition was similarly expressed through the legislation which was passed in the same period.

In 1795, the British parliament passed the Seditious Meetings Act and the Treason Act. These are better known collectively as the Two Acts or the Gagging Acts. The main purpose of the Seditious Meetings Act was to limit the number of people able to meet publicly to fifty, effectively curtailing any actual or perceived radical efforts to commit violence (or merely to protest) in large groups. The law considered any room, building, or outdoor space to fall

---

49  See Omissi.
50  See Epstein.
51  See Kidson. 'Nadin Jo' is a reference to Joseph Nadin, the deputy constable who arrested Hunt and others at Peterloo.

within the definition of 'public' spaces – accordingly, the Act targeted vibrant lectures and public debates as well as large demonstrations. The Treason Act made it an offence to even consider hurting, imprisoning, or killing the king. John Thelwall,[52] a notable radical speaker and educationist, believed that the Two Acts were directed against his efforts in particular. Thelwall felt that the measures ended his lectures and impacted his 'own freedom, life and well-being. Now, the general crisis is upon him, personally – that is, he draws it upon himself.'[53] The London Corresponding Society avoided suppression under the Two Acts, but was subsequently suppressed under the Corresponding Societies Act of 1799.

A similar Act was approved in 1817. The Seditious Meetings Act was passed by Lord Liverpool's government after being introduced by Lord Castlereagh. It continued to restrict public meetings to a maximum of fifty people, but it introduced the possibility that permission could be granted to larger meetings if enough notification was given to the authorities, or if the gathering had been requested by an official. In reality, this simply forced the barrier against public gatherings higher, and gave the authorities further powers of prohibition. Unlike the 1795 Act, which was a blanket ban, the 1817 Act also entitled justices of the peace to attend meetings and disperse them if they deemed them to be unlawful or likely to incite sedition. The legislation affected Hampden Clubs too. Upon hosting a national convention, the clubs were suppressed by the Acts almost immediately.[54]

After Peterloo, and the wounded response by radicals to the massacre, the government again felt it necessary to enforce an Act to limit meetings. The Seditious Meetings Act 1819 was passed in December. It restricted meeting sizes to fifty, but was the first Sedition Act to be extended to Ireland. It also banned the use and display of banners, flags, and ensigns at meetings – an illustration of just how powerful radical material culture was considered. This Act was part of a battery of legislation which became known as the Six Acts. These Acts sought to counter supposed revolutionary activity and to work against the radical press. For example, the Unlawful Drilling Act 1819 combatted radicals who practised marching by making it illegal for anyone other than municipal or military bodies to receive drill training. The Blasphemous and Seditious Libels Act increased

---

52 John Thelwall (1764-1834) was a leading radical orator in the late eighteenth century who also wrote on elocution. Thelwall was involved in the London Corresponding Society, founded by Thomas Hardy in 1792. Along with several other radicals, Thelwall was arrested on charges of high treason in 1794. However, the claims against the radicals were weak and no convictions were recorded.
53 Poole, S., 33.
54 See Cannon.

# Introduction.

the maximum sentence for publishing or authoring anti-establishment texts to fourteen years, and the Newspaper and Stamp Duties Act was designed to make cheap radical literature more expensive by closing a loophole which radicals had been using: previously, radical publications avoided paying tax because they published opinion rather than news. Many radicals thought that these Acts were Draconian, and that they threw the spotlight on the Pittite government's paranoid thirst for repression.[55]

## V. Peterloo

From various industrial towns around Lancashire, then, reformers marched to St Peter's Field, Manchester, on Monday 16 August 1819. This section will provide an overview of the event itself, as well as the cancelled meeting of the week before.[56] The day of Peterloo has featured in various political and social histories, although arguably it does not always receive the attention it deserves (nor, generally, does political radicalism in the post-Napoleonic era).[57] The following account is taken from contemporary sources, and supplemented by retrospective scholarly debate.

Members of the Manchester Patriotic Union Society had decided to organise a mass platform meeting in Manchester. Crucially, it would be focused not just on Manchester reformers; rather, they aimed to co-ordinate it so that reformers from across Lancashire would attend. Joseph Johnson, who was later found guilty at the York trial, invited Henry Hunt to be the main speaker at the event. The original meeting was to be held on 2 August, but was delayed until Monday 9 August as Johnson's letter to Hunt was intercepted by government spies.[58] This second date was then abandoned too. The meeting had to be rearranged: it was deemed illegal by the Manchester magistrates, who apparently believed that it was really an attempt to elect an MP. In order to avoid this charge, the reformers circulated notices for a new meeting which intended 'to consider the propriety of adopting the most LEGAL and EFFECTUAL means of obtaining a reform in the Common House of Parliament'.[59] St Peter's Field was chosen as the site of the event. It was a large croft in the centre of Manchester, making it

---

55   See Hollis.
56   See Read.
57   For historical overviews of the Peterloo Massacre, see Read; Marlow; Riding. For academic analyses of the day, as well as connections between Peterloo and other events and theories, see the collected volume *Return to Peterloo*, edited by Robert Poole; and Katrina Navickas's 2016 book, *Protest and the Politics of Space and Place*.
58   See Reid.
59   Taylor, J. E. (1820), 23.

## Hunt and Others.

a practical spot at which reformers could congregate.

The day arrived, and St Peter's Field started to fill up from early in the morning. Many in attendance wore their best clothes (or at least their second-best clothes, according to Elizabeth Healey's account), and were looking forward to an exciting day. The various marching regiments of reformers from Oldham, Middleton, Saddleworth, Stockport and elsewhere began to enter the field. Banners were an important part of the procession, and these colourful artefacts were used to decorate the hustings. Notable banners included the Middleton flag (which survives to this day) and the 'black flag' of Saddleworth.[60] The black flag was frequently mentioned in the subsequent trial, and the prosecution presented it as proof of the reformers' seditious purposes. It proclaimed the bold words, 'Equal Representation or Death', and the precise meaning of these words would occupy the court for some considerable time. The Oldham Female Reformers carried a 'most elegant' banner too; it was beautifully designed, reading 'Major Cartwright's Bill, Annual Parliaments, Universal Suffrage, and Vote by Ballot', and in the one corner there was a depiction of Justice holding her scales and sword.[61] The female reformers from Royton brought two red flags with them, one bearing the powerful statement: 'Let us [women] die like men, and not be sold like slaves'.[62] And then there were the liberty caps, which were considered to hold a prominent place in the procession. Accounts of the meeting often included the number of caps that witnesses noticed, and this was used to suggest that the meeting was for seditious or revolutionary purposes.[63] Songs, ballads, and oral culture were important aspects of radicalism and reform communities and the singing of certain songs was used as evidence for insurrection.[64] Other features of the meeting which were eventually exploited by the prosecution included the reformers' organised marching in rank and file, and the language they used. For the prosecution, the performative behaviour of the Peterloo reformers and their use of material culture were particularly emphasised.

---

60   The Middleton banner is currently exhibited in the People's History Museum in Manchester, along with many other banners telling the history of political radicalism in Britain.
61   Hunt claims in the trial that the banner did not include the sword. However, several reports and witness statements suggest that Justice was indeed holding a sword, and she was often depicted in this manner, so it would not be unlikely. (See TNA: PRO TS 11/1086, and *Morning Chronicle*, 19 August 1819.) It is possible that this was the banner which caused women to descend upon Mr Tate's house: they believed him to have the Oldham Female Reformers' banner, as he reportedly waved a banner as fleeing reformers went past. (See *Morning Chronicle*, 20 August 1819; Philips.)
62   Urban (ed.), 172.
63   Early newspaper reports noted that the presence of the liberty cap was an 'overt act' and asserted that its potent symbolism inspired the initial charge of high treason against Hunt (*Caledonian Mercury*, 21 August 1819).
64   See Morgan.

# Introduction.

Mary Fildes, chairwoman of the Manchester Female Reformers, rode to St Peter's Field in a barouche with Hunt.[65] She carried a sign which asked for 'Order!' – this was one of the many ways in which reformers would attempt to regulate the behaviour of the assembled crowd. Other female reformers were present elsewhere in the meeting. Dressed in all white to symbolise liberty (or possibly in the style of the Vestal Virgins),[66] they turned out in remarkable numbers. John Tyas, the reporter for *The Times* who was present at Peterloo, recalled them during the evidence he gave at the trial:

> There were a great number of women and children present. Many of them marched in ranks, like the men. I saw two female parties in particular, who came in at the head of divisions. They appeared to be dressed in their best clothes on the occasion.

Along with people who were attending the meeting to support the cause of reform, others attended as bystanders or out of curiosity. These included a group of women ('of the lower order') who shouted at the processing female reformers, 'Go home to your families and leave sike-like [ie, suchlike] matters as these to your husbands and sons, who better understand them'.[67] Similar scorn was on display elsewhere. Mary Waterworth, of the Stockport contingent, was called a 'profligate Amazon' for riding on a barouche and carrying her society's banner.[68] Ruth Mather has suggested that female reformers were using their society and meeting spaces as a way of discussing the feminine need for reform, as well as sharing women's experiences of industry and poverty.[69] Gender boundaries were sensitive, and perceived transgressions were treated harshly. Bush's analysis of the injuries inflicted upon Peterloo's women outlined the extent to which 'female reformers … could expect no quarter if they behaved like men'.[70]

By the time Hunt's barouche arrived at the field, a huge crowd had gathered. Contemporary estimates ranged from 30,000 to 120,000, but scholarship

---

65  Mary Fildes was an active radical in the Manchester area. Other notable women in the Manchester Female Reformers society included Susanna Saxton, Elizabeth Gaunt, and Sarah Hargreaves. Fildes was very passionate about the cause of reform and clearly idolised leading radicals of the time. Her sons were called Thomas Paine Fildes (born 1818), Henry Hunt Fildes (born 1819), and John Cartwright Fildes (born 1821).
66  See Riding.
67  *Leeds Intelligencer*, 23 August 1819.
68  *Morning Chronicle*, 19 August 1819. At the trial, Hunt challenged this characterisation of Waterworth. Henry Horton, the reporter in question, defended his statement: 'I called her a profligate Amazon because I thought her appearance in the manner and place where I saw her justified the observation. … I never saw a lady present colours at the head of a regiment.'
69  See Mather.
70  See Bush (2004).

## Hunt and Others.

usually agrees on around 60,000. Hunt was welcomed to the hustings with great noise and spoke for perhaps ten minutes before his speech was interrupted. In response to a cry of alarm that the yeomanry were approaching, Hunt directed the crowd to give three cheers to signify their peaceful intentions.[71] It soon became apparent that these sentiments were not shared by the Manchester Yeomanry,[72] a group of volunteer cavalrymen who were, in normal circumstances, mainly local shopkeepers and property owners. As the yeomanry charged the crowd, they also targeted banners and caps of liberty, destroying and trampling them in the dirt, and their violent actions left the ground 'strewed with bleeding bodies of men and women, bruised, cut, and trampled upon'.[73] Samuel Bamford was at the centre of the pandemonium:

> I saw a party of cavalry in blue and white uniform come trotting, sword in hand, round the corner of a garden wall ... waving their sabres over their heads; and then, slackening rein, and striking spur into their steeds, they dashed forward and began cutting the people... The cavalry were in confusion: they evidently could not, with all the weight of man and horse, penetrate that compact mass of human beings and their sabres were plied to hew a way through naked held-up hands and defenceless heads; and then chopped limbs and wound-gaping skulls were seen; and groans and cries were mingled with the din of that horrid confusion...
>
> Over the whole field were strewed caps, bonnets, hats, shawls, and shoes, and other parts of male and female dress, trampled, torn, and bloody.
>
> Several mounds of human being still remained where they had fallen, crushed down and smothered. Some of these still groaning, others with staring eyes, were gasping for breath, and others would never breathe more.[74]

The devastation reverberated around Manchester and, once news broke, around the country.

The number of injured and dead has varied in both contemporary and scholarly analysis.[75] Michael Bush's recent research puts the number of dead at eighteen, and at least 600 injured, with trampling being a major cause of injury.[76] John Knight's eyewitness account, by contrast, contained a less extensive list, but it captured radicals in the process of compiling evidence to frame and emphasise the atrocity. In 1820, the Metropolitan and Central Committee was formed, with

---

71  *Leeds Mercury*, 21 August 1819.
72  The Manchester and Salford Yeomanry formed in 1817 in response to the growing radicalism in the north-west of England.
73  *York Herald*, 21 August 1819.
74  Bamford (1844a).
75  Some accounts include an unborn child, surname Gaunt, in their figures.
76  Bush (2005).

# Introduction.

one establishing member being John Cam Hobhouse.[77] One of their aims was to provide relief or compensation to those injured at Peterloo – in pursuit of this objective, they also compiled a list. They placed the figure at 430, and gave valuable details about the injured men, women, and children, descriptions of their injuries, and their occupations and ages. Here are the names of those who died at a peaceful petition advocating for the extension of the right to vote:

- John Ashton
- John Ashworth
- William Bradshaw
- Thomas Buckley
- Robert Campbell
- James Crompton
- Edmund Dawson
- William Dawson
- Margaret Downes
- William Fildes
- Samuel Hall
- Mary Heyes
- Sarah Jones
- John Lees[78]
- Arthur O'Neill
- Martha Partington
- John Rhodes
- Joseph Whitworth

Numerous reformers, including Hunt and Bamford, were arrested at Peterloo. They were taken to the New Bailey, Salford, in a mirror-image mock procession of that morning's congregation: constables beat the arrested participants with truncheons, and two at the front carried seized reform banners

---

77 John Cam Hobhouse (later granted the title Lord Broughton) was a Unitarian and social reformer. He was good friends with Lord Bryon and later Sir Francis Burdett. After being defeated in the 1819 by-election for Westminster, he became its MP in the general election of 1820 and was an important radical MP in parliament. A pamphlet expressing his views on aristocratic privilege landed him in trouble, and he was imprisoned in Newgate. During this imprisonment, he helped found the Metropolitan and Central Committee and began his inquiry into Peterloo. He denounced William Hulton, one of the Manchester magistrates, as a liar and argued that the Peterloo meeting was peaceful in its intent and that reformers' behaviour had demonstrated this.

78 John Lees, a Waterloo veteran, died on 7 September 1819; he had been injured by sabres and truncheons. An inquest was held into his death and no verdict was found. The inquest drummed up a lot of radical literature and newspaper coverage.

## Hunt and Others.

– the spoils of war.[79] Later, the prisoners were moved to Lancaster Gaol, located in the mediaeval castle. Conditions in the gaol were desperate. During subsequent hearings at Lancaster, frequent references were made to Elizabeth Gaunt, who was ill and described as 'pale, emaciated, and almost fainting from weakness'. She was released without charge after spending eighteen days in solitary confinement.[80] Eventually, Hunt and the others were charged with several offences, all amounting to conspiracy and rioting, and were able to pay their bail and leave Lancaster.

### VI.
#### 'All liberated from the damned Bastille of Lancaster': Processions in Lancashire and London

Upon being released from Lancaster Gaol (or 'Bastille', as it was referred to, consciously evoking the French Revolution), Hunt and his associates were honoured by a huge celebratory procession across Lancashire. This visited numerous towns across the county, and then it reached Manchester. By the radical press, it was considered (in a hyperbolic statement) to surpass the 'triumphal entries of Roman conquerors'.[81] Throughout the towns of Lancashire, reformers and supportive crowds expressed their enthusiasm and support. Gifts of fruit were made, and flowers covered the roads the carriages had to pass over. Crowds would cheer and applaud, shouting acclamations: 'Hunt and Liberty'; 'Hunt forever'.

The procession, as this description implies, focused largely on Hunt, who was being cast as a hero, and was arguably a radical celebrity. He even had poems written in his honour:

> Hail, glorious Champion of a Sacred cause,
> Undaunted advocate of freedom's laws.[82]

It was possible to buy an engraved portrait of Hunt, and various ceramics were produced with his image transferred onto them.[83] Radical interest in the massacre and its subsequent legal by-products ensured that Hunt's words and experiences were broadcast through published reports and, in one case, even

---

79  See Taylor, J. E. (1819), no. 2.
80  *Caledonian Mercury*, 4 September 1819.
81  See Taylor, J. E. (1819), No. 3, 70.
82  *Manchester Observer*, 25 September 1819.
83  Transfer-print pottery was a popular form of ceramic in the early nineteenth century. The pottery would depict political leaders and movements as well as literary scenes. See Katz-Hyman; Lucas.

# Introduction.

a song.[84] At Preston, Hunt's favourite horse Bob died, and there were rumours that Bob had been poisoned. Bob received a funeral and, as a mark of respect to the fallen horse, he was buried standing upright in the garden of Mr Huffman, a Preston radical.[85] On several occasions, while Hunt continued to process through Lancashire, his carriage had its horses unhitched so that it could be pulled by hand – a gesture of popular respect and admiration.[86] In Blackburn, the female reformers of Blackburn presented Hunt with the liberty cap which they had made, and which had been present at Peterloo.

Another large-scale procession occurred in London. Again, it centred around Hunt and, again, hyperbole and enthusiastic accounts appeared in the radical press. This procession was considered greater than the entry of the Emperor Joseph into Brabant.[87] The *Black Dwarf* records that the crowd in London was great and excited, as evidenced by 'the waves of hats and handkerchiefs, the clapping of hands, [and] the shouts of applause mingled with the sound of musical instruments'. The journal also includes its own contribution to events: as Hunt passed the *Black Dwarf* offices, a long red streamer appeared from their window to great surprise and acclaim.[88] The radical response to the release of those arrested at Peterloo emphasises not only the popularity of Hunt, but also his commercial potential. When accounts of the trial were published, they invariably ensured that Hunt's name appeared front and centre – that, if nothing else, would surely sell copies.

## VII.
### 'We mourn for our murdered countrymen': The Radical Response

Alongside these celebratory events, reformers continued to meet publicly and in large-scale gatherings. Peterloo elicited a nationwide response. The reaction was not contained to Manchester, or even Lancashire: instead, people up and down the country were horrified by the actions of the yeomanry and magistrates. The decision to meet in response to the violence at Peterloo was a

---

[84] Reformers were angered by the chairman's actions at a hearing at the New Bailey, Salford, on 27 August. Hunt was questioning a witness, but the chairman kept intervening to shut the examination down: Don't answer that question'. This resulted in a song based on the hearing, with the chorus being: 'Shocking suggestion! Don't answer the question, Don't answer! Don't answer! Oh! Dear!' (*Manchester Observer*, 11 September 1819.)

[85] As an aside, a later account suggested that, seven years after his interment, Bob was dug up and his hooves made into snuff boxes, with one being gifted to Hunt. See Huish.

[86] See Taylor, J. E. (1819), No. 5.

[87] *Manchester Observer*, 18 September 1819.

[88] *Black Dwarf*, 15 September 1819.

## Hunt and Others.

particularly brave and striking form of solidarity.

Of course, not everybody was angered or saddened by the 'Manchester occurrence'. The Prince Regent sent his hearty thanks to the magistrates for their actions.[89] The *Lancaster Gazette* reported that 'in surrounding the hustings, and in dispersing the meeting yesterday, the spirit and promptitude of action so admirably displayed by the Yeomanry Cavalry was accompanied by a temper and forbearance which have been spoken of by persons of all parties in terms of admiration'.[90] Here, it is possible to see how the authorities and the Tory press were trying to create a narrative which legitimised the violent dispersal of the reformers. This version is not widely accepted within research or scholarship today; instead, the debate more often concerns the intent of the yeomanry.[91]

Across the country, radicals and reformers responded to Peterloo by continuing to meet. At a reform meeting in Halifax on 4 October 1819, numerous banners were present including one that said, 'Proud look; lying tongue; and hands that shed innocent blood: Peterloo Massacre'.[92] A meeting in York moved to the sound of the Dead March and carried a banner dedicated to 'the immortal memory of the Reformers killed at Manchester, August 16th, 1819'.[93] These meetings, and others like them, allowed reformers to share their anger and shock in public, and on a local and national level.

There was also a print response to Peterloo. Important prints included one by George Cruikshank, entitled *Britons Strike Home*, which depicts the Manchester Yeomanry striking down reformers with axes (rather than sabres). A notable figure is a female reformer holding a baby while trying to stop a fat yeoman from hitting her child. Cruikshank's print did not hold back from showing the violence of Peterloo. Richard Carlile also distributed a print, dedicated to Henry Hunt and the female reformers of Manchester, entitled *Peterloo Massacre (or Battle of Peterloo)*. The print shows Hunt, Mary Fildes, and other reformers on the hustings looking on in horror at the fearful carnage around them. Radicals and reformers utilised prints to circulate their anger and their opposition, and to ensure that the violence of the yeomanry stood at the forefront of popular discussion.

---

89   See TNA: PRO HO 41/4 f.496.
90   *Lancaster Gazette*, 21 August 1819.
91   This debate can take numerous perspectives. E. P. Thompson considered there to have been premeditated intent from the yeomanry, whereas Donald Read attributed the tragedy to mismanagement, poor choices, and panic. The main outlier in this debate is Robert Walmsley, who argues that there was no attempt by the authorities to be violent whether through premeditation or poor choices: instead, it was a series of unfortunate events.
92   *Leeds Mercury*, 9 October 1819.
93   *Manchester Observer*, 2 October 1819.

# Introduction.

## VIII. 'Singled out': The Defendants

Although the trial became inextricably associated with the name of Henry Hunt, nine other defendants were tried at the same time. Hunt was, of course, one of the major figures of radicalism and the reform movement, but it is worth providing a brief biography for each of the defendants. All five convicted men were important names within the politics of the late Regency period – not merely Hunt alone – and their significance is reflected and reinforced by the fact that they were 'singled out' by the authorities as leaders of the meeting at St Peter's Field. Five men were acquitted at the trial, and a short biography is provided for them too.

The Gentleman Radical: Henry Hunt

Henry Hunt (1773-1835) was one of the figureheads of the reform movement in the post-Napoleonic period. Alongside William Cobbett and Major Cartwright,[94] Hunt led the campaign for political change and generated great support for the cause; indeed, it was this fame and renown that led to his being asked to visit Manchester to chair the meeting on 16 August 1819. Owing to his talent for speaking, he was popularly known as 'Orator Hunt'. His powerful voice served him well at the mass platform meeting (a form of protest and petitioning for which Hunt was a particular advocate). In contrast to Bamford, Johnson, Moorhouse and Knight, however, Hunt was a landowner, and had not originated among the emergent working classes of the industrial parts of Britain. He has therefore been characterised as a 'gentleman radical' by Epstein and Belchem, but it is worth noting that social hierarchy in this period consisted of a complex series of stratifications.[95]

In his memoirs, Hunt attempted to distance himself from the gentry, perhaps preferring to construct a particular identity and portray certain characteristics over others. This has generated a clash between, on the one hand, Hunt's self-presentation (non-gentry), and, on the other, the modern historian's view of him (very much the gentry). Of course, we have to treat autobiographical sources with care, and, with this in mind, the trial represents an important source for the class intersections and divisions between Hunt and his co-defendants.[96] At the

---

94    Cobbett and Cartwright were significant figures in radicalism. William Cobbett – a strong proponent for parliamentary reform and Catholic emancipation – eventually became the MP for Oldham. Cobbett, originally a loyal Tory farmer, shifted his political allegiance when he came to believe that reform would benefit the rural workforce.
95    See Belchem and Epstein.
96    See Griffin.

## Hunt and Others.

same time, it is perhaps useful to consider the transcript of the trial in the same manner in which we would consider Hunt's autobiography: at the trial, Hunt is performing publicly, seeking to convey a particular identity, to give a certain impression of himself.

Historians have not always described Hunt in the kindest of terms. 'Vain, self-serving and arrogant', he is particularly known for his ego, and he did not necessarily help himself in this regard.[97] Remembering his childhood, he recalled his father's impassioned response to his early reading of Hector's speech to Andromache:

> He wept over me with rapture, and he exclaimed aloud, in a sort of frantic ecstasy, 'The name of HUNT will again be recorded in the page of history, and I feel that you, my dear boy, are destined to restore the fame of our family; and I hope to live to see you prove yourself worthy of your ancestors.'[98]

Hunt's memoirs may be vitiated by such moments of self-indulgence, but his prison writings are among his most important. Through them, he attempted to construct an identity predicated on honesty and trustworthiness. Hunt's efforts to initiate prison reform will be discussed below.

Hunt appeared on several of the most important stages that Regency radicalism had to offer. His major contributions – Peterloo aside – came in the Spa Fields Riots of 1816 and the Smithfield meetings of 1819. Both these events were mass platform meetings at which Hunt was an important speaker, but neither escaped satirical comment or criticism. Smithfield was the location of London's historic meat market, leading Charles Williams to depict Hunt in *The Smithfield Parliament ie Universal Suffrage* as an ass preaching to a crowd of horses, cattle, sheep and pigs. The implication is clear: listening to reformist rhetoric will lead you to slaughter.

### 'Let us perish, or be free!': The Radical Poet, Samuel Bamford

Samuel Bamford (c. 1788-1872) was an active radical in the 1810s. Born in the small industrial town of Middleton, near Manchester, he received an education through the local grammar school and in later life, became a weaver. An important figure in his life was his wife, Jemima, whom he would affectionately call 'Mima'. Jemima was also a loyal reformer: she was present at Peterloo and received praise from the radical baronet, Sir Charles Wolseley, after responding to a group of soldiers who threatened to shoot her in the head

---

97 Zamoyski, 143.
98 Hunt (1820), 4.

# Introduction.

with the words, 'Blow away! Hunt and Liberty! Hunt for ever!'[99] Mima and Samuel enjoyed a long marriage.

Bamford was a distinctive political writer, using poetry to express his beliefs. He wrote at least two poems which appeared to allude to Peterloo, including 'A Song of Slaughter':

> Ah, behold their sabres gleaming,
> Never, never known to spare,
> See the floods of slaughter streaming!
> Hark the cries that rend the air!

John Gardner has analysed Bamford's poetic works, and has characterised him as a 'Jean Valjean figure'.[100] Bamford, for his part, implausibly denied having written on Peterloo or the 'Manchester affair' at all, despite his contributions to the lively radical press. One poem, written about Henry Hunt, perhaps suggests that Bamford's attempt to disclaim his Peterloo verse was necessary because he had glanced over his shoulder at the repressive social context. What was the message of this stanza if not that the violence of the authorities would be met with violent reprisals of the very sort which the authorities most feared?

> TOUCH him, aye! touch him, if you dare;
> Pluck from his head one single hair –
> Ye sneaking, coward crew:
> Touch him – and blasted be the hand
> That graspeth not a vengeful brand,
> To rid our long oppressed land
> Of reptiles such as you.

In the 1810s, Bamford was militant in his radicalism and not unopposed to the use of force. In his later work, however, he attempted to construct a new identity which simultaneously emphasised his role in the energetic post-Napoleonic years and obscured his more extreme ideas and actions.[101] His autobiography, *Passages in the Life of a Radical*, is a valuable insight into a working class experience of the reform movement in Lancashire and a repository of personal stories and anecdotes about various reformers, including, of course, the ubiquitous Hunt. E. P. Thompson deemed Bamford to be 'the

---

99   See Bamford (1844a).
100  See Gardner (2007).
101  See Hilton.

## Hunt and Others.

greatest chronicler of nineteenth century radicalism'.[102]

Alongside his writings, Bamford was involved in meetings and reform societies. In 1817, he was arrested on charges of sedition and treason for supposedly being involved in a revolutionary group which aimed to perpetrate violence against property and persons in the Manchester area, including – notably – the property and person of Mr Joseph Nadin, the chief constable who would later arrest Hunt at Peterloo.[103] All of this led to Bamford's imprisonment at the New Bailey in Salford, and Bamford wrote about his prison experience in a pamphlet entitled *Account of the Arrest of Samuel Bamford*. By 1835, it was possible for Bamford to claim that he had been 'confined in a greater number of English prisons, for the cause of reform, than any other Englishman living'.[104] In an eloquent expression of how prison made him conceive of the world, Bamford wrote on Abingdon Jail:

> It seemed to be an epitome of the great world we had left, only there were not any spinning or weaving going here ... but all the degrees of luxury and want ... all the extremes and contrarieties of our English condition might here be observed.

Bamford was one of the five found guilty at the Peterloo trial, and he was sent to Lincoln Castle to serve his time. Following his sentencing, Bamford wrote this poem of love and devotion to Jemima:

> I never will forget thee, love!
> When summer sheds her golden ray;
> And thou shall be my comforter
> Amid the winter's cheerless day!
>
> Oh! they may bind but cannot break,
> This heart, so full of thine and thee;
> Which liveth only for YOUR sake,
> And the high cause of LIBERTY.

As time went by, Bamford's militant radicalism softened, and he found solace in his beloved countryside. A key theme in his poetry is his affection for nature and the outdoors;[105] he later wrote books about walking.[106] He is probably best remembered, however, as a key working-class figure in post-Napoleonic

---

102 Thompson, 637.
103 *Lancaster Gazette*, 5 April 1817.
104 *Sheffield Independent*, 4 April 1835.
105 See 'A View from Tandle Hill' for an example of the way in which Bamford's political beliefs connected to the Lancashire landscape. The poem is about the hope that reform is just over the horizon; Tandle Hill, near Oldham, was a regular meeting spot for reformers.
106 See Bamford (1844b).

# Introduction.

radicalism, apparent both through his presence at meetings and through his carefully articulated writings.

## Chairman of the North: John Knight

John Knight (1763-1838) was a passionate reformer involved in numerous mass meetings in the Lancashire area. Indeed, Knight chaired the first meeting of the Blackburn female reformers, and it was he who read their first address. Along with Joseph Johnson and James Wroe, Knight was a founding member of the Patriotic Union Society in Manchester. He had a respected reputation in Lancashire and was considered a figurehead of the north-west reform movement by fellow radicals. He was, accordingly, the chairman or a delegate at numerous gatherings, including one in Oldham on 7 June 1819, where endeavours were undertaken to better co-ordinate radical activities. Peterloo, which occurred later the same summer, should be seen in the context of this effort to unite geographically disparate radicals.

Following Peterloo, Knight continued to attend meetings across the north of England. During one lively meeting at Skircoat Moor, near Halifax, Knight and a Baptist minister, Parson Ellis, had repeatedly to call for silence from the crowd in order to ensure that the resolutions could be read by the chairman. The risk of another Peterloo must have loomed over him, but his association with the defining massacre of the reform movement must also have given him considerable popular credibility. It is hard to believe that his pleas for the meeting to 'be as quiet as possible' would have been as influential if they had emanated from a less notable source.[107]

Eventually, it was Knight's continued presence at meetings which proved to be his undoing in the eyes of the law. In addition to the charges he faced with regard to Peterloo, he was sentenced to prison for two years for his role in a meeting at Burnley, Lancashire, in November 1819.

He was later involved in the process of unionising the north of England. At the West Street Rooms, Oldham, Knight chaired a meeting on 14 September 1829, advocating for parliamentary reform.[108] The Oldham Political Union had at its helm two of the old guard of radicalism, Knight and William Fitton,[109] and

---

107 *Leeds Mercury*, 9 October 1819.
108 *Manchester Times*, 12 September 1829.
109 William Fitton was from Royton and was part of the large division of reformers who set off to Peterloo from this burgeoning industrial town. Fitton was arrested and charged with sedition for his involvement, but the charges were dropped. Royton had a lively political community with numerous meeting rooms. He is the cousin of James Taylor, the 'Royton Poet', and was a friend of John Fielden, who later became the radical MP for Oldham.

## Hunt and Others.

between them they led many meetings, commemorating Peterloo, supporting Hunt, and, in Knight's case, using the union rooms as a schoolroom.[110] There were significant connections between the union and the local Methodist Unitarian church, underscoring the importance of dissenting religions in the radical tradition.

### Bearer of the Black Flag: 'Dr' Joseph Healey

Although lacking in formal qualifications, Joseph Healey (1780-1850) was known by the title of 'doctor' in radical circles. Some literature refers to Healey as a 'quack', and suggests that he believed that he had inherited his medical abilities from his father, but it is perhaps kinder to describe him as an 'apothecary' working within the limits of the resources and knowledge available to him. Unlike his co-defendants, Healey was virtually illiterate, but nonetheless ardent in his desire for parliamentary reform. In 1816, operating under the heavy influence of Major Cartwright, he was involved in the creation of a Hampden Club in Oldham. Healey was active and visible within Lancastrian radical circles, marching into Peterloo with the Saddleworth and Lees contingent who carried the infamous black flag: 'Equal Representation or Death'.

Healey and Bamford were fine friends and, prior to Peterloo, each had experienced interrogation. Following the suppression of the Blanketeers, the authorities, whose restlessness was unassuaged, believed they had uncovered a huge insurrectionist plot in the Manchester area. At Ardwick Bridge, a group of reformers was broken up, and the authorities spun the story that up to 50,000 reformers across the north of England were planning to attack local officials, burn mills, and liberate the Blanketeers. This kind of narrative was perfect for propping up the government's use of emergency measures and its suspension of *habeas corpus*. Shortly after the 'existence' of the conspiracy was announced, several reformers were rounded up as suspected insurrectionists. Healey, Bamford and several other prisoners were taken in irons to London and were questioned by the Home Secretary, Lord Sidmouth, and the Foreign Secretary, Lord Castlereagh. Their families were not informed of their arrest and extradition to Whitehall (Jemima Bamford tried to find out what had happened from John Knight, but he refused to help her; this was later a sore point between Knight and 'our Sam'). During the examination of the supposed insurrectionists, Healey was asked to spell his name. In a broad Lancashire accent, he answered, 'Haitch, hay, haa, el, hay, wye', bewildering his interrogators. As he could not write very well, he produced a business card reading, 'Joseph Healey, Surgeon,

---

110  See Navickas.

# Introduction.

Middleton, Please take __ Spoonsful of this Mixture Each __ Hours'.[111] Bamford was released on bail, but the hapless Healey was imprisoned indeterminately. The suspension of *habeas corpus* meant that it was not necessary even to imagine a charge against him.

Elizabeth Healey, Joseph's wife, was also a passionate reformer. On the day of Peterloo, Joseph had suggested that she should stay at home, but Elizabeth, who was feeling unwell, dismissed her husband's advice and went into Manchester anyway. Forgoing the crowd, she watched the meeting from a distance, situating herself in a house on Windmill Street. She therefore avoided the carnage, but saw the massacre unfold before her; she was interviewed about her experience by Bamford. Her account includes a description of a middle-aged woman, killed in the tumult, being carried helplessly into the sanctuary of the property.

A Brush with Death: Joseph Johnson

Joseph Johnson (1791-1872) was a fairly successful brush manufacturer from Manchester, and a member of the Manchester Hampden Club which had been formed by Knight. In 1818, Johnson was also involved in the creation of the *Manchester Observer* (being one of its owners) and, in 1819, he was one of the founding members of the Patriotic Union Society (becoming its secretary). As described in the overview of Peterloo, Johnson was central to the organisation of the meeting, ensuring that it included reformers from beyond the boundary of Manchester and that it attracted a star speaker. Prison, however, appeared to break Johnson's radical spirit. His young wife died during his incarceration, and the governor of Lincoln Castle did not give him leave to attend her funeral. He largely disengaged from politics after his release, but did host William Cobbett[112] during Cobbett's 1830 tour of the north.[113]

The Acquitted: Moorhouse, Saxton, Jones, Swift, and Wylde

As previously mentioned, there were ten defendants at the Peterloo trial in York, half of whom were acquitted of the charges against them. Not much is known about Robert Wylde, Robert Jones, George Swift or James Moorhouse. Wylde lived in Ashton-under-Lyne, a growing industrial town south of Oldham, and may have been much younger than the other defendants – he is referred

---

111  See Marlow.
112  Cobbett's tours of the country are documented in his book *Rural Rides*. He took on the role of a journalist, particularly reporting on the plight of the countryside and rural workers.
113  See Cobbett.

## Hunt and Others.

to as 'the boy'. However, an account of the examination at Lancaster Castle guessed that he was, in fact, about twenty-three years of age.[114]

Robert Jones was a rag dealer from Manchester, and was presumed to be about twenty-five. Witnesses at the trial suggested that he was involved in helping to put the hustings up, and that he may have spoken to the crowd before Hunt's arrival. A newspaper report called him 'a person of mean appearance, but ... rather vain of his eloquence'.[115]

George Swift was a shoemaker from Manchester, aged nineteen at the time of the massacre. He had also helped to erect the hustings. While he was being held in the New Bailey in the days after the massacre, Swift wrote his account of events in a letter to his brother: this text became known as the 'Swift Narrative'.

James Moorhouse was a stagecoach proprietor, an auctioneer and a staymaker from Stockport, and a 'jolly-looking elderly gentleman'.[116] On the day of Peterloo, he led the Stockport procession to the meeting.

Much more is known about John Thacker Saxton (c. 1776-1835). Both Saxton and his wife, Susanna, were visible in the radical Manchester scene. Susanna was the secretary for the Manchester Female Reformers (formed in July 1819) and the author of several radical pamphlets. At the Peterloo meeting, it was the intention of the female reformers to give Hunt a beautifully-made flag. In an address later published in a letter, the women declared:

> May our flag never be unfurled but in the cause of peace and reform! and then may a female's curse pursue the coward who deserts the standard![117]

After the massacre, this injunction became a rallying cry amongst radicals, urging one another to continue to pursue reform in the face of repression, to keep up the momentum for change.

John Saxton was involved in writing and publishing the *Manchester Observer*, along with fellow defendants Knight and Johnson. Tyas, the reporter

---

114   See Taylor, J. E. (1819).
115   *Caledonian Mercury*, 23 March 1820. This newspaper reported an amusing courtroom moment: Jones had lent his copy of the indictment to 'a reporter of a country paper'. The reporter then handed the copy to another individual. Jones lost his patience and said to the judge, 'My Lord, that man has thrown away my indictment. Ax him to give it me back again.' Another newspaper described Jones telling a man who was wearing a white hat in the galleries that, if he was a defence witness, he must leave the courtroom. His manner – and the fact that the man with the hat was not a witness – 'called forth a general laugh' (*Morning Post*, 20 March 1820). The similarity between Henry Hunt's symbolic headwear and the man's own hat must have led Jones to an inevitable (albeit incorrect) conclusion.
116   *Caledonian Mercury*, 23 March 1820. A 'staymaker' was a maker of corsets.
117   Huish, 218. Jacqueline Riding has suggested that the use of the 'curse' may be a reference to the Lancashire Witches.

# Introduction.

from *The Times* who witnessed the massacre from the hustings, reported that the yeomanry attempted to kill Saxton. In a prophetic statement contained in a letter which he wrote to *The Times*, Saxton argued that the massacre of peaceful men, women and children would do little to halt the movement for reform:

> I beg leave to conclude with reminding you ... that our cause grows and gathers strength with the plunderings of our enemies; whilst their rapacity must not only destroy the means of their own existence, but must, ere long, turn them to the destruction of each other.[118]

Unlike his fellow *Observer* writers, Saxton was acquitted at the trial, possibly because he argued that he was present at Peterloo as a journalist. He, along with the seven committee members of the Manchester Female Reform Society, went on to address the crowd at the first anniversary commemoration of the massacre. In the last years of his life, Saxton lived in Hertford – hardly, one would think, a hotbed of radical feeling to compare with Lancashire – where he nevertheless served as the enthusiastic editor and publisher of a paper called the *Hertford and Ware Patriot* (later changed to the *Radical Reformer and Hertford and Ware Patriot*).

## IX. Landscape of Justice: The Trial and its Buildings

The York Lent Assizes of 1820 arrived, and the trial began.[119] It was no brief affair. Originally, the trial was to be held in Lancaster: Hunt was one of the radicals to request a relocation, believing that by moving the trial away from Lancashire, a fairer jury would be empanelled.[120] The defendants probably also wanted to have more time to prepare their defences; and it is also possible that the unsatisfactory inquest into the death of John Lees influenced the decision to move elsewhere. Lees had received sabre wounds at Peterloo and had subsequently died from his injuries. Edward Meagher, a yeoman, was identified as the murderer by reformers but, despite the weight of the evidence, no verdict was found against him. Tensions were running high again in Lancashire. Yorkshire looked comparably calm.

The number of witnesses called by the prosecution and the defence – more than eighty in total – inevitably contributed to the trial's duration.[121] Prior to the

---

118 *Times* (London), 25 November 1819.
119 Before the abolition of assizes by the Courts Act 1971, quarter sessions were held around the country to deal with more serious offences. The assizes have a long history, dating to the twelfth century.
120 See Poole, R. (2006).

## Hunt and Others.

trial, Hunt was busy campaigning to become the MP for Preston (in an election he eventually lost, accruing eighteen per cent of the vote in a four-horse race). He went via Manchester to York; he had time to make a speech, leaning his head and one arm out of an upstairs window, announcing his confidence that he would 'record a verdict of guilty against them', the 'butchers of Peterloo', as if the authorities were on trial, instead of him.[122] The widespread support for Hunt was again visible on his journey to the trial. Around a mile from Leeds, he was welcomed by a throng of radicals, some of whom hand-pulled his chaise to his accommodation.[123] One report put the size of this crowd at 60,000, and suggested that his adherents were willing to hand-pull Hunt all the way to York.[124] On their own north-eastern journey to York, Bamford and the witnesses for the defence took a spectacular and symbolic route across the Pennines. Reportedly, two groups of around 140 men marched to the trial, carrying a banner saying, 'The Truth, the whole Truth, and nothing but the Truth'.[125] During the trial itself, Hunt would often be followed back to his lodgings on Coney Street by a loyal band of Manchester radicals.[126]

The York Assize Court, now called the York Crown Court, is a neoclassical building designed by John Carr (perhaps as early as 1765) and completed in 1777. There are two different courtrooms: the crown court and the civil court. Both courtrooms had their galleries enlarged in 1812, and some remodelling then took place in 1818. Each courtroom is of a similar rectangular footprint. The original oak panelling survives to this day, although it has been rearranged, along with the seating.[127] The façade of the building includes a depiction of a cap of liberty. This provoked a moment of wit during the trial: when the prosecution described the apparently threatening symbolism of the black flag ('Equal Representation or Death'), Hunt retorted that, by that logic, the liberty cap could be construed as revolutionary. How could 'that which was approved by all in York be deemed a crime in Lancashire'?

The court sits within a landscape of justice. It is one of three buildings surrounding a circular patch of ground called the Eye of the Ridings: here,

---

121 One newspaper report suggested that the Crown was aiming for around a hundred witnesses, and that Hunt would call between five hundred and a thousand (*York Herald*, 11 March 1820).
122 *Morning Post*, 16 March 1820. The address occurred in the residence of a Mr Chapman; Mr Chapman's parlour was too low down to properly address the number of people who had gathered to welcome Hunt to Manchester.
123 *Lancaster Gazette*, 18 March 1820.
124 *York Herald*, 18 March 1820.
125 *Morning Post*, 18 March 1820.
126 *Morning Post*, 21 March 1820.
127 Royal Commission on the Historical Monuments of England.

# Introduction.

elections for the Ridings of Yorkshire were held until 1832. To the south-east of the court stands the Debtors' Prison, a baroque building dating from 1705. To the north-east of the Debtors' Prison, and to the east of the court, is the Female Prison, a neoclassical building completed in 1780. To the north of all three buildings is Clifford's Tower, the last remnant of the mediaeval castle which once stood on the site. Collectively, these buildings form a striking quartet, expressing power, authority and centuries of precedent, in which justice was, or was not, delivered.

Locally and nationally, there was fascination with the trial. As well as the witnesses who made their way to York, 'the extraordinary interest excited by this trial caused multitudes to pour into York several days before its commencement'.[128] On the opening day, the desire to witness the proceedings first-hand was intense, with people jostling for seats. In the rush to grab a seat in the gallery, some people took to scaling the walls, and others 'forgot all decorum to the fairer sex'. The courtroom filled quickly, with around twenty journalists from London and provincial newspapers present: the reporters gained early access, getting to the best seats ahead of the public.[129] The boxes and galleries were filled by eight o'clock, with the box reserved for the Manchester magistrates also quickly occupied.[130] The magistrates had been allocated space in the attorneys' box, behind the journalists, but, in the dash to find a good seat, 'it was invaded by many who had no claim to sit there', and some of the invaders refused to give up their position until they were 'expelled by order of the magistrates on their arrival'.[131] The defendants arrived at a quarter past eight and sat at the barristers' table.[132] The courtroom was a packed, dynamic space, and, to those watching, its activities occurred at the blurred interface between civic participation and entertainment. The public appetite for more, however, remained as healthy as ever. Just after seven o'clock on the morning of the second day, when the courtroom doors were opened, the inward rush was 'excessive' and 'a number of ladies encountered the pressure of the crowd' – and this was two hours before the defendants arrived, and two and a half hours before the judge took his seat.[133] On day seven – admittedly an exciting one, since Hunt was in the middle of calling his witnesses – the court remained 'crowded to excess'.[134] The written transcript is merely a starting point for our imagination

---

128 *Examiner*, 19 March 1820.
129 *York Herald*, 18 March 1820.
130 *Leeds Mercury*, 18 March 1820.
131 *Morning Post*, 18 March 1820.
132 *Morning Chronicle*, 18 March 1820.
133 *Morning Chronicle*, 20 March 1820.
134 *Morning Chronicle*, 25 March 1820.

## Hunt and Others.

in this regard: the testimony was given in a crowded public environment, and some of defendants palpably appreciated the importance of their performance, to be considered separately to the cogency of their defence. The judge and the jury were not the only spectators at the theatre – the onlookers and the journalists were the conduits by which the defendants' political philosophy would reach the consciousness of the nation.

Then there were the witnesses. Their accounts of the Peterloo meeting were not merely descriptive; they also showed how the contested details of Peterloo were remembered and reconstructed in the memories of those present. Hunt took the opportunity to cross-examine every single witness: this was a policy which hinted at the performative value of the trial; a lawyer, by contrast, might have recommended a more targeted approach. Not everybody enjoyed the show, and the author of a private letter published in several newspapers was distinctly unimpressed:

> Hunt's trial continues, and is likely to continue, going on as he does; he may make it last as long as that of Warren Hastings did.[135] His endless cross-examinations render it quite impossible to guess, with any tolerable chance of coming near the mark, at what time any particular set of witnesses will be disposed of. The course he takes is the same in every case. With great insolence he amuses himself with a rude banter on everyone who gets into the witness's box.[136]

The same writer felt similarly towards Hunt's co-defendants. He is the source of Robert Jones's unflattering character reference, given above, and he described Healey as 'the gin-drinking doctor' whose combative courtroom manner appeared to have been derived naively from popular theatre. Hunt, to another commentator of matching sentiment, was simply an 'impudent fellow'.[137]

Still, opinion pieces of this sort were part of York's complex landscape of justice, a physical and philosophical space in which people could imagine and construct their version of Peterloo, seven months after the massacre itself. Through performance, oratory, discussion and the transmission of ideas – all catalysed by the charming vagaries of the adversarial system – the dead lived again, reassembled in endless, kaleidoscopic variations, rewound to their stabling inns and their drilling points in the Lancashire fields, and scrutinised

---

135 Warren Hastings was an English statesman in the 1700s. He was impeached in 1788 for crimes in India. At the hearing in the House of Commons, it took Edmund Burke two days to read the twenty counts against Hastings, and the whole process lasted for 148 days, spread across seven years.
136 *Caledonian Mercury*, 23 March 1820.
137 *Royal Cornwall Gazette*, 25 March 1820.

## Introduction.

from every possible political angle, with benevolence and sympathy by one witness, and with fear and suspicion by the next.

After ten days, in what might seem like a pusillanimous compromise, five of the ten defendants were found guilty of 'assembling with unlawful banners for an unlawful assembly, for the purpose of moving and inciting the liege subjects of our Sovereign Lord the King to contempt and hatred of the government and constitution of the realm, as by law established, and attending at the same'. Even then, there was an unedifying moment as the jury were sent back out of court, with advice ringing in their ears, to consider exactly which part of the indictment their guilty verdict applied to.

X.
'My incarceration in this infamous Bastille':
The Prison Experiences of Hunt

Following the verdict, the five convicted men were dispersed between three different prisons. Hunt was sent to Ilchester Gaol near Yeovil; Knight was sent to Lancaster Gaol; and Bamford, Johnson and Healey to Lincoln Castle. It is possible to get an idea of their experience through this description of a standard cell at Ilchester:

> Each story containing five cells, nine feet by six, and eight feet six inches high, fitted with perforated iron bedsteads, and straw, changed either monthly or oftener, as needful; a blanket, and a coverlet, or rug. Each cell has a double door; the outer iron-gated, the inner of wood ... The cells have each a semicircular window, half glazed, half open, with sloping boards, and have a view into the Keeper's garden.[138]

During his imprisonment, Hunt was busy with his correspondence and the writing of his memoirs. However, he also decided to continue a business venture which he had begun in January 1820: breakfast powder.[139] Hunt's Breakfast Powder was made from roasted rye and meant to be a cheap substitute for coffee or tea. The venture soon ran into legal problems. Selling foodstuffs as a coffee substitute (and thereby depriving the government of the tax levied against sales of the real thing) was against the law in the Regency period, and the authorities believed that Hunt had advertised his Breakfast Powder in violation of the act;

---

138 Neild, 288.
139 Several versions of breakfast powder were produced, including one made by Thomas Worth, agent for the *Black Dwarf*, a radical journal (*Norfolk Chronicle*, 24 December 1819); and another by a Mr Dynes from Ipswich (*Ipswich Journal*, 25 January 1823).

## Hunt and Others.

they therefore seized his apparatus and rye. After a drawn-out affair, in the course of which breakfast powder was discussed in parliament, the Court of Exchequer introduced a new Excise Act which permitted 'the manufacture and sale of scorched or roasted corn, pease, or beans, by *persons not being dealers* in coffee, cocoa, tea, tobacco, or snuff'.[140] The press, meanwhile, accused Hunt of ripping off poor people. The *Morning Post*, adopting a strikingly sarcastic tone, claimed that, by assembling the same 'cheap materials' found in Breakfast Powder, a fair simulacrum could be made at home for four pence a pound – a third of the retail price of Hunt's product:

> The friends of the people, the advocates of their rights and liberties, are giving a notable instance of their disinterestedness to the wretched Radicals whose distress they pretend to commiserate. ... [Breakfast Powder is] prepared, of course, not for the benefit of the vendors, but wholly and solely for the relief of the people.[141]

Hunt also occupied himself by attempting to secure prison reform, especially at Ilchester. According to his memoirs, it was by far the worst prison in the entire country – worse, he said, than Newgate. It was certainly in need of repair. There were issues with dirty water and poor-quality sewers, and these problems were exacerbated by the frequent flooding which occurred beside the River Yeo. Of the 6678 prisoners incarcerated at Ilchester between 1811 and 1821, 4058 had to receive medical assistance including Hunt himself: 'I have been attended by three physicians, and have taken the prescriptions of them all; have been four times bled, and survived the whole'.[142] Hunt's criticisms, articulated in a publication entitled *A Peep into a Prison*, feed into the contemporary concerns of the prison reform movement, which was gathering pace in the early nineteenth century.[143] Another prisoner at Ilchester, James Hillier, perhaps inspired by Hunt's pamphleteering, decided to petition the House of Commons for an inquiry into the state of the gaol, emphasising the poor health of the prisoners and the debauched behaviour of the gaolers. Ultimately, Hunt and Hillier were successful in removing the prison's governor, the tyrannical William Bridle, from his post.

---

140  *Royal Cornwall Gazette*, 15 June 1822.
141  *Morning Post*, 26 January 1820.
142  Hunt (1821), 217.
143  The early nineteenth century saw the prison reform movement begin to accelerate, with ideas abounding for practical changes, the need for moral instruction, and the role of architecture and space. Penal transportation was causing enormous stress on the punishment system because of its cost (see Herrup); Ignatieff suggests an association between the shift to larger prisons and the emergence of capitalism. Sir Francis Burdett, the radical MP, was also involved in prison reform, with his efforts largely focusing on Coldbath Fields Prison.

# Introduction.

## XI. The Trial's Importance

Thematically, the trial of Henry Hunt *et al* does not stand alone. It connects to numerous other significant actions of the Regency and pre-Regency periods: trials which reveal the fears and anxieties of the authorities, and which imagine the courtroom as a space in which to perform. Radicals and reformers recognised that trials provided valuable opportunities to disseminate their ideas, and that the question of whether they were found guilty or not was rather a separate one. Trial transcripts were widely published and would often recreate whole speeches, with a curious double effect: the publication of the proceedings of a trial for sedition could contain a seditious or libellous speech.[144]

The repressive 1790s were punctuated by the trials of radicals. Among the most familiar was the trial of Thomas Paine in 1792; Paine, who was represented by Thomas Erskine, a notable lawyer and politician, was found guilty of seditious libel. Erskine later defended Thomas Hardy, John Horne Tooke and John Thelwall in the treason trials of 1794 – all three were acquitted.[145] The power of performance continued to pay dividends. William Hone, the radical satirist, was tried in 1817 on charges of publishing blasphemous and seditious works. After three seven-hour speeches, his wit and his ability to communicate an argument led to his acquittal.[146] In the same year, James Watson and Arthur Thistlewood were tried for high treason for their involvement in the Spa Fields Riots. Watson's spirited defence of his actions undermined the indictment, and he was acquitted; Thistlewood followed when it was shown that the Crown's chief witness was fraudulent.

There are three notable Regency trials in which the successful prosecution of radicals for high treason resulted in the death penalty being exacted: the 1817 trial of the Pentrich conspirators, and the 1820 trials of the Cato Street conspirators and the Scottish Insurrectionists.[147] If the severe charges against them had not been downgraded before the commencement of the trial, it is possible that a similar fate may have befallen the Peterloo defendants. The usual mode of execution required the condemned person to be hanged until dead and then beheaded, in public. But the public spectacle of the execution

---

144  Richard Carlile took advantage of this privilege by reading Thomas Paine's *Rights of Man* in court.
145  Erskine also defended James Hadfield, who was accused of attempting to assassinate King George III at the theatre. Hadfield was acquitted by virtue of insanity.
146  See Porter.
147  To find out more about treason trials generally, as well as Regency ones, see Steffen. Arthur Thistlewood, James Ings, Richard Tidd, John Brunt and William Davidson are the last people to have been hanged and beheaded in England, whilst James Wilson, Andrew Hardie and John Baird are the last to have been hanged and beheaded in Scotland.

## Hunt and Others.

of dissenting radicals cut both ways, stoking feelings of resentment among reformers, creating martyrs to the cause, and radicalising the living.[148] The 1820 trials are a supplementary chapter to the Peterloo narrative: the conspirators and insurrectionists' anger at the maltreatment of reformers gathered to petition peacefully was one of the reasons for which they considered violent action themselves.

Both Hunt and Bamford had been on trial before. Hunt's first experience was not for sedition – rather, it was over some pheasants which the plaintiff, Lord Bruce, argued were on his land, and which Hunt had no right to kill. Hunt was imprisoned, and it was while he was incarcerated that he met Henry Clifford, a radical lawyer, who introduced him in turn to famous radicals such as Hardy and Tooke.[149] As noted in Bamford's biography, Sam was sent to prison in 1817, and wrote about his experiences; and the Peterloo defendants who were most closely involved with the *Manchester Observer* knew the financial cost of being charged with seditious publication. Eventually, the back of the newspaper was broken by its legal fees and fines. The dangers of speaking out were impossible to ignore, and the Peterloo trial is part of the longer history of the state's attempts to suppress radical thought and action.

### XVIII. Contextual Value

Historians have often examined the loyalist and conservative responses to post-Enlightened radicalism through the lens of Edmund Burke. This tendency has simplified a complex and multifaceted experience, and has underplayed the potential of the wealth of additional sources – including trial records – which supplement our understanding of the period. Through the trial of Henry Hunt, it is possible to observe the authorities' fears and anxieties in original ways, and this creates new opportunities for new readings.

We briefly explored the class implications of the trial above – but it is a theme worth returning to. The transcript and its associated coverage present several permutations of class relationship: the defendants with one another, the defendants with the judiciary and the representatives of state, the defendants with the spectators, and the spectators with the defendants, for example. The

---

148 The Scottish Insurrectionists' executions were greeted by angry crowds who considered that the executions were state-sanctioned murder. At his execution, Wilson's head was displayed to the crowd and the announcement was made: 'This is the head of a traitor'. A journalist recorded the disagreement of the masses. 'Vehement cries of, "It is false, he has bled for his country," were heard from different quarters.' (*Glasgow Herald*, 1 September 1820.)

149 Belchem (1985).

## Introduction.

starkest class division existed between the privileged Hunt and the other four guilty men. How did these divisions and differences affect how the defendants performed, spoke or behaved during the trial? Were their shared political and philosophical standpoints enough to occlude their class differences? How do the prosecution's attempts to justify the violence of the yeomanry link to wider establishment and middle class readings of reform, radicalism and sedition? And what about the spectators? Did class define one's likelihood to take an interest in, and even attend, the trial? Was the crowd heterogeneous, or homogeneous? What does attendance at a political trial tell us about polite society?

Of course, Peterloo was a landmark moment in the history of suffrage. The verdict against the guilty men defined it, retrospectively, as an illegal meeting – it said little about the language they used, but merely about the question of assembling 'with unlawful banners' in the first place (Hunt had already told the court that he 'did not well understand the law of flags'). By shifting the focus from seditious speech to the idea of unlawful action, the prosecution was able to establish in practice that meetings could be framed as seditious or illegal irrespective of the content of their language.[150] To what extent did this subtle shift open up new avenues for official prosecution and repression?

For the historian, the trial's multiple witness accounts of Peterloo provide a unique insight not only into the manner in which the events of the day unfolded, but also into the manner in which people were remembering them. Witnesses describe the demonstration's material culture (clothing, banners and flags, liberty caps, walking sticks, swords, and so on) in rich detail. Material culture was also an important focus for the prosecution, who sought to prove that the meeting was violent in its intentions by emphasising the presence of certain items including brickbats, stones, and 'truncheons'. What can these accounts, when cross-referenced and combined, tell us about the mindset of the reformers? What was the function of material culture at this mass platform meeting?

The significance of the trial was recognised at the time: 'the circumstances,' one commentator wrote, 'though local in the immediate sphere of operation, involve some questions of national importance'.[151] Transcripts of the trial became part of a vibrant print culture in which news, gossip, and current affairs were much sought after. Versions were published by several different individuals – an indication of the attention which the trial received, the size of the popular market, and Hunt's distinctive commercial viability. The press also covered the trial, dedicating countless columns to the testimony, day after

---

150  See Lobban; Tilly and Tilly (eds.).
151  See Fisher, 4.

day. The defendants can rarely have found their political principles so easy to disseminate, and there are clear indications that some of them readily grasped the opportunity to perform. How can trials generally be considered performative? How – if at all – would a modern trial for sedition be handled differently? How do we, as twenty-first century readers, imagine the space in which Hunt and his co-defendants operated?

## XIX. Conclusion

The themes that emerge from the transcript of the Peterloo trial are familiar: fears and anxieties of the authorities and the establishment; the connections between radicalism and revolution; the trial as a performance space; the role of class. They invite the reader to consider the trial within its wider context and history, and within the narrative of radical repression. The trial also offers a unique insight into the events of the day, and the ways in which they were remembered and represented by opposing political forces. It is therefore a unique and vital account of an episode which should be central to our understanding of the country's political development – a microcosm of political resistance, and a theatrical event in which prosecution and defence performed a battle of words.

# Introduction.

## BIBLIOGRAPHY.

Bamford, S., *An Account of the Arrest and Imprisonment of Samuel Bamford, Middleton, on Suspicion of High Treason* (Manchester: 1817).

*Passages in the Life of a Radical* (London: Simpkin, Marshall and Co., 1844). [1844a]

*Walks in South Lancashire and on its Borders* (Blackley: 1844). [1844b]

Belchem, J., 'Henry Hunt and the Evolution of the Mass Platform' in *The English Historical Review*, 93 (369) [1978], 739-773.

*Orator Hunt* (Oxford: Oxford University Press, 1985).

Belchem, J. and Epstein, J., 'The Nineteenth-Century Gentleman Leader Revisited' in *Social History*, 22 (2) [1997], 174-193.

Burgess, G., and Festenstein, M., *English Radicalism, 1550-1850* (Cambridge: Cambridge University Press, 2007).

Bush, M. L., 'The Women at Peterloo: the Impact of Female Reform on the Manchester Meeting of 16 August 1819' in *History*, 89 (294) [2004], 209-232.

*The Casualties of Peterloo* (London: Carnegie, 2005).

Cannon, J., 'Hampden Clubs (1812-17)' in *A Dictionary of British History* [2009]. Available at: www.oxfordreference.com/view/10.1093/acref/9780199550371.001.0001/acref-9780199550371-e-1614 (subscription required).

Cobbett, W., *Rural Rides* (London: 1830).

Crick, J., *'Pristina Libertas:* Liberty and the Anglo-Saxons Revisited' in *Transactions of the Royal Historical Society*, 14 [2004], 47-71.

Dolby, T., *The Trial of Henry Hunt, Esq., [et al] for an Alledged Conspiracy to Overturn the Government, etc.* (London: 1820).

Epstein, J., 'Understanding the Cap of Liberty: Symbolic Practice and Social Conflict in Early Nineteenth-Century England' in *Past and Present*, 122 [1989], 75-118.

Fisher, H., *An Impartial Narrative on the Late Melancholy Occurrences in Manchester* (Liverpool: 1819).

Gardner, J., 'Peterloo, Cato Street, and Caroline: Poetry and Popular Protest, 1819-1821' (PhD Thesis, University of Glasgow, 2002). Available at: theses.gla.ac.uk/6872/1/2002GardnerPhD.pdf

'The Suppression of Samuel Bamford's Peterloo Poems' in *Romanticism*, 13 (2) [2007], 145-155.

Griffin, C. J., *Protest, Politics and Work in Rural England, 1700-1850* (Basingstoke: Palgrave Macmillan, 2013).

Harrison, M., *Crowds and History: Mass Phenomena in English Towns, 1790-1835* (Cambridge: Cambridge University Press, 1988).

Herrup, C., 'Punishing Pardon: Some Thoughts on the Origins of Penal Transportation' in Devereaux, S. and Griffiths, P. (eds), *Penal Practice and Culture, 1500-1900: Punishing the English* (London: Palgrave Macmillan UK, 2004), 121-137.

Hewitt, R., *A Revolution of Feeling: The Decade that Forged the Modern Mind* (London: Granta, 2017).

Hilton, T., 'Introduction' to Bamford, S., *Passages in the Life of a Radical* (London: MacGibbon & Kee, 1967).

Hobsbawm, E. J., *The Age of Revolution: 1789-1848* (New York: New American Library, 1965).

Hollis, P., *Class and Conflict in Nineteenth-Century England: 1815-1850* (London: Routledge, 2016).

# Hunt and Others.

Huish, R., *The History of the Private and Political Life of Henry Hunt, Esq., His Times and Contemporaries* (London: John Saunders, 1835).

Hunt, H., *Memoirs of Henry Hunt Esq. Written by Himself in His Majesty's Jail at Ilchester* (London: T. Dolby, 1820).

*Investigation at Ilchester Gaol, In the County of Somerset, Into the Conduct of William Bridle, the Gaoler, Before the Commissioners Appointed by the Crown* (London: T. Dolby, 1821).

Ignatieff, M., *A Just Measure of Pain: the Penitentiary in the Industrial Revolution, 1750-1850* (Harmondsworth: Penguin, 1989).

Katz-Hyman, M., 'Doing Good While Doing Well: The Decision to Manufacture Products that Supported the Abolition of the Slave Trade and Slavery in Great Britain' in *Slavery & Abolition*, 29 (2) [2008], 219-231.

Kidson, F., *Traditional Tunes: A Collection of Ballads* (Oxford: Taphouse and Son, 1891).

Lobban, M., 'From Seditious Libel to Unlawful Assembly: Peterloo and the Changing Face of Political Crime, c. 1770-1820' in *Oxford Journal of Legal Studies*, 10 (3) [1990], 307-352.

Lodge, D., *After Bakhtin: Essays on Fiction and Criticism* (London: Routledge, 1990).

Lucas, G., 'Reading Pottery: Literature and Transfer-Printed Pottery in the Early Nineteenth Century' in *International Journal of Historical Archaeology*, 7 (2) [2003], 127-143.

Marlow, J., *The Peterloo Massacre* (London: Rapp & Whiting, 1969).

Marrison, A. (ed.), *Free Trade and its Reception, 1815-1960* (London: Routledge, 2003).

Mather, R., '"These Lancashire Women are Witches in Politics": Female Reform Societies and the Theatre of Radicalism, 1819-20' in Poole, R. (ed), Return to Peterloo (Manchester: Manchester History Review, 2014), 29-64.

McElligott, J., 'William Hone (1780-1842), Print Culture, and the Nature of Radicalism' in Hessayon, A. and Finnegan, D. (eds.), *Varieties of Seventeenth- and Early Eighteenth-Century English Radicalism in Context* (Burlington: Ashgate, 2011), 241-260.

Miller, H., 'Popular Petitioning and the Corn Laws, 1833-46' in *The English Historical Review*, 127 (527) [2012], 882-919.

Miller, N. C., 'Major John Cartwright and the Founding of the Hampden Club' in *The Historical Journal*, 17 (3) [1974], 615-619.

Morgan, A., *Ballads and Songs of Peterloo* (Manchester: Manchester University Press, 2018).

Muddiman, J. G. (ed.), *Trial of King Charles the First* (Edinburgh: William Hodge & Co., 1928).

Navickas, K., *Protest and the Politics of Space and Place, 1789-1848* (Manchester: Manchester University Press, 2016).

Neild, J., *State of the Prisons in England, Scotland and Wales* (London: J. Nichols, 1812).

O'Gorman, F., *Voters, Patrons and Parties: The Unreformed Electoral System of Hanoverian England, 1734-1832* (Oxford: Oxford University Press, 1989).

Omissi, A., 'The Cap of Liberty: Roman Slavery, Cultural Memory, and Magic Mushrooms' in *Folklore*, 127 (3) [2016], 270-285.

Philips, F., *Exposures of the Calumnies Circulated by the Enemies of Social Order and Reiterated against their Abettors against the Magistrates and the Yeomanry Cavalry of Manchester and Salford* (London: Collins, 1819).

Phillips, J. A., *Electoral Behavior in Unreformed England: Plumpers, Splitters, and Straights* (Princeton: Princeton University Press, 1982).

# Introduction.

Pickering, P. A. and Tyrrell, A., *The People's Bread: A History of the Anti-Corn Law League* (London: Leicester University Press, 2000).

Plowright, J., *Regency England: The Age of Lord Liverpool* (London: Routledge, 1996).

Poole, R., '"By the Law or the Sword": Peterloo Revisited' in *History*, 91 (302) [2006], 254-276.

'French Revolution or Peasants' Revolt? Petitioners and Rebels in England from the Blanketeers to the Chartists' in *Labour History Review*, 74 (1) [2009], 6-26.

Poole, S., *John Thelwall: Radical Romantic and Acquitted Felon* (London: Pickering & Chatto, 2009).

Porter, R., *Flesh in the Age of Reason* (London: Penguin, 2004).

Pratt, J., *An Impartial Report of the Proceedings in the Cause of the King versus Henry Hunt [et al] for Conspiracy* (Manchester: 1820).

Read, D., *Peterloo: The Massacre and its Background* (Manchester: Manchester University Press, 1958).

Reid, R., *The Peterloo Massacre* (London: Random House, 2017).

Riding, J., *Peterloo: The Story of the Manchester Massacre* (London: Head of Zeus, 2018).

Royal Commission on the Historical Monuments of England, *An Inventory of the Historical Monuments in York: The Defences* (London: RCHME, (1972).

Steffen, L., *Defining a British State: Treason and National Identity, 1608-1820* (London: Palgrave, 2001).

Taylor, J. E., (ed.) *Peterloo Massacre* (Manchester: J. Wroe, 1819).

*Notes and Observations, Critical and Explanatory, on the Papers Relative to the State of the Country* (London: Effingham Wilson, 1820).

Taylor, M., 'British Conservatism, the Illuminati, and the Conspiracy Theory of the French Revolution, 1797-1802' in *Eighteenth-Century Studies*, 47 (3) [2014], 293-312.

Thompson, E. P., *The Making of the English Working Class* (London: Victor Gollancz, 1963).

Tilly, C. and L. A. (eds.), *Class Conflict and Collective Action* (Beverly Hills: Sage, 1981).

Turner, M., 'The "Bonaparte of Free Trade" and the Anti-Corn Law League' in *The Historical Journal*, 41 (4) [1998], 1011-1034.

Urban, S. (ed.), *The Gentleman's Magazine: and Historical Chronicle*, Vol. 89, second part (London: 1819).

Walmsley, R., *Peterloo: The Case Reopened* (Manchester: Manchester University Press, 1969).

Waterman, A. M. C., 'The Nexus between Theology and Political Doctrine' in Haakonssen, K. (ed.), *Enlightenment and Religion: Rational Dissent in Eighteenth-Century Britain* (Cambridge: Cambridge University Press, 1996), 193-218.

Wood, G. D., *Tambora: The Eruption that Changed the World* (Princeton: Princeton University Press, 2014).

Zamoyski, A., *Phantom Terror: The Threat of Revolution and the Repression of Liberty, 1789-1848* (London: Harper Collins, 2014).

## Hunt and Others.

## Archival Sources.

The National Archives: Home Office collection. PRO HO 40/9/146.
'The Birmingham Hampden Club'.

The National Archives: Home Office collection. PRO HO 41/4.
'Disturbances Entry Books: Miscellaneous'.

The National Archives: Treasury Solicitor papers. PRO TS 11/200.
'Papers relating to the prosecutions: (1) for high treason (arising from the riots in London in 1816); (2) for a misdemeanour (sending a challenge to Lord Sidmouth to fight a duel in 1818); (3) for high treason and other offences (arising from the 'Cato Street conspiracy' in 1820).'

The National Archives: Treasury Solicitor papers. PRO TS 11/1086.
'Court records'.

The National Archives: Treasury Solicitor papers. PRO TS 11/1133.
'Society for Constitutional Information: Resolutions and Orders'.

## Acknowledgements.

Thanks to Jonathan Finch, Claire Boardman and David Kitchener for their insightful comments about the book throughout its development.

Many thanks to the Working Class Movement Library for their assistance and knowledge during research trips.

# Leading Dates in the Case of Henry Hunt et al.

**1815**

    April and
following months    Eruption of Mount Tambora.

    18 June    Battle of Waterloo.

**1816**

    15 November    Peaceful gathering at Spa Fields, Islington.

    2 December    Spa Fields Riots.

**1817**

    10 March    The Blanketeers set off from Manchester. Their march to London is quickly suppressed.

    31 March    The Seditious Meetings Act (1817) gains Royal assent.

**1818**

    4 August    The Tories, under the Earl of Liverpool, achieve a parliamentary majority in the general election.

**1819**

    2 August    Plans are made to hold a mass platform event in Manchester on this date; the event is postponed by one week.

    9 August    The mass platform event is postponed for a further week.

    16 August    The Peterloo Massacre. Numerous reformers arrested.

**1820**

    16 March    Trial of Henry Hunt *et al*: first day.

    27 March    Trial of Henry Hunt *et al*: tenth and final day. Hunt, Bamford, Knight, Healey and Johnson convicted; Moorhouse, Jones, Saxton, Swift and Wylde acquitted.

    26 April    Henry Hunt applies (unsuccessfully) for a new trial.

    15 May    Hunt, Bamford, Healey and Johnson sentenced to imprisonment.

TO THE

# INHABITANTS
## OF
# Manchester
### And Neighbourhood.

**FELLOW COUNTRYMEN,**

Our enemies are exulting at the victory they profess to have obtained over us, in consequence of the postponement, *for a week*, of the PUBLIC MEETING intended to have been held on Monday last.

The Editor of the London Courier, (although he admits that we are only *checked* not *subdued*) appears to be as much rejoiced as if *he*, and his *coadjutors*, had for a time escaped unhurt from the effects of an Earthquake or some other great National Calamity; his *blood-thirsty imitators* of the local press of Manchester, cannot disguise the fears of their employers, although I am informed that they attempt to do it, by resorting to the most vulgar and impotent abuse. To reply to any of their malignant and contemptible efforts, would only tend to drag them forth, for a moment, from their natural insignificance and obscurity; therefore you will bestow on their petty exertions the most perfect indifference; for as they are beneath your anger, so you will not even suffer them to attract your notice.

You will meet on Monday next my friends, and by your *steady, firm, and temperate* deportment, you will convince all your enemies, you feel that you have an *important* and an *imperious public duty* to perform, and that you will not suffer any private consideration on earth, to deter you from exerting every nerve, to carry your praiseworthy and patriotic intentions into effect.

The eyes of all England, nay, of all Europe, are fixed upon you; and every friend of real Reform and of rational Liberty, is tremblingly alive to the result of your Meeting on Monday next.

OUR ENEMIES will seek every opportunity by the means of their sanguinary agents to excite a Riot, that they may have a pretence for SPILLING OUR BLOOD, reckless of the awful and certain retaliation that would ultimately fall on their heads.

EVERY FRIEND OF REAL AND EFFECTUAL REFORM is offering up to Heaven a devout prayer, that you may follow the example of your brethren of the Metropolis; and by your *steady, patient, persevering,* and *peaceable* conduct on that day, frustrate their HELLISH AND BLOODY PURPOSE.

Come, then, my friends, to the Meeting on Monday, *armed* with NO OTHER WEAPON but that of a self-approving conscience; determined not to suffer yourselves to be irritated or excited, by any means whatsoever, to commit any breach of the Public Peace.

Our opponents have not attempted to show that our reasoning is fallacious, or that our conclusions are incorrect, by any other argument but the *threat of Violence*, and to put us down by the force of the *Sword, Bayonet,* and the *Cannon*. They assert that your leaders do nothing but mislead and deceive you, although they well know, that the eternal principles of *truth* and *justice* are too deeply engraven on your hearts; and that you are at length become (fortunately for them) too well acquainted with your own rights, ever again to suffer any man, or any faction, to mislead you.

We hereby invite the Boroughreeve, or any of the *Nine wise Magistrates*, who signed the Proclamation declaring the meeting to have been held on Monday last, *Illegal*, and threatening at the same time all those who *abstained from going* to the said Meeting; we invite them to come amongst us on Monday next. If we are wrong it is their duty as *Men*, as *Magistrates*, and as *Christians*, to endeavour to set us right by argument, by reason, and by the mild and *irresistible precepts of persuasive truth*; we promise them an attentive hearing, and to abide by the result of conviction alone. But once for all we repeat, that we despise their THREATS, and abhor and detest those, who would direct or controul the mind of man by VIOLENCE or FORCE.

I am, my Fellow Countrymen,

Your sincere and faithful Friend,

## *Henry Hunt.*

*Smedley Cottage, Wednesday, August 11, 1819.*

J. WROE, PRINTER, OBSERVER OFFICE, MARKET-STREET, MANCHESTER.

"Placard issued by Henry Hunt, calling the inhabitants of Manchester to a public meeting on Monday [16 August], 'armed with no other weapon but that of a self-approving conscience; determined not to suffer yourselves to be irritated or excited, by any means whatsoever, to commit any breach of the Public Peace'."

Published under Creative Commons licence
from manchester.ac.uk (English MS 1197/22 / JRL18090809)

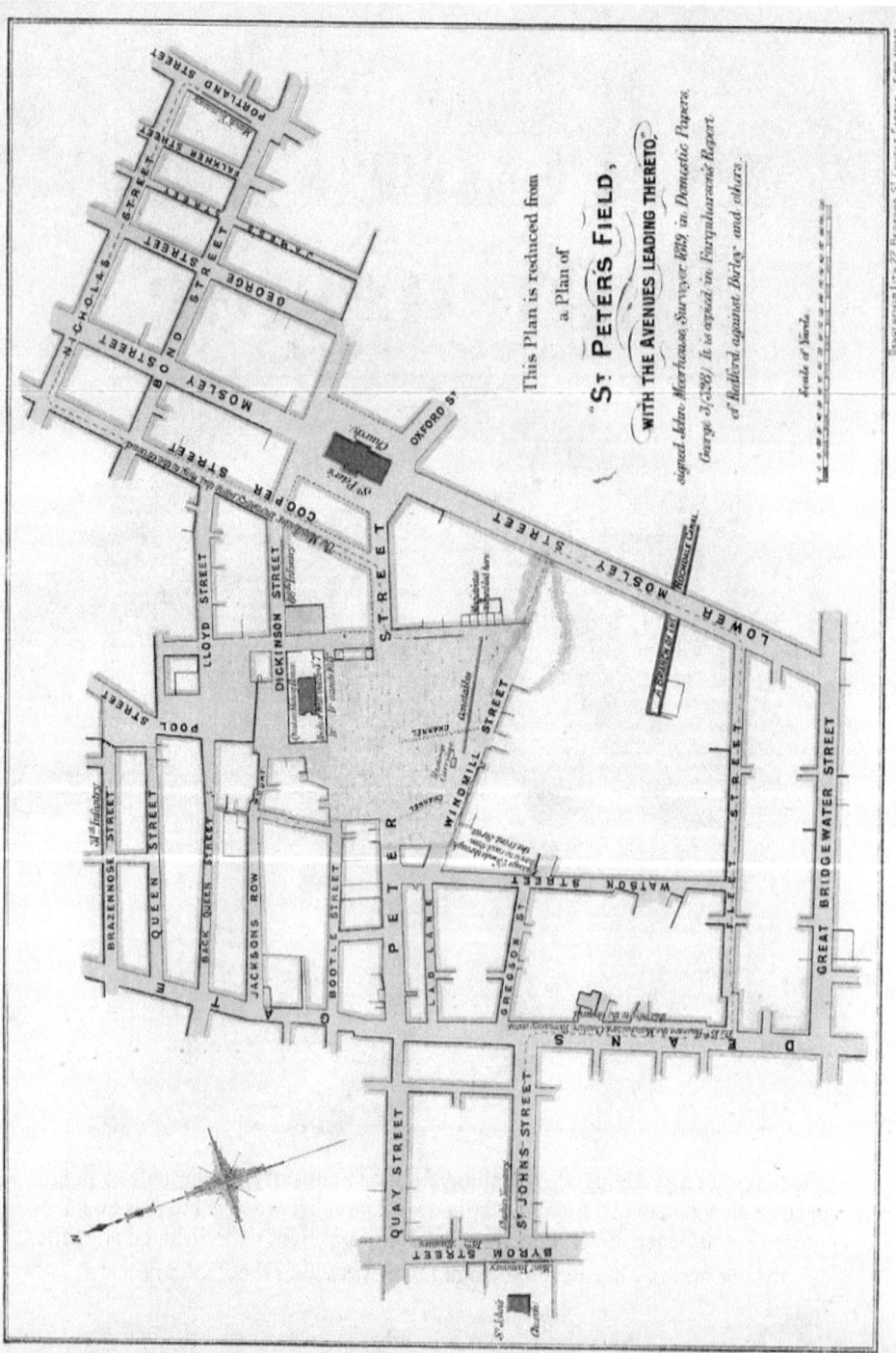

Portrait of Henry Hunt,
by Adam Buck, c.1810

Names & Condition of those persons who were taken to the Manchester Infirmary in the course of Monday & Tuesday, 16 & 17 Augt 1819.

28

1. John Wrigley — Warrington — fractured ribs — much bruised
2. John Mellor — Burslem — slightly wounded. O.P.
3. James Lees — Saddleworth — do — do
4. Willm Taylor — Middleton — sabre wound in the head
5. Willm Robinson — Salford — contusion — cured
6. Edmd Dawson — Saddleworth — sabre wound on head
7. Owen McCabe — near Bury — fractured ribs — not dangerous
8. Edward Lennaway — Manchester — contusion — not dangerous
9. Benjamin Seed — Manchester — fractured thigh
10. Shot Heywood — Pendleton — fractured ribs & contusion
11. John Scotfield — Oldham — slightly wounded — cured
12. Edwd Lancaster — Manchester — slightly wounded O.P.
13. Thomas Blinston — Manchester — both arms fractured
    Robert Ratcliffe — Stockport — bruised leg O.P.
14. John Bridge — near Bury — much bruised
15. J. Whitworth — Hyde — shot in the head — since dead } New Cross
16. James Jackson — Ardwick — 2 shots in the thigh
17. Samuel Jackson — Salford — shot in the leg — amputated
18. Mr Campbell † — Manchester, dangerous
19. John Ferguson — Manchester — shot
20. John Ashton — Oldham — dead
21. Daniel Bowers — Manchester — contusion O.P.
22. Mar. Whitaker — do — very much bruised
23. Ann Barlow — Oldham — fractured ribs & much bruised
24. Elizabeth Rigby — Manchester — contused ankle
25. Betty Wild — Manchester — bruised — contusion not dangerous
26. Nancy Jackson — Chadderton — broken arm — very bad
27. Ann Roberts — Manchester — slightly wounded — cured
28. Abigail Jackson — do — fractured ribs & much contused

† This person, a special constable, was dreadfully abused by the Mob & struck by a spent ball, as he was going to his work.

Out Patients of 40 who applied during Monday & Tuesday & were dressed by far the greatest part were hurt by falls, by being ridden over, & crushed. There appears to have been very few instances of sabre wounds amongst this class of Patients.

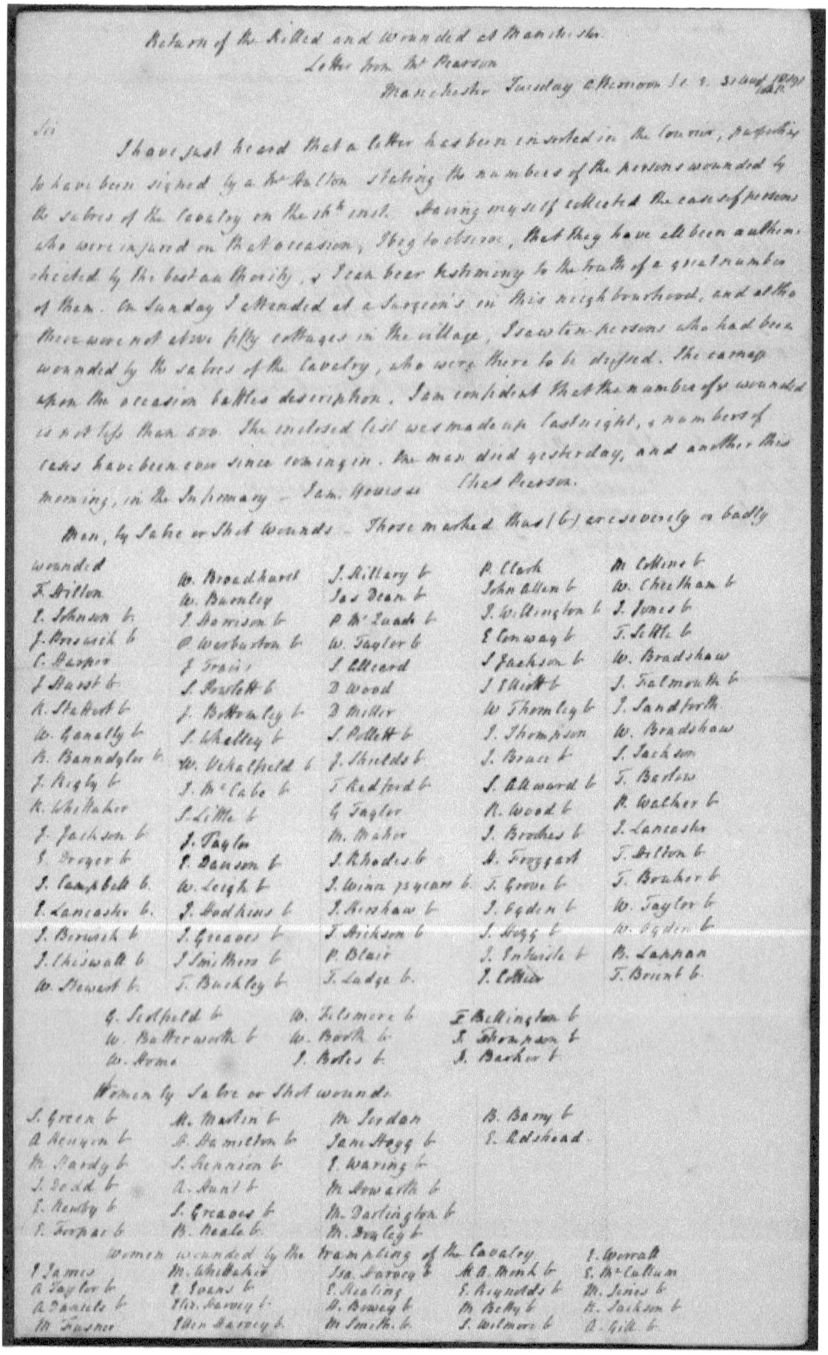

Return of the Killed and Wounded at Manchester.
Letter from Mr Pearson
Manchester Tuesday afternoon [illegible] 31 Aug 1819

Sir

I have just heard that a letter has been inserted in the Courier, purporting to have been signed by a Mr Hulton stating the numbers of the persons wounded by the sabres of the cavalry on the 16th inst. Having myself collected the cases of persons who were injured on that occasion, I beg to observe, that they have all been authenticated by the best authority, & I can bear testimony to the truth of a great number of them. On Sunday I attended at a Surgeon's in this neighbourhood, and altho there were not above fifty cottages in the village, I saw ten persons who had been wounded by the sabres of the cavalry, who were there to be dressed. The carnage upon the occasion baffles description. I am confident that the number of wounded is not less than 500. The enclosed list was made up last night, & numbers of cases have been ever since coming in. One man died yesterday, and another this morning, in the Infirmary – I am. Yours &c Chas Pearson.

Men, by Sabre or Shot Wounds – Those marked thus (b) are severely or badly wounded

F. Dillon
E. Johnson b
J. Berwick b
C. Harper
J. Hurst b
R. Stafford b
W. Ganolly b
B. Banndyler b
J. Rigby b
R. Whittaker
J. Jackson b
S. Brozer b
J. Campbell b
E. Lancaster b
J. Berwick b
J. Chiswall b
W. Stewart b.

W. Broadhurst
W. Burnley
J. Harrison b
O. Warburton b
J. Travis
S. Bowlett b
J. Bottomley b
S. Whalley b
W. Uchalfield b
J. McCabe b
S. Little b
J. Taylor
E. Dawson b
W. Leigh b
J. Hodkins b
J. Greaves b
J. Smithers b
T. Buckley b

J. Hillary b
Jas Dean b
P. McQuade b
W. Taylor b
J. Ellcard
D. Wood
D. Miller
S. Pollett b
J. Shields b
T. Redford b
G. Taylor
M. Maher
J. Rhodes b
J. Winn 75 years b.
J. Hinshaw b
T. Atkinson b
P. Blair
T. Ludge b.

P. Clark
John Allen b
J. Willington b
E. Conway b
S. Jackson b
J. Elliott b
W. Thornley b
J. Thompson
J. Bruce b
S. Allwood b
R. Wood b
J. Brookes b
A. Froggatt
J. Grove b
J. Ogden b
J. Hogg b
J. Entwistle b
J. Collier

M. Collins b
W. Cheetham b
J. Jones b
T. Little b
W. Bradshaw
J. Falmouth b
J. Sandforth
W. Bradshaw
J. Jackson
T. Barlow
R. Walker b
J. Lancashire
T. Dillon b
T. Barker b
W. Taylor b
W. Ogden b
B. Lannan
T. Brunt b.

G. Sidfield b
W. Butterworth b
W. Horne

W. Filemore b
W. Booth b
J. Boles b.

E. Billington b
S. Thompson b
J. Barker b

Women by Sabre or Shot wounds

S. Green b
A. Kenyon b
M. Hardy b
J. Dodd b
E. Newby b
E. Fennar b

M. Martin b
A. Hamilton b
S. Kennison b
A. Hunt b
S. Greaves b
B. Neale b.

M. Jordan
Jane Hogg b
E. Waring b
M. Howarth b
M. Darlington b
M. Braley b

B. Barry b
E. Redshead.

Women wounded by the trampling of the Cavalry

J. James
A. Taylor b
A. Daniels b
M. Fusner

M. Whittaker
E. Evans b
Eliz. Harvey b.
Ellen Harvey b.

Isa. Harvey b
E. Healing
A. Bewey b
M. Smith b.

A.A. Monk b
E. Reynolds b
M. Betty b
S. Wilmore b

E. Worrall
E. McCallum
M. Jones b
H. Jackson b
A. Gill b

"Copy [in the hand of W.R. Hay] entitled 'The Return of the Killed and Wounded at Manchester - Letter from Mr Pearson', dated Manchester, Tuesday afternoon 31 Aug 1819."

Women wounded by the Truncheons of the Special Constables, or crushed by the Multitude.

| | | | |
|---|---|---|---|
| A. Wellworth b | S. Wood b | S. Pierce b | S. Marsden |
| C. Penin b | S. Golding b | B. M— | A. Walk |
| M. Ashcroft b | A. Reynolds b | S. Croft | |
| S. Thorp b | M. Lewis b | S. McGrath b | |
| A. Roberts b | M. Crofts b | B. Lockshut b | |
| A. McGarth b | C. Coleman b | S. Chiswell b | |

Men wounded by the trampling of the Cavalry

| | | | | |
|---|---|---|---|---|
| A. Canlike b | S. Barlow b | R. Morand b | Ed. Slanaphy b | G. Flint b |
| J. Green b | W. Owen b | J. Grice | W. Robinson b | J. Cook b |
| D. Coyle b | J. Bell b | J. Teasdale b | T. Clark | J. Taylor b |
| J. Wise b | P. Martin b | J. Carthy | T. Ratcliffe b | J. Smith |
| J. Thornbury | — Pilly b | J. Groth b | O. McCollum | |
| A. Benford b | R. Walton b | J. Parr b | J. Prince b | |

Men wounded by the Truncheons of the Special Constables or crushed by the Multitude

| | | | | |
|---|---|---|---|---|
| A. Harrison b | J. McConnell b | A. White b | J. Hargrave b | J. Jones b |
| J. Walker | C. Washington | G. Croft b | J. Foster | J. Cook |
| A. Steel | J. Leadbeater | P. Wolf b | W. Renshaw b | |
| J. Steel | A. Campbell | P. Reynolds | D. Webster b | |
| J. Baker | I. Blundstone b aged 70 | J. Haywood b | J. Bell b | |

Top: Medal commemorating the Peterloo Massacre
Bottom: A commemorative handkerchief

*Courtesy People's History Museum*

"Universal Sufferage or the Scum Uppermost!!!!!"
Hand coloured engraving by Georges Cruikshank,
printed by George Humphrey, July 1819

*Courtesy People's History Museum*

Mr Justice Bayley

James Scarlett,
Barrister for the Prosecution

"A Slap at Slop and the Bridge-Street Gang,
a short news sheet published in 1822, by W. Hone."

*Published under Creative Commons licence
from manchester.ac.uk (R27129 / JRL1119149)*

# LENT ASSIZES, YORK CASTLE

Thursday 16 March to Monday 27 March 1820.

Before Mr Justice Bayley.

The King

against

Henry Hunt

| Samuel Bamford | Joseph Healey | Joseph Johnson |
| Robert Jones | John Knight | James Moorhouse |
| John Thacker Saxton | George Swift | Robert Wylde |

for Conspiracy to Excite Terror and Rioting.

---

Mr Littledale, Mr Scarlett, Mr Serjeant Hullock
and Mr Serjeant Cross
*appeared for the prosecution.*

Mr Barrow appeared as Counsel for Mr Moorhouse,
and Mr Holt for Mr Saxton.

# First Day – Thursday 16 March 1820.

This morning the long-expected trial of Mr Hunt and the other defendants, indicted for a conspiracy on 16 August last at Manchester, commenced at York. At a very early hour in the morning some persons of the first respectability in the county were admitted. By an arrangement considerately made by the high sheriff and his deputy, with the aid of Messrs Brook and Bulmer, and the attention of Mr Stavely, the governor of York Castle, the reporters for the London press were admitted through a private entrance at a quarter before seven in the morning. The box for the jury in waiting, and the seats usually occupied by attorneys, were reserved for the magistrates of the county, their own box being insufficient to afford them accommodation, the attendance being so full. The ladies, who in general grace country courts with their presence in fascinating groups, were not deterred by the impending risk attendant upon the terrible pressure of the crowd, and many of them had obtained admission before the Castle gates were thrown open to the public.

Long before the court sat, the prelude to the more serious business of the day was filled up by a variety of incidents which occurred among the persons who were so fortunate as to obtain early admission. The galleries were kept locked until the hour of public admission, but many who had got access to the body of the court, and who were there prevented from occupying seats otherwise appropriated for visitors, adopted the expedient of ascending the galleries without putting themselves to the intermediate trouble of mounting a flight of stairs. They scaled the walls, and helped themselves to the front seats without ceremony.

At ten minutes past eight o'clock, the court was thrown open, and the rush into every part of it was tremendous. In less than a minute every corner was crowded almost to suffocation, and the assemblage which then filled the court presented a most singular spectacle. Ladies, apparently of rank, were hustled about by the yeomen of the county, and for a moment the usual courtesy which all men wish to pay the fair sex was suspended. The general decorum was only forgotten for a moment, for, owing to the excellent arrangements made by the official persons who had the superintendence of the court, no more were admitted in the first rush than could obtain accommodation without any greater inconvenience than that usually encountered in crowded meetings.

Immediately before the judge entered, Mr Hunt, Mr Moorhouse and the other defendants, ten in number, with Mr Pearson as their solicitor, took

## Hunt and Others.

their seats at the barrister's table. The Rev. Mr Ethelston, the Rev. Mr Hay, Mr Sylvester, Mr Hulton, Colonel l'Estrange, Colonel Fletcher, and the rest of the Manchester magistrates were also in the throng; but such as were subpoenaed as witnesses were ordered out of court until they were called upon for examination. Witnesses on both sides withdrew by order of the court. Lord Howden was also present.

At nine o'clock the defendants were arraigned, and they severally pleaded Not Guilty. They were charged with a conspiracy to alter the legal frame of the government and constitution of these realms; and with meeting tumultuously at Manchester on 16 August last with 60,000 persons, many armed with sticks which they carried on their shoulders like firearms; and with bearing flags and banners, on which were inscriptions and devices calculated to inflame the minds of his Majesty's subjects against the constituted authorities of the state. There were several counts, varying the form of the indictment, but in substance implicating the accused in a conspiracy against the state.

The following jury were sworn to try the case:

William Hall, Esq. (foreman).
Thomas Robson, Esq.
William Chaytor, Esq.
Timothy Hutton, of Clifton, Esq.
Thomas Parker, Esq., of Layton.
George Beswick, Esq.
John Hutton, Esq., of Marsh.
John Chadwick, Esq.
George Atkinson, jun. Esq.
William Selby, Esq.

A tales was prayed, and the following names added to the special list: Septimus Bromley, of Sculcoates, near Hull; and George Addy, Esq.

The last juror expressed a desire to be exonerated from attending on this Jury, but as he had no personal objection, the court declined excusing him, and the abovenamed gentlemen constituted the jury. Defendants conducting their own defence were permitted to remain at the counsel table, where Mr Hunt took his station.

Mr Barrow appeared as Counsel for Mr Moorhouse, and Mr Holt for Mr Saxton.

Mr Littledale opened the pleadings, and, at half past nine o'clock, Mr Scarlett proceeded to address the jury.

**Mr. Scarlett**  They had heard, he said, from his learned friend who opened the pleadings, the nature of the charge preferred against the defendants which they were now about to try. It was impossible not to perceive that

# First Day – Thursday 16 March 1820.

**Mr. Scarlett** this prosecution arose from certain recent transactions, which had very much agitated the public mind – transactions that were combined with circumstances of great political importance, and which were calculated to create a most extensive and powerful interest in the country. It was, therefore, to be supposed, that hardly any one of the gentlemen of the jury could be a total stranger to those matters which this prosecution now brought under their consideration. At the same time, he felt a perfect confidence in addressing himself to gentlemen of their description, and he was sure they would agree with him when he said that they owed it as a duty to the country, and to the proper administration of public justice, to dismiss from their minds all impressions favourable or unfavourable on this subject, and, as far as lay in their power, to forget every conception they had previously formed on a question of such vital importance. It was for them to wait till they had heard all the evidence connected with the case, and then to decide by it, and by it alone.

For his part, he must commence by stating his peculiar satisfaction that this case came to be tried before a special jury of the county of York. Looking to the question which was to be tried, in a constitutional point of view, and on public grounds, it was exceedingly desirable that the parties accused should be arraigned before a jury that could not possibly be affected by local or personal prejudices. If he had an important cause to decide, he knew no set of men before whom he would sooner have it discussed than before an enlightened and experienced jury of that county, the gentlemen of which had long held a high and proud character for entertaining a proper sense of public duty and of private honour.

On the part, therefore, of the prosecution, as well as on that of the defendants, he was perfectly satisfied with the choice that had been made. It gave to him an opportunity of addressing men wholly unprejudiced, who were devoid of any local feelings, and would give way to no impression save those which arose from the case itself as it should be hereafter developed. They must be aware that the charge arose out of transactions which took place in the month of August last, in the county of Lancaster. The parties were accused of having convened a meeting at Manchester, the object of which was to excite fear and terror in the minds of his Majesty's subjects; this was the short description of the crime alleged against the defendants. The circumstances which occurred at the time of the meeting were matter of evidence, and would throw considerable light on the projects of those who took part in the proceedings. The individuals who appeared before them as defendants were singled out as having been among the leaders of those who assembled at the meeting alluded to.

With respect to public meetings in general, it was requisite for him to say a few words in the outset as to his conception of what constituted a

# Hunt and Others.

Mr. Scarlett  legal assembly in this country. It was undoubtedly the privilege of the people of England, stating the proposition in a broad and unqualified manner, when they suffered under any grievance, to assemble at a public meeting, and to pursue the lawful mode of address. But the meeting in question was not of this description: it was of a nature unknown to the constitution.

In former times it was customary for counties, towns, districts, or particular classes of individuals, united by one common interest, in the pursuit of one common object, to meet together. Thus, for instance, where a particular trade was affected by a particular law, the parties interested met to petition for its repeal. If a particular class of persons were oppressed by any grievance, they also assembled together to petition for its removal. If a Lord-Lieutenant, or the High Sheriff of a county, were informed that the freeholders had to complain of something that operated against their interests, the practice of the constitution enabled him to call a meeting for the purpose of petitioning either the throne or the parliament. But he had never heard it stated by any lawyer, and he trusted he should never hear it decided, that it was a right, sanctioned either by the law or constitution of this land, for any person who pleased to call all the people of England together in one place, there to discuss political measures, and to lay down particular modes by which they might obtain redress.

He would tell them why such a proceeding could not be legal. No man could deny that the great physical force of every community consisted in the mass of the people; and those who looked for the most extended reform admitted that all power and all right were derived from the meetings of the people at large. Therefore it was clear that the people, when they met to frame the groundwork of constitution, went back to the origin of society, and annihilated that state of things which had previously existed. Let it be imagined that the bulk of the population met together to discuss public affairs, and to take into their own consideration such measures as they might deem proper for the alteration of the existing order of things – it was evident, as all power and right were derived from the people, that they would in that case resume their original functions, and the government must be for the time dissolved. Hence it followed, beyond all controversy, that public meetings of the people, without any legal foundation, whether they assembled from their own private will or under the direction of some demagogue who for a time possessed some influence over their minds, for the purpose of carrying into effect, by such means and in such manner as they might think proper, an alteration in the constitution of the county could not be a lawful assembly as the

# First Day – Thursday 16 March 1820.

Mr. Scarlett

constitution at present existed.[152] If they could suppose a case – of which indeed modern times gave no example – a case in which a vast number took a part in the government, it would not shake his position. History told them that Athens was the most perfect specimen of a republican government. There, 30,000 citizens met to discuss matters of state. But as this was a component part of the government itself, as it was interwoven with their system, such a meeting was undoubtedly constitutional. But even at Athens, free as its constitution was with respect to the citizens, who were allowed to express their opinions on questions affecting the state, still the greater part of the inhabitants were consigned to slavery, and were not allowed to interfere in the business of the state. These were all the remarks he would offer to point their attention to the character of the meeting which they were called on to consider. He took it in the outset as a principle not to be contested that the people of England had a right to meet for the purpose of petitioning against grievances, when those meetings had no factious disturbance in view, when they were not intended to alarm the minds of peaceable and moderate men. He hoped that nothing would ever be done to interfere with this right, for which their ancestors had successfully fought; but that, as it had been handed down to them unimpaired, so would they hand it down unimpaired to their posterity.

He would now proceed to notice the different individuals who were charged in the indictment. Of Mr Hunt it was unnecessary that he should say anything, because his name had appeared so much of late connected with these transactions as to leave no doubt on the mind of any man as to his character and avocations. The others were more obscure; they were very little known, and he should therefore state who they were, premising that they were charged with assembling, and inciting others to assemble, to disturb the public peace. John Knight had formerly been in business; his occupation had latterly been that of an itinerant orator. Joseph Johnson was a brushmaker, residing in or near Manchester, and he believed was also in the habit of attending public meetings. Of John Saxton all the description which he had was that he was some way or other connected with the office of a paper called The *Manchester Observer*. Joseph Healey was an apothecary. James Moorhouse was a coach-master, residing at Stockport. George Swift carried on the business of a shoemaker at Manchester. Of Robert Wylde he knew nothing but that he lived near Ashton-under-Lyne. Samuel Bamford and Robert Jones were individuals in humble circumstances. The jury would find, by unquestionable evidence, that these persons were connected in some sort of secret design. He would be able to show the course which the

---

152 'County' sic in transcript. Should read: 'country'.

# Hunt and Others.

**Mr. Scarlett** parties respectively took when he called his evidence, and therefore it was not necessary for him at that moment to state the specific acts of each; it would be sufficient to give a general view of their proceedings.

To begin, then, with Mr Hunt. It appeared that some time in the month of June in the last year, a meeting took place in Smithfield; he knew not by whom it was assembled, nor was it of any consequence. It created, however, considerable alarm in the metropolis. Resolutions were, however, passed at that meeting, inculcating on the minds of the people of England that the time was come when some extraordinary and unprecedented measure was to be taken. Indeed, those resolutions went to disfranchise all those, who, according to the established law of the land, were invested with political and representative power. It was known that Mr Hunt was the person who proposed these resolutions, among which there were two inviting and recommending the people of England to resist the payment of taxes, declaring that they were not bound to obey any laws enacted by the parliament as it was now formed; and therefore, for some reason which the mob in their enlightened wisdom had found out, calling on them to pay nothing towards the revenue till such a parliament was assembled as they conceived it was proper and fitting they should have. He alluded to this meeting, of which Mr Hunt was the head, as the probable cause of his being subsequently invited to preside at a meeting at Manchester. That, he believed, was the result of the Smithfield meeting.

It appeared that on 9 August a meeting was projected to be held by the people of Manchester for the purpose of considering public grievances and discussing the question of parliamentary reform, and also to elect a representative, to be returned by themselves, to sit in parliament. This was a measure which no man could contend fell short of the highest misdemeanour which could be committed. It was a denial of the authority of all law and an interference with the prerogative of the King himself, without whose sanction, from the earliest periods, no person had the right to return members for parliament. It was well known by those who understood the history of the country that parliaments had originally been called by the Crown, and that a long series of circumstances and many happy accidents had concurred to place parliament in the situation in which it at present stood.

But to return to the history of these proceedings: on 8 August, Mr Hunt arrived at a place called Bullock Smithy, about nine miles from Manchester and three miles from Stockport. He was here joined by Moorhouse, who took him to Stockport, and on the morning of the ninth they were joined by Johnson. The party made a progress towards Manchester, accompanied by Sir C. Wolseley and others. The notice of

# First Day – Thursday 16 March 1820.

**Mr. Scarlett**

a meeting at Manchester had, it seemed, attracted the attention of the magistrates, and the meeting was prohibited by them. By their orders, placards were stuck up in the town stating that the people were called upon to do a thing highly illegal. Mr Hunt, it appeared, was extremely angry at this prohibition, or rather at the conduct of those who were to have met together in yielding to it; and they would find that on the evening of the ninth he was haranguing the people, and speaking of the magistrates who prohibited the meeting by the appellation of 'Number 9' in allusion to nine tailors.[153] He used terms of extreme reproach and contumely in mentioning these gentlemen, declared that he conceived the object of the people to be legal, stated his opinion that they were acting in a weak manner to yield to the suggestions of the magistrates, and inviting them to meet him on 16 August. The obscure situation of most of the people residing at Manchester – their habits of labour, and the moderateness of their circumstances – had induced them to pay some respect to the magistracy, who constituted the sole authority there, as there was no corporation, or any body of that description.

Their conduct when the prohibition was issued afforded a sort of security that they were rather disposed to take the advice and obey the authority of the local magistrates; but when Mr Hunt came down to Manchester (he having been occupied in assembling mobs at other places) and said that the people behaved pusillanimously, and that the time was come for acting, he induced those persons, in the face of the constituted authorities, to determine on a meeting. He gave notice that a meeting would be held on 16 August – not a meeting of the inhabitants of the town of Manchester, but of the population of the surrounding country. Having given this notice that the meeting of the ninth was adjourned to 16 August, he proceeded to the residence of Johnson, near the town of Manchester, which he understood to be called Smedley Cottage. Whilst he was there, he would show the jury that Mr Hunt received a visit from Knight, another of the defendants. As Mr Hunt had acquired a sort of popularity in the town of Manchester, which it was not difficult for a man to do who headed a mob, and spoke the language of sedition, he proceeded to mature the plan of the meeting.

The magistrates now received information on which it was very difficult

---

153 Apparently a reference to the idiomatic expression, 'It takes nine tailors to make a man'. This can be variously understood as a pejorative estimation of the value of the labouring classes by comparison to the aristocracy; or as a revolutionary threat suggesting the potential of the majority to unseat the minority if popular consent for the status quo is withdrawn. Here, Hunt allegedly repurposes the phrase, inverting the social roles it implies by reducing the magistrates to the status of tailors, and making the unrepresented and disenfranchised beneficiaries of future electoral reform into '[gentle]men'.

# Hunt and Others.

**Mr. Scarlett** to act. They were informed that movements had taken place among the people composing the immense population of the neighbourhood of Manchester, in the dead hour of the night, five, six, and even ten miles off, which were of a nature quite unprecedented. The magistrates thought it necessary to take measures for the preservation of the peace: they felt that the calling of a meeting by a person who had no connexion with the town, who had no property in or about it, was likely to lead to serious mischief. They determined to ward off the evil; and the prudence of their determination appeared evident when they were informed that on 15 August, in the night time, a number of persons assembled at a place called White Moss, and had been observed going through the evolutions of military discipline in such a manner that no one who had seen soldiers performing their exercise could entertain a doubt that the persons thus employed had some ulterior object in training at such an hour. The two persons who gave the information drew near to these individuals – so near that they were discovered and pursued; they were followed by bodies of men detached from the main body, and, when overtaken were beaten most unmercifully. One of them, of the name of Murray, was discovered to be a special constable: he was obliged, in order to save his life, to fall on his knees, and abjure his allegiance. This circumstance would give the jury some idea of what the object of these people was.

Mr Hunt here interrupted the learned counsel. He wished to know how the learned gentleman meant to connect this circumstance with the charge alleged against him and the other defendants.

Mr Justice Bayley said the learned counsel was, perhaps, introducing this as a matter which would be connected by collateral evidence with the general charge.

Mr Hunt objected to the introduction of the circumstance which the learned counsel was stating as having nothing at all to do with the specific charge.

Mr Justice Bayley said he had a right to suppose that the learned counsel would not introduce any circumstance which was not material to his case, and that he would not advert to any fact which he did not believe that he had evidence to prove. If he acted otherwise, the result would be beneficial to the defendant's case, and certainly not to his.

Mr Hunt said he felt himself happy in being placed under his Lordship's protection.

Mr Scarlett proceeded. He had, he said, too long been acquainted with the duties of his profession to introduce, to the prejudice of the defendant, matter which he did not think he was warranted in stating. He would inform the defendant, if it were any pleasure to him, that he would endeavour to connect him deeply and criminally with the circumstances

# First Day – Thursday 16 March 1820.

of which he had just been speaking.     Mr. Scarlett

On the morning of 15 August, circumstances took place which appeared to throw some light upon those motions which were observed in various parts of Manchester and its vicinity. The magistrates of Lancashire having received an intimation that a gentleman from London had been preaching his dissatisfaction to the populace on account of the prohibition of the meeting of the ninth, and that he had declared his intention to hold a meeting on the sixteenth, deemed it prudent to take those precautions which were necessary when vast assemblies of the people were assembled together for any purpose whatsoever.

It was now his duty to open a scene, which, he would venture to say, in the whole history of public meetings in this country, had no equal. What was this meeting intended to be? Was it to be a meeting of the inhabitants of the town of Manchester? Was it ultimately not a meeting as it was reported it would be? Although the notice was not so definite as to exclude persons who were not inhabitants of Manchester, yet, as it was published in that town and was more especially disseminated amongst the people there, the inference was that the meeting was intended for the inhabitants of that place.

But what occurred on the morning of 16 August? He here begged of the jury to direct their eyes to the map which he held in his hand. The learned gentleman then proceeded to illustrate his observations by pointing out the situation of Manchester and the different villages in its neighbourhood. This, said he, was the position of the town of Manchester – a town containing in itself an immense population: second, perhaps, only to that of London. Manchester was divided into twenty-four townships, and was far more populous than other parts of the kingdom. That population consisted for the most part of the laborious and industrious order of persons, although there certainly were many who possessed much wealth and property there. The very nature of such a population rendered it necessary to observe more than usual precaution when they were assembled together without any definite object. But, in addition to the danger which might be apprehended from a meeting of inhabitants, it was found that greater evils might be apprehended from the influx of vast numbers of strangers. On the morning of 16 August, it appeared that bodies were seen advancing towards Manchester from various places, some of them at the distance of ten or twelve miles from that town. They were provided with banners, the inscriptions on which he would by-and-by describe to them, and they marched upon Manchester with all the regularity of an army. From Rochdale, from Lees, from Middleton, from Oldham, from Stockport, and from many other places which would be named in evidence, parties might be seen

## Hunt and Others.

**Mr. Scarlett**  marching towards Manchester.

Indeed, from every point of the compass persons might be observed arriving there, manifesting all the discipline of soldiers, and differing from them only in this: that they had not uniforms and arms. At Middleton, Mr Bamford was seen placing in marching order a body of 2,000 men; they were without uniforms, but he displayed talent sufficient to put them through their evolutions. He addressed them, and gave to each pieces of laurel leaf, that they might distinguish one another. Two thousand more were seen marching from Rochdale. It would also be found that Mr Healey, another defendant, advanced from Oldham with a body of men. He would not say that this defendant commanded that body, but he would prove expressions of a very extraordinary nature uttered by him when he was, as it were, singing in triumph, in anticipation of the glories of that day. The town of Manchester was, in fact, surrounded by an immense force, who appeared as if they were going to invade it. Every road which approached the town was covered with parties marching in a military manner.

This was going on, he believed, up to eleven o'clock in the day and, amongst those who were advancing to the town, some of the individuals who had been training at White Moss were recognised. It was necessary that they should pass the house of Murray the constable, who had been extremely ill and unable to remove from his bed in consequence of the bruises he had received. The party stopped opposite his house and huzza-ed, and gave evident tokens that they recollected the proceedings of the former day. They hailed him either to confirm him in the abjuration of the former day, or to intimate to him that if he gave information he might expect their vengeance. At eleven o'clock, Mr Hunt and his party were preparing to enter the town from the residence of Johnson. He came in an open barouche, and he, Johnson and Moorhouse were seen to approach the place where the meeting was assembled. Mr Hunt was attended by a triumphant band; the Middleton and Rochdale force had united – they became his guards – and thus surrounded he advanced into the town of Manchester.

The first place, he was told, which they approached was the house of Murray the constable. When they came opposite to it, Mr Hunt took the command of the body; he stood up in the barouche, and commanded them to halt. The same expression of feeling was then shown as had previously been manifested by the party which had gone before him, and much hooting and hissing took place. Mr Hunt then made his way to Deansgate and, on passing the Star Inn, where the magistrates were assembled on one of the most arduous duties they could possibly be employed in, he ordered his corps to stop again, and the magistrates were assailed with

# First Day – Thursday 16 March 1820.

groaning, hooting and hissing – a pretty good exemplification of the manner in which they would have been treated had he been in authority. He next passed the place where the headquarters of the constables were held, whom they also treated in the same manner. Mr Hunt ultimately proceeded in triumph to the place of meeting, which had been previously visited by the other defendants.

**Mr. Scarlett**

While the forces which he had described were assembling, Saxton, Swift, Knight and all the remaining defendants were employed in preparing hustings for Mr Hunt. The magistrates determined that a line of constables should be formed from the house in which they assembled to the cart on which the hustings were formed; and it would be proved that when those parties found that the constables approached so near to them, they caused the hustings to be removed fifteen yards farther back; and the mob (he did not mean offence by using the word) formed in great strength around the waggon in order to protect it. Speeches were made by two or three of those whom he had mentioned – particularly by Jones, who said it was the direction of the committee (so that there was, it seemed, a committee) that they should take close order till Mr Hunt came. They were then to open and let him pass, after which they were to close immediately; and they were to take particular care not to let any but friends enter, as their enemies were abroad. The jury would also find that most of the parties when they approached were provided with large sticks which they shouldered and brandished as they marched along. They were all provided with ensigns and banners and advanced either six or four abreast with a firm military step, and presenting every appearance of troops upon their march. When they arrived at St Peter's area, the word of command was given, and they wheeled off with perfect regularity, and took the ground which their commander directed them to occupy. One of them, Healey, was particularly active on this occasion; and indeed everything connected with the entrance of those large bodies of men bore the appearance of an established and cultivated habit of military discipline.

Next came Mr Hunt with the largest band, consisting of more than 4,000 men. He ascended the hustings and his partisans took their places around, displaying their flags and banners. On some of these flags they would find described the words 'Equal representation or death'. What could be the object of such a sentiment as this? He spoke to the jury as men free from all prejudice; but he took it for granted that they were men who at least wished for no violent revolution, for no reform except that which could be effected by legal means. He would ask them to lay their hands on their hearts and say what good object could those have in view who exhibited a flag bearing such a motto. They were not met there

# Hunt and Others.

**Mr. Scarlett**  to discuss whether the present state of the House of Commons was the best that could be imagined. Good and wise men differed on this point; but, whatever difference of opinion might be entertained upon such a subject, of this he was sure: that there was no man who considered the question rightly that would not stand by the law and constitution of the country, if threatened with violence, as they were now administered; that would not resist to the uttermost an attempt to make a forcible alteration in the present system. 'Equal representation or death' was by no means a vague expression, and he thought the mob, with all respect for those who had a better opinion of their understanding, had better attend to their different avocations instead of discussing political opinions for which their education did not always qualify them.

Were the mass of the people to be told, by those who urged them on, that equal representation was to be purchased even at the expense of their head? Were doctrines to be disseminated which no man durst utter with his lips, though he might display them on his banner? Were they to be taught to consider equal representation as the sine qua non of their existence, and that they should rather perish than not secure it?

Another banner bore the inscription of 'No Corn Laws'. He came not to that court to discuss whether the law on the subject of corn were good or otherwise; he had his opinions on the question, but it would not be decorous or proper to state them there. He knew that wise men might sometimes frame a mischievous law; but it was not to be removed by riot and violence. He would suppose every honourable gentleman in that box was as much an enemy to the Corn Laws as the persons who thought themselves most aggrieved by them; but would it not be a most dangerous thing to say to a mob of 60,000 persons for the purpose of getting rid of such a measure, particularly when the minds of the people were irritated and inflamed – would it not, he asked, be an appeal of the most inflammatory nature to say to them, 'We will have no Corn Laws; we will force the legislature to do as we please'? This was not an election appeal. What object could it have but to inflame their feelings – to induce them to decide on a question with respect to which they were ignorant and those who affected to instruct them were not well informed?

Next came the inscription of 'Annual Parliaments': there were men in this kingdom, and no doubt respectable and honourable men, who thought annual parliaments would be very useful: but would any of those individuals say that such a proposition was to be carried by violence as the sine qua non of their existence? Let the people meet to petition for reform – let them submit to parliament what they thought expedient for the public good – and no man could complain. But was it the business of a public meeting to dictate to parliament, and to declare that they would

# First Day – Thursday 16 March 1820.

effect a certain object, or they would have nothing?     **Mr. Scarlett**

The next inscription was 'Universal Suffrage and Election by Ballot'. These two points, with annual parliaments, were the three pretexts which were advanced for calling this assembly. Seeing that Mr Hunt (whom he had heard defend himself on other occasions, who had more talent than the mere itinerant orators who travelled about from place to place) was at the head of that meeting, he felt considerable surprise that he did not perceive that those three terms, taken together, meant nothing but an entire subversion of the constitution; but as long as these questions were sub judice, what right had any man to say, 'We will, in spite of all opposition, have these three things'? To do so was illegal; and it was most unfit that, on the subject of public grievances, the mob should be suffered to dictate to the legislature. Let them meet and petition: let the weavers and shoemakers and other artisans in this kingdom who were destined to get their bread by the labour of their hands inform the legislature of the best course to be pursued with respect to public affairs if they had more wisdom than those by whom they were now conducted. The law enabled them to do this: but let not demagogues state to them that those three points were the only things which could be got to serve them; they ought not to do so, for this reason: because, when the mob got hold of a grievance, they were apt to consider it as the great source of all their evils, and they were at length led to believe that the removal of that alone would operate as an effectual panacea to cure the whole of their complaints. The ridiculous folly of a mob had been exemplified in a most humorous manner by that eminent painter, Mr Hogarth. It was found necessary many years ago, in order to prevent a confusion in the reckoning of time, to knock eleven days out of the calendar, and it was supposed by ignorant persons that the legislature had actually deprived them of eleven days of their existence. This ridiculous idea was finely exposed in Mr Hogarth's picture, where the mob were painted throwing up their hats and crying out, 'Give us back our eleven days'.[154] Thus it was at the present time that many individuals who could not distinguish words from things were making an outcry for that of which they could not well explain the nature.

Another inscription was 'Let us die like men and not be sold like slaves'. Who, he should be glad to know, had been selling the people of Oldham, of Rochdale, of Middleton, and of the other places, the inhabitants of which went to Manchester that day? He never heard of any such sale; but some person, who did not choose to speak these words, thought fit to place it on his banner. The pole to which one of the banners was affixed was surmounted by a pike-head, painted red as if to show the

---

154   A reference to Hogarth's 'An Election Entertainment' (c.1755).

# Hunt and Others.

**Mr. Scarlett** sanguinary feelings of those who bore it. Another flag had painted on it a dagger. God forbid the time should ever come when they should see any man who had the courage to declare to the people of this country that the dagger was the instrument by which lost rights were to be recovered. But he was afraid that, though no man had the courage or audacity to preach such a doctrine to a mob, yet that there were persons who had insinuated that the dagger was a fit weapon to be used – and he would make no farther comment on the consequences which such a doctrine had led to. A dagger was not the weapon which Englishmen were wont to use, and he trusted that those who said our rights were lost and wished to regain them would not declare to the people that they should arm themselves with such an instrument because, he was sure, the moment the people imbibed such a feeling, they might give up all idea of a free constitution, of morality, or order, of all that was dear to them. He had thus described the form in which the people assembled, and the progress of the meeting.

What was that meeting? Was it a meeting of the people of Manchester, or the county of Lancaster? No.

Was it a meeting of a particular trade to procure the repeal of some obnoxious bills? No.

Who assembled at it, and who presided over it? Were the former inhabitants of Manchester? And was the latter any person interested in the welfare of the town, or intimately connected with the county? No.

These were questions, however, which must be left to the jury to decide. This at all events, he knew: that the effect of the meeting, whatever might have been the design of those who called it, was to strike terror into the minds of his Majesty's subjects. Would any man whatever tell him that the respectable inhabitants of Manchester must not have felt great alarm when they saw the shoemakers, the weavers, the journeymen of all descriptions, advancing towards that town as if to invade it? The law had determined that any meeting of people, even for a legal object, in such array and such numbers was an unlawful meeting. But did it require law books to tell them that? Why had they laws to prevent the rude hands of power from destroying and devastating property?

But if they were to be told that a mob might be suffered to advance from every part of a county, to the terror of the peaceable inhabitants, their laws would be of little use, and it would be better to return to a state of nature – to sink into the original mass – and declare that force must be repelled by force. Let individuals look to the consequence of such a system. If meetings of this description were to be tolerated, it would be impossible to sustain the constitution of the country, except by means of such an increase of the military force as no good man, as no man who loved the constitution, wished to see established in a time of peace. The common civil power could not do anything against such numbers; for

# First Day – Thursday 16 March 1820.

what could sixty constables effect against as many thousand individuals?

The magistrates of Manchester, finding the meeting drawing together in this manner, perceiving parties coming from different quarters, and not knowing to what distance the ramifications of the system might have extended – perhaps to Birmingham, or more distant places; seeing also that the assembly was headed by a man who had no local connexion with the town, thought it necessary to interpose. They proceeded to do so, particularly as it was deposed by various persons in the town that they felt considerable alarm. They in consequence issued warrants, and the defendants were taken into custody. With what passed afterwards he had nothing to do; his task closed here.

He would now briefly recapitulate the offence which was imputed to the defendants. They were accused of having met together in great numbers, with flags and banners, to excite alarm in the minds of his Majesty's subjects. This was charged as an unlawful meeting, and they were arraigned for having taken a part in it. If this were proved (and, although he could not be responsible for the evidence, he believed it would be proved), the jury must return a verdict of guilty. At the same time, he called on them to bestow their best attention to all that the defendants might urge in their own behalf, as it was a maxim of law that every indulgence should be extended to an accused party.

(Mr Scarlett's speech lasted one hour and thirty-five minutes.)

THOMAS FIDLER, sworn and examined by Mr Serjeant HULLOCK.

Where do you live, Mr Fidler? — I keep the Red Lion, three miles from Stockport.

Do you recollect Mr Hunt calling at your house in August last? — Mr Hunt came with a servant on the afternoon of 9 August last; he baited his horse, and dined at my house

Do you know Mr Moorhouse? — I do.

What is he? — He is a coach proprietor and auctioneer at Stockport.

Do you recollect Mr Moorhouse coming to your house about the same time? — Moorhouse came immediately after in a post-chaise with his brother, and inquired for Mr Hunt, who had just left my house.

What did he do then? — After stopping five or ten minutes, he went off in the direction Mr Hunt went, towards Stockport.

Was Moorhouse in the neighbourhood before Mr Hunt left your house? — When Moorhouse first came in the neighbourhood of my house, Mr Hunt was at my house, but the former did not then enter.

How long did Mr Hunt stop at your house — About four hours.

*Cross-examined* by Mr BARROW.

# Hunt and Others.

**Thomas Fidler**

Did Mr Hunt meet Moorhouse at Bullock Smithy? — The report was not true that Mr Hunt was met by Moorhouse at Bullock Smithy, and conducted on to Stockport.

State all you know of what occurred at that time. — All I know is that Mr Hunt had gone from my house before Moorhouse came there.

Do you know Moorhouse perfectly well? — I have known Moorhouse intimately these dozen years, and he is in the habit of stopping at my house when he passes that way.

Is he in the habit of attending public meetings? — I have heard he attended public meetings since 16 August; but I cannot state it as a fact. Before that time I never heard that he did.

*Cross-examined* by Mr HUNT.

Is your inn much frequented? — Mine is the principal inn at Bullock Smithy.

Moorhouse, you say, stopped opposite your house in the morning, but did not call; but he called on his second visit when I was gone? — Yes.

Was it generally known that I was there? — It was a matter of public notoriety that you was there.

How long did I stop? — About four hours.

Did Mr Johnson, of Manchester, call? — No.

Did any other person call? — One Jump did, and asked to see you; he was admitted.

Do you know any of the other defendants? — I know none of the other defendants; all I know is that, by your permission, I conducted three successive parties of two each into your room.

Was the door locked? — The door was not locked, anybody who inquired was admitted.

Did you see anything to excite your suspicion of a plot? — I know of no plot carried on there.

*Re-examined* by Mr Serjeant HULLOCK.

Did the parties admitted to Mr Hunt appear to be friends or strangers? — The parties admitted to Mr Hunt were strangers to him.

**Henry Lomas**

HENRY LOMAS, sworn and examined by Mr Serjeant CROSS.[155]

Did you live at Stockport on 8 August last? — I kept the White Lion, at Stockport, on 8 August.

Do you recollect Mr Hunt and either of the other defendants calling

---

155 Lomas died on 21 February 1834, and was still the landlord at the White Lion at the time of his death.

# First Day – Thursday 16 March 1820.

there about that time? — Late on that night, Mr Moorhouse and Mr Johnson came to Mr Hunt at my house; and also early on the following morning, when they were joined by a stranger and a crowd of persons. I saw the gentleman who was called Sir Charles Wolseley, and at a late period of the morning of 9 August, Parson Harrison joined them.

Have you observed such crowds frequently at Stockport? — Such crowds were not customary at Stockport except when Mr Hunt was making his speeches. They went (or some of them) into Mr Moorhouse's house, where chaises were getting ready in the yard. One gig was also there into which Mr Hunt and Sir Charles Wolseley entered, and Moorhouse and Johnson went into a chaise and went off all together towards Manchester.

**Henry Lomas**

*Cross-examined* by Mr BARROW.

Do you know Mr Moorhouse? — I know Mr Moorhouse perfectly well, and that he worked stages on that line of road.

Does he not take in horses to bait? — I don't know that he takes in other horses than his own to bait. He took in Mr Hunt's, certainly, at that time. I can't say that Mr Moorhouse has been in the habit of addressing public meetings, but he certainly had two, three, or four crowds about this time, when he used to be speaking to large meetings on the road.

*Cross-examined* by Mr HUNT.

What line of business do you follow? — My business is a publican.

You also keep a chaise to let, do you not? — I do.

Mr Moorhouse also keeps a chaise to let? — He does.

You are rivals, then? — I am not a rival of his.

Have you known meetings at Sandy Brow? — I have known public meetings at Sandy Brow, and attended them.

Have you seen Mr Moorhouse at either of those meetings? — I never saw Mr Moorhouse there; if he had, I should have recollected it.

You are something besides a publican. Have the goodness to say what other capacity you sometimes act in. — I am one of the yeomanry, and was called upon in that way to attend the meetings; the same cause led me to Manchester on 16 August.

You said that crowds attended on Mr Hunt and Moorhouse? — I have said that crowds were there to hear Hunt's and Moorhouse's speeches.

Have you seen such crowds after the Duke of Wellington? Did you see such a crowd follow Mr Cross after the Derby trials? — I never saw crowds about the Duke of Wellington, nor around Mr Cross, the learned counsel, after the Derby trials.

Did you attend the Manchester meeting on 16 August? — I was at St

# Hunt and Others.

**Henry Lomas**

Peter's Field, Manchester, on the sixteenth.

What company did you serve in on that occasion? — [Here the witness smiled.] I was in the Cheshire yeomanry at the dispersion of the Manchester meeting.

Why did you laugh? — I laughed because it was a fine day, and we had no right to be called out.

What did you observe on that occasion? — I saw no particular transaction that day.

You had on your uniform and were armed? — I had on my uniform, and had sword and pistols.

Did the people march in military order? — I saw no marching in array, except among the yeomanry and soldiers – no invasion of Manchester. But I saw flags and banners.

At what time did you arrive on the ground? — I was at St Peter's Field betwixt one and two o'clock, and remained perhaps an hour, or an hour and a half.

What did you see transacted? — I saw nothing particular but the people running one way or another.

What did the Cheshire yeomanry do — The Cheshire yeomanry remained still – they cut nobody, though I saw some people down.

Did not the cutting the people down attract your attention? — It did not attract my particular attention.

Did you observe who it was that smote the people? — I cannot say who cut the people.

At what time did you leave Stockport? — I do not know at what time I left Stockport; it might be about seven or eight o'clock: between that and one. I was where Captain Newton choosed to take me in the neighbouring county.

What were you doing while the people were endeavouring to get away? — The Stockport troop had nothing to do with the running away of the people.

Did you get any of the flags? — I saw some flags which the cavalry had in their hands. How they came into their hands I cannot say.

Did not the Stockport get a few flags? — Some colours got into our hands – two, I believe – but how I don't know. We took back one of the flags to Stockport. I never saw it since.

Were your swords drawn or sheathed when you came upon the ground? — Our swords were drawn before we came upon the ground, by order of our officers.

[To other questions this witness answered:] When we got to the ground, the people were all running away except a few. We halted at the instant and dispersed nobody; I saw no resistance made to the Stockport troop;

# First Day – Thursday 16 March 1820.

saw persons going to the meeting, but not in battle array. I saw nothing to call for the interference of our troop. We were formed to the left of the 15th, but not in sight of the hustings; nor could I see what was going on in the turnpike road.

**Henry Lomas**

Mr SCARLETT here objected to the relevancy of this course of examination.

Mr Justice BAYLEY explained to Mr Hunt that what followed the meeting of 16 August could not affect his case. The charge against him was for a conspiracy entered into previous and upon that day, before the dispersion. He might, however, question the witness a little out of the line, if he meant to impeach his credibility.

Mr HUNT thanked his Lordship, and said that was his object.

MICHAEL BENTLEY, sworn and examined by Mr Serjeant HULLOCK.

**Michael Bentley**

I live at Heaton Norris, near Stockport, and was there on 8 August last, and saw Mr Johnson there in the evening of that day in a gig with Mr Hunt, going towards Stockport. I saw Mr Hunt with the gentleman they called Sir Charles Wolseley on the following day.

*Cross-examined* by Mr HUNT.

You know Mr Johnson? Is he here? — I know Mr Johnson, but do not see him here.

Are you a yeoman? — I am not.

What line of life have you followed? — I was formerly in a counting house.

Were you at the meeting on 16 August? — I was at St Peter's Plain on 16 August.

How did you go? — I went there in a coach.

Where were you stationed, and what did you observe? — I was stationed behind the hustings, and did not see the people commit any illegal act before the appearance of the military.

Did you observe a disposition to riot and commit violence? — I saw one or two men act very rough and insolent.

How many people do you think there were assembled? — I think there were about fifty thousand or sixty thousand persons, but I only saw one or two who were a little rough.

What was your motive for going to the meeting? — I went from curiosity. I saw the Stockport people advancing; they did not alarm me. I was alarmed afterwards when the cavalry appeared.

Were the persons who behaved insolently armed? — I saw no arms with the persons who behaved insolently; I saw nobody cut that day.

# Hunt and Others.

**Michael Bentley**

I saw one constable hurt; he was pressed down in consequence of the people going from the cavalry. When the cavalry approached, I was a little alarmed and got amongst the constables, some of whom I knew.

You knew some of the constables, you say? — I knew Mr Nadin. I saw an opening of constables, a body forming two rows from the house where the magistrates met, up to the hustings.

Did you see Mr Nadin there? — I saw Mr Nadin on the spot, but I did not see him insulted by any one.

Did you hear me address the people? What did I say? — I heard you address the people, and request them 'to be quiet and peaceable'.

What was the general conduct of the people before the arrival of the cavalry? — With the exception of one or two persons who forced their way through the constables, I saw nothing but peace and quietness among the people until the cavalry arrived.

[To other questions witness answered:] I do not know Mr Platt or Mr Derbyshire; I do not know that the persons who behaved riotously were among those charged here this day.

*Cross-examined* by Mr BARROW.

I know Mr Moorhouse, but do not particularly recollect whether he was on the hustings. I saw him in the carriage. I do not know what became of him after he left the carriage.

*Re-examined* by Mr Serjeant HULLOCK.

Though I do not recollect having seen Mr Moorhouse on the hustings, I remember having seen him in the carriage. Mr Hunt, Mr Johnson and two or three ladies were also in it. The carriage was a long time coming to the hustings. There were plenty of banners; one of the ladies, who sat on the coach-box, carried a flag. The carriage approached close to the hustings, and persons came out of it. I saw Johnson on the hustings, but whether Moorhouse transferred himself from the carriage in which I saw him to the hustings or not, I cannot say. I passed the Stockport people in the morning; they amounted to upwards of a thousand.

I heard a few words of Mr Hunt's address. He said, 'If any people break the peace they must put them down, keep them down, and make them be quiet'. I cannot recollect any other words.

By THE COURT.

I cannot judge how many of the people Mr Hunt could make hear him in so large a concourse.

**Mary Cadman**

MARY CADMAN, sworn and examined by Mr LITTLEDALE.

I know Mr Hunt. I saw him at Manchester on 8 August. Did not make

# First Day – Thursday 16 March 1820.

the bed for him there.

*Cross-examined* by Mr BARROW.

I had been a servant at Moorhouse's: he was a good, religious man, and used to read the Bible very often to his family and servants. Witness went to the meeting on 16 August. There were a number of women and children there. Was not a servant to Mr Moorhouse then. Moorhouse took his wife there. She was then in the family way. She saw no children there belonging to Moorhouse: he has eleven children; six by his present wife.

**Mary Cadman**

SAMUEL MORTON, sworn and examined by Mr Serjeant CROSS.

I lived near St Michael's church, at Manchester, on 9 August; saw a crowd near his house on that day; there was a great noise that Johnson, Hunt, and Moorhouse were coming. They came on a large piece of ground near the church, opposite the sign of the Church public house. Hunt and Johnson were in a gig, and Sir C. Wolseley and some others in a chaise. There was a large collection of people, about a thousand. Mr Hunt got on his legs, and addressed the people. Among other things, he began making allusion to the Manchester magistrates: he compared them to nine tailors on a shopboard. This, witness supposed, was for forbidding the meeting, which he (Mr Hunt) said was a legal one. He encouraged them to be firm and come forward, and no doubt they would prosper.

**Samuel Morton**

Mr HUNT: Will your Lordship tell the witness to say how I encouraged them?

Mr Justice BAYLEY: You will, by-and-by, Mr Hunt, set all that right by your own examination.

Witness went on. He advised the people to be firm: he (witness) saw several placards forbidding the meeting. They were up in several parts of the town. They were signed by nine persons, five of whom he knew to be magistrates. There was a great multitude of people, and a noise. He could not say that Hunt made any particular allusion to those papers; but he told them there would be a meeting on the sixteenth, and to come forward then. There was a loud huzza, and cries of, 'We will, we will'. Mr Hunt waved his white hat. Johnson was by Hunt's side; he waved his hand a little. It continued from half an hour to three quarters. They then went off to Johnson's house. There were many thousands moving about on Monday the sixteenth: he saw them from Withy Grove. He saw Mr Hunt, Johnson, and others, he believes, in a carriage. There were people after them five or six abreast. They kept step very well, like soldiers: he could not tell the numbers, but it was nearly half an hour before they passed, and they continued moving all that time. They came either

# Hunt and Others.

**Samuel Morton**

from the Oldham or the Rochdale road. He heard a bugle blow, which appeared as a signal for their halting: they halted during the half-hour he mentioned. They had a black flag with 'Liberty or Death'. These were the words, or similar – 'No Corn Laws' upon another.

Mr Hunt here wished for the production of the flags, as their production would be the best evidence. It appeared they were taken.

The Judge said there was only evidence as to two being taken.

The witness continued: There were several other flags with caps of liberty at top. One had 'Hunt and Liberty' on it: he saw them come opposite to Mr Murray's house. Murray is a constable. Murray was very ill at that time, and in his bedroom. They hissed opposite the house. They also shouted out that they wanted some White Moss humbug. They were halted at that time. The carriage had gone on, and was not then in sight. The town was very tumultuous, and, for myself, I was alarmed. I had lived in the town forty years, and never saw anything so tumultuous there before. Public business did not go on as usual. I did nothing. I was afraid. There were so many running up and down, it was hardly safe.

*Cross-examined* by Mr BARROW.

He did not mean to say that Moorhouse was in the carriage on that day.

*Cross-examined* by Mr HOLT.

Did not know Saxton. [Saxton was here pointed out to him, and witness said he was a stranger to him.] He did not see him on the ninth or sixteenth.

*Cross-examined* by Mr HUNT.

What is your line of business, sir? — I am a fustian manufacturer.

What was it that disturbed you? — The people running up and down in the streets.

Was this before or after the procession? — This was after the procession.

Where do you carry on your business? — I carry on my business at my own house.

Was that in the street where the crowds were? — No.

What induced you, then, to leave your home and business? — I was going about my business when I saw the people at Withy Grove. I was alarmed.

When you saw this, of course, you returned home for safety? — No, I did not go home to my own business, but went on a little further, to the corner of Hanging Ditch. This was a stone's throw from Withy Grove. I was alarmed at the black flag. I thought they were going to level something.

# First Day – Thursday 16 March 1820.

Have you any family? — I am a married man, and have a wife and seven children.

You took care of them? — I took care where they were: they were at the house: there were none of them at Peterloo, as you call it.

Are you quite sure that none of them were at the meeting? — I depend on what they told me. I never went to the meeting. My lad was at his work in High Street.

Why did you not go home? — The reason why I did not go home to my family was that I wished to see the crowd pass. I saw the black flag. I thought there would be a disturbance and a fight.

Did you see any fighting? — There was no fighting, but something that I did not like. There was a trumpet blowing, and they generally fight after blowing the trumpet.

What is your definition of a riotous meeting? — My meaning of a riotous meeting is a number of people racketing together. There were several weavers came up to Hunt without coats. There were many women and grown-up girls. Could not say whether women walked arm in arm with the men.

Did the women appear to be alarmed? — I could not say whether they were alarmed. I saw several whom I knew at the procession on the sixteenth.

How long did you remain a spectator? — I went home about one o'clock to dinner, though I was alarmed.

Did your fears subside after you had dined? — I was as much afraid after dinner as before.

If you had been at home attending your business, you would not have seen this procession. — Sir, if you had continued at home, there would have been no meeting.

How long have you been in York? — I have been in York since Sunday.

Have you seen any procession? — Saw the processions of the candidates in the city. Saw the bands of music and the flags, but was not afraid. There was no black flag there. His opinion of the difference between the two meetings (that at Manchester and the election at York) was that the one looked like war and disturbance, and the other like merriment and rejoicing. [Some approbation was here manifested, which Mr Justice Bayley strongly condemned.] His reason for making this difference was that he had heard of the intended meeting at Manchester, and, seeing the people coming, he was afraid.

Were not some of the people in the York procession drunk? — There were some of the people in the York procession drunk. The sober procession looked more like war than the drunken one. Did not see a flag with a bloody pike on it at York, nor a flag with the motto 'We will

*Samuel Morton*

# Hunt and Others.

**Samuel Morton**

conquer our enemies'. Witness could not say whether the allusion to the conduct of the magistrates at Manchester did not arise from the wording of their notice.

*Cross-examined* by Mr JOHNSON.

You spoke of levelling; are you not a leveller of property yourself? — Witness objected to the question, but on a little explanation it appeared to refer to the witness having been discharged from Lancaster gaol under the Insolvent Debtors' Act, and that he had not since paid any of his former debts; but he had acquired no funds to do so.

**James Standering**

JAMES STANDERING, sworn and examined by Mr LITTLEDALE.[156]

I saw Mr Hunt on 9 August at the bottom of Blakeley Street, Manchester. He had just then got up in his gig to address the people. Witness was at his work, but was drawn to the spot by curiosity. There might have been about a thousand persons there; he heard Mr Hunt say that the first thing he heard of the postponement of the meeting was at Bullock Smithy. There were nine signatures to the paper, which fulfilled the old proverb that 'nine tailors made a man'. He also said something about a notorious quorum. He was astonished at anyone being sent to Liverpool to know whether the meeting was legal or not; he knew himself that it was legal. He also said that there was another meeting to be held on the following Monday, but witness did not hear him say whether he should attend it or not. Here the placard from the magistrates, warning the people not to attend the meeting of the ninth, was put into witness's hand, and he said he saw similar ones in Manchester.

*Cross-examined* by Mr HUNT.

Did you write down my words at the time? — I did not take notes at the time, but he afterwards wrote it for a man who was employed by the police. This was about a fortnight after. Did not hear Mr Hunt say that he had important business to do, and that he must return before 16 August. Did not recollect hearing Mr Hunt say that the magistrates had threatened with their indignation all who did not attend the meeting.

**John Chadwick**

JOHN CHADWICK, examined by Mr SCARLETT.

Lives at Manchester, and is a shoemaker. He went on the ninth to meet Mr Hunt; he met him at Ardwick Green. There was a gig with Mr Hunt and Johnson in it, and a chaise with Sir C. Wolseley, Parson Harrison and Mr Moorhouse in it. There appeared to be about three hundred people coming in with them. The crowd increased as they went along; he heard

---

156 'Standrig' in transcript – but 'Standering' or 'Standring' are probably to be preferred.

# First Day – Thursday 16 March 1820.

**John Chadwick**

Mr Hunt say in a loud tone, 'Shout, shout, shout'. He repeated that till he got opposite the *Observer* office. There they stopped, and Mr Hunt whirled his hat, and the people near him shouted, and the others joined. They appeared to understand him. They then went on to Johnson's house, and shouted again; Mr Hunt said, 'Three times three'. This was opposite St Michael's church; he then told the people to come on one side and he would tell them his errand to Manchester; he then drawed his gig on one side, and said that he had been invited to Manchester by the Manchester committee and that he and his gig and his political Bob (his horse) had set out together. He had come as far as Coventry, where he saw the *Courier* newspaper, which stated that the Manchester magistrates had put down the reformers at Manchester, and that he (Hunt) would be afraid to show his face there as they would make him smell gunpowder. Afterwards he said that he had seen the proclamation at Bullock Smithy, and such a proclamation never came from a shop-board of tailors: he also added that he would have the *Courier* to know that he was not afraid of gunpowder. He then turned to the Stockport people and said he hoped to see them all on the sixteenth, and that they would bring as many of their friends and neighbours as they could with them.

Witness knew where White Moss was. On 15 August, he got there before daylight; White Moss is about five miles from Manchester. There was a great number, about two or three hundred at first, but they kept increasing all the morning. They came from different roads. Witness went there from curiosity; they fell in ranks like soldiers when the horn was blown. This was about daylight; witness also fell in. The people fell in to the companies belonging to the place they came from. Every company had a person to command it; they then marched about the field for two hours and, when the word was given to fire, they clapped their hands. The words 'Make ready, present, fire!' were given as if they had guns, and at the word 'Fire!' they clapped their hands. They afterwards fell into a large body, and made the spectators fall in also. Witness falled in at first, but he very soon after falled out. Did not know any of the commanders there.

Mr HUNT objected to this evidence. The witness had sworn that he knew none of these people.

Mr SCARLETT said he would show that some of these people had attended Mr Hunt.

Mr HUNT said it mattered not unless some of those persons were among the accused.

Mr SCARLETT said he hoped Mr Hunt would not be allowed to disturb the proceedings of the court.

Mr Justice BAYLEY: Mr Hunt has a right to take the objection, and I

# Hunt and Others.

**John Chadwick**

am doubting whether this is evidence.

[The witness was sent out.]

Mr SCARLETT said he was about to show that some of those persons who were training and who assaulted Murray had attended the meeting of 16 August, and had also cheered opposite Murray's house. He would show that Mr Hunt and his party had done the same. This he conceived was perfectly regular.

Mr Justice BAYLEY: When you have shown that any of the persons of the White Moss party were at the meeting on 16 August, then it will be evidence, but I think you had better prove that first.

[Witness was again called to the box and examined.]

WITNESS: I was at the meeting of 16 August, and the first person I saw was a man I had seen at White Moss with a letter brought from Manchester. After the letter came the parties formed into a square, like four walls, and the man who was to read the letter was in the centre. The letter was not read as they said there was no name to it, and they would have nothing to do with it. The man then joined them. The man who was to have read the letter was the person who led up the Middleton and Rochdale parties on Monday. This man was drilling the men, and giving the word of command. I saw Murray, the constable, on the Moss, and heard the people call 'Spy, spy!' and then run after him. There was another man with Murray. I left the ground about six o'clock. I went the next day at eleven o'clock to Johnson's house to meet Mr Hunt. I went with a party from the Union schoolroom at Manchester. I did not see Mr Hunt go from Johnson's, for I joined the Rochdale and Middleton party, who were going on to the meeting. I saw Mr Hunt go on to the meeting afterwards from Johnson's house. Johnson, Knight, and a person they called Carlile were with him in an open-topped chaise. Some of the people walked in ranks near it, but the rest walked irregularly. They shouted as they came to Johnsons's, and also at the Exchange; and opposite Murray's house they hissed hard. There was a woman on the coach with the coachman. She carried a flag.

*Cross-examined* by Mr HUNT.

I live at number 30, Miller Street, Manchester; I have lived there nine years. I work a little for myself. I know you are Mr Hunt. When you bid the people shout, I did not join them. I went through mere curiosity and nothing else. I stayed up all the night I went to White Moss. The man who went with me is named William – I do not know his other name. He saw all I saw at White Moss. I never told those who brought me here that another person had been with me at White Moss. I have frequently talked over the matter with the man who went with me. I do not know where he

# First Day – Thursday 16 March 1820.

**John Chadwick**

lives. The story I have told here has been taken down in writing by Mr Milne; he never asked me whether anybody had been with me. I went to him of my own accord to speak the truth; I went to him last Thursday. I never went to him before that time.

There were about three hundred persons at White Moss when I got there. There were some scores who did not fall in until they were forced. They said to us, 'You must all fall in, for we'll have no lookers-on'. When I first came, they had not fallen in – they were all sitting down. There are roads close to White Moss, and persons passing could not miss seeing the people marching. When I fell out of the ranks, I went into the next field, lest I should be made to fall in again. I think there were as many spectators as persons marching. I left them about seven in the morning, and went home. I do not recollect any other words used but 'march' and 'counter-march'. When they said, 'March!' the men walked up the field. I think when they said, 'Counter-march!' they marched back again, not backwards, but to the place from which they came. I did not see them raise their arms in the attitude of firing; I did not see the people in the carriage hiss or take any notice of Murray's house; any person who should state the contrary would state what is false.

[Witness described the flags borne by the different parties on the sixteenth.]

I heard shouting and cries of 'Hunt and Liberty'. There was no disposition to do mischief manifested by the crowd; they were all gay and cheerful. If any person was to swear that the people marched by with you four or five abreast in a riotous manner, they would swear a falsehood. I saw no swords, pistols, or bludgeons. I saw some walking sticks with some of the people. If any of them had had weapons calculated to do mischief I must have seen them. I never cheered on any occasion. When I got to Peter's Field, I stood near the house where the magistrates were. When the cavalry came in, I was rather alarmed, but not before.

Peter's Field was full of people who were all standing peaceably. I saw nothing to the contrary. They remained so till the cavalry began to go down. As they were going to the stage, I quitted the field. They came in with their swords drawn, and in a sort of a trot. I went away because I thought there would be danger. There were many others running as well as me. I went to White Moss as it was well known in the town that drilling was going on there.

*Cross-examined* by Mr ROBERT WYLDE.

I left Manchester about twelve o'clock on the night of the fifteenth, and arrived at White Moss about six o'clock in the morning. It was daylight between two and three in the morning. It would be a hard job for me to

# Hunt and Others.

**John Chadwick**

tell you the road I took to White Moss.

*Cross-examined* by Mr JOHNSON.

Some of the people went before Mr Hunt's carriage on the sixteenth. You may call it marching if you will. I can't say whether they went six abreast. I was before the carriage, and do not know how those behind it went. I heard no sound of bugle, nor any order for hissing given at Murray's.

*Re-examined* by Mr SCARLETT.

I went to Blackley, and then crossed the fields to White Moss. The nearest turnpike road to the Moss is a mile and a half distant. The nearest village is Blackley, which is a mile off. There were some stout lads who marched before the carriage of Mr Hunt. I was then in Ashton Lane.

[The placard calling the meeting of 9 August in order to consider of the best means of obtaining a radical reform in the House of Commons was then put in.]

Mr Hunt objected to it as evidence, unless it could be shown that he had been a party to its being published.

Mr Justice Bayley said the pamphlet had not yet been proved.

**James Murray**

JAMES MURRAY, sworn and examined by Mr Serjeant HULLOCK.

I live at Manchester. I know Mr Shawcross; I went with him on the night of 14 August. Mr Rymer and his son were with us. We went to White Moss. We left Manchester on purpose to go there, and reached it by daylight. Hearing some persons near us shouting and hallooing, we lay down to prevent our being seen. We then got to the Moss where the men were drilling; there might be 600 or 800 hundred of them. The plot of ground was square. They were in squads, and there was a drill sergeant at the head or end of every squad. They were marching when I went up. I heard the words 'march', 'wheel', and 'halt'. It appeared like a camp; the men obeyed the orders given to them. I remember the words 'eyes right', 'dress', and 'forward'. I was close amongst them on the left hand. The first words said to me were by a drill sergeant, who bid me fall in. I knew the man – his name was Catterall. I said I thought I would fall in soon.

The different sergeants began to shift their squads and look steadfastly. I did not like his looks, and thought of shifting my ground, when I heard the cry of, 'Spy!' It ran along the lines, and I heard the words, 'Mill them, damn them, mill them!' I then heard a cry of, 'They are constables!' and the answer to that was, 'Damn them, murder them!' I moved off, and moved off, and so did Shawcross, but were followed by eighty or ninety

# First Day – Thursday 16 March 1820.

men. They overtook Shawcross, beat him, and knocked him in the ditch.

Mr Hunt here submitted that this was not evidence. This was proof of an assault for which men had been convicted and punished.

Mr SCARLETT contended that he had a right to examine this witness. His object was to show the connection between the men at White Moss and those assembled on 16 August. The charge against the accused was that of conspiring to disturb the King's peace. Now, the conduct of those assembled at White Moss --?

Mr HUNT said that he felt as fully as anyone the grossness and illegality of the conduct of those persons at White Moss, but he hoped the court would not implicate him and his fellow defendants in it upon such testimony as that already given.

Mr Justice BAYLEY said the only question was whether those assembled on the fourteenth had not intended to give those assembled on the sixteenth that superiority which military training gives, and, if so, whether it is not evidence to show the intention of the parties in assembling.

[Mr MURRAY's examination continued.] From twenty to thirty men followed and overtook me. They began to beat me with sticks and kick me most violently with their clogs. I desired them to give over, that that did not look like a Reform in Parliament; it was, I said, very different treatment from that received by prisoners of war. They asked me how we would treat them if we took them prisoners to Manchester. I said we would treat them as prisoners, and not murder them. They continued beating me, and one said, 'Shall we kill him out and out and put him in the pit, or let him go?' A young man said, 'He has had enough'; another, 'If he has any more, he'll die'. They then desisted, and held a consultation, after which one of them asked me if I would consent to go down on my knees, and never be a King's man again, and never name the King any more? I said yes, as I considered my life was in danger. I fell upon my knees; the words I now mention were proposed to me, and I repeated them. They then let me get up. One man struck me twice after I got up, and that was all.[157]

I went to Middleton, as I was unable to go to Manchester. I was unable

---

[157] *Carlisle Patriot*, 5 February 1820, reporting the Manchester Quarter Sessions of 27 and 28 January 1820: 'John Catterall was indicted for a violent assault upon Mr James Murray of Manchester on 15 August at White Moss, the nature of which we particularized at the time. Upwards of five hundred men were practising the military exercise, of whom the prisoner was one. The case was proved, and the jury immediately returned a verdict of guilty. The court sentenced him to three years' imprisonment in Lancaster Castle, and to find sureties in £50 each, and himself in £100, for his good behaviour for five years afterwards.'

# Hunt and Others.

**James Murray**

to stir after I got to bed. I was the next day removed to Manchester where I was confined to my bed. On the next day, the sixteenth, I heard the sound of bugles, and, on being removed to the window, I heard the cry of, 'Halt!' The crowd then halted near my door. I looked out, and saw the streets filled with people. Those in the centre were in ranks about six abreast. The bugle was again sounded, and I heard the word, 'March!' and the party moved on, and began to hiss very loud. Many of them had sticks. They had several flags and banners with them. Those who marched in line amounted to between 5,000 and 6,000 men. Besides these, there was a large crowd of men and women. I could not identify any of them; I was unable to go out that day. This was about eleven o'clock. About one o'clock, another crowd of men, women, and children, came past my house. There was an open carriage in which I saw Mr Hunt and Mr Johnson, and I think another person. I do not think it stopped at my door, but it moved very slow. The whole of the crowd hissed and pointed at my windows. I think those in the carriage looked at my house.

[To a question from the judge.] I am sure they looked up as they passed. I think those in the carriage were standing. There were near 4,000 persons, many of whom were women and children. The road from Smedley Cottage does not run past my house; by going that way they went 500 or 600 yards out of the way.

*Cross-examined* by Mr HUNT.

I am not employed by the police; I am a confectioner; I am a district constable, sworn in by the magistrates. I went to White Moss in consequence of the alarmed state of the country, as well as of my family and myself. I went of my own free will. I told several persons I would go, as I had heard of drilling. I believe I told Nadin. I got nothing for my trouble from the police.

There was a subscription for the wounded at Peterloo, and I got a part of it to pay my doctor's bill. I got £15. I will swear that I never arranged with Nadin or any other person, nor was I employed by anyone to go there. It was my own act and deed. On my oath, to the best of my belief, Nadin did not know I was going. I saw no lookers-on at White Moss. They were all at drill except myself and those who went with me. I did not notice the lookers-on. There were some persons at a distance, who might be lookers-on for what I know. There were not many looking on in front of the ranks. If there were two hundred lookers-on, I must have seen them. They had no arms. I did not hear them say, 'Make ready, present, fire!' but if it had been said, I must have heard it. I first mentioned this to Joshua Pollet.

My depositions were made in my bedroom before Mr Norris and Mr

# First Day – Thursday 16 March 1820.

Trafford, on the same day that I was attacked. On the twenty-first I went before a magistrate in order to correct an omission which I had made in my depositions. They were put down on a slip of paper, but I do not recollect whether I swore to them or not. I think myself a religious man. I go to church and chapel. I know Robert Meagher.[158] I do not recollect any particular conversation with him. I do not recollect any particular conversation between Meagher, Samuel Morton, and myself. Perhaps I do not like the Reformers, but I do not recollect using any violent language against them. I never said that I would rather be rowed to my own house in a boat in the blood of the Reformers than walk upon the pavement. I once said that if it was to come to an action, I would not give up to the Reformers, even were I to fight up to my knees in blood. I went one night to the Cock public house, and, being a King's man, they were all at me; I had a good deal of ale, and I do not recollect what I did say; I will not swear that I did not use the words you mention.

James Murray

I know a Mr Chapman, at Manchester; I went not long since in a coach with him to Liverpool. There were six in the coach. We spoke of Reform; I do not recollect saying that if I had the command of the troops on 16 August, I would have put every bloody rascal of them to death. I swear I did not say so.

Mr HUNT here cautioned the witness, and repeated the question. — I did not say I would make the troops fire, and put all present to death. I will not swear that I did not say this. I was sober in the coach. On my oath, I did not say so to my knowledge. Mr Chapman did not call me to account for saying so. I told Mr Chapman I would not believe a reformer upon his oath, and I now repeat it. I would not believe any reformer on his oath. Some words about firing might fly out of my mouth, and my enemies might have misconstrued it against me.

I do not recollect seeing you at the Spread Eagle, Hanging Ditch. I was one of a party of King's men who once went into a private room in that house in which you were. The boroughreeve and constables were going their rounds and I joined them, but I do not recollect the door being broke open; I swear it.

*Cross-examined* by Mr JOHNSON.

I never took money from my wife and went off to Liverpool with females of loose character. I never made any offer of myself to serve the office of special constable.

JOHN SHAWCROSS, sworn and examined by Mr Serjeant CROSS.

John Shawcross

---

158  Sic in transcript. Presumably read: 'Edward Meagher'.

# Hunt and Others.

**John Shawcross**

I am a clerk at the police office, Manchester.

[The printed placard announcing the intended meeting of 9 August was shown to witness, who said such bills were posted up as early as 23 July in the public streets at Manchester. He was also shown the prohibitory placard issued by the magistrates, which he said was placarded in a similar manner. The witness then corroborated the evidence of last witness, Murray, respecting the outrage committed upon him by the people assembled at White Moss.]

*Cross-examined* by Mr HUNT.

I know most of the defendants, and accompanied Murray to Lancaster Castle to see if I could identify the parties. White Moss was about a mile and a quarter across. The men there were in squads, as if under leaders. Heard nothing said about 'firing', 'marching', 'counter-marching'. Heard nothing said of that kind at all, except wheeling to the right and left. The people did not call upon him to fall in; they never said anything of that kind, nor did he ever give them any hopes that he would join them by and by. No such proposition was made to him. If anybody said so, it was not true.

In answer to questions from Mr Justice Bayley, he said the squads appeared some of them awkward, and some perfect in drilling.

To a question of Mr Hunt: The people who went to White Moss did not go secretly, but set up a hooting every ten minutes; they were very noisy on the way.

**John Heywood**

JOHN HEYWOOD, sworn and examined by Mr LITTLEDALE.

I live near Manchester, and was there on Sunday morning, 15 August. While there a man came up to me and said, 'Here, lads, is another spy!' They then beat me with sticks as fast as they could.

He saw the same body of men marching from Middleton towards Manchester, with flags and a cap of liberty. As they came along, they said they would give me what they gave me short the day before if I followed them. One of them said, 'That's he that was at the Moss the day before'. I went, on the same day, within four miles of Smedley Cottage, and saw Mr Hunt addressing the people there.

*Cross-examined* by Mr HUNT.

I saw one of the parties who beat me since: he is now convicted for it, and lodged in Lancaster Castle.[159] They did not use the sticks as arms, nor

---

159 *Carlisle Patriot*, 5 February 1820, reporting the Manchester Quarter Sessions of 27 and 28 January 1820 and having previously described the conviction and sentencing of

# First Day – Thursday 16 March 1820.

was there any command of, 'Make ready, fire!' Nor did they give me any hint to join them. I heard Mr Hunt speak that day from Smedley Cottage, but what he said I don't know. I saw him throw up the sash before he spoke from the window; I was standing in an adjoining meadow.

In answer to a question from Mr Scarlett, he said he stood about 400 yards from the window.

*[At six o'clock the court rose, and adjourned the further hearing until the following morning. Mr Hunt was loudly cheered as he passed home to his lodgings.]*

**John Heywood**

Catterall for the assault on James Murray: 'David Kay, for a similar kind of assault upon John Heywood on the same day and whilst the radical troops were exercising, was found guilty and sentenced to two years' imprisonment at Lancaster Castle; to be bound to keep the peace for three years afterwards, himself in £100 and two sureties in £50 each'.

# Second Day – Friday 17 March 1820.

*The court was crowded this morning soon after seven o'clock. The rush, when the doors were thrown open, was excessive, and a number of ladies again encountered the pressure of the crowd – they were, however, accommodated with such places as could be spared near the bench. At nine o'clock, Mr Hunt entered, accompanied by the other defendants. He seemed in excellent spirits. Mr Harmer and Mr Pearson assisted him as yesterday. Mr Hunt was cheered by the people through whom he passed on his way to the court. Mr Justice Bayley took his seat on the bench at half-past nine o'clock. Many persons of rank in the county were also present. The first witness called was:*

WILLIAM MORRIS, sworn and examined by Mr Serjeant CROSS.

I am a weaver, residing five miles from Manchester, near White Moss. I know a place called Smedley. In the course of the month of August last, I saw many groups of people near Middleton; Samuel Bamford (one of the defendants) used to be among them. Early on 16 August, about nine or ten o'clock, I saw many hundreds of people put into regular form at Middleton, with two flags. Twenty-five men were in each section. I know not who formed them into sections, nor how many there were, but there certainly was a large number collected that day in the township – two or three thousand at the least. They marched off four abreast after being first drawn into the form of a square in the inside of which was placed a chair, on which Samuel Bamford stood and said, 'Friends and neighbours, I have a few words to relate. You will march off this place quietly, not to insult any one, but rather take an insult; I do not think there will be any disturbance or any to-do; if there is, it will be after we come back. There is no fear, for the day is our own.' I did not hear him say anything more.

He got off the chair and spread laurel among the men who were to command the sections; they put it, some into their breast, and others in their hats. It was after this they marched off four abreast. Before they went away, a large number of people came, also arranged in form, from Rochdale, with a band of music before them, and bearing two flags which had an inscription, but I do not recollect it. Both bodies, which were nearly of equal numbers, joined, and then went off together, each with a cap of liberty. The men had nothing in their hands but bits of switches, or small sticks.

Before that day, I saw the Middleton people forming and arranging, both in the fields and high roads. Bamford was with them different times.

<sub>William Morris</sub>

# Hunt and Others.

**William Morris**

On 8 August, they talked of a row at Manchester, but I cannot say that any of the defendants were there. On the sixteenth, Bamford was in the front of the people. I know John Whitworth, who was a private in the 6th Regiment of foot; he was drilling the men, but not on 16 August. John Heywood, who was a private in the sixteenth Dragoons, was doing the same.

*Cross-examined* by the defendant, BAMFORD.

I am swearing the whole truth. I did not see who put the men in form on the morning of the sixteenth; but I saw you address them from the chair, and heard you recommend them to be peaceable, and did understand you wished them to continue so the whole of the day. There were two flags, but I heard you say nothing of what they were to serve for. I was only a dozen yards from you, and I think I could very well hear what you said. I do not recollect your saying, that, when they got to Manchester, every man was to remain around his own banner, nor that they were to return home quietly and orderly after the business of the day, and that if any stragglers were on the ground, they were not to form with them, but to look out for their own banner.

Many thousands went before and followed the Middleton and Rochdale people, who were not formed with them in the march; they mixed up with them, as well as a good deal of women and children. I know your wife by sight, but it is not everywhere I see her that I recollect her. I did not observe her or your child in the crowd that day. The crowd appeared promiscuous. I know there were many people and stragglers at the right and left of you, but none in form except those you led up.

Barrowfield was the place where I first saw you with the men. I have seen many processions with music at Middleton – of the Orangemen, and Odd Fellows – they had flags and inscriptions. I was at Middleton on the proclamation of His Majesty George IV, and I saw then a procession of the Odd Fellows bearing a flag.

Mr Justice BAYLEY: I am unwilling to interrupt you, but how does this bear upon the point?

Mr BAMFORD: I mean to show that it is a common practice in this part of the country to have these sort of processions. I know what marching is, for I learned it when I was a soldier. You can tell what they were to do, as you were with them.

*Cross-examined* by Mr HUNT.

It is twenty-five years since I was a non-commissioned officer in the 104th Regiment; I remained so as long as I stayed in the service. I was in the habit of a soldier for three years, but I never took an oath, and was

# Second Day – Friday 17 March 1820.

therefore not sworn to the oath of allegiance. I did not on that account feel myself bound to remain with the regiment any longer than I thought proper. When I had seen as much of the service as I liked, I wished them good morning. [A laugh.] I considered myself to be with them, but not as a soldier, though I wore the clothing. When I thought I had been there long enough, I made the best of my way home. I was never told that – being a deserter, and having violated my oath – I would not be a good witness in a court of justice. I entered the regiment as what was called a mushroom sergeant. [Loud laughter.] I had so much a man for enlisting on the recruiting service. I have been in Ireland, but never happened to see Orange clubs marching there as at Middleton. I never saw the Orangemen with shillelaghs to defend themselves, but I have seen them with common sticks.

Mr HUNT: You were not alarmed then? — No, I was not, nor was I alarmed at your set. [Laughter.] I saw no depredations committed on their march, nor can I tell whether people were alarmed or not by them. I saw them insult nobody. The high road from Middleton to Manchester is within half a mile, or thereabouts, of Smedley Cottage. I had nothing to do with Smedley Cottage; it was the learned counsel's [Mr Serjeant Cross's] question that put it into my head. I will not swear that they did or did not play 'God Save the King'.

[He added, with warmth, on Mr Hunt's pressing the question:] I did not expect those loyal tunes would be played by them. I did not hear them play disloyal tunes, nor 'The Rogue's March' (which perhaps I think is yours), nor 'The Deserters' (which maybe I'd have taken to myself). [Laughter.] I saw none of them drunk on their way to Manchester. I do not know anything to the contrary of Bamford's being a peaceable man. Some of the people had small sticks.

Mr HUNT: Were any of them large enough to whip an infamous cause out of court?

The JUDGE said this was not the time to make an observation.

**William Morris**

JOHN EATON, sworn and examined by Mr LITTLEDALE.

I live at Middleton and am a plumber and glazier. On the morning of 16 August, I saw a great many people assembling, and Samuel Bamford among them and in front. They had music and flags (two): the inscriptions were 'Liberty, Strength, and Unity' and something with a cap on a pole. Bamford had a bunch of laurel in his hand and many others had a little of it in their hats. Some had also little walking sticks, and were proceeding towards Manchester by the new road.

*Cross-examined* by Mr BAMFORD.

**John Eaton**

# Hunt and Others.

**John Eaton**

One flag was green and another blue. I saw nothing but small sticks; there were no poles except such as had the flags and cap of liberty. I don't know whether I could tell your wife, but there were many women and children – three, and four, and five abreast – who appeared to partake of the conviviality of the procession. These were principally in the Rochdale division. I do not think they were in the Middleton. The people did not seem sullen and sulky; they had no angry looks, but were more, as it were, in joy. I have some little property, and was then on my premises. I felt no occasion to go home and shut my doors when I saw this procession; if I saw anybody else doing it, perhaps I might. The processions of the Orangemen and Odd Fellows (one of whom I am) often move in regular order.

I am not a reformer. I know nothing about radical reform, except that it creates a great noise up and down the country and perhaps it would be as well to lay it aside. I could not suppose the reformers had any particular regard for me. I said nothing about the legality of the Manchester meeting, except that you ought to know best what you were going for.

*Cross-examined* by Mr HUNT.

I have often walked to our Orange processions, and understand them, but I do not understand yours, and of course did not walk with it. Our flag is called the Union, but it has no inscription. I don't know Mr Fletcher, the magistrate, but that he is in our lodge.

**Joseph Travis**

JOSEPH TRAVIS, sworn and examined by Mr Serjeant CROSS.[160]

I live at Oldham and am a grocer. I remember on 16 August parties of men passing through at nine o'clock, on their way to Manchester. They marched past. I saw 'Saddleworth' on one of their flags. After they were passed, I was sent on after them by the magistrates to count the number that passed. There were five divisions: Royton, Crompton, Chadderton, Saddleworth and Oldham flags with their names at the head of each. Each division was formed into marching sections; they were irregularly formed, some being two, some four, and others eight or up to twelve abreast. There were about two paces between each of the sections, and a man or commander marched on the left flank of each; they had bugles and flags, and marched like soldiers to Bent Green. I counted 864 marching in ranks but there were many hundreds of stragglers went besides, and some of them frequently went into the ranks; occasionally,

---

160  Whether Mr Travis's appearance as a witness for the prosecution affected the shopping habits of the denizens of Oldham is not known, but he was declared bankrupt in October 1821.

# Second Day – Friday 17 March 1820.

they got into a little disorder owing to the stragglers who fell in, and then the man at each section gave the words, 'Halt! Eyes left!' His command was obeyed, and they speedily formed and went on when the word, 'March!' was given. One leader I saw was Dr Healey of Lees. He led the Saddleworth and Lees divisions. I know the doctor.

**Joseph Travis**

Here Mr HUNT rose to express his apprehension that Mr Milne of Manchester, who assists the Solicitor of the Treasury for the prosecution, was communicating with some of the witnesses. He had, he said, repeatedly seen him go out of court, and he was informed he had seen some of the witnesses. Of course it followed that, when witnesses were to be kept apart, the only intention of so placing them was to exclude them from any communication with the previous business of the court. It was but just this moment that he saw Mr Milne hand out a letter; he hoped the court would send after it, and ascertain the purport of the communication.

Mr Justice BAYLEY immediately asked Mr Milne to whom this letter was addressed. The latter answered, 'To G. F. Merry'. The under-sheriff followed the messenger, and in a minute or two returned with the letter, which the judge opened, and, after perusing it, informed Mr Hunt that it contained nothing respecting the pending business of this trial.

Mr SCARLETT, on behalf of Mr Milne, felt it right to say that the letter was in reply to an application from Mr Merry for a copy of his depositions.

Mr Justice BAYLEY repeated that there was no impropriety in the matter.

Mr HUNT said that the appearance at first looked suspicious.

[Examination of witness resumed.] The crowd kept increasing while I remained in sight, and marched (as I have already said) in regular order, as soldiers do.

*Cross-examined* by Mr HUNT.

I was employed by the magistrates to do this as a special constable, or else I should not have gone. While I was with the magistrates, I left my father – who was seventy-one years – to take care of my shop. I was not alarmed when the men passed; I saw no reason to fear; I have been a soldier myself. I do not recollect what was on the flags; I went with Mr Chippindale, a gentleman at Oldham, to count the people; he wrote down as I counted. We have talked over the matter together. I do not know that he is here. I believe that he is not. I was forced to come on. I saw no drunkenness, no rioting, no threats, no ill usage. I do not know whether Mr Chippindale was a special constable. He is not an attorney. I was not at all alarmed; nor did I see any reason why I should, as these

# Hunt and Others.

**Joseph Travis**

people passed with the black flag, though the look of it I did not like. I did not stop the flag, which had upon it 'Saddleworth, Lees, and Mossley Union' and something like two hands grasped, and the word 'Love' also. I did not see what the learned counsel called the bloody dagger upon it. I did not see such a thing upon any of the flags.

I do not know the particular reason why Mr Chippindale is not here today, though he was subpoenaed, and though his signature as well as mine was to the deposition which went into the solicitor for the prosecution. I have not heard he was let off by the other side.

I saw no caps of liberty among the people, but I have seen the stone cap at the top of this castle; a stone cap is not a cap of liberty, it is only the figure of one. [Laughter.]

**John Ashworth**

JOHN ASHWORTH, sworn and examined by Mr LITTLEDALE.

I was working as an engineer at a factory at Oldham on 16 August when I saw the Saddleworth and Royton divisions come there and join another division which came up before them. They formed altogether, and went on ten or twelve abreast to Manchester by the new road. There might be from three to five thousand, exclusive of stragglers. [He then described the banners nearly in the same terms as the last witness.] Many called out to me by name to go with them, but I said they were a week too soon for me; that I could not go till Saturday. Some of them also said they would make a 'Moscow' of it before they came back; this occurred at eight o'clock in the morning of the sixteenth.

*Cross-examined* by Mr HUNT.

I live at Manchester but am no relation to Ashworth the constable, who was killed there on the sixteenth.[161] I have a wife and children who were at Manchester that day while I was working at Oldham. They did not alarm me about this 'Moscow' business. I was surprised to see so many people, and I said at the time to those about me that the words were terrible. I was repairing the factory steam engine, and could not go to look after my wife at the time. I sent off no messenger to her. Only one or two said 'Moscow'. I saw the cap of liberty with the people, but never saw one before or since. I am not a man of that principle that bothers my head about caps of liberty or things of that kind.

**William Standring**

WILLIAM STANDRING, sworn and examined by Mr SCARLETT.

---

161  John Ashworth, the proprietor of the Bull's Head inn, was serving as a special constable on the day of Peterloo. He was 'shockingly trampled on and mutilated, and presented a most horrible spectacle', in the words of one reporter. (*Kentish Weekly Post*, 24 August 1819.)

# Second Day – Friday 17 March 1820.

**William Standring**

This witness was a publican residing at Failsworth, between Oldham and Manchester, and described his having seen the crowds assemble in his neighbourhood about nine o'clock in the morning of 16 August. He saw Dr Healey while the division halted: many of them, and among the rest the doctor, came into his house and had a glass of gin, and said, 'Victory, my lads, and success to the business of the day'. The doctor also hoped the people of the house were true to the cause.

*Cross-examined* by Mr HUNT.

I have retired from the public business, and live now with my brother-in-law. I have my living still to get by my industry. On that day I was much alarmed for my property. I did not, however, remove it to any place of safety. It has been sold since at Oldham, but no person's name was to the bills advertising the sale. I have been in a court of justice before now, as a witness. I was once charged for breaking windows one night when I was full. I have had the misfortune of being confined in the lunatic asylum, but was not latterly in a state so as to feel unnecessary fear. I have been a special constable, but was never in the pay of the police.

**Jeremiah Fielding**

JEREMIAH FIELDING, sworn and examined by Mr LITTLEDALE.

I am a merchant and was on the road between Manchester and Cheetham Hill on the morning of 16 August. I met there on the road numbers of people passing towards the town; there were two or three thousand in one group, and they marched four or five abreast with music and flags.

*Cross-examined* by Mr HUNT.

There were no women and children with them when I saw them, nor did they insult anybody.

**James Heath**

JAMES HEATH, examined by Mr SCARLETT.

I reside at Cheetham Hill. I saw a party proceeding to Manchester on 16 August [which he described nearly as the last witness had done. He saw a party of three and one of those three persons, looking earnestly at witness, said to him, 'You will not sleep in that house tonight'. Witness went to Manchester in the afternoon.]

*Cross-examined* by Mr HUNT.

Knew Mr Nadin; did not know all the police runners; could not swear that they were not connected with the police at Manchester, but he did not believe them to be persons of that description.

# Hunt and Others.

**Roger Entwistle**

[ROGER ENTWISTLE being called, it was answered that he was out of the way. Mr Hunt suggested that he should be called as 'Clerk of the Racecourse', as he was better known by that title than by the name of Roger Entwistle.]

**James Duncough**

JAMES DUNCOUGH, sworn and examined by Mr LITTLEDALE.

I am a cotton-spinner, and reside at Hollinwood, within five miles of Manchester. I was going to that town on the morning of 16 August, and saw on the road a body of at least 2,500 men. They were going in the direction of Manchester. One man said to me, 'Well, captain, how do you do?' I had been a captain in the local militia. I heard some of them say, as they passed Hollinwood, 'We are going to Westhoughton'. I formerly had a mill there which was burned down in the year 1812, at the time of the Luddites. It was purposely set on fire. A mill was afterwards built on the spot.

*Cross-examined* by Mr HUNT.

I was at Manchester on 16 August. I was not acting as a constable. I saw you on the hustings, and also before Mr Buxton's house. I took no part in the transactions of the day. I left the ground before the cavalry came up, for I thought it was unsafe to remain there without a protection. I saw you before Buxton's house after the meeting was dispersed. I left the field before the cavalry came, and I returned again through curiosity. Both visits were made through curiosity. I certainly thought it safer to be on the ground after the cavalry arrived than before.

I am not a medical man, and did not assist in dressing the wounds of any of the individuals who were injured on that day. I did not see any person wounded. I sent a cartload of goods to Manchester on that morning. I cannot speak as to what particular goods they were: our cart always goes out early in the morning, at seven or eight o'clock, and when I sent the goods to Manchester I believed they would reach the town before the meeting began. On that account, I was not afraid of sending them on that day, but if they were not likely to reach Manchester before one o'clock I certainly should have been afraid to transmit them. I have a warehouse there and, though I might be afraid to send the goods to Manchester at a late hour, I should feel no apprehension when they were once safely arrived there as they would be locked up in a secure warehouse. I returned from Manchester the same evening, and on the road had a short conversation with an officer of the 6th Dragoon Guards respecting the transactions of the day. I told the officer I could give him but a very imperfect account of the meeting, as I left the ground before the cavalry arrived and did not return till after the crowd was dispersed. I

# Second Day – Friday 17 March 1820.

did not ask him, or any other officer, whether he had been at Manchester that day.

Of course I could not say that in consequence of his absence he had lost all the fun. I never made use of such an expression. I did not go to Manchester exactly through curiosity: my business lies in Manchester, though I live in the country, and it is my duty to attend my warehouse; but I had no motive whatever, except curiosity, in going from the warehouse to the meeting. I knew it would be dispersed in consequence of notices issued by the boroughreeve and constables. The notices did not state specifically that the meeting would be suppressed, but, from the language and tenor of the publication, I thought it was very likely that it would be put down. I have no copy of the placard, but the substance of it was a recommendation to the people to keep their families and servants at home. I do not think the notice was signed by any magistrate; it was the recommendation of the boroughreeve and constables. I went, notwithstanding that recommendation to the meeting. Of course I went at my own risk; I should have run considerable risk if I had remained.

When I left St Peter's Field – the first time – it was crowded with people; when I returned, it was in the possession of the soldiery; at that time, they were taking you out of Mr Buxton's house. I had a factory at Westhoughton burnt down some years ago. It was, I believe, the only one entirely burned. Four persons were convicted and hanged for the offence. I do not know that one of them was a boy, though I have heard it stated.[162] I was then at Gibraltar. I understood it was burned down by the Luddites, who entered it in the open day. I never heard that the crime was perpetrated by the black-faced spies of Bolton, and, if I had, I would not have believed it. The prosecution was commenced before I left Gibraltar. I believe my name was inserted in the indictment as one of the prosecutors. Did not hear of any factories being burned within the last two or three years, since the period when great meetings began to be held for parliamentary reform.

By Mr SCARLETT.

There were from 60,000 to 100,000 persons on the ground. They were, with the exception of those who came through curiosity, persons belonging to the labouring classes. The whole ground, about six or eight

**James Duncough**

---

162 *Leeds Mercury*, 20 June 1812: 'Manchester, June 16 – About twelve o'clock on Saturday, the awful sentence of the law was put into execution upon the eight unfortunate persons condemned at the late Special Assize at Lancaster, viz., Jas. Smith, Thos. Kerfoot, Job Fletcher, and Abra. Charlson, for burning, &c., Messrs Wroe and Duncough's Weaving Mill at West Houghton [sic]; John Howarth, John Lee, and Thos. Hoyle, for breaking into the house of John Holland of this town, and stealing bread, cheese, &c.; and Hannah Smith, for committing a highway robbery, by stealing potatoes at Bank Top in this town.'

# Hunt and Others.

**James Duncough**

statute acres, was covered with people. Those who were mere lookers-on stood at a distance. At that time, many persons, especially weavers, were out of employment. I stayed until Mr Hunt reached the field, and I left just as he began his address. There was much shouting. I observed fifteen or twenty banners. I did not think the town of Manchester was safe when such a multitude of people were congregated together from different parts.

[In answer to a question by the court, witness said that, in his opinion, the number of people assembled on that occasion was calculated to inspire the inhabitants of the town with a great degree of terror.]

**Roger Entwistle**

ROGER ENTWISTLE, sworn and examined by Mr SCARLETT.

I am an attorney of Manchester. From ten to twelve o'clock on 16 August, I was at the Albion Hotel, Piccadilly, opposite the infirmary, which is on the line from Stockport. I saw a large body of people marching into the town like regular soldiers, with banners and also caps of liberty. Several among them appeared to have the command of different parties, and moved about a yard from the rest, at the side of the front ranks. They had very large sticks, some walking with them, and others bearing them upon their shoulders. When the coach which headed them came opposite the White Bear, Mr Moorhouse came out of it. One of the men said to me as he marched by that before night he would have as good a coat on his back as I had. I then went to St Peter's Field where I saw the special constables in front of Mr Buxton's house. Mr Hunt had not then arrived, and they were preparing the hustings, and the constables formed a line between it and Mr Buxton's. Soon after I saw Mr Hunt, Mr Moorhouse and several others come up in an open carriage. I saw Mr Hunt get upon the hustings; several thousands, at the very least upwards of 100,000, were there at the time, and many of them were chanting 'Britons never shall be slaves'. There were very few Manchester people there except out of curiosity, but they chiefly consisted of the labouring classes from the adjacent country. The meeting was most certainly calculated to inspire alarm and terror in the minds of the peaceable inhabitants of the town.

I heard Mr Hunt's address from the hustings; he commenced by congratulating the meeting on the adjournment from the ninth, as they had thereby doubled the number in the cause. Shortly after, the military (infantry) made a movement in the direction of Dickinson Street. Mr Hunt immediately pointed to them and said, 'Your enemies are among you! If they attempt to molest you, get them down, and while you have them down, keep them down.' Soon after the Manchester cavalry came up to the front of Mr Buxton's house. Hearing that warrants were likely to be used, I did not think it safe to remain any longer near the hustings,

# Second Day – Friday 17 March 1820.

and retired towards Mr Buxton's house. The moment the cavalry came, there was a great shouting from the mob.

**Roger Entwistle**

*Cross-examined* by Mr HUNT.

My profession is that of an attorney; I am also the clerk of the Manchester racecourse. I was examined on oath at the Oldham inquest, but I cannot say I said one thing at Oldham and another here. What I said at each place is true. I was on the Albion steps when the people entered the town on 16 August, with a number of respectable persons, among whom I class myself. The Stockport division was preceded by the coach in which was Mr Moorhouse. When the coach stopped at the White Bear, the division went on to the meeting. Notwithstanding my first alarm, I went to St Peter's Field, where my apprehension became greater at the sight of such a multitude. My alarm was on account of the immense number, and from knowing their minds were very much inflamed from the seditious publications about that time published. I have seen large parties coming out of the *Manchester Observer* office after purchasing such works, and I have heard them recommending their friends to purchase them; and at different times heard some people express their feelings at reading such things, particularly the people from about Hollinwood, Royton and Oldham, who used to crowd round the *Manchester Observer* office on Saturdays.

There were very few Manchester faces at the meeting. I know that many Manchester people bought the seditious works, but the reason they had not the same effect upon them as on the country people was that one set bought them from curiosity, and the other to take home and read. The meeting consisted entirely of the lower orders, such as weavers and the labouring classes. I admit that many of them (the Manchester people) would have attended the meeting if they had not been confined within the factories. My own opinion is that when you said, 'Keep them down', you alluded to the military, and wished not to be molested, but that if you were, you wished the people to keep them off if possible. The people were peaceable at the time you addressed them. My impression was that you congratulated the meeting on its adjournment from the ninth to the sixteenth. I will not swear that I did not use the word 'postponed' in giving my evidence at Oldham. On my oath, it is not my knowledge of the law respecting adjourned public meetings which induces me to use that word now.

Though I was alarmed, I wished to hear what you had to say, and therefore I went to Peter's Field. I saw the yeomanry cavalry advance at a sharp trot from Mr Buxton's house. I went to the meeting by myself and returned with you to the New Bailey. I went with the military, and I did not

# Hunt and Others.

**Roger Entwistle**

think it safe to go alone amongst the mob who were in the streets. When I went to the meeting, I thought it perfectly safe to go by myself. I saw two or three wounded persons – a woman, in particular; she was carried into Mr Buxton's house. Seeing such a concourse of people, with the flags, particularly a black one, which more resembled a pall than anything else, and bearing an inscription, 'Equal Representation or Death', I felt much alarmed. I felt all this fear before the yeomanry arrived, as I did not know what would be the result when the meeting broke up.

I do not remember the particulars of my evidence at Oldham. I stated at Oldham that I saw danger the moment I saw the parties coming from Stockport. I might have said at Oldham that I saw no danger until the cavalry approached, but I then feared some danger might ensue. My reason for stating that was that there had been no previous acts of violence, but when they arrived within ten yards of the hustings, they were assailed with sticks, stones, and brickbats. My fear was of what would be the result of the meeting when it broke up. I did not hear a report that the meeting was to be dispersed by the military. I heard that there was a warrant issued against you, and that you were to be arrested.

I was not in London since last May. I should call a man one of the lower orders, who was imprisoned for debt or misconduct. I never was so imprisoned. The assignees of a bankrupt and myself have been served with a petition in Chancery, and the case is now pending. Mr Partington, of London, is the attorney against us. I was never in the Fleet Prison in my life.

Mr HUNT: Then I apologise for asking these questions. I assure you, I have no wish to offend you. I received information from a person in court, which induced me to question you in this manner.

[The examination was resumed.] I stated at Oldham that I was near the constables on the sixteenth nearly all the time. I knew the Yeomanry Cavalry were to be brought up. They, as well as the special constables, were ordered out in the morning. I was walking up and down Peter's Field from eleven until you were arrested. I was not insulted, but I saw several gentlemen who were. Some person said, 'He,' pointing to another, 'is a spy; he,' pointing to another, 'is a special constable'. I was not called a spy. I am not a spy. I was not hurt. I did not wave my hand to the cavalry when they came in. The black banner was not like a flag; it was not square; it had letters upon it. I did not see two hands, and the word 'Love' upon it. There was one flag with a bloody dagger painted upon it. It was painted red; I was not near it, but it appeared to me like a dagger. I swear this. I have never seen that flag since.

*Examined by* Mr BARROW.

# Second Day – Friday 17 March 1820.

**Roger Entwistle**

I saw Mr Moorhouse in a coach on that day. I conceived he was leading the Stockport party. When I first saw the coach, it was 200 yards from me; it was near Portland Place. I will swear that the coach did not stop at the White Bear, Piccadilly, ten minutes before the Stockport division came up. It came immediately before them. I saw females in it, but I did not see them alight. I know Moorhouse; he is proprietor of a stagecoach which comes daily to Manchester. I do not think I ever saw him drive it himself. I believe the coach stops daily at the White Bear. The men who came after the coach were called the Stockport division. I knew some of those who composed it to be Stockport men. I particularly recollected one who carried a flag.

*Re-examined* by Mr SCARLETT.

The black flag was extended by a stick being fastened to the top of it, so that it hung square. All the flags and caps of liberty were at one time on the hustings. I cannot say it was while Mr Hunt was there or not. I find that some person has published the Oldham evidence. I have read the book. I think if my evidence in that book was compared with what I now have said today, they would agree.[163]

FRANCIS PHILIPS, sworn and examined by Mr Serjeant HULLOCK.[164]

**Francis Philips**

What are you, Mr Philips? — I am a merchant and manufacturer at Manchester.

Do you remember anything particular of 16 August last? — I remember

---

163 *Liverpool Mercury*, 22 August 1828: 'A most shocking instance of self-destruction took place at an inn in Manchester on Saturday last. Mr Roger Entwistle, many years clerk of the racecourse, was found quite dead, hanging to the top of a door, with the blood flowing from a deep gash in his throat. From his bedroom below being covered with blood, he must have cut his throat there, and then walked into an adjoining room, tied a handkerchief once round his throat by the middle, and afterwards made a noose by tying the two ends together; this noose he had thrown over the corner of the door, and thereby suspended himself, with his feet nearly touching the ground. The unfortunate gentleman had been confined to his room for some time by indisposition. A verdict of insanity was returned.'

164 This was not Philips's first brush with history. *Caledonian Mercury*, 16 May 1812: 'Francis Philips of Longsight Hall, near Manchester, deposed that he was standing near the fireplace in the lobby when he heard the report of a pistol. He saw Mr Perceval walk forward, stagger, and fall on his knees; and heard him exclaim, "I am murdered!" twice. He rushed forward, caught him in his arms, supported his head upon his shoulder, and assisted in carrying him into the Secretary's room, where he soon after died in his arms – it might be ten, five, or fifteen minutes, he was so extremely agitated that he could not state the precise time. He did not hear him utter a word from the time of his first exclamation until his death.' Spencer Perceval is the only Prime Minister of the United Kingdom to have been assassinated.

# Hunt and Others.

**Francis Philips**

16 August. I was on horseback about eleven o'clock on that day, and rode towards Stockport. Mr J. Birley was with me.

Did Mr Birley and you meet any persons going to the Manchester meeting? — We met at Ardwick Green, about a mile and a half from Manchester, a large body of men coming towards the town.

Marching in the way soldiers do? — They were marching in every way like soldiers, except that they had no uniforms. They marched in files, and were three abreast.

Had they music and flags? — They had no music, but carried two flags. There were persons marching at the sides who acted as officers, and kept the files distinct; the order was beautiful indeed.

What do you suppose might be their number? — The body amounted to about 1,400 or 1,500.

Were they armed? — They had no arms, but many of them had sticks. I noticed one with a large stick or club, which he shook at me.

[To other questions witness answered:] The officers gave the words 'left' and 'right' to keep the men in better order. He returned to Manchester by a less public road. He went immediately to where the magistrates were assembled. Witness was a special constable on that day. He went to St Peter's area, and in a short time after the same party arrived in nearly the same order which he had seen them marching before. He knew them by the banners, one of which had the inscription, 'No corn laws' on it. When they arrived at the area, there were many parties assembled there, and others continued to arrive in different directions. One party was extremely numerous, infinitely more so than that from Stockport. St Peter's area is about 150 yards square, but he could not say exactly. There was music there, but he did not attend particularly to it. There was a sort of raised place for a hustings or stage around which the people were assembling. Mr Hunt afterwards arrived, accompanied by an immense multitude. There was a great noise and shouting on his arrival; witness never heard such a noise, and never saw so large an assemblage in his life before. The impression produced on his mind by the meeting was that of very great alarm. The meeting was of a nature calculated to excite considerable alarm in the minds of the inhabitants of Manchester. He did not see any of the defendants but Hunt.

Hunt began to address the people apparently with energy, but witness could not hear a word of what he said. Not one half of those present could hear him. Only a small portion of the witnesses could. Saw Mr Nadin with a party of the police, but did not see Mr Hunt taken. Most of the shops in the town were closed on that day. Witness gave directions to his porter to keep his doors fast shut if the crowd should advance, and he did so because he considered the town in imminent danger. He

# Second Day – Friday 17 March 1820.

dismantled some firearms, lest the crowd should come to take them.

Francis Philips

*Cross-examined* by Mr HUNT.

What did you say you were, Mr Philips? — I am a merchant and manufacturer.

You are something of an author too, I believe, occasionally? — I have written and published an account of this transaction.[165]

[Mr HUNT handed witness a pamphlet, asking if he knew it as an old friend.] — This is the first edition.

Not quite so correct, I fear, as it should be? — I afterwards published a second, more correct.

Did you sell many copies? — I published a thousand of each edition, the greater part of which I sold. I also gave a great many away.

I know it. You are like many other authors, who, if they did not give their works away, would find it difficult to get them off their hands. You sent some to London, to members of Parliament? — I sent some to London, and several to members of Parliament.

Did you not endeavour to publish your work before Parliament met? — The publication was intended to have been before the meeting of Parliament, but it did not take place until a few days after it. I wished to give facts to the public.

On your oath, sir, did not Mr Birley command the Manchester cavalry on that day? — On my oath, I do not know that Mr Birley commanded them on that day. He was at the head of the corps, but I do not know whether he or Major Trafford commanded them.

What did you see done which you considered insulting? — I consider the shaking of the stick at me as an insult.

[Here Mr HUNT read an extract from Mr Philips's pamphlet, in which it was stated that no direct offence was given before the yeomanry appeared.]

[Cross-examination resumed.] I heard many taunting expressions used on the field to every man who wore a good coat and went amongst the crowd. I went a private road on my return from Stockport, as I could not go with equal speed on the high road without danger to the crowd which had passed. I considered that the Stockport men marched very well indeed.

I do not admit that either of my editions of the book giving an account

---

165 *An Exposure of the Calumnies Circulated by the Enemies of the Social Order and Reiterated by their Abettors against the Magistrates and the Yeomanry Cavalry of Manchester and Salford*, by Francis Philips of Longsight Hall, near Manchester, November 1819.

# Hunt and Others.

**Francis Philips**

of the Manchester business states a falsehood. I considered the town of Manchester and the magistrates to be in great danger. I ordered my porter to close the gates if anything occurred – not for the purpose of keeping the workmen in. I gave my men orders to keep their wives and children at home that day. They acted with great propriety as far as I saw.

I only saw the first advance of the yeomanry; and after the regular troops came upon the field, I saw the Cheshire Yeomanry come upon the field in a hand canter, but I do not know whether they acted or not. I saw some infantry near Peter's Field, and I also saw two pieces of artillery brought up after the crowd was dispersed. I saw very little of the battle: the dust and the number of constables prevented me from seeing what took place. I saw no blood spilt.

Mr Justice BAYLEY observed that questions of this kind ought not to be put. That blood had been spilt he believed, and he was sorry for it. The question was not how the military had acted, but whether the meeting was a legal one, and, if so, whether it was conducted in that peaceable and orderly manner that would preclude any alarm from being infused into the public mind. To this point Mr Hunt had a right to examine the witness.

Mr HUNT: I do not think I can better prove that the meeting was quiet and peaceable than by showing that the people, so far from holding up a finger in resisting a wanton and violent attack upon them, every man fled from the fury of the military. I bow, however, to your Lordship's decision.

[Cross-examination resumed.] The people were peaceable on that part of the field where I stood. I should have thought it excessively imprudent in the magistrates to have sent the constables into such a large assembly, closely wedged together as that was. I never went near the hustings. I have not admitted that the soldiers charged the people.

Mr HUNT was proceeding to inquire into the conduct of the yeomanry when Mr Justice BAYLEY interrupted him. It was a point which he meant to leave to the jury, whether a body assembling in such numbers as to excite terror in the public mind was not illegal. A meeting might be illegal though its purpose was legal, by using illegal means to attain it; or a meeting might become illegal from the manner of it, as it might from its numbers create an alarm in the public mind. This was his opinion, so he should state it to the jury.

Mr HUNT said, without impugning his Lordship's view of the question, he hoped he should be allowed to show that the fears entertained were excited by erroneous notions. When an experiment was made to try the temper of a meeting by sending a few straggling drunken soldiers among them, as if to seduce them to try their power, he hoped he would be

# Second Day – Friday 17 March 1820.

allowed to show that the people, so far from offering any resistance, fled for their lives; indeed, several of them lost their lives without even attempting resistance.

**Francis Philips**

Mr Justice BAYLEY said Mr Hunt was at liberty to ask any questions tending to show what the conduct of the meeting had been.

[Examination resumed.] The people were very closely locked near the hustings. I saw them from the steps of the magistrates' house. Those near the hustings had their hats off. They were as close to each other as they could stand. I did not see them arm in arm.

I did not hear one word of what you said on the hustings. When you were upon the hustings, I was about seventy-five yards from you. It was natural that those who wished to hear you should crowd round the hustings, but not in the manner they did.

[In answer to the Judge.] The wish to hear alone would by no means make them crowd as they did.

[In answer to Mr Hunt.] It appeared to me that they were disciplined troops who came to protect you, or fight for you, as they might be called upon, or as occasion offered. I never have seen disciplined troops surround a man in such a way in order to fight for him. The crowd appeared to be ready to fight for you, as you gave them the command. Those persons would have kept the constables from you. The line of constables did not extend to the hustings. I tried to get to the hustings, but failed. I do not think the line of constables extended to the hustings at any time of the day.

I saw the Manchester Yeomanry Cavalry when they were formed. I did not see them ride down any persons in coming into the field. They behaved with the greatest propriety, as far as I can judge. I am convinced they were sober. I spoke to some, and they evinced not the slightest inebriety. I saw Nadin, but I do not recollect having any communication with him. I did not see him make any attempt to reach the hustings without the aid of the Yeomanry. It would have been madness to attempt it.

REV. DR JEREMIAH SMITH, sworn and examined.[166]

**Rev. Dr Jeremiah Smith**

Resided in Manchester; is head master of the grammar school; was near the Star on the sixteenth; saw a large body of men in Deansgate. It was that party that conducted Mr Hunt to the ground. Saw him in an open carriage; was in the house next the Star Inn; the coach stopped;

---

166 Smith had been headmaster at the Manchester Grammar School since 1807. The school's website describes him as a 'good scholar [who] could keep the boys in order without beating them and [who] is reputed to have used the cane only once in his career at Manchester'.

# Hunt and Others.

**Rev. Dr Jeremiah Smith**

and the party stopped also – shouted, hissed, and groaned – opposite the Star Inn. Did not know whether the magistrates were then there or not. Saw or heard no signal, but it seemed to be done by consent. Mr Hunt, he thought, was sitting. There was music and banners; could not say accurately what the numbers were. It was not practicable to get along the street; he acted upon that judgement, for he did not go home that moment as he intended. The crowd next stopped at the shambles nearer the ground; they marched at first irregularly, but near the carriage, both before and after it, there was great regularity; the men marched in rows in a practised step. When they arrived in King Street, the same thing occurred as opposite the Star, but, being further off, witness did not see it so distinctly. Heard shouting, hissing, and a clapping of hands. A white handkerchief was displayed from some window. The police office is in Back King Street.

The mode in which they proceeded was most certainly calculated to inspire alarm, many of them seeming to be countrymen. The body itself was considerable, and connecting it with what he heard to be in St. Peter's Field, he became very anxious. Most of the shop windows were closed, but the doors, as far as he recollected, were opened. Witness shut his own windows, and locked both his front doors. The crowd round Mr Hunt had not at all the air of a deliberative body.

*Cross-examined* by Mr HUNT.

Witness is master of the Greek Grammar School of Manchester; had a great number of boys; dismissed them on that day after breakfast. The number of day scholars and boarders was 110, fifteen being boarders. They were sent home immediately after breakfast; did not think it prudent to keep them in school, thought it better to send them home to be under the care of their respective parents. The usual hour of breaking up was half past twelve, and witness thought it safer to let them home at ten than at half past twelve. This alarm rose principally from what might occur in the course of the afternoon. No insult was offered to witness as he passed through Deansgate. Did not recollect to hear that any of his boys were hurt on that day. Recollected when George IV was proclaimed the other day in Manchester, did not see any windows closed upon that occasion.

*Examined* by Mr SCARLETT.

When he dismissed the boys at ten, it proceeded from an apprehension that some disturbance might arise; had he kept them till twelve, he would have felt much perplexed how to act. He did not know where the parents of all lived.

# Second Day – Friday 17 March 1820.

JOHN BARLOW, examined by Mr Serjeant HULLOCK.

I keep the Coach and Horses in Deansgate, about sixty yards from the police office. I remember 16 August. I was at home from ten o'clock in the morning until evening. I saw a number of people marching in bodies, in the same manner that soldiers do when drilling. I saw a carriage in the crowd, in which there were four persons. There was a woman in front with a flag. When they got near the police office they stopped the carriage for a few minutes. A number of them turned their faces towards the police and gave three cheers. The persons in the carriage looked towards the police. There were several banners, upon one of which was 'Equal Representation or Death'. The cheers were very loud. I closed the shutters for fear of having the windows broken, and burned candles. Two of my neighbours closed their windows also. I remained at home, as I felt alarmed lest there should be some mischief.

*Cross-examined* by Mr HUNT.

I have lived thirty years in Manchester. I remember the Proclamation of the Peace; there were great crowds, but not so large as this. There was much cheering and shouting. It was near my house, and also near the police office. No offence was offered to me. I felt great alarm during the whole of the sixteenth. I saw the proclamation of George IV; there was a great crowd; they marched very well, but I think they had not had so much drilling as the meeting on the sixteenth. The latter had sticks, and several shouldered them as soldiers do muskets.

I may have mentioned this to some of my servants, but there are none of them here at present. I do not know whether the crowd who assembled on the Proclamation of the Peace had banners; I know they had no such flags as those used on the sixteenth. There never was half so many persons assembled at Manchester races as I saw pass my door on that day. I cannot tell whether ten thousand, twenty thousand, fifty thousand or one hundred and fifty thousand persons passed my door on that day. I do not know how many persons I have seen at Manchester races at once.

THOMAS STYAN, sworn and examined by Mr SCARLETT.

I am a gunsmith residing in Market Street, Manchester. I saw numbers of people pass my shop on the morning of 16 August. They continued passing from eleven o'clock. I shut my shop for fear the windows should be broke, as I saw great crowds coming down the street. I kept my shop shut till two o'clock.

*Cross-examined* by Mr HUNT.

I know Richardson, the gunsmith. I do not know that he sharpens the

# Hunt and Others.

**Thomas Styan**

swords for the cavalry. The crowd which caused me to shut my shop was going in a great hurry. There was no mischief done to my shop. The first time I shut my shop was about eleven o'clock. Soon after, some shutters were taken down. I know Mr Molyneux, my next neighbour; he does not know when the shutters were put up better than I do. The first time I opened the door and part of my windows was between two and three. I do not recollect I ever had occasion to shut my shop before.[167]

**Edmond Simpson**

EDMOND SIMPSON, sworn and examined by Mr Serjeant HULLOCK.

I am a hatter and reside in Deansgate. I saw several bodies of people pass on 16 August; they commenced passing about ten o'clock, and ended at one. They had music and colours. When Mr Hunt came up, there was music with him; he came up at a quarter past one. The people marched about nine or ten abreast, and some part of them went in regular step. I shut my shop before ten o'clock, and kept it shut all day. I closed both doors and windows. I was afraid there would be a disturbance, and I was very much alarmed, and so were my family, at seeing them march in that manner. I have a wife and five children. I looked out of the upstairs window.

*Cross-examined* by Mr HUNT.

I was very much alarmed on that day; I was not afraid of the cavalry at all. I did not hear a report that the cavalry would attack the people. I did not open my shop that day.

[In answer to the Judge.] Between four thousand and five thousand persons passed my house.

**Matthew Cowper**

MATTHEW COWPER, sworn and examined by Mr SCARLETT.

I am an accountant at Manchester. I went to the meeting of 16 August, about twelve o'clock. I have some memorandums which I took on the ground. I think that about 100,000 persons were assembled; I measured the ground, and made the best calculation I could as to the number who could stand on a square yard of ground. The meeting seemed principally

---

167 Mr Styan's windows survived intact for another eight days. *Lancaster Gazette*, 4 September 1819: 'A little after seven o'clock on Tuesday evening, the 24th ult[imo], a slight alarm was occasioned in Market Street, Manchester, by an explosion of gunpowder. It proved to have taken place in the shop of Mr Styan, a gunsmith. Mrs Styan had imprudently been striking a light in the shop; a spark fell on some loose powder, which took fire, and communicating with a quantity in some scales, the whole exploded. Every pane of glass was shattered to atoms, and the materials blown across the street. Mrs Styan ran out in flames, and was much burnt.'

# Second Day – Friday 17 March 1820.

composed of the labouring classes. The people stood so close that I could not get so near to the hustings as I wished. I saw the flags. I have an account of some of the inscriptions which were upon them. One was 'No Boroughmongers', reverse, 'Unite and Be Free'; another, 'Equal Representation or Death'; a third, 'Taxation without Equal Representation is Tyrannical and Unjust'. There were several others.

Matthew Cowper

I was on the field when Mr Hunt and his party approached. Several who followed the procession had white paper or rags in their hats. I heard some of them say to the others, 'Lads, take care of your white rags'. Before Mr Hunt's arrival, I saw several on the hustings. Johnson was with Hunt. I saw Mr Saxton and Mr Knight on the hustings. I saw others whose names I do not know. [Here witness pointed out Swift and Jones as two who were on the hustings.]. Mr Hunt, on taking the chair, made a speech. I heard the whole of it. I took notes of it on the ground, and they are now in their original state. It is thus [here witness read his notes]:

'Gentlemen, I must entreat that you will be peaceable and quiet, and that every person who wishes to hear must keep order; and all I ask for is that during the proceedings you will be quiet. We will endeavour to make ourselves heard, but it is impossible for us to be heard by the whole. We wish our fellow countrymen who do hear us will communicate to those who do not. It is useless to observe upon the intended meeting of last week; only to observe that those who by their malignant exertions, in taking advantage of a few illegal words, expected they had triumphed – instead of which it has produced two-fold numbers –' there were cheers – 'and now we have triumphed.'

He went on to state that two or three placards, signed by two or three obscure individuals --

While he was saying this, some companies of foot soldiers appeared in Dickinson Street, and formed. Mr Hunt then spoke on, but I did not take notes any further; I shall give the substance from memory.

[Witness went on to state as follows:]

He said, 'Never mind, they are only a few soldiers, and very few compared with us; we are a host against them'. In my judgment the meeting was such as to inspire very great fear in the inhabitants of the town of Manchester. My apprehension did not arise from what I then saw, but from previous circumstances, and from information communicated to me.

*Cross-examined* by Mr BARROW.

I know the appearance of Jones; I never heard that he was a carpenter employed to build the hustings.

# Hunt and Others.

**Matthew Cowper**

*Cross-examined* by Mr HUNT.

How do you do, Mr Cowper? I hope you are well; I have had the pleasure of seeing you before. [Mr Hunt then went on to examine him.] What is your occupation? — I am an accountant.

No other occupation? — I have no other occupation but those of an accountant and law-stationer.

Recollect yourself? — I am secretary to a committee, but that arises out of my other occupations. I was secretary to a committee composed of three hundred gentlemen, in aid of the Civil Power.

Are you not employed by the police? — I am not in the employ of the police.

Have you any connection with the ministerial newspapers? — I occasionally communicate with the *Courier* and *Morning Post* – London papers.

Did you not send an account of the meeting in question to one of those papers? — I sent up an account of the Manchester meeting to the *Courier*.

Did the *Courier* people publish it? — I think my report did not appear. I believe they selected from the other papers.

Have you always been in the line of business you are now? — I have been in the service of a professor of the law for nine years.

Do you not expect to be employed in the Excise department? — I have been under instructions for the Excise.

Were you not, at one time, clerk to a brewer at Bolton? — I was, earlier in life, a clerk to a brewer; to Dawes and Fogg, of Bolton. Perhaps twelve months.

What was your father? — My father was in the Excise; he was supervisor of the district in which the brewery is situated.

How came you to leave Messrs Dawes and Fogg? — [Witness at first declined answering; at length he stated as follows:] I applied to my own use money belonging to the firm, and Messrs Dawes dismissed me in consequence. That money I have repaid to Mr Dawes, with compound interest, up to the time of payment. I took the money out of the till, and was detected. I know John Roscoe; he was servant to Messrs Dawes. I have repaid in all, with interest, £25. It is some months ago since I paid this money; it was the first money I could command. The reason of my not paying it sooner was that my father's death left three younger brothers to be supported by me. It was to Mr Fogg I paid the money.

How long is it since you returned this money? — It was paid three months ago. I did not take so much as £25 from my master's till, but, it being left to my discretion, I thought I ought to do my utmost to repair the injury.

How long have you been in business? — I have been three years in

# Second Day – Friday 17 March 1820.

business.

Did you tell the counsel for the prosecution this story? — I never told Mr Scarlett, Mr Maule, or Milne, this story. I did not know you knew it.

Was the money you took marked? — The money which I took was stamped. If I had known that you were acquainted with it, I should have had Mr Dawes here, as he would willingly come forward for me.

Do you not think that you have been favoured through your father being supervisor of the district? — I do not know that my father being a supervisor of the district and having great power over my master was the reason why I was not prosecuted.

What are you to receive for your services on this occasion? — I have not been paid by the magistrates or police, except for being secretary to the committee in aid of the Civil Power. The accounts of the committee were passed at the parish table.

Don't you know this money was paid out of the parish rates?

Mr Justice BAYLEY said this was not a relevant question.

[To other questions witness answered:] I was within a dozen or fifteen yards of the hustings on the day of the meeting. I stood between the hustings and the house where the magistrates were. I saw no disturbance. I went purposely to take notes of what you or anyone else should say. The reason why the observations respecting the soldiers were not written down was that, all attention being directed to them when they appeared, I ceased to use my pencil; the cavalry were coming up at the time. I took down the heads of your discourse at the time, and the remainder I filled up from memory. All I have read is not down in my notes.

Mr Justice BAYLEY: Let me look at these notes. [The notes were handed in.] I think there are the materials of such a speech.

[Cross-examination continued.] I have a good memory. I wrote out my notes and handed them over to Mr Norris, the magistrate. I have not seen them since. I did not hear you say, 'Put them down, and keep them down'. I turned when the cavalry came, and you might then have said it without my hearing you; it was not said before the cavalry appeared. None but the editor of the *Courier* employed me to take notes of what passed. [Witness repeated the inscriptions on the flags.] There was no bloody dagger on the black flag. The inscription on the black flag attracted my attention particularly; I had not time or I would have taken all the inscriptions. The black flag was attached to a pole as the other flags were. I saw no difference between them. I saw a barbed point to one of the flag-poles: it was painted red. The top of the pole was not a fleur-de-lis. I did not see two hands and the word 'Love' upon the black flag.

*[The Court adjourned at seven o'clock.]*

Matthew Cowper

# Third Day – Saturday 18 March 1820.

*This morning the same anxiety was manifested to obtain admission which marked the struggle of those who were anxious to be spectators on the preceding days. The ladies seemed still as curious as ever, and the obvious eagerness of their anxiety again induced them to enter the court through privileged avenues as early as seven o'clock in the morning. Each side of the judge's seat on the Bench, was, as usual, graced by the presence of rank and beauty, and Mr Justice Bayley displayed to them that courteous affability for which he is so eminently distinguished. At eight o'clock, the public gates were thrown open, and the galleries and area became filled in the usual manner by a mixed throng, who rushed into every seat and corner of the court that were not defended by constables for the magistrates, attorneys and jurors.*

At nine o'clock, Mr Hunt and the other defendants, with the solicitors, entered the court and occupied their usual places. A few minutes previous, Mr Justice BAYLEY entered the Court, and addressed Mr BARROW, one of the counsel for some of the defendants, in the following terms:

Upon a question which arose yesterday, I stated that we could not here enter into a consideration of the conduct of the yeomanry cavalry on 16 August. Whether that be proper or improper we are not now trying. But, when I say this, I beg the defendants particularly to understand that it is open to them to show the conduct of every part of the people collected at the meeting on that day with a view to establish their peaceable character or the tendency of their acts; also with the view of showing that there was no desire manifested by them to resist the civil authorities. Into all this they may fully enter, but not into the propriety or impropriety of the conduct of the yeomanry. I mention this now to have what I said yesterday explicitly understood, if it was not so at the time; and also for the purpose of allowing you, if you please, to call back any witness you may desire to put questions to relative to the character of the meeting, but whom you may not, perhaps, have examined on that subject through any misapprehension of what fell from me yesterday.

Mr BARROW said the defendants would avail themselves, if necessary, of his Lordship's kind permission.

Mr Hunt, who had entered the moment after his Lordship made this communication, was apprised of it by the judge's considerate repetition of what he had just said. Mr HUNT then said:

My Lord, I was quite aware of your Lordship's meaning yesterday. I know we are not here to try the conduct of the yeomanry cavalry on 16

## Hunt and Others.

August, but whether the defendants are guilty of a conspiracy to form and attend an illegal meeting, and to inquire whether any illegal act had been committed by that people when assembled. I wish to show the animus of that meeting, more particularly as the opposite side have travelled out of the record, and attempted to show that we were concerned in instigating some individuals to inspire terror into the minds of peaceable people, and have produced witnesses to identify us, as it were, with those who wanted to take a man's good coat off his back – who wanted to make Manchester another Moscow – and, thirdly, who wish to represent that I pointed to the soldiers and then said to the people, 'There are our enemies; get them down, and keep them down'. If I can show that, instead of these statements being true, as regarded the people assembled, they evinced a conduct exactly the reverse of that ascribed to them, and that their whole demeanour was orderly and pacific, then I imagine there will be an end to the indictment.

Mr Justice BAYLEY: I neither meant yesterday – nor do I mean now – to exclude any evidence the defendants may have to offer respecting the conduct of the people assembled on the particular day.

Mr HUNT: I had hoped we should have been spared the trouble of calling any evidence to show the character of the meeting, so little has been said to impeach it; but as the other side has travelled farther, we shall be obliged to trouble the court with our witnesses.

Mr Justice BAYLEY: If you wish to put any question to the witnesses of yesterday touching the demeanour of the meeting, I shall call them back to answer you.

Mr HUNT: If I shall find it necessary in the course of the day, I'll take the liberty of troubling your Lordship.

[The trial was then resumed.]

**Joseph Mills**

JOSEPH MILLS, sworn and examined by Mr Serjeant HULLOCK.

Is a publican living at Manchester. Was on St Peter's Field on 16 August. Saw a large party arrive there. They were marching in files to the number of three thousand or four thousand. The defendant Healey led them up like a military party. There was a trumpeter with them. Healey took the black flag from a man in his party and got with it into a cart around which the people closed, and he addressed them, and desired them to be steady and firm to their cause, for their enemies were at hand. The people cheered him. There was a trumpeter near him and a cap of liberty.

He also saw Wylde (another of the defendants) on that day, leading up a party. [Wylde was not in court at this moment, but the witness gave an accurate description of his person.] He saw Wylde that morning

# Third Day – Saturday 18 March 1820.

coming to the field with a party of about two thousand. They were the first that formed round the hustings. They had marched in regular files, six abreast, in military order. When they came to the hustings, Wylde halted them and said, 'Link your arms', which was done quite round the cart. Afterwards, he said, 'Fall back, and keep as you are', meaning, as witness understood, to keep their arms linked. They fell back upon the constables, and gave greater room round the cart. They were so linked five deep.

About one o'clock, Mr Hunt came in a carriage with Moorhouse and Johnson, and got upon the hustings. Saxton had been there for more than half an hour before this. He spoke several times to the crowd, but witness could not hear what he said. The crowd cheered him. At the time Mr Hunt arrived, there were more than 60,000 persons present. The meeting was of a nature, in his judgement, calculated to inspire terror and alarm into the minds of the people of Manchester. He was at several meetings before and saw them coming to them, but they never came in such a way as they did. Never saw so large a meeting before. Those who attended former meetings came to town two or three together at their own leisure, but at the present they came quite in a military array.

*Cross-examined* by Mr HUNT.

How long have you been a publican? — I have been a publican since last October twelvemonths.

What were you before? — One of Nadin's runners, as they are called.

You look very well. — I am jolly and well [witness was a fat, jovial-looking man], and would be glad to see you look so well, Mr Hunt.

What were you doing at the meeting? — I was, like many others, a special constable on that day.

Are you sure you saw Dr Healey heading a party? — I am quite sure Dr Healey came up, heading his party, which formed round the hustings with a trumpeter. [He here repeated his direct evidence, and said that Healey might have recommended the people to be peaceable, though I did not hear him.]

You should call them squadrons, not parties? — I call them parties, not squadrons; the latter are dragoons, Mr Hunt.

Have you not had conversation with some of the witnesses who have been examined? — I have conversed with none of the witnesses since this trial about what has transpired in court.

Were you insulted at the meeting? — None of the men insulted or assaulted me, nor did I see them molest anybody – except shouting.

They had music, you say. What tunes did they play? — When you came up, they played 'See the Conquering Hero Comes'. [Laugh.]

*Joseph Mills*

# Hunt and Others.

**Joseph Mills**

Do you think that amounted to an assault? — I did not think that an insult or an assault.

Did you hear 'God Save the King' and 'Rule, Britannia!' played? — I don't think I heard 'God Save the King' or 'Rule, Britannia!' played.

Will you swear they were not? — I won't swear they were not.

Where were Healey's party stationed? — Healey's men formed at the back of Mr Wylde's.

Did they link their arms? — The former, I think, did not link arms; the others did, and by the forming and keeping room pushed back the constables, who were then but about a dozen or fourteen yards from the hustings.

Is it not a common thing to be so linked at meetings? — I never saw such a thing done at a meeting before, and it alarmed me as well as many others.

You complained of it then, of course? — We did not complain of being pushed back, nor ask them for a more direct communication with the hustings.

What did you hear Wylde say? — Wylde ordered them to be firm and steady.

Did you observe anything remarkable in his appearance? — He had a tradesman's apron on.

Had he said anything treasonable or improper, you would have heard it? — If he had said anything treasonable or violent, I should have, as a special constable, noticed it.

Will you swear that he did not recommend peace and order? — I will not swear that he did not recommend peace or order.

Did you see any constables assaulted? — I saw no act of violence committed by anybody in the crowd upon the constables.

How did we seem? Merry, or displeased? — When you came, they shouted, and you seemed all merry together.

When did Saxton arrive? — Saxton was there half an hour before you. You said they must be quiet; if not, to pull them down and keep them quiet. I did not hear you tell the people to pull the soldiers down and keep them down. I heard you say nothing so foolish or wicked.

*Cross-examined* by Mr BARROW.

Was on the ground before the hustings were erected. Did not see Moorhouse there.

*Cross-examined* by Mr HOLT.

He believed Saxton was on the hustings before Mr Hunt came. He was either on the hustings or on a cart near them. He did not know that Saxton

# Third Day – Saturday 18 March 1820.

was a reporter to a newspaper at Manchester. He could not recollect whether he saw him with pen, ink and paper there.

*Cross-examined* by Mr HEALEY.

Did you or did you not tell me, the week before, that if I attended that meeting you would take me into custody? — I did not.

Did you or did you not say to one of your customers, that when you saw me on the hustings you marked me down for your bird? — I did not; but I was over near where I lived at that time, and was called where you were. This was on 8 August, and he knew me very well, my Lord, as I once took him up to Lord Sidmouth's office. He asked me, 'You have not another warrant for me, Mills?' 'No,' said I, 'I have not.' 'Then,' said he, 'sit down and take something with us.' We then talked over our travels together when we were in London.

HENRY HORTON, sworn and examined by Mr SCARLETT.

Were you at Manchester on 16 August last? — I was at the Manchester meeting on 16 August.

For what purpose did you attend? — I attended to take notes for a paper.

Did you observe what was going forward in different parts of the field? — I was at several parts of the field at different times. I saw several parties come into the field in regular order.

At what time did you arrive? — I was there about half past eleven o'clock.

You saw the flags. What sort of flags were they? — I saw the flags and banners; one of them was surmounted by something like a dagger painted red.

Did you see the constables? — Before Hunt came, there was a line of constables formed from the hustings to Mr Buxton's house; did not observe that the hustings were removed.

Did you see Jones? — Saw the defendant Jones.

What did he say? — He exhorted the meeting to be peaceable, and mentioned something to the effect that the committee had ordered, on the Saturday preceding, to form round the hustings at six yards' distance, and to lock themselves arm in arm in order that they might not be broken in upon. I don't give these as the precise words; they were preparing the hustings at that time. There was no particular movement then, but afterwards the people locked arm in arm.

Did you see Wylde? — I saw the defendant Wylde, and heard him address the people to the same effect. Mr Swift, one of the defendants, also addressed the meeting, and received a better hearing than the other.

# Hunt and Others.

**Henry Horton**

What did Swift say? — Swift also exhorted them to be peaceable until their chairman came; to be quiet, and not give their enemies an opportunity of exercising that power which he knew they were ready to do. 'Let us prove,' said he, 'that we are not mad, as they say; but if we are mad, it is the most pleasant insensibility I ever experienced in my life.'

Were you certain these were his words? — I am certain these were the words he used. I took notes up to this time, but after this I was getting nearer the hustings and I found it more prudent to put my notes and my pencil in my pocket. I was now near the hustings, which were surrounded by people about eight or nine deep on one side, and five or six on the other. The people locked arms. I entered into this arrangement that I might not be remarked, and two persons were locked with me, one at each side. I was not the locker but the locked. It would have been impossible for any man to have forced his way to the hustings then. There was a body of six or seven deep between the constables and the hustings.

Did you see Mr Hunt come? — I was present when Mr Hunt came.

Did you observe who was with him? — Moorhouse was in the carriage with him, I believe.

How did they get to the hustings? — The people opened to make way for him. When he got on the hustings, the flags and banners were brought nearer.

Did Mr Hunt speak, and what did he say? — Mr Hunt addressed the meeting in front, and requested them to be quiet, and not to interrupt by calling, 'Silence', as that made more noise than anything else. This was in front, and I was at that time behind the hustings. Hunt turned round, and said something to the same effect at the other side; he added, 'If any one attempt to destroy our tranquillity, I hope some persons will be found with courage enough to put them down, quiet them, and keep them down'. A man behind me said, 'Why, that's killing them', but this was in a low tone, and could not be heard on the subject. Hunt then turned round to the front of the hustings, and addressed those before him. He began by requesting that no persons would call, 'Silence', as the calling of that made more noise than anything else.[168] He then congratulated them on their assembling, and thanked them for the honour they had done him in electing him chairman of so large a meeting. He then said that it was unnecessary to allude to the meeting which was to have taken place on the Monday before; but the magistrates, in thinking that they had triumphed on that occasion, had been the means of doubling their numbers on the present. He would not then allude to those placards which were signed by Jack Short and Tom Long, or some such insignificant individual. Mr

---

168 Probably an error in the transcript, repeating the witness's previous evidence.

# Third Day – Saturday 18 March 1820.

Hunt was here interrupted by the appearance of cavalry, which had come near Buxton's house. This created some confusion near the hustings, and Mr Hunt made some observations which were lost in the noise. Hunt then said, 'Stand firm, my friends – they are in disorder already. Let us give them three cheers.' The cheers were accordingly given. The soldiers then came on, and took the men on the hustings.

**Henry Horton**

What became of you then? — I was thrown back from the hustings by the pressure of the crowd. There was great confusion.

The meeting you saw was very numerous? — The meeting was the largest I ever saw. I was not acquainted with Manchester, and had not seen such meetings there.

What do you suppose was the number of persons present? — I cannot exactly judge of the numbers present, but I think they were not less than 60,000.

Of what description were the people, generally? — They were in general the working classes.

Did you consider it a dangerous meeting? — The meeting, in my judgement, was calculated to excite considerable terror and alarm in Manchester.

*Cross-examined* by Mr BARROW.

You are a reporter you say, and arrived on the ground at eleven o'clock? — I came down as a reporter for a London paper, and was on the field at eleven o'clock.

Did you observe Jones doing anything? — Jones was assisting in putting up the hustings.

Do you know that he is a millwright? — I don't know that he is a millwright.

What did you hear him say? — He exhorted them to be peaceable.

Is it not customary to have some sort of barrier at public meetings? — He did not know whether it was usual to have some barrier at public meetings to prevent the crowd from pressing on the hustings.

Did you not think it a judicious precaution? — It was a necessary and safe measure, perhaps – or it might be so – to form this barrier themselves by linking around, so as that a little space should be kept, and all anxious to hear. And this was accompanied by an exhortation to be peaceable.

*Cross-examined* by Mr HOLT.

I heard Jones and Swift address from the hustings, but to my recollection nobody else before Mr Hunt came. I was within six yards of the hustings, and if anybody else came up to speak from the hustings, I must, I think, have heard them. But still possibly it might have occurred, as there were

# Hunt and Others.

**Henry Horton**

preliminary matters to which I did not pay much attention. These whom I have mentioned spoke merely to the same effect repeatedly, and it is very likely that others may have done the same. I think I should have certainly noticed Saxton if he spoke and was cheered – it must have attracted my attention. I can't, however, conclude that he did not speak, for the observations of the speakers were to the same effect and, as they were all strangers to me, I could not positively say who did or did not. If Saxton did come forward and speak, I think I must almost of necessity have noticed him. I don't recollect Saxton on the hustings, but can't speak positively, as all the persons there at the time were strangers to me.

*Cross-examined* by Mr HUNT.

What papers are those which you refer to? — The papers I hold in my hands are two of *The New Times*, containing my accounts of the transaction at Manchester, which are the same as I have verbally given in court.

You attended the meeting as a reporter? — I was sent down as reporter to *The New Times*.

Are those reports printed exactly as you sent them? — The accounts in those papers are not perhaps exactly the same as I sent – that is, verbally so, for they were drawn up in a hurry, and may require verbal corrections. It is not usual to alter the tenor of my reports, but hasty verbal inaccuracies may be corrected.

What other occupation have you? — I have no other occupation than that of a reporter on *The New Times*, and an occasional correspondent for some country papers.

Do you not, occasionally, communicate with the Manchester police office? — While at Manchester, I was frequently at the police office to gain information of passing occurrences.

Are you acquainted with Mr Nadin? — I know Mr Nadin.

You exchange intelligence with the police? — I do not communicate any information to the police office as well as I receive it from thence. I merely reported for the paper I have mentioned.

Have you never been employed by the Solicitor for the Treasury? — I was never employed by the Solicitor to the Treasury.

Have you not seen Mr Maule? — I never saw Mr Maule until a month ago.

Have you ever been at Halifax? — I never was at Halifax, except passing through on my way here.

What other papers did you send your account to? — I sent no communication of the Manchester business to any other London paper than *The New Times*.

# Third Day – Saturday 18 March 1820.

What appeared, then, in that paper, we may look upon as coming from yourself? — What appeared in that newspaper was from my pen. The communications which I sent were of occurrences under my eye.

**Henry Horton**

It was all yours? — I believe there was a letter sent to the paper from Manchester, but from whom I did not know.

Did you never say that it was a made-up report? — I never told anyone that my report was made up from what I heard from other London reporters. That was not the fact.

You were locked in, you say, amongst the people? — I was locked in among the people.

You must, being so high bred a gentleman, have been curiously situated among the lower orders. Did you get anything unpleasant in the crowd? — I felt no inconvenience; nobody threatened to take my good coat off my back. I was certainly alarmed.

How came you to omit 'the putting down and keeping down' in your account that you sent up? — Because I wrote the report in a private room, the moment I got out of the crowd: I, without reading it over, sent it by an express to town. I afterward noted down more particulars on refreshing my recollection, and then I remembered that passage in your speech as well as another which I did not know I omitted until the paper reached Manchester. It is not my practice to omit material and transmit trivial points. I did not recollect the omission before I saw any other paper. I never sent up to have it corrected, as I had other things of more consequence to attend to.

Did you understand when I said, 'Keep them down,' that somebody was to be put to death? — It certainly never struck me that by making that observation – 'Keep them down, et cetera' – you meant to put anyone to death.

Were the military in view when I said so? — There were no military in view when you said, 'Keep them down, et cetera'. It was when you spoke to the people at the back of the hustings.

Were you near enough to see whether I pointed to anybody? — I was very near you at the time, and did not see you point to anyone.

Then those who have said I pointed to the soldiers and said, 'There are your enemies, put them down, et cetera, et cetera,' are not correct? — Certainly not, according to my recollection.

Have you your original notes? — I have not got my original notes, though I knew for what I was coming here.

What became of your original notes? — The notes I took on the field I lost on the same day in Mr Perry's offices – the solicitor, at Manchester.

Have you ever inquired for them? — I made the greatest inquiries after them, without effect.

# Hunt and Others.

**Henry Horton**

Have you a transcript of them? — I have not brought down my manuscript reports to the papers; they may be lost or not, I never saw them since they went.

Is your recollection at this time perfect as to the occurrences of that day? — I refreshed my memory from the account in the papers which I hold in my hand. Though there is a verbal difference between parts of the written and the printed account, yet there is no alteration of any matter of fact.

Did you hear me endeavour to incite the people to riot or disorder? — I did not hear you exhort the people to any act which had a tendency to lead them to violence and disorder.

[Holding in his hand a number of *The New Times* of 18 August.] Look, sir, at the early part of the report in this paper. Is it yours? — Yes, I wrote it.

[The paragraph referred to stated the arrival of Mr Hunt and others at the hustings, in a coach, accompanied by 'Tyas' in the coach.]

Is it true? Can you swear to it? — I cannot swear to it. I was told Tyas was one.

Did you not know Mr Tyas? — No. I was also told Saxton was there. I received my information on the field as well as I could. I don't recollect seeing Saxton in the field.

Is this passage – in which you speak of a lady who was on the box of the coach as 'a profligate Amazon' – your writing? — It is.

Where did you get that information? — I received it from some person who told me who were the parties, for I did not know any of them myself. I called her a profligate Amazon because I thought her appearance in the manner and place where I saw her justified the observation.

Have you never seen a lady present colours at the head of a regiment? — I never saw a lady present colours at the head of a regiment.

[Mr Hunt read from the *New Times* report: 'The soldiers advanced and surrounded the hustings when Mr Nadin, with the utmost resolution, seized hold of Johnson first, and then of Hunt, and afterwards of several others whom he handed to his assistants, and the latter carried them immediately to the New Bailey. The banners were the next objects to which the police officers directed their attention, and with very little resistance they got possession of the whole of them. The scene that now ensued was truly awful! The shrieks of women and the groans of men were to be heard at some distance. Every person who attended out of curiosity, finding his personal safety at risk, immediately fled, and where was then the boasted courage of these mad-headed Reformers? They were seen retreating in all directions with the utmost speed. The crush was so great in one part of the field that it knocked down some

# Third Day – Saturday 18 March 1820.

outbuildings at the end of a row of houses, on which were at least twenty or thirty persons, with an immense crush.[169] As I was carried along by the crowd, I saw several almost buried in the ruins. Others, in their anxiety to escape, had been trampled on by the populace, many of them to death. A feeling of sauve qui peut appeared now to fill the mind of everybody, and the dreadful result is not yet known. Among the spolia opima they say are to be reckoned sixteen banners with seditious inscriptions and six caps of Jacobinism.']

What do you mean by six caps of Jacobinism? — Those were red caps of Liberty, with 'Henry Hunt, Esq.' on them.

Why did you call them caps of Jacobinism? — It was the colour and the shape, not the inscription, which gave me this notion of them.

Have you seen the cap of Liberty on this castle? — I have not examined this castle, nor been struck with the cap and pole surmounting it.

Did you not see many hurt? — I did see several people hurt near the outhouse by the pressure of the ruins.

And some cut? — I saw nobody cut while I was there.

From whom did the groans proceed? — The groans proceeded from the crowd getting away from the field.

Did the field then attack the people? — I know as well as you the field did not attack them. I presume they were endeavouring to get away on the appearance of the soldiers, and not from any act done them by the soldiers, certainly.

How did you escape? — I escaped amid the pressure of the crowd.

Have you never said you were cut at? — No one attacked me, no one cut at me with a sword, no one cut at my hat with a sword: nor did I ever tell such a thing to anyone.

Have you never said that you carried a constable's staff for protection? — I had no constable's staff on that day, nor ever said I saved myself from a blow of a sword by holding up a constable's staff on the day of 16 August.

Never to a reporter? — I never said such a thing to any brother reporter, nor that a yeoman who struck at me exclaimed, 'Damn you, why did you not show that staff before?' I have certainly told people that I was coming here as a witness for the prosecution, and might have said 'against Hunt', but I never said, 'I would do for him in the witnesses' box'.

[Mr Hunt again read from the report: 'Had it not been for the interference of Nadin, the deputy constable, whom these men have particularly calumniated, it is certain that Hunt would not now have been alive, for the military were determined to cut him to pieces.']

**Henry Horton**

---

169   Sic in transcript. Perhaps 'crash' is to be preferred.

# Hunt and Others.

**Henry Horton**

Who told you that? — I cannot recollect now, but I was told it by somebody between the meeting and twelve at night.

Cannot you recollect who told you this? — I do not recollect. It was an occurrence which I heard and, as it struck me to be a forcible circumstance, I mentioned it, though I cannot think it was likely to be true.

How came you to insert 'it is certain' when you say you did not believe it to be true? — I did not think it likely; yet, having heard it, I felt it right to mention it as it was related to me, and I certainly wrote 'it is certain' merely stating what had been communicated to me.

You are employed, you say, by the proprietors of *The New Times*. Who are the proprietors? — I am employed by the proprietors of *The New Times*, the only one of whom I know is Dr Stoddart.

Is he not a relation of yours? — He is no relation of mine.

Did you not know that I had bills found on an indictment for libel against that paper? — I did not know when I wrote that account that you had bills found upon an indictment against that paper for an alleged libel. Though I knew you were proceeding for some libel, I did not know it was for urging people to assassinate you. I did not write what you call a libel. I know nothing about it.

Did you not know that Mr Tyas, instead of being a delinquent, was, like yourself, a London reporter? — No; I never saw him until the Manchester meeting.

[Mr Hunt read on further: 'The yeomanry were supported by the Hussars. At the moment when Hunt was seized, there could not have been fewer than 50,000 persons on the ground. The loyal inhabitants of Manchester, and loyal they certainly are, felt themselves imperatively called upon to rescue the town from the odium cast on it by the toleration of these meetings. It is solely from such feelings that they have acted, and in so doing they have certainly set an admirable example to the community at large; for, though irritated to a very high degree, they have conducted themselves on this unhappy occasion with the greatest temperance and moderation.' He then turned to a leading article in the same paper, which stated that 'the wretch' who was foremost in the meeting changed countenance, and that his 'grin of malice' gave way to a pallid and sallow hue.]

Is that your writing? — It is not.

By whom was it written? — I don't know.

Is it true? — It is true that you looked pale at the approach of the military.

And that my lips quivered? — I have nothing to do with the garnishing of it. You certainly looked pale, as I have mentioned.

# Third Day – Saturday 18 March 1820.

Were not the shrieks of the women and the groans of the men calculated to appal the stoutest heart? — I heard no shrieks at that time, nor until afterwards.

You saw me make no resistance to the constable's staff? It was an instant surrender? Did I resist? — I saw you make no resistance, but it was rather a seizure than a surrender. I think it was Nadin who seized you. I heard no question put by you to the officer of cavalry. I saw Nadin take Johnson off the hustings by the leg, and it appeared to me he was about to do the same to you, but as I had turned round at the moment, I can't say exactly how he took you.

*Cross-examined* by Mr BAMFORD.

With whom did you communicate at the police office? — I occasionally saw Mr Nadin at the police office and got accounts of public business from him.

Did Mr Nadin tell you Mr Hunt was to be cut to pieces? — It was not him who communicated to me the intention of cutting Mr Hunt to pieces.

Have you not occasionally communicated with Mr Milne and Mr Cowper? — I never communicated with Mr Milne, but I have with Mr Cowper, the accountant – sometimes at his own house, and sometimes in the street. Between the time of the meeting and the night, I communicated with a number of persons whom I don't now recollect.

From your appearance, I should presume you have the honour and manners of a gentleman. Why not then have communicated to Mr Hunt the intention to cut him to pieces? — I did not hear it until after the meeting, and of course could not have made a previous communication.

*Cross-examined* by Mr SWIFT.

I know you, though I did not see you until the meeting at Manchester. I refer these words to you as having uttered them in your speech (some few sentences, recommending peace and good order). Your speech was, I think, applauded, and so was that of everybody who spoke.

*Re-examined* by Mr SCARLETT.

Do you know of any indictment against the paper for a publication to urge anybody to assassinate Mr Hunt? — I know there is a charge of libel for something like calling him 'a coward'. It relates to some occurrence at the Westminster election between Mr Dowling and Mr Hunt, on the hustings. There is nothing, I think, in that article inciting anybody to assassinate Mr Hunt. I have no recollection of hearing Mr Saxton address the meeting, but I occasionally left the field. I was not near the hustings the whole time. There might have been others speaking, though I did not

## Hunt and Others.

**Henry Horton**

hear them. As near as I could, I sent a faithful relation of what I saw and what was told me by others. I never used the expression, 'I'd do for Mr Hunt,' or that I had a constable's staff on that day, either to Mr Tyas or Fitzpatrick, which protected me from yeomen's sabre blows.

**James Platt**

JAMES PLATT, sworn and examined by Serjeant HULLOCK.

Was a constable belonging to the police in Manchester. Was on the ground at St Peter's area on 16 August. Saw defendant Healey, at the head of many hundreds, go up to the meeting, where he got into a cart and appeared to address them. I did not hear what he said. There was a black flag with the party, with the words 'Lees, Saddleworth, Mossley' upon it. Saw other parties besides this. One was coming very near the church. Some of them had sticks, and were marching three and four abreast. Saw Mr Hunt arrive with a much larger party. Knew Bamford and saw him on the hustings, but could not say how he got there; he apparently shouting with the rest.

*Cross-examined* by Mr BAMFORD.

Did you hear me shout? — I did not hear you shout, but you appeared to do so. There was an immense shout, in which you appeared to join. I considered it a shout of defiance to the constables on the ground. There was a waving of hats and sticks. At the time of these shouts, the people kept their faces towards the constables rather than towards Mr Hunt. Mr Hunt had then come upon the ground. There were all sorts of noises made. He had heard shouts and huzzas from respectable meetings. He would not say whether their shouts were not like that he heard at the meeting of the sixteenth.

*Cross-examined* by Mr HUNT.

How and where did you first become acquainted with the police office? — About five years ago I first became connected with the police.

Do you understand what is meant by a 'flimsy'? What is the present value of a flimsy? — I cannot say what the price of a flimsy, or forged note, is now.

But five years ago a flimsy was worth ten bob (10s). — The price of a flimsy then, in the flash language, was ten bob (ten shillings).

That was, that a £1 bad note was sold for 10s.? — Yes.

How did you find this out? — My knowledge of this arose from the circumstance of my father having had several forged notes passed upon him which, out of aggravation, I wished to detect the utterers. I went to the people and by inveiglement I got them to offer me some of them, and I went off that night to the Bank of England with the notes. I succeeded

# Third Day – Saturday 18 March 1820.

in detecting several, and I would do the same again. I gave £2 16s for the £5 note, and 8s for each flimsy. The man who sold me the notes is now at large in Manchester.[170] I was not suspected as an accomplice.[171]

James Platt

This was the commencement with Nadin? — This was the cause of my first introduction to Nadin.

Have you inveigled any more since? — I have inveigled several others since.

Any of them been hanged? — One of them was hanged.

What did you get for that? — I will not tell how much money I got for the conviction of that man.

Have you appeared against others and got them convicted? — I have appeared against several others, and all were convicted.

[To other questions witness said:] I saw Mr Hunt, Johnson, Bamford, Healey and Moorhouse on the hustings; would swear that I saw Moorhouse on the hustings. I was about thirty or forty yards between the magistrates; would not say that the people did not cheer Mr Hunt on his arrival; was not hurt on the field; did not see the people commit any breach of the peace where I was.

JONATHAN ANDREW, sworn and examined by Mr SCARLETT.

Jonathan Andrew

I reside at Hendam Hall, near Manchester; was one of the constables of the town on the sixteenth; have property in the town; went to the place of meeting; there were some additional constables found necessary; went, upon the ground at 12 o'clock, and a line of constables was made from the hustings to Mr Buxton's house. At first, the hustings were nearer to Mr Buxton's house, but they were afterwards moved off some yards; saw them removed; they consisted of a cart, with planks upon it. Saw a great number of persons arriving and marching like soldiers; they marched five or six abreast; a great many of them had sticks, and some carried them on their shoulders as soldiers do their muskets; there were others who had their sticks differently. When each division arrived they set up a shout, and were answered by those on the hustings; they shouted, and flourished their sticks.

---

170 On Tuesday 3 September 1816, at the Lancaster Assizes, Peter Montgomery (alias Hulme, alias Hughes) was convicted of uttering four forged Bank of England notes to James Platt on 6 October 1812. He was sentenced to death, but the sentence was apparently commuted.

171 Reporting of the case begged to differ (the word 'accomplice' apparently meaning, in this case, an accomplice of law enforcement): 'Platt was not an accomplice; but though he had been one, and though his testimony would in consequence require to be received with caution, still there was evidence sufficient to convict the prisoner, without reposing any reliance upon what he said, except when confirmed by Nadin' (remarks of Mr Raine, prosecuting counsel, reported in the *Evening Mail*, 9 September 1816).

# Hunt and Others.

**Jonathan Andrew**

Was near the hustings, and saw Jones speaking. When Hunt came, the crowd was immense; estimated them at between 60,000 and 70,000 persons; they consisted chiefly of mechanics and labourers, and very few of the higher orders attended. The impression on my mind created by the meeting was that so large a meeting could have no other tendency than to overawe the respectable inhabitants of Manchester and its authority.

*Cross-examined* by Mr BARROW.

I did not know that Jones was employed as a mechanic to put up the hustings.

*Cross-examined* by Mr HUNT.

I think the division that carried their sticks shouldered was that which was accompanied by a black flag bearing the inscription 'Equal Representation or Death'. I saw them marching into the field with sticks shouldered like muskets. The sticks were of different sizes, but they were, for the most part, very large and thick. With few exceptions, the people all carried sticks. I calculated the number of persons present at 60,000 or 70,000. I cannot say what number of sticks they had amongst them. The sticks were very large, both with reference to length and thickness. They were different from common walking sticks, but I was not near enough to examine them minutely. The sticks varied materially in size, according to the size of the men, but I believe they were from four feet to four and a half long. I did not perceive, with the division carrying them, a flag inscribed 'Mossley, Oldham, and Saddleworth Union'. Every fourth or fifth man seemed to have a command; those who commanded had, in general, sticks in their hands. The division of which I have spoken consisted of between three thousands and four thousand persons; I cannot state with any degree of accuracy the number that carried sticks. I am positive, however, that more than one in ten, or more than one in five, carried sticks. When they came on the ground, the division shouted and waved their sticks in the air.

I had no particular companion on that day, and do not know that any person in particular witnessed with me what I have stated. We had a hundred constables on the ground that day, but I do not know one of them by name who saw the transaction to which I speak. After the people shouted, they marched as near as they could to the hustings, in the same manner as that in which they had entered the field. I heard no word of command given, no direction to shoulder arms. I have not called these sticks muskets. I could not, for the different divisions were not playing at soldiers. I did not see the people strike the constables with those sticks.

I observed other divisions march to the ground. The persons who formed

# Third Day – Saturday 18 March 1820.

them in general carried sticks. I was in almost constant communication with the magistrates, and therefore it was possible the people might have used their sticks against the constables without my being aware of the fact. There were very few women or girls present.

    I was on the ground when you arrived, but not sufficiently near the hustings to hear what was said. I did not observe the people commit any violence. I did not see any other arms except those sticks; neither pistols nor swords. I did not see any person wounded except at the infirmary; and, though on the ground, the constables did not, in my sight, make use of their staves.

*Jonathan Andrew*

THOMAS HARDMAN, sworn and examined by Mr LITTLEDALE.

    I was a special constable on 16 August. When I first got to the ground (about eleven o'clock), there was but a few people assembled; soon after, several parties came in in regular military order, carrying sticks. Those that I saw carried them in the left hand as soldiers do muskets, and seemed to have command over the others. They marched towards the hustings and were cheered as they went up. I heard two persons speak from the hustings before the whole party arrived. The first speech was, 'There has been an order given to stand six yards back from the stage, otherwise you will afford your enemies an opportunity of rushing in with their cavalry and all their corruption'. The other speech was soon after – I know not which was first – it was as follows: 'If you had ever so stout hearted a leader, you will do no good unless you stand firm to your post'. Both these speeches were made before Mr Hunt arrived. Jones spoke one of the speeches – the first, I believe. I know not who spoke the other.

    I saw Mr Hunt come up in a barouche, attended by a large crowd. I was then at a distance, and could not judge how many came up with him. He got upon the hustings, which were at that time removed eight or ten yards farther from where the constables stood than they were on their first erection. I think there were 60,000 or 70,000 persons present. The alarm in Manchester was very great.

*Thomas Hardman*

*Cross-examined* by Mr BARROW.

    I have an uncle named James Hardman, a brewer. Jones was some time since employed by him as an engineer and millwright. I do not know that Jones was employed to erect the hustings. I was between fifteen and twenty yards from the hustings when he spoke. A Mr Green was with me, and also heard him. I do not know anybody else who was present at the time. Mr Green is here. I think the words are correct as Mr Ellis, who was near me, wrote them down. I am not positive that it was Jones who made the first speech, but I believe that he did.

# Hunt and Others.

Thomas Hardman

*Cross-examined* by Mr HUNT.

I am a dry-salter and acted as a special constable on that day. I can't say that a reporter standing within five yards of the hustings and taking notes is likely to be more correct than myself. I saw the Oldham division marching in in regular order. I never saw a copy of the indictment against you. The expression of one of the men who appeared to be a leader attracted my attention to the Oldham division. The commanders had sticks which they carried in their left hands as soldiers do muskets.

I did not see any of the men make use of their sticks. I saw no black flag. The sticks were very large ones, but not so long or so large as a musket. They were of different sizes. Some were three or four feet long, and about half as thick as my wrist. I saw no persons injured that day. I remained on the ground till you were taken to the New Bailey. I accompanied Mr Hay to London.

Did you give the same evidence before His Majesty's ministers as you have given here? — Does your Lordship think I ought to answer that question?

Mr Justice BAYLEY: You may answer it. — I did. I am not a magistrate.

Mr HUNT: Did you compare the evidence given to ministers with what you now say? — I do not think proper to answer that question.

Mr Justice BAYLEY: I think you may say whether the evidence given on both occasions be correct.

Mr SCARLETT: I object to this question.

Mr Justice BAYLEY [to Mr Hunt]: Do you mean to contradict the evidence of this witness?

Mr HUNT: If I can show that he has equivocated, I think I have a right to do so.

Mr Justice BAYLEY: You may ask any question tending to invalidate the testimony of the witness.

Mr SCARLETT: I object to this question.

Mr HUNT: If he gave different testimony at different times, I wish to know where and how he corrected his opinions.

Mr SCARLETT: The defendant has no right to inquire into what has taken place elsewhere unless he mean to contradict the witness; it is under a pledge of this sort that such questions are allowed. But how can the witness be contradicted in this instance without calling some of His Majesty's ministers into court, which cannot now be done. If the witness say that he has not given the same evidence in both places, then the inference will be against his testimony, and I shall have no opportunity of showing the contrary. If Mr Hunt can contradict the witness in any legitimate form, I have no objection to his going on.

# Third Day – Saturday 18 March 1820.

Mr Justice BAYLEY: I am of opinion that a general question of this kind might be asked, not for the purpose of being received as evidence, or of contradicting a witness, but in order to go to his credit, and of seeing if his evidence was substantially the same.

Mr HUNT said that sooner than put any question likely to disturb the verdict when given, he would waive the question.

Mr SCARLETT: Don't be afraid, Mr Hunt. If you are acquitted, the Crown will not move for a new trial.

Mr Justice BAYLEY said that if a judge reject evidence he ought to have received, or receive evidence he ought to have rejected, there is good ground for an application for a new trial.

Mr HUNT waived his question, and the examination proceeded.

WITNESS: Captain Henly of the Manchester Yeomanry Cavalry is a cousin of mine. He was on duty that day.

*Re-examined* by Mr LITTLEDALE.

The expression which attracted his attention to the Oldham division was used by a man who carried a stick; he said, 'Who said we Oldham lads durst not come here today?' I heard nothing else.

JOSEPH GREEN, sworn and examined by
Mr Serjeant HULLOCK.

After confirming the last witness as to the mode of marching to the ground, and as to the language used by Jones, said: I heard no word given. I saw no arms, no muskets. Some of the people had sticks. The meeting was calculated to produce the most alarming sensations. It certainly appeared to me more like the beginning of a general rising of the neighbourhood than of a meeting for any peaceable purpose, especially for the purpose of deliberation. I conceive deliberation to have been impossible. In my judgement, they were by far too great a body for any person to be heard from the middle to the extremity; therefore they could not deliberate. As to the numbers, I estimated those who formed the ring – who took off their hats, shouted and felt a lively interest in the business of the day – at about 40,000. In consequence of what I saw, I joined in an affidavit at my own instance, relative to the business. I went from the ground where I stood to the magistrate's house for the purpose of making the affidavit.

*Cross-examined* by Mr BARROW.

Except the young man (Mr Ellis), I do not recollect the names of any of those who were standing near me when the speech which I have quoted was delivered. Persons nearer than I was must, if they paid attention,

## Hunt and Others.

**Joseph Green**

have heard better than I did, but that depended in a great measure on the degree of attention that was given. I did not think the speech contained anything extraordinary but, an intimation having been given to me that undoubted information should be procured of what actually took place, I caused the speech to be written down. I know Henry Horton, the reporter of *The New Times*. At the period of the meeting, I was not acquainted with him. If he had been near the hustings, he ought to have heard that speech.

*Cross-examined* by Mr HUNT.

I am a manufacturer. The person who intimated to me a desire that correct information should be obtained was Mr Moore, who is one of the head constables of Manchester and connected with the police. Mr Ellis was near me when the speech was delivered by Jones. I had a perfect recollection of the words, and so had Mr Hardman, and from our dictation they were written. Ellis did not write what he heard Jones say, but what was dictated. I was boroughreeve in the year 1816-1817. Several meetings during that period took place in St Peter's Field. That which took place in March 1817 attracted my particular attention for a variety of reasons, especially the extraordinary nature of its object. I know of no person being killed on that occasion. It was what was called 'the blanket meeting'. I know of no person being killed at that time between Manchester and Salford.

I saw all the divisions march to the ground on 16 August. The people had no arms. They did not insult me, nor did I see them insult any other person. I recollect a meeting held in January 1819 at which you presided. It was a small meeting compared with that of 16 August. I recollect many other meetings more numerously attended than that of 1819. I was present at that meeting for a short time. I did not then hear of any violence connected with it. I saw you returning from it. I was near enough to see the hustings fall on that occasion, but I did not know that the accident was caused by the pressure of the crowd. Whatever the hustings consisted of on 16 August, whether of one cart or two, they were removed (soon after I arrived on the field) from their original position. I do not remember having seen any planks.

I know Matthew Cowper. He is, I believe, a respectable man. I understand he took down an account of the proceedings. I have been also informed that William Horton, another reporter, attended for the same purpose, but, although I may vary in my account of Jones's speech in some slight degree, I can swear that what I have stated is the sense of what he said, if indeed it can be called sense. Jones certainly made use of the word 'corruption'. What he meant I know not, for I never could

# Third Day – Saturday 18 March 1820.

make sense of the expression. I saw one person who had been hurt on 16 August.

Joseph Green

*Re-examined* by Mr Serjeant HULLOCK.

I saw the meeting in the June preceding; it was not to be compared with that of 16 August. The people on the former occasion went to the meeting individually. I never heard that any of them proceeded thither in bodies. I saw Mr Hunt at the meeting in January. He had no property or connection in Manchester; he did not pay as a householder when he was there. I believe he resided with Mr Johnson.

JOHN ELLIS, sworn, described the flags and the manner of marching to the ground. He then proceeded:

John Ellis

After I got on the ground, before Mr Hunt came, I observed a person address the crowd from the hustings. I did not distinctly hear what he said, but I copied it down from the dictation of Mr Hardman and Mr Green. [Here witness read the words imputed to Jones and stated in the evidence of Messrs Hardman and Green.] I heard the speech imperfectly. There was a small alteration in the position of the hustings while I was on the ground. They were removed about half a dozen yards. I saw Mr Hunt arrive and observed him address the crowd, but I could not hear what he said. I think there were 60,000 or 70,000 persons present. Such an assembly must have produced a very appalling effect on the inhabitants in general.

*Cross-examined* by Mr BARROW.

Mr Hardman, Mr Green and myself were together for a part of the time, observing what was doing and listening to what was said.

Did you hear the words? — I did not hear the words which I wrote down. I am not hard of hearing. I do not know the person who addressed the crowd, nor can I say whether the speeches were delivered from the cart or after the hustings were completed.

*Cross-examined* by Mr HUNT.

I was a special constable on 16 August. I was not attending much to what was said. I wrote the words that had been quoted from, I believe, the dictation of Mr Hardman. I wrote them either while the person was speaking, or so immediately afterwards that they could not escape my memory. I heard them myself imperfectly, and cannot speak to their accuracy.

I saw the different bodies march in. They crowded round the hustings. As the parties came to the field, they had a most imposing appearance.

# Hunt and Others.

**John Ellis**

I believe the greater part of them left the field before two o'clock, but do not particularly recollect seeing any of them going away in crowds. I witnessed the dispersion, and certainly the people did not go away in the same manner as they had entered the field. I cannot describe the way in which they quitted it because, as the field is very extensive, I could see but a small part of them.

Nothing occurred to excite my particular attention between one and two o'clock. My attention was chiefly taken up by a person of the name of Ashworth, who was crushed in the crowd. He was crushed, as I conceive, by a crowd not of horses but of men. I did not see the crush but I judged from the way in which he was hurt. He was crushed on the breast. I saw no cut; neither did I see any blood. Ashworth was not stripped in my presence. When I saw him he was alive. He did not speak to me. I do not know whether he could speak or not. He died soon afterwards. I did not see him when dead. According to my judgement, if any persons swore that he died by cuts, they did not swear correctly.

I took down the inscriptions on the flags as fairly as I think it was possible to do. I neither added to nor subtracted from any of them. I did not pay more attention to the black flag than to the others. I saw several caps of Liberty in front of the court.

Mr HUNT: Look at the banner of the Nottinghamshire militia; is that a cap of Liberty on it? — I believe so.

There is a sword to protect this cap of Liberty. Were there any swords to protect those at the meeting? — No. I saw sticks in the hands of the people; they did not use them. I was, however, knocked down in the hurry of dispersing the crowd. I was not knocked down by a brother constable, nor by a horse, but by a person whom I did not know, who struck me a violent blow.

**William Hulton**

WILLIAM HULTON, Esq., sworn and examined by Mr SCARLETT.

You are, I believe, a magistrate? — I am a magistrate of the county of Lancaster and was at Manchester on 16 August.

Where did the magistrates first assemble? — The magistrates first assembled at the Star Inn and then adjourned to Mr Buxton's house, which overlooked St Peter's area.

At what time? — We assembled between ten and eleven o'clock, and received information on oath relative to the approach of large bodies of people.

Did you observe the movements of the different parties? — As chairman of the bench of magistrates for the counties of Lancaster and Chester, much of my time was taken up in writing, but I frequently looked out of the window and saw large bodies of men approach. The

# Third Day – Saturday 18 March 1820.

first came by Mosley Street towards St Peter's Square with banners and music. They were apparently divided into sections, and had persons walking at the side who, from time to time, seemed to give the word of command. This observation more particularly applied to the first body, for the others were too far off to be so minutely observed. All the bodies, however, proceeded regularly and in a remarkable manner, for they did not march straight to the hustings but wheeled when they received the word of command. The persons in command went up to the hustings and deposited their colours. They were regularly received with loud huzzas. The men appeared to me to be beautifully exact in coming up to the hustings, but I could not mark their motions afterwards. The division which advanced from Mosley Street by St Peter's Square marched with particular precision.

**William Hulton**

Did the division which came with Mr Hunt march with equal precision? — I could not see what sort of order was kept by the division which came with Hunt.

How many were there, do you suppose, in the first division? — I should think, having seen regiments reviewed, that the first division consisted of four thousand or five thousand men.

Had they music and drums? — They had music, but I do not know whether they had drums.

You saw the division which escorted Mr Hunt? — I observed the division which escorted Mr Hunt. He was in a carriage in which I believe were also Johnson, Moorhouse and Carlile. The extraordinary noise which was made on the approach of Hunt induced me to walk to the window and mark what was going forward. The hustings were moved in the course of the morning: this I knew because it had been the desire of the magistrates to form a line of constables from the hustings to the house where the magistrates were; but I observed that a number of men had rushed in, locked their arms together and surrounded the hustings.

You saw all this, in the situation in which you were placed? — I could perceive from the window different people coming forward to address the meeting. From the situation in which I was placed, I had a view over almost the whole of St Peter's area.

What in your opinion was the number of persons met? — The number of persons assembled was estimated at 50,000.

Was the meeting of such a description as to inspire terror? — The meeting did undoubtedly inspire terror in the minds of the inhabitants. I received depositions on oath to that effect, and I myself marked the extraordinary way in which the people approached.

Mr HUNT: I desire that those depositions may be produced. — I have not got them.

# Hunt and Others.

**William Hulton**

Mr Justice BAYLEY: You must speak, then, as to your own opinion: you cannot state the opinions of others.

[Witness continued.] Many gentlemen stated to me that they were greatly alarmed, and, looking to all the circumstances, my opinion was that the town was in great danger. The population of Manchester and Salford, according to the census of 1805, was 100,000 souls. Manchester was a large place, and contained many shops and warehouses. The magistrates, in consequence of these proceedings, deemed it necessary to issue a warrant for the apprehension of the supposed leaders, which was given to Nadin – either in the presence of one of the chief constables of the town, or else it was handed to him by the constable. I cannot say whether the warrant was brought back after it had been made out. In giving the warrant to Nadin, he said he could not execute it without military aid.

Mr HUNT objected to hearing what Mr Nadin said.

[Witness continued.] He refused to serve the warrant without military aid, and made use of this remarkable expression --

Mr Justice BAYLEY intimated to the witness that he could not state the observations of Nadin.

[Witness continued.] The reason Nadin gave was perfectly satisfactory. I then wrote two letters, the one to the commander of the Manchester Yeomanry, the other to Colonel l'Estrange, requiring them to come to the house where the magistrates were, which they accordingly did. A troop of the Manchester Yeomanry soon arrived from the Mosley Street end. The troop came at a quick pace, and formed in a line under the wall of the magistrates' house. The moment they appeared, the crowd set up a tremendous shout. They groaned and hissed, and those men who had sticks shook them in the air. I saw those sticks lifted up in a menacing manner. I had a full view of the whole. I can positively swear that I saw the sticks flourished in this manner, and I even heard the expressions of some of the people who were near the military.

Whilst the cavalry were forming, some of those persons who were nearest to them turned or advanced towards them. After the mob had set up this shout, the cavalry waved their swords. They then advanced. I believe the boroughreeve was with them when they formed for that purpose. From the appearance of the crowd and from their general conduct, I conceive it was totally impossible for the constable to serve the warrant without the assistance of the military. I wrote at the same time to Colonel l'Estrange and the commander of the Manchester Yeomanry and I supposed the two forces would have arrived at the same moment on the ground, but I was informed that, from the appearance of the crowd, it was thought that it would be dangerous for Colonel l'Estrange to lead his

# Third Day – Saturday 18 March 1820.

men through a narrow pass where there was only room for a single soldier at a time. He afterwards brought up two troops of the 15th Dragoons, and two of the Cheshire Yeomanry. When the Yeomanry and the constables approached the hustings, I saw stones and brickbats flying in all directions. I saw what appeared to me to be a general resistance. In short, when Colonel l'Estrange arrived at the magistrates' house with the 15th and Cheshire Yeomanry, I conceived the Manchester Yeomanry to be completely beaten. The crowd closed the moment the Yeomanry had entered, and when Colonel l'Estrange arrived and asked what he was to do, so convinced was I of their perilous situation that I exclaimed, 'Good God, sir, don't you see how they are attacking the Yeomanry?' My idea of their danger arose from my seeing sticks flourished in the air, as well as brickbats thrown about. I believe the Yeomanry went in about four abreast, but their horses being raw, unused to the field, they appeared to me to be in a certain degree of confusion. They must penetrate through the crowd to get to the hustings and, as fast as they advanced, the crowd closed in around them. I saw distinctly from the window where I stood an immense body of people between the house and the Yeomanry when they advanced to the hustings. In a very few minutes some of the parties were taken into custody.

**William Hulton**

On my saying to Colonel l'Estrange, 'Good God, sir, don't you see they are attacking the Yeomanry? Disperse the crowd!' he advanced, and the dispersion of the crowd took place. I am not sure whether Colonel l'Estrange advanced with the whole or only with a part of his force. Having spoken to him, I left the place. I do not know how many prisoners were brought in.

*Cross-examined* by Mr BARROW.

There were four persons in the coach which brought Hunt. There were a man and woman on the dicky.[172] The woman waved something that looked like a white pocket handkerchief.

*Cross-examined* by Mr HUNT.

Are you sure, sir, you have stated the facts? — I declare that I have related everything exactly as I saw it.

Did you see me so distinctly as to know me? — I could not see distinctly so as to know you on the hustings. I mean that I could not distinguish your person from that of another.

How far do you think you were from the hustings? — The hustings were, I believe, about 300 or 400 yards from the window where I stood, but though I saw a map of the place, with the admeasurement, I cannot speak exactly to the fact.

---

172   The folding seat at the back of the carriage.

# Hunt and Others.

**William Hulton**

Then, I am to understand, that although you could not distinguish me from another, you could perceive that the people were linked arm in arm round the hustings? — I could not distinguish you from another, but I could perceive the persons locked together round the hustings because they formed a complete cordon, and were bare-headed. I believe solemnly that those people near the hustings were locked arm in arm.

You saw them linked? — I saw them linked, I believe, by the arms. They were as close together as ever they could be, and were distinguished from the rest of the crowd.

You swear this, notwithstanding the distance? — Though the distance was so great as to prevent me distinguishing an individual on the elevated hustings, still I and others could see the persons beneath locked together.

From your own knowledge, you swear this? — I swear this from my own knowledge and observation, and not from what I was told.

Can you, sir, standing in that elevated situation, and looking round on the comparatively small number of persons in this court, see whether their arms are locked?

[Here a very considerable tumult of approbation was manifested, partly in the galleries, but principally in the lower part of the court. His lordship strongly commented on such impropriety of conduct, and a man was immediately brought into the witness box, who was accused of having joined loudly in it. His lordship, after a suitable admonition, committed him to the Castle Gaol. The trial then proceeded.]

Mr HUNT: You will now look round to the benches, where that crowd is elevated, one above another, and say whether you can see what they are doing with their arms? — Must I answer that, my Lord?

Mr Justice BAYLEY: You may declare whether the opportunity you had of viewing the meeting on 16 August was better than that which you have of seeing the people now present. — I had a much better opportunity of seeing the persons at the meeting than I have of observing those in the court.

Mr HUNT: Could you see the arms of the persons then? — I could see them wedged and, I believe, linked together.

Could you see any part of their arms? — I could distinctly see the outside men linked.

Then, from the appearance of the others, you believe the rest were linked? — I have no doubt of it. I described before what I will state again: that I saw a body of men ten deep whom, on my oath, I believe to have been linked arm in arm, and many of whom I had an opportunity of ascertaining were so linked. There was a space within this circle which admitted the hustings and also some of the mob. I could distinguish the circle from those who were nearer the hustings because the men who

# Third Day – Saturday 18 March 1820.

composed it were bare-headed. When you came upon the ground, there was immense shouting.

**William Hulton**

Did you understand it to be a shout of applause, or of defiance? — I conceived it to be applause, huzza-ing.

Were the people looking towards the carriage when they shouted? — I cannot say whether the people were looking towards the carriage when they manifested this applause.

Did you see them turn and shout towards the constables? — I did not see the people turn towards the special constables and applaud them; but many circumstances might have occurred while I was not at the window.

I speak merely of what took place at a time when you stated that you were at the window. Did any portion of the people, when I was advancing, turn round, and give a shout of defiance to the constables? — Not that I know of. The shouts of applause that were bestowed on you had great influence with me in signing the warrant, because you brought with you a great accession of strength to the numbers already collected.

You say, depositions were made 'before me', in the singular number; and a warrant was issued 'by me', in the singular number. Were you commander-in-chief of the magistrates on that day? — I was president of the Lancashire and Cheshire magistrates.

Why did you use the singular number? — I did not know that I used the singular number. The warrant was signed by me and others.

At what time was the first deposition made? — The deposition with respect to the alarm of the town was made about half past eleven or twelve o'clock.

At what time was the last? — The last deposition was made immediately after you ascended the hustings.

By whom? — It was made by a person named Owen. He could not swear to your person, but it was made after the carriage had drawn up and the people had alighted.

Have you the warrant now? — I have not got that warrant. I delivered it into the constable's hands. It is often the case for a constable to return the warrant when it has been served, but as there were magistrates senior to me in age and service it was not returned to me.

Can you recollect the terms of the warrant? — I do not know the exact terms of that warrant, as I have not seen it since.

To whom was the warrant given for execution? — It was placed in the hands of Nadin, and directed him to arrest Hunt, Johnson, Knight, and Moorhouse.

Was Owen's affidavit made before the warrant was granted? — Owen's affidavit was made before the warrant was granted, and after you had ascended the hustings. When the warrant was made out, I had a very

# Hunt and Others.

**William Hulton**

strong idea that its service would be a task of great difficulty.

Did you or your constables call to the people to make way for your approach to the hustings? — Neither I nor any of my constables, to my knowledge, called on the people to make way for the constables to approach the hustings.

Did your brother magistrates elect you to the chair on this occasion? — I was not elected chairman of the magistrates on this occasion because no one else would undertake the task; the situation was offered to no one else.

Were you ever in the army? — I was never in the army. I was for a short time in the local militia.

I believe you saw very little service until that day? — I don't call it service.

The letters to the two military commanders were sent at the same time, you say? — The letters to Colonel l'Estrange and the commander of the Manchester Yeomanry were sent at the same time. The reason why the two forces did not arrive at the same time was because it was deemed prudent that, instead of Colonel l'Estrange proceeding through a very narrow street, he should advance to the area by a circuitous but more open route.

Cannot you recollect what were the terms of the warrant? — I think the warrant granted on the oath of Owen set forth that you, Moorhouse, Johnson, and Knight, were proceeding through the town in a car.

Then, as I was in a barouche, that was not correct.

Mr Justice BAYLEY: You cannot make any remark on the warrant unless it be produced in court.

Mr HUNT: Did the cavalry in forming wave their swords? — The cavalry in forming waved their swords and advanced to the hustings.

Do you recollect the pace with which they advanced? — If I were called on to state the particular pace in which they advanced, I would say it was something of a trot, or rather prancing; the horse were fidgeting in consequence of the noise, and they were not in good order.

Did not some of them gallop? — I saw none of the cavalry galloping. The pace I wish to describe was between walking and trotting. I believe they advanced to the right of the constables, but the line of constables had, I believe, been previously broken. The letters I sent to the officers were written in conjunction with all my brother magistrates. The space which the cavalry made in their approach was immediately filled up by the people.

Was not the space blocked up with the constables? — I cannot say that it was filled up by the constables on the right and the people on the left, endeavouring to escape. I only know the space was immediately

# Third Day – Saturday 18 March 1820.

filled up. I think decidedly that the space was filled up for the purpose of closing them and cutting them off.

**William Hulton**

Mr Justice BAYLEY: Do you think it was done to pull them off their horses and injure them? — I certainly do, my Lord. The impression made on my mind at the time was that the people closed in order to injure the yeomanry.

Mr HUNT: Will you swear that the constables were not mixed with the people? — There might be some constables mixed with the people; I could not see them.

Was not the space filled by Nadin and his party? — I do not know that the closing was effected by the rushing in of Nadin and the constables. I believe the people wished to close on the cavalry.

On your oath, sir, did not the people fall back at the sight of the military? — I will swear that many of the people did not fly when the first body of cavalry rode amongst them. They fled when they saw the second. The moment Colonel l'Estrange advanced with his squadron, the general flight, according to my belief, took place.

Were there not many children in the crowd? — I saw very few children in the crowd. I cannot undertake to swear that I saw one.

There were many women? — There were a good many women, undoubtedly. I heard the women particularly noisy in hissing and hooting the cavalry when they first appeared. When the yeomanry advanced to the hustings, I saw bricks and stones flying.

At the yeomanry? — I have not stated that they were levelled at the yeomanry, nor can I swear it. I wish to convey to the jury that those stones and bricks were thrown in defiance of the military. I saw them attacked, and, under that impression, I desired Colonel l'Estrange to advance. I said, 'For God's sake, see how they're attacking the yeomanry – save them!' or words to that effect. There was not time for me to consult my brother magistrates as to sending in more military, but they were with me at the window and I should certainly conceive they heard me. I did not take the responsibility on myself. They, at that moment, were expressing fear themselves.

What fears? Fears that the people would hurt the yeomanry, or the yeomanry destroy the people? — I have answered that. They saw the perilous situation in which the yeomanry were placed. I do not recollect how many of the magistrates were with me. Some of them endeavoured to get into the crowd, but without effect. I and my brother magistrate, Mr Tatton, tried to get into the crowd, but were repulsed. That was after the first body of cavalry had arrived and proceeded with the constables towards the hustings. The attempt was made before the dispersion, and subsequent to the advance of the cavalry.

## Hunt and Others.

**William Hulton**

Did you or any of the other magistrates attempt to persuade the people to disperse? — Neither I nor any of my brother magistrates attempted to persuade the people to disperse.

You saw some of the parties come in beautiful order? — I saw some of the parties march into the field in beautiful order.

And this thing, which was so beautiful, created alarm in your tender heart? — That body, which marched so beautifully, did create great alarm in the town. Several of those persons had large sticks – I won't say shouldered like muskets, but they had them up to their shoulders. This applied principally to the party that entered from Mosley Street. The others I could not see.

Why did you leave the window? — Because I had given my orders to Colonel l'Estrange.

Was the carnage too horrible to look at? — I would rather not see any advance of the military.

Then you gave orders for that which you had not the courage to witness? — I gave orders to Colonel l'Estrange to advance to the support of the yeomanry: I never thought it would be necessary to disperse them violently as I thought they would disperse on the apprehension of those named in the warrant; and I will add that we had no previous intention whatever of dispersing the crowd. I witnessed none of the scenes that took place after. I went downstairs just as Mr Hunt was brought in prisoner.

Did you see any of the killed? — I did not see any of the killed.

Nor wounded? — I believe I did see one man wounded who was brought into Buxton's house, but I would rather not swear it.

Are you sure you saw none of the wounded? — I saw none at the time, but I have some faint recollection of having seen a wounded person – a woman-carried in a chair – two or three hours after. I saw a woman brought into Buxton's house in a faint state but not wounded, as I can recollect.

On your oath, will you say you did not see a woman wounded? — I did see one woman in a faint state and advanced in pregnancy, and blood flowing from her bosom. I think that is the woman to whom I alluded.

Do not you recollect another fainting and some water being required for her? — I do not recollect having had a woman in a fainting state pointed out to me and a person asking for a little water for her. I was so busy looking at you, sir.

Do you recollect having said to Colonel l'Estrange in Buxton's house, 'There, sir, is your prisoner; march him off to the New Bailey. I commit him to your care.' — I do not believe I did. I do not recollect some person pointing out to me the danger which there would be in sending you

# Third Day – Saturday 18 March 1820.

among the yeomanry and constables ['Who had been already attacking me,' added Mr Hunt.] I wished to send you in a coach. I did not think it safe to send you among the crowd. I had heard that Mr Hunt had been struck, but I will not swear it.

**William Hulton**

By Mr SCARLETT.

I and another magistrate (Mr Tatton) attempted to force our way into the crowd, but could not effect it. We had our horses ready saddled to have ridden in if it were possible, and then we attempted it on foot, but could not succeed. I positively swear that we had had no previous intention of dispersing the crowd; or, if other magistrates had such intention, it was not known to me. Our first thought of dispersing the crowd was when we found the yeomanry in danger. We found it absolutely impossible to execute the warrant by the aid of the police alone. We conceived at first that Mr Hunt was not sufficiently identified with the multitude, till we had depositions to the active part he was taking in the meeting. Our reason for ordering the execution of the warrant was that from the information we had received and our own observation we considered the town in imminent danger from the crowd, and that the men named were the leaders. I think I saw one man brought into Buxton's house wounded.

By THE COURT.

I have acted as magistrate for nearly nine or ten years; I have acted as such since I came of age. I do not live at Manchester. I live at Hulton, twelve miles from it. There were ten magistrates present. It was a large meeting of magistrates; the magistrates of Cheshire and Lancashire were called on to act together on this occasion. Nothing but a conviction of the existence of imminent danger could have induced me to order Colonel l'Estrange to do what he did. I think that I ought to have been struck out of the commission if I had acted otherwise; I should not have discharged my duty if I had not done so. If the constables had not informed me that it would be impossible to execute the warrant, I should not have ordered the Manchester yeomanry to advance.

By THE COURT, at the request of Mr Hunt: Had you heard that a warrant had, under similar circumstances, been peaceably executed at a large meeting in Smithfield? — I certainly had, and this was one reason which induced me, when I had consented to sign the warrant, to order its execution at the meeting. And, my Lord, I beg to add that I also wished the public should know that it was the leaders of these proceedings and not the people who were objectionable. I never heard till this moment that Mr Hunt had, on the Saturday preceding the sixteenth, offered to surrender himself if there was a warrant against him. I had heard that Hunt had called and asked whether they had a warrant against him, but no more.

# Hunt and Others.

**William Hulton**

By Mr BARROW.

I never gave it a thought whether the warrant was to operate only on those who were on the hustings; it was against Hunt and others.

By THE COURT.

I could judge by the motion of a large body whether they had their arms locked without actually seeing their arms.

*[Here the gentleman's examination closed, and Mr Justice Bayley observing to the jury that they must now be fatigued, he would have the court adjourned to Monday.]*

# Fourth Day – Monday 20 March 1820.

*The moment the galleries were opened they were crowded to excess. The whole of the seats in the lower part of the court were filled before eight o'clock by females of the most respectable appearance. At nine o'clock, Mr Justice Bayley entered the court and, the different defendants having taken their places, the counsel for the prosecution proceeded to examine the following witnesses.*

JOHN WALKER, sworn and examined by Mr SCARLETT.

John Walker

I am an attorney at Manchester and have resided there all my life. I was at the meeting between eleven and twelve o'clock on 16 August. I saw several bodies of persons arriving there. I saw a cart as a hustings, from which a line of constables extended to Mr Buxton's house. The leaders of the first division, on coming up, got into the cart and ordered it to be removed a little. It was not removed far. Wylde was one of the persons who got into the cart. I did not know him then, but I saw him the next day at the New Bailey. He headed a party and ordered them to place themselves three deep round the hustings. He had before ordered the cart to be removed. I do not know the other man. He was taller than Wylde. The people obeyed Wylde's orders.

The division had a cap of Liberty with Hunt's name upon it and said, as they came up, they were the Ashton division. Ashton is eight miles from Manchester. The next division that came up was, I think, the Stockport; they had a cap of Liberty. Stockport is seven miles from Manchester. The Saddleworth, Lees, and Mossley Union came up with the Oldham party. Their leaders, as they arrived, ordered them how to place themselves. They had all flags. Wylde said, 'Stand firm to your post – if you have a leader of ever such strong nerve, it is impossible he can do if you cannot stand firm'. This was addressed to the different columns or divisions ranged round the hustings. The taller man told them to link arm in arm round the hustings. He said, 'Every man who knows his neighbour and who is staunch to the cause, and by that means you will keep your enemies from the hustings'. I took this down at the time. The persons assembled obeyed this order.

I was close to one of the divisions; the people were probably fourteen or fifteen deep when these words were used. I fell back as they kept forming between me and the hustings. I could distinctly observe that they were linked arm in arm; I have no doubt of it. They were about fourteen

# Hunt and Others.

**John Walker**

deep. I cannot say that all were linked; I could see some of the back rows linked, and also some of the row immediately preceding them. After the party was so formed, Wylde gave an order to fall back six yards from the hustings; it was after the directions to link arm and arm. There was a little falling back, but not to the extent of six yards; I receded as they fell back. They still continued the linked position. The taller man said, 'The word of command has been given to fall back six yards. Unless you obey, you'll give your enemies an opportunity of letting in the cavalry amongst you.' The same man soon after added, 'I do not see any of our enemies amongst us. If I did, I would tell them, and probably they might wish themselves in another place.' After this was said there was a further falling back. As I was placed, I could not see whether any opening was left to the hustings. I then left the ground. I was absent half an hour.

I returned about one o'clock. Mr Hunt and a number of others were then on the hustings. Johnson was there also. I was fifty yards distant. I heard Mr Hunt desire the people not to call out, 'Silence,' but to keep silence; and if their enemies would not keep order, to put them down and keep them down, or something to that effect. In my judgement, it was not possible to penetrate the crowd near the hustings without absolute force. They formed a solid body; I saw no aperture; this body was formed between the extremity of the line of constables and the hustings. There were upwards of fifty thousand persons present. The division I saw marched to the ground in a military manner, as I conceive, and as each division came up they were cheered by those previously assembled and by the crowd. I have seen as many men assembled at Manchester races as I have that day. The crowd consisted of the lower class of people. The crowd so assembled was calculated to overawe, to intimidate, and to create fear and alarm in the minds of the people of the town. This was the impression on my mind. I felt fear and alarm, as I thought it would create a disturbance.

The distance of Oldham from Manchester is about eight miles. Mossley and Saddleworth are farther; the former is ten or twelve miles distant; Rochdale, twelve miles.

*Cross-examined* by Mr HUNT.

I have always been an attorney at Manchester. I was a special constable on 16 August. When I left the ground, I went up Mosley Street to Mr Fielding's for the purpose of getting a little refreshment. I was overheated – there was a great crowd – it was very dusty. My person, not my spirits, was over-heated. Mr Fielding is not a magistrate. While I was absent, I did not see any magistrate. In the course of the day I went to Mr Buxton's house and then saw one of the magistrates. I was not employed

# Fourth Day – Monday 20 March 1820.

by them. I was not an amateur constable. I acted as a special constable, considering it to be my duty to protect the peace of the town as far as I could. I did not conceive myself under the orders of the magistrates: I was sworn before a magistrate, but I conceived that I ought to take my orders from the chief constable.

John Walker

I did not go to the meeting as an amateur reporter. I made use of an old letter on which I wrote the words that were uttered, for it struck me as being very extraordinary that they should be made use of on such an occasion. I do not attend meetings for the purpose of reporting speeches. I cannot say whether persons who were nearer than I was to the hustings and who were in the habit of reporting speeches would take the words down more correctly than I did. I cannot answer for other people. I do not know a reporter of the name of Horton.

I only saw one magistrate at Mr Buxton's. Mr Norris was the magistrate I saw: he is the stipendiary magistrate of Manchester. I communicated my fears to Mr Norris. I merely said, 'I am afraid there will be a disturbance'. I had thought it necessary, before my going to the ground, to draw up a deposition of what I saw in the morning. It was probably ten o'clock, or a little earlier, when I drew up the deposition. I don't know whether Sergeant Cross was or was not in Manchester at the time. The deposition was not shown to him. There was no conversation between me and Mr Norris as to the relevancy of that affidavit to meet the question. I drew up the affidavit at the police office. I was induced to make this affidavit in consequence of several circumstances. In the first place, a knowledge that large parties had been training in different townships round Manchester, and information that those persons meant to march into the town with caps of Liberty – revolutionary emblems, as I considered them – and that the meeting was calculated to overawe the town, to create disturbance and to produce riot and confusion. Those were the reasons which induced me to make this affidavit, and the same feelings were expressed to me by several other gentlemen. There were thirty or forty gentlemen in the police office at the time, who all concurred with me in opinion. I cannot say that these gentlemen knew the facts of their own knowledge; but I believe they heard them from others. A dozen of them joined with me in the affidavit. I might have got a greater number to join me if it were necessary, but several of them went away to the meeting. On recollection, I believe twenty or thirty persons joined me in the affidavit. We wished to prevent such large bodies from approaching the town. I thought it was wrong to allow such vast numbers of people to enter Manchester. The subject had been discussed the day before (Sunday) at the police office. None of the magistrates were present either on the Sunday or the Monday at the police-office that I saw. I was at the police office at noon on the Sunday. At that time

# Hunt and Others.

**John Walker**

about half a dozen or a dozen of the persons who afterwards met there on Monday were present. The purport of the affidavit was not stated on the Sunday, though the general subject was then discussed. I then declined making any affidavit. Nobody urged or asked me to make an affidavit. Several gentlemen had drawn up statements as to their fears of what was likely to occur the following day which they thought ought to be submitted to the magistrates. Those gentlemen were respectable inhabitants of Manchester.

Mr HUNT: Let me have some of their names.

Mr Justice BAYLEY: I cannot allow that question because it does not bear on the question of the legality of the meeting of the sixteenth in St Peter's Field.

Mr HUNT: If the witness be directed to withdraw, I will state my reason for asking the question. [The witness then withdrew.]

Mr HUNT: I wish to know whether certain persons who have been examined in this court and have stated that depositions were made so late as half past eleven o'clock – on which the magistrates acted – were present at the police office when Mr Walker swore to his deposition before ten o'clock, and whether they joined in it.

Mr Justice BAYLEY: Then you cannot ask a general question. You must inquire whether A or B was there, and so on.

[Examination continued.] I think I saw Mr Green on the Sunday, but I had no conversation with him. I have no recollection of Mr Green's discussing this subject. Mr Green was at the police office on the Monday morning between ten and eleven. I don't recollect seeing Mr Jonathan Andrew at the police office on the Sunday. I think he was there on the Monday, but I am not sure. Mr Philips was not, I think, at the police office on the Sunday. He was, I believe, on the Monday, but not when the depositions were drawn. There was no conversation on the subject of any affidavit. It was done wholly by myself. Mr Entwistle was not at the police office either on the Sunday or Monday.

I knew previously to the Sunday that training was going on and that circumstance, connected with the intelligence that a great body of people were to march into Manchester in a particular manner, induced me to draw up my deposition. I was under considerable apprehension of danger on Monday morning before ten o'clock. These apprehensions were excited both by what I knew of my own knowledge and what I heard from others. The fact of training, which I learned from those who had actually seen it (having been deputed for that purpose), was one great reason for my conduct. I had seen a considerable number of persons coming into the town, which created great alarm in my mind. I saw several bodies marching into the town on the Monday morning,

# Fourth Day – Monday 20 March 1820.

before I made the affidavit. Their appearance did not give me any idea as to whether they had been training or not. I live upwards of a mile from Manchester, on the Cheetham road. I left home to go to Manchester about nine o'clock, but before I left my house I saw numbers of people proceeding to Manchester. There was nothing so particular in the manner of those people as to create alarm. My fears were excited not only by what I saw, but what I heard. There was nothing striking in the appearance of those whom I saw at that hour; therefore, my fears were chiefly excited by what I heard. The people I saw passing by my house before nine o'clock did not march in regular order. They had no flags or banners, no revolutionary emblems.

John Walker

The deposition was not fairly copied at the time I left the police office to go to the ground. I left it to be copied and to be brought to me for the purpose of going before the magistrate and swearing it. There were alterations made in the draft. They were the suggestions of my own mind. The gentlemen to whom I have alluded did not sign the draft at the police office. It was signed at Mr Buxton's house. Before I drew up the draft, I did not see anything in the town of Manchester to excite my alarm. My deposition was, in effect, 'that I understood training had been carried on in different townships round Manchester; that great bodies of people meant to enter the town with flags, caps of Liberty, and other revolutionary emblems; and that, if they did so, they would overawe the town, and it would be attended with mischievous consequences'. My opinion was that such an assemblage would be illegal. I did this in order that the magistrates might be acquainted with my opinion and that of others, leaving it to them to decide on what was to be done. I suggested nothing. I offered my opinion because I thought the people ought to be stopped from coming into the town. There was no discussion at the police office between me and my friends relative to my affidavit. When I swore it, I had not seen any bodies of men with flags and banners and caps of liberty, marching in. I was informed that they would so march in from different places where they were training. I do not recollect whether the persons who gave me my information stated that they had seen any of these revolutionary emblems, but it was perfectly well understood that the people meant to march into the town in that manner.

I calculated at the time that there were 50,000 persons present. I believe I have seen as many at the Manchester races. I could not see a great way at each side of me, but a number of the persons immediately before me on the field had sticks. One man near me had a bludgeon which appeared to be cut from a hedge. He held it over his shoulder till another man nodded to him, and he removed it. I do not know whether that bludgeon is here today. He did not hold it as a soldier would a musket; the man

# Hunt and Others.

**John Walker**

who pointed to it also carried a large bludgeon; neither of them made use of their bludgeons on my head. I was neither insulted or assaulted by any of them. I saw several divisions marching to the ground, but, from my position, I could not see whether they carried sticks or not. I saw the black flag, but I do not think I was present when it arrived. I heard part of what you said. It was to this effect: 'Don't cry, "Silence," but keep silence; that will produce order; and, if our enemies endeavour to prevent order, put them down and keep them down'. The military had not then arrived. I do not recollect whether you pointed to any particular person when you used those expressions. I have no recollection of your pointing to the soldiers as the enemies to which you alluded, and whom you wished to be put down and kept down.

*Re-examined* by Mr SCARLETT.

Mr Hunt might probably have been ten minutes addressing the people. I did not hear all he said. I could not, from my position, see any soldiers in Dickinson Street. I had been apprised of the intended meeting on the sixteenth, and also of that which was to have been held on the ninth but which had been postponed. I understood Mr Hunt was in the neighbourhood and was to preside. I had reason to conclude, before I went to the ground, that the information I had received was correct and my ideas on the subject were in consequence confirmed, though I had drawn up the draft of an affidavit. I did not swear to it until I had been on the ground and seen several divisions arrive. I recollect having seen a notice of a meeting to be held on 9 August posted up in Manchester. I saw placards for the meeting of the ninth which appeared to me to be illegal – it was that portion which related to the election of a representative or legislatorial attorney for Manchester.

Mr SCARLETT here intimated that it purported to be for the election of a member.

Mr HUNT said, with great warmth, that Mr Scarlett was continually putting words into the mouths of the witnesses. In this instance the expression was 'legislatorial attorney'.

Mr Justice BAYLEY: It signifies very little; but, for the decency of the court, I wish objections to be stated calmly.

Mr HUNT: I wish, my Lord, you would compel the gentleman to be decent.

Mr SCARLETT: I am not conscious of having manifested any indecency during this trial. On the contrary, I have submitted to much which I consider indecent.

Mr Justice BAYLEY: I believe other people have submitted to it also; I know I have.

# Fourth Day – Monday 20 March 1820.

Mr SCARLETT: I certainly feel for your Lordship's situation.

Mr Justice BAYLEY: The better way will be to have no angry discussion. I will go through the cause as equally as I can and I will interfere with either side when I see it necessary.

[Examination continued.] The objectionable part, that which was illegal, in the placard of 9 August, was omitted in the advertisement for the meeting of the sixteenth. I do not act as secretary to the Pitt Club in Manchester.

JOHN WILLIE, sworn and examined by Mr Serjeant HULLOCK.

I know Johnson, the defendant. I am acquainted with a house kept by a publican of the name of Slater at Manchester. I saw Johnson at Slater's house on 6 August; at that time, placards had been put up, postponing the meeting advertised for the ninth to the sixteenth. We were talking of the preparations that were making by the 'big' men of Manchester with respect to the approaching meeting when Johnson said, 'The great people think because it is put off that it is entirely done away with; but they are under a mistake, for we shall be ready on the sixteenth for anything the soldiers can bring against us'. There was a great deal of talk about the 'Ludding', and Mr Horsfall's being shot near Huddersfield.[173] Johnson said that when Horsfall was killed there was a body of men combined together to go to London and upset the House of Commons, or something of that sort; and, he observed, the reason they did not go was because they had not enough to support their families in case they were sent to prison or came to any harm. The conversation lasted for three quarters of an hour or an hour.

*Cross-examined* by Mr JOHNSON.

I am a butcher, and never followed any other business. I never was employed as a spy in Manchester. I know a man of the name of Henry Moore; I owe him something.

Mr Justice BAYLEY: What has that to do with the present inquiry?

JOHNSON: I wish to show that Willie is a most abandoned character and not to be believed on his oath.

Mr Justice BAYLEY: Then you must call witnesses to the fact. — My Lord, I am ready to answer any question Mr Johnson likes.

[Witness then proceeded with his evidence.] I had a conversation with you at Slater's; you spoke to me there; you wanted afterwards to know what passed before the magistrates, but I refused to state it except in a

---

173  Mr W. Horsfall, a manufacturer, was shot in a Luddite attack while riding from Huddersfield to his home in Marsden on Tuesday 28 April 1812; he died two days later.

# Hunt and Others.

John Willie

private room. I did not state in my deposition that you meant to get into the barrack and take away the cannon.

*Cross-examined* by Mr HUNT.

I and Johnson were taking a glass together. I was not drunk. I thought it a serious business which Johnson ought to keep to himself. I said – after he was gone – if Nadin was there, he would have taken him up; I believed the statement, for Johnson declared it was a fact. I did not know Johnson at the time, and therefore asked the landlord who he was. He told me he was Johnson the brush-maker and great reformer. I thought many persons had been taken up for a deal less than Johnson said. I took no measure for having him apprehended, for I never troubled my head with such like.

Slater was in company the greater part of the time, but some of the conversation was addressed to me personally, when Slater left the room. The part directed to me alone was that in which Johnson, speaking of the meeting of the sixteenth, said, 'We shall be ready prepared for anything the soldiers can bring against us'. I and Slater have talked over this matter together, but not much. Slater is here. Slater did not tell me he did not recollect that part of the conversation relating to the sixteenth of August. It was not in consequence of anything Slater said to me since I came here that I recollected he was out of the way when that part of the conversation took place. Slater did not say anything about taking up Johnson; I did not expostulate with Slater as to the impropriety of allowing such words to be spoken in his house. We did not think much about it then, and wanted to hear what he had got to say. We asked him no questions.

I did not inform Nadin of the circumstance. I did not take any measures to have Johnson apprehended. I and the landlord had some little conversation about the matter after Johnson went away; I believe I did not communicate to the landlord the important statement which Johnson made to me during his absence. Johnson told me and Slater what I have stated, although I was a perfect stranger to him. I have had some conversation with Slater on the subject, but I cannot recollect when first I mentioned the matter to him. I believe it was before I made my deposition. I said Nadin would have taken Johnson into custody had he been present not for any particular part of this conversation, but for the whole of it put together. I have seen Slater here, but we have had no conversation on the subject. We are both subpoenaed to speak to this conversation, but we have not talked the business over.

*Re-examined* by Mr Serjeant HULLOCK.

Except Slater's servant-woman, no person was present at the

# Fourth Day – Monday 20 March 1820.

conversation but myself, Johnson, and Slater. Johnson introduced the subject of the soldiers by referring to the preparations of artillery, et cetera, that were making at the Barracks, at which he laughed. After I had been at the magistrates', Johnson saw me passing his door, and sent his man after me. I went to his shop, where there were two or three gentlemen. Johnson said, 'So, you have been with the magistrates?'

I answered, 'They sent for me'.

'And were you,' asked he, 'fool enough to go to them? They had no authority to send for you.'

I told him I did not inquire whether they had or had not authority. But, as they had nothing against me of which I was afraid, I had no objection to go. He then asked me to tell him candidly what passed before the magistrates. I said, if he would go into a private room in the York Inn opposite, I would tell him, but I would not tell him in his shop. Johnson said he was not afraid of having what passed publicly known. I then bid him goodnight, for I felt that he treated me ill in bringing me into his shop amongst a parcel of people. I thought they wanted to get something out of me. They were not like workmen, but spies, 'attorneys, and such like'.

JOSEPH SLATER, sworn and examined by Mr Serjeant CROSS.

In August last I kept a public-house at Manchester. On the sixth of that month, I recollect Johnson and the last witness being at my house. I began a conversation with Johnson by saying that I understood he and Nicholas Whitworth were to be returned members of parliament for Manchester. He said it was all nonsense, for, even if they were elected, they would not be allowed to sit in London. I then went out, leaving Willie and Johnson together. On my return I found Willie speaking of the attack on Mr Cartwright's mill.[174] I said that was the time when Mr Horsfall was shot. Johnson observed, 'Do you know, Mr Slater, there was a set of men at that time who intended to go armed to London to disperse the House of Commons?' I ridiculed the idea that such a set of ragamuffins could overturn the House of Commons. He said he knew it to be a fact, and that if the subscriptions had been large enough to support their families while they were away or in case they failed, they would have gone. I again ridiculed the idea, and Johnson said, 'Oh! but recollect when Bellingham shot Mr Perceval what confusion there was; Lord Castlereagh was scrambling to get out at one door, and Mr Canning

---

[174] William Cartwright, a manufacturer at Rawfolds, had been shot at three times (without injury) by May 1812. The murder of Horsfall and the attacks on Cartwright were connected.

# Hunt and Others.

**Joseph Slater**

at another; and when Bellingham was taken, they were near tearing him to pieces. They all strove to get hold of him.'[175] He then observed, if one man could frighten them, he was sure it could be done.

There was some conversation about the meeting of the sixteenth. On last Saturday week, Johnson came to my house. He knew I was subpoenaed and he said to me, 'You know, Mr Slater, I said I heard it for a fact'. I answered, 'No, you declared that you knew it was a fact'.

*Cross-examined* by Mr HUNT.

I keep the Bay Horse in Manchester. I asked Johnson whether there would be a meeting on the sixteenth and he said there would. I cannot recollect anything more being said on that point. I was not in the room at the time. The conversation was chiefly about Cartwright's mill. I ridiculed and laughed at the idea thrown out by Johnson. Do not know whether Willie joined in the laugh. Willie did not say that he ought to be hanged for using such expressions. Soon after Johnson went away, Willie said, 'It was well for that gentleman that Nadin was not present, for, were he to hear him speak in that manner, he would have him'. Willie and I have seen each other frequently since we came here, but he never told me what he had to prove. I knew he was coming here to prove something that Johnson had said about 16 August. I was aware of the fact, because I knew he was subpoenaed. Willie had told me he was coming for that purpose, but he did not say exactly what he was to prove; neither did I tell him what I was going to prove. I am sure Willie never told me what he was to prove relative to 16 August, neither on the day when the conversation took place, nor at any other time since. I did not ask him whether anything particular had occurred while I was out of the room.

I thought it was a very foolish and wicked story which Johnson told; I thought it wicked to relate such a story, and wicked also as it referred to the persons who were said to be connected with the business. Johnson declared that he knew it to be a fact. I have heard him say many foolish things; but when he spoke of persons coming to town to disperse the House of Commons, he was serious. I related the story in the evening, without thinking anything of it. I did not think it necessary to give information about it. I know it is the duty of a publican, if he hear seditious conversation in his house, to inform the proper authority. It appears that I did not do my duty on that occasion. If I were to relate every foolish conversation that passes in a public house, I should do nothing else.

---

175 Spencer Perceval, prime minister of the United Kingdom, was assassinated in the House of Commons by John Bellingham on 11 May 1812. See previous note re: Francis Philips.

# Fourth Day – Monday 20 March 1820.

*Cross-examined* by Mr JOHNSON.

Joseph Slater

I know the reason why Johnson came to my house. I had a good breed of pigs, and he wanted one of them. I met him at his door; he asked how the sow was getting on; I took him by the arm and we went to my house together. I rallied him on the report that he and Nicholas Whitworth were to be returned to parliament, and he said it was false – that he had no such intention, or something to that effect. When I saw Johnson on Saturday week, he observed that if I said nothing more than what he uttered on 6 August, I should be a good witness for him. I did not see Willie until he met him at my house.

I never heard Johnson say in my life that he would overturn the House of Commons, or that he approved of such a proceeding. Mr Horsfall was shot in the year 1812. I don't recollect Johnson expressing his horror at the murder of Mr Horsfall, or at the burning of Duncough's mill, but there was much conversation and Johnson might have expressed such a sentiment, though I don't recollect it. I have been once or twice to Mr Norris and Mr Milne for my deposition, but I did not get it. Mr Milne did not promise to give me a copy of my deposition.

*Re-examined* by Mr Serjeant CROSS.

I wished to see my deposition because the circumstances to which it related had taken place so many months since. Johnson related the circumstances in question as facts, as things which he knew would have taken place but for the reasons he stated. I am not sure that Johnson said, when I spoke of his being returned to Parliament, that it was nonsense and there would be no election. I have no reason to suppose that he did.

JOHN SHAWCROSS, *re-examined* by Mr LITTLEDALE.[176]

John Shawcross

[A newspaper (the *Manchester Observer*) being put into his hand, deposed] that he purchased it in July last at the shop of Mr Wroe in Manchester. It is a paper that used to circulate very much in Manchester.

*Cross-examined* by Mr HUNT.

I saw placards posted up, calling a meeting on 9 August. I also saw placards declaring the intended meeting to be illegal. I am a clerk in the police office. It was my peculiar duty to look after these placards. Some of those calling a meeting on the ninth were taken down. I believe, in consequence of the notice issued by the magistrates, the meeting advertised for the ninth was abandoned. I afterwards saw placards announcing the meeting for 16 August. I do not know the express words

---

176  By 1825, Shawcross – like Travis before him – was bankrupt.

# Hunt and Others.

**John Shawcross**

of that placard. I believe some of them were taken down. I have no knowledge of the opinion of the magistrates as to that part of the placard announcing a meeting for 9 August which they considered illegal. I was in the habit, almost weekly at that time, of buying the *Manchester Observer*.

I did not attend the meeting of the sixteenth of August. I believe a number of sticks, staves and pikes have been brought here. There are also some flags, banners, and caps of liberty. They are in the custody of Mr Nadin.

**Michael Fitzpatrick**

MICHAEL FITZPATRICK, sworn and examined by Mr SCARLETT.

I attended a meeting held at Smithfield on 21 July. Mr Hunt was the chairman of that meeting. Certain resolutions were then passed in the presence of Mr Hunt. [Certain papers being handed to witness, he said:] I recollect obtaining these papers from Mr Hunt at the time, as the resolutions. When I received them, they were on one long slip which had been cut for the convenience of printing. I was at the time a reporter on *The New Times* newspaper. One of my colleagues was so soused in the mire that he could afford me little assistance, and it unfortunately fell to my lot to get to the hustings. Hearing people crying out against *The Times* and *The New Times*, I did not for some time like to advance. I endured the pressure of the crowd for half an hour. I then endeavoured to get a place on the waggon. I spoke to the persons who were in attendance – a sort of beadles with white staves for the purpose, I suppose, of keeping the peace – but they would not let me up. I then spoke to Mr Hunt, who said he was glad to see me for he knew I would write a fair report, and he gave me these papers.

I heard the resolutions read. There did not appear to be a decided arrangement between the chairman and those about him as to the mode in which they should be put. They were first read as they followed in the slip. Mr Hunt first proposed that they should be put separately, as was the usual course, but, though read separately, they were put in the mass. They were greatly applauded, particularly the eighth and ninth. The most violent were the most applauded.

*Cross-examined* by Mr HUNT.

I had considerable difficulty in getting to the hustings. The people were crowded very thick indeed round them. I have frequently found it to be the case where you have presided, to my great inconvenience. I felt no personal alarm, but I felt that species of alarm for my wearing apparel which made me put on my worst coat. If the attendance of constables were indicative of alarm, certainly it might be inferred that some apprehension

# Fourth Day – Monday 20 March 1820.

existed in the minds of those who sent them there. I observed no riot or violence. The meeting was exceedingly large, but I have seen larger. I have been at so many meetings where you have presided that I cannot, at the moment, name one which I conceive to have been larger. I never, within my own personal observation, saw any tumult or violence at any of the meetings when you had the honour to preside. I cannot make a calculation of the number of persons who attended the meeting of 21 July.

**Michael Fitzpatrick**

I recollect Mr Harrison being arrested on the hustings at Smithfield. That circumstance excited no disturbance. I believe that those who were forty or fifty feet from the waggon knew nothing about the transaction – it went off so quietly. Harrison, I rather think, had, at the time, addressed the meeting. I cannot decidedly say whether Harrison had or had not addressed the meeting when he was taken unless I saw the newspaper, as I did not report the whole of the proceedings. I think you introduced Harrison as 'the Reverend Mr Harrison', or 'Parson Harrison' of some place in the country in order to induce the people to listen to him. You said to the people – as far as my recollection goes, before the arrest took place – 'Here is Brown – 'or Wontner '– the marshalman, going to take Parson Harrison; will you let him go?' and then, with a good-humoured shrug of the shoulders, you turned to the parson and said, 'You had better go quietly'. You then said, 'If they come to take me, will you let me go?' The people cried, 'No, no'. You, however, said, 'Yes, but I would go. If I am wanted, here I am.' And then, with another good-humoured shrug, you asked one of the marshalmen whether he had anything to say to you? He answered he had not. Harrison asked your advice, and you told him to go away quietly, which he did. The business of the meeting then went on peaceably. The marshalmen, attended by a few constables, made the caption without the aid of any military force.

I believe, when you gave me the resolutions, you said you were particularly desirous of accommodating me, as I came from *The New Times*. I did not imagine when I received them that I should ever be called on to produce them in a court of justice. I believe I asked you for a copy of them. At the time that you handed me the copy of them, I rather think that a part of the resolutions had been read and an individual was occupied in reading the remainder, you having previously stated that your lungs were not in as good order as usual and for that reason you would decline reading them. They were read, in the first instance, in continuity, and a question arose whether they should be passed singly or altogether. I believe, in consequence of your desire to get the business over, it was agreed that they should be put altogether. None of them had passed, I imagine, at the time I received the copy from you.

# Hunt and Others.

**Michael Fitzpatrick**

I have the pleasure of knowing Mr Horton; he is on the same establishment with me; I have heard that he is a relation of Dr Stoddart, but he himself has told me that he is not. I never had any conversation with him about the scenes he witnessed at Manchester. Though we are on the same concern, I had not interchanged five words with him till I met him in York this day week. I never observed any tumult or riot at any of the meetings at which you were present.

*Re-examined* by Mr SCARLETT.

I have often attended meetings at which Mr Hunt presided, but I generally left them before they terminated. There might be riot after I went away. When crowds passed *The New Times* office after those meetings, I have seen the office windows shut. I believe the first meeting at which I saw Mr Hunt preside was that which was held at Spa Fields. I think that it was impossible that the resolutions could have been heard by all the persons present, taking the meeting at from fifteen to twenty thousand persons; they could not have been heard by more than a tenth. It depended in a great measure on the way in which the wind blew. The wind was blowing against Mr Hunt.

[The resolutions of the Smithfield meeting of 21 July 1819 were then put in and read.]

Mr HUNT contended that this was not the best evidence that could be given that these were the resolutions passed at the meeting. The original resolutions should be produced, and a notice served to produce them. He did not publish the resolutions. They were passed at a deliberative assembly.

Mr Justice BAYLEY asked if what was read corresponded with the copy that was published. — Yes.

Mr Justice BAYLEY said he had taken a note of Mr Hunt's objection.

*[The case for the prosecution here ended.]*

**Mr Barrow**

MR BARROW, on the part of Moorhouse and Jones, submitted that there was not any evidence upon which to send the case of his clients to the jury.

He was interrupted by Mr Justice BAYLEY. His Lordship observed that the learned counsel had better confine himself to the fourth and fifth counts of the indictment. Those counts charged the defendants with assembling in an unlawful, formidable, and menacing manner. It would be for the jury to consider whether the meeting was an unlawful one, and, if so, whether the defendants Moorhouse and Jones had taken a part in the proceedings as innocent persons or as partisans. He must observe that there was not that absence of evidence which would warrant his directing the jury to acquit the two defendants. They might be found

# Fourth Day – Monday 20 March 1820.

guilty of some of the acts charged, without the criminal intention.     **Mr Barrow**

Mr BARROW bowed to his Lordship's opinion. He then proceeded to address the jury on the part of the before-mentioned defendants. First then, he begged to state that he held in his hand a copy of The Old Times in which Mr Scarlett's opening speech appeared, and thus much he could say: that whoever was the reporter, it was given nearly word for word.

Mr Justice BAYLEY: Have the proceedings, then, been published? I am very sorry for it.

Mr HUNT: Yes, my Lord, the accounts are in town from London.

Mr Justice BAYLEY: It is very wrong. I am sure the gentlemen of the jury have not seen them.

The learned counsel proceeded to read the preliminary observations in opening the case, in all of which he fully concurred, but in none more than that in which his learned friend had so highly and so justly eulogised the gentlemen of the county of York. Had his clients had an opportunity of choosing the county in which they would be tried, they would have selected that of York; so far, therefore, both parties were satisfied.

He begged now to call back the minds of the jury to the fourth and fifth counts of the indictment. The fourth count stated that the defendants had maliciously, unlawfully and seditiously conspired with other persons unknown to cause discontent and disaffection in the minds of His Majesty's subjects, and to excite hatred and contempt against His Majesty's Government and the Constitution of the Realm; and the fifth charged them with having assembled for the above purposes. The seventh count also charged them with having riotously and routously assembled to the terror and alarm of the inhabitants. To this point the jury would have to direct their patient attention, and no doubt they would, with the most unbiased judgements, decide whether his clients were guilty of all or any of the charges against them. Let them look to the evidence and say whether it was possible that any part of the evidence adduced went to affect either Moorhouse or Jones. His learned friend on the other side had stated on opening the case that this was an indictment against the ringleaders of the meeting. Now, where was it shown that either of his clients had acted in that capacity?

First, with respect to Moorhouse, they would observe where and when he had been introduced into the business, and they would observe what had been his conduct from that period up to 16 August, when all the defendants were apprehended. The first evidence respecting Moorhouse was that he had taken a ride to Stockport to meet Mr Hunt, who was invited to preside at a meeting at Manchester for the purpose of petitioning the Crown for a redress of certain grievances. He went as far as Bullock Smithy, and, not finding Mr Hunt, he returned. He was next found in company with Mr Hunt, whom he had invited to take a bed at

## Hunt and Others.

**Mr Barrow** his house. On 9 August, Mr Hunt, in his own carriage, accompanied by Sir C. Wolseley and followed by Johnson and his wife, who was then in a state of pregnancy, proceeded to Manchester. The parties calling the meeting having found that there was something objectionable in the placard by which it was announced, acquiesced in the objection of the magistrates and the meeting was not held. From this it was clear that if the object of Moorhouse had been to attend an illegal meeting, he would not have acted as he did. On the contrary, he would have persevered, instead of doing which he had at once given up all idea of attending the meeting of the ninth when declared illegal. Mr Moorhouse was a married man, the father of eleven children, and his wife was at the period in question in a state of pregnancy. But he took his wife with him to Manchester on 16 August. He would put it to the jury as men, as husbands, as fathers, whether any man would have done this whose object in going to a meeting was to cause a riot, or to excite terror or dismay in the minds of the inhabitants? The good sense of the jury would at once show that it was impossible to suppose any man so base as to be capable of acting in such a manner. Whatever was his intention, then, it certainly was not that of creating riot and confusion.

From the ninth to the sixteenth of August, there was no communication or connection between Moorhouse and Mr Hunt or any other of the present defendants. Was it, then, a crime to have been seen at this meeting? If so, then one half of Manchester was guilty; and if any man should be found wicked enough to stir this question again, he had only, on learning the names of any persons who had attended, to bring forward the evidence produced on this trial in order to convict as many as he pleased. It appeared from the evidence that Moorhouse was not seen in connection with any of the other defendants from the ninth to the sixteenth of August. On that day, according to the evidence of Mr Entwistle, he was seen heading the Stockport party through Piccadilly into Manchester. Now, the fact was this, and so it would be made to appear in evidence, that Mr Johnson was on that day plying his coach in the usual manner.

[Here the learned counsel proceeded to detail the movements of defendants as they were afterwards detailed in the paper of Moorhouse himself.] Was he seen upon the hustings? No; it was certainly hinted at, but he should prove that witness to have been mistaken. He was not on the hustings; he could not have committed the riot of which he stood charged, for if in the crowd – and any man might have been there – he only stayed about two minutes. Was it likely in so short a period he could have been guilty of the riot and conspiracy laid to his charge? The only division he was said to have been connected with was the Stockport.

# Fourth Day – Monday 20 March 1820.

He happened to be in front of it but not, as had been represented, in a formidable manner, and not with a flag, nor with violent language. What connection had he then with the White Moss drilling or with any of the other divisions on that day?

**Mr Barrow**

As to poor Jones, there was nothing to inculpate him in such a charge. He was seen by Mr Horton, the reporter, who heard uncertain expressions – but they were only exhortations to peace and good order. It was certainly alleged that he recommended them to lock arms to prevent the hustings being broken down; yet it was imputed to him that he meant to create a riot and confusion. The poor man was only employed to build up the hustings; all he had to do was this; he was no member of any committee, but proud of his hustings-building situation, he became an orator. The reason was this: he was only to have 25s for putting up the boards, which were borrowed. He was therefore interested in having the people kept back from shaking them to pieces, whereby he would have lost all. Indeed, it was God's mercy he got them back, for, a short time before, the populace carried away the boards erected in a similar manner on the hustings, and the architect lost them all owing to the want of Jones's foresight in recommending them to lock arms, which ultimately saved his borrowed boards.

[The learned gentleman then contended that the definition of an illegal meeting given by the other side was wrong.] Who was to say numerically where order ceased and disorder began? Who was to say the parties that ought to attend and those who ought not? Mr Moorhouse was transported with a desire to see Orator Hunt deliver his elocution and his law, in both of which he was, like Demosthenes of old, to guarantee the success of the cause of liberty. Poor Jones, hearing the cheering for the orators before the great Demosthenes came, determined to have one for himself, and so he mounted and made his speech and got cheered in his turn. The poor man has, however, now got enough of it. He lost his 25s and will, he had no doubt, in future, act upon the good old maxim, 'let no cobbler go beyond his last'.

[Here the learned counsel read the following narrative from Mr Moorhouse's account of the transaction:]

'My Lords and Gentlemen of the Jury, I am charged with combining, conspiring, confederating and agreeing to overthrow the Government of this country by force and threats. Now, gentlemen, I am persuaded if there be any such combining, conspiring, confederating and agreeing, it will be found to be amongst my prosecutors: it will be them that will be found guilty of that most abominable crime – conspiring to deprive me of my liberty, and for what I know not.

'Now, gentlemen, you will be surprised when I inform you that five of

## Hunt and Others.

Mr Barrow  the persons with whom I am charged with having conspired, et cetera, five of them – viz. Smith, Wylde, Jones, Bamford, and Healey – I never in my life was in company with, until the day on which we were all brought into court together, which I believe was on 27 August last. I shall therefore, I think, be entitled to your acquittal of conspiring along with them. With respect to Mr Knight, Mr Johnson and Mr Saxton, I never exchanged half a dozen words with any one of them in the whole course of my life, previous to our confinement in the New Bailey.

'Now, gentlemen, with respect to Mr Hunt, it is necessary in this stage of the business to inform you I am what is commonly called a coach proprietor – that is, I employ coaches to travel between the towns of Stockport and Manchester – and it sometimes happens, though not often, that a passenger may want a bed who from a variety of circumstances may prefer a private house to a public one. I was applied to by someone to inform them where a bed could be had, to which I replied, 'I have a good bed, provided the room will be approved of, it being small'. The room was seen and approved of, and on the evening of 8 August, Mr Hunt slept at my house, and left on the ninth for Manchester in company with Sir Charles Wolseley. From that day until 16 August, I never either saw or heard anything from Mr Hunt.

'On the sixteenth, in the morning, a little after ten o'clock, I left Stockport with one of my coaches and, near the second milestone, I passed the procession from Stockport, consisting of near one thousand men and boys and near one hundred women and young girls, several of them being the wives and daughters of the men. Their conduct was perfectly peaceable. At the midway, while watering my horses, the procession passed again, and we did not overtake them until we got into Longsight, a little on the Manchester side of which we left them, and got into Manchester ten minutes before them. While the procession was passing the White Bear, Piccadilly, it was proposed by some of the passengers to take the coach on the ground for their accommodation, to which I consented provided they would agree to pay me one shilling each for the accommodation of standing on the roof. But this was done at the suggestion of my son, who said otherwise there would be so many crowding on that the roof would be broken in, and I should have £10 damage done to the coach though I might not make £1 by it. Upon this it was given up.

'I went to the ground a little after twelve o'clock, where I saw an immense concourse of people assembled. After I had been there some time in conversation with various persons who all appeared to be delighted with the orderly manner in which the various processions came upon the ground; with joy beaming on every countenance; and several I heard declare it the most gratifying sight they ever beheld in the whole

# Fourth Day – Monday 20 March 1820.

**Mr Barrow**

course of their lives. Someone pointed out the constables, formed in two lines with a space betwixt them from the hustings to the house, where I was informed the magistrates were sitting; and credit was given to the magistrates for the judicious plan they had adopted to bring before them anyone who might be guilty of disturbing the peace of the meeting. This was actually the opinion I had formed of the purpose for which the constables were thus placed.

'After listening for some time to the music, which was playing a variety of national airs, and, amongst the rest, "God Save the King", I went into Deansgate to get a little refreshment, where I had not been long before Mr Hunt was announced; and upon going into the street near the Dog Tavern, on the carriage passing where I stood, Mr Hunt perceived me in the crowd. He called out to me, saying, "Moorhouse, will you get into the carriage? We will make room for you." In an instant the door was opened; I was seized by the arm by John Collier and instantly shoved into the carriage, but before I had time to take away my hand, the door was hastily shut, and three of my fingers were caught and most severely trapped so as to give me very great pain, and immediately on the carriage arriving at the hustings I got out and went to the public house to get some brandy to allay the pain.

'I remained in the public-house until the dispersion had in a great measure taken place, and, on going downstairs to leave the house, I found Mr Twemlow at the front door for the purpose, as I supposed, of preventing any one from going out that way. He directed me to the back door and I left the house in search of my wife, who was at that time six months advanced in her pregnancy. I was near two hours before I met with her, during which I was several times informed she was thrown in a cellar-hole and crushed to death; but, thank God, it was not so. We met at the Flying Horse and while drinking a glass of wine and water and returning God thanks for delivering her from the perilous situation which she was in (being betwixt the constables and the carriage at the time the cavalry surrounded the hustings), two police officers, Platt and another, came into the room and told me I was their prisoner. I demanded their authority; they produced their staves. I observed, "That is no authority. You must produce a warrant, and I will go with you," to which Platt replied if I did not choose to go without a warrant, he would fetch some soldiers who would not be trifled with. I then rose up and went along with them to prison. This took place between four and five o'clock in the afternoon of Monday. I remained in the New Bailey from that day until 27 August, on which day I was admitted to bail.'

The learned counsel concluded by entreating the jury not to send such a man before the world convicted of a conspiracy.

# Hunt and Others.

Mr Holt

## Mr SAXTON's defence.

Mr HOLT said that little devolved upon him to say in behalf of his client, Saxton, who was only late yesterday tacked in evidence to this prosecution. Their object was to comprehend in the charge all who were included in the indictment; but he hoped, if the jury would hear him, he should disconnect Saxton from the other defendants in a fair and open manner to have a verdict of acquittal. The temper of the times, the prejudices which were unfortunately excited by extraneous events against the defendants – all these were circumstances calculated to excite prejudice against them.

Mr Justice BAYLEY: Here at least there can be no prejudice or passion brought to bear against them, beyond what the fair import of the evidence is calculated to bear.

Mr HOLT expressed his perfect assurance that in this court no such prejudice could be excited against them. Indeed the Court of King's Bench had shown this in relaxing from the ordinary rule, and removing the trial to this place.

The indictment stated three charges. The first was the heavy and solemn charge of traitorously and unlawfully conspiring by collecting an immense assemblage of people to create a change in the Government by force. The next charge was that of a seditious assembly; laying aside all conspiracy, the charge then resolved itself into that. The third states a charge of riot, tumult and disorder. Probably they would be told to separate the individuals as they were affected by the indictment, and bring its force to bear upon some of them and not against others. He then proceeded to suggest to the jury such arguments as, in his opinion, drew a distinction between Saxton and the other defendants. He, according to the evidence, was not known to a single other individual charged with this conspiracy; with them he was never found to act even in the least subordinate part. The prosecutors commenced their allegation of conspiracy with the Smithfield meeting, and they then went on to 8 August at Bullock Smithy, with neither of which places had Saxton the smallest connection, so that from 1 July to 8 August in any of these acts the name of Saxton did not appear. Neither with the training at White Moss did he appear to have the smallest identity. He begged also to impress upon them that Saxton was not seen in any of the marching arrays, as it was called, which characterised the meeting of 16 August.

He was then about to refer to Mr Scarlett's speech in the House of Commons, in which that learned gentleman expressed the great difficulty he had in making up his mind upon the question of the legality or illegality of the Manchester meeting, when Mr Justice Bayley said

# Fourth Day – Monday 20 March 1820.

that a speech made in the House of Commons could not be introduced into that court. The facts might not have been known in the place alluded to, and it is upon the facts disclosed here alone that any argument could be founded.

Mr Holt

Mr HUNT said that everything that came out in court had been already before the House of Commons.

Mr HOLT resumed and said that he merely referred to the circumstance to show the doubt that arose in the most acute legal minds upon the Manchester question. With reference to the law of the case as laid down in Mr Scarlett's opening speech for the prosecution, it was only since 1815 that restrictions had been put upon public meetings which interdicted them from assembling during the sittings of Parliament or meetings of the Courts of Westminster Hall within one mile of such places. If the learned gentleman's law were good, why not prevent the Spa Fields meeting and others which had been repeatedly held up to the year 1820? This was not a cause of Athens, or of Sparta; it was one of Manchester: a cotton-spinning, not a classical district; and the question was, ought they not to be permitted to do what had been repeatedly done under the eye of the law in London? A priori, there was nothing to constitute this meeting illegal. Even if it were, Saxton had no participation in the crime, for he was present for a lawful purpose, namely to take notes for a newspaper establishment.

If not, then, guilty of the charge of conspiracy, was he of the second? If he was, the meeting must be first proved to be a seditious one, and he must be found participating in their seditious acts. In looking at this point they must overlook the late restricting laws, and consider how the law stood in August 1819. There was then no law to limit such meetings. Would any man deny that the people of Norfolk might not have then met on the subject of the Corn Laws, which they might suppose to affect their staple article of growth? The people of Manchester might feel the same interests in the cause-of Reform, and might equally meet in whatever numbers wished well to that question. It was said they met in marching array – was there any law to prevent men entering a town in a breadth, and with measured military step? It ought rather to be called civil array, for there was just the same reason to give it the one name as the other. Was there any law to prevent them entering Manchester in order, instead of disorder? They had indeed been told that the people were armed with sticks which were carried like muskets, but what proof had they that they were not the ordinary walking sticks which men usually carry in the streets? If they were otherwise, why not produce even one of the deadly weapons, for they knew that many of them and the flags were taken in triumph on the field? Why not call Mr Nadin if he could prove

## Hunt and Others.

Mr Holt    any such fact? Well, they had music, but playing what? None but tunes to which every loyal heart must cordially respond. Neither arms, pikes, nor staves were among them, but some few who came from a distance had common walking sticks. Again, upon the banners, with the single exception of that with the inscription of 'Equal Representation or Death', where was there anything seditious (and even it was overstrained reasoning that could make sedition out of that)? There was no sedition in recommending annual Parliaments: although, he confessed, there was a very unwise recommendation, yet sedition was quite different. The same proposition had been long ago made by the former Duke of Richmond, so that this was not a die for their own mint, but an old doctrine kept up in continuity. Mr Jeremy Bentham also had repeatedly written the same doctrine in books he had often addressed to the peeple.

[He then took a review of the history of Parliaments from ancient times to show the various terms of their continuance, and dwelt upon the practice urged by many that they were once held annually.] An ensign, then, bearing the inscription of 'Annual Parliaments' could not be illegal, though he knew many disputed the wisdom of their revival, if even that they had ever existence; but it was said that 'Equal Representation' (with the alternative, 'Or Death!') was illegal. If anybody had perhaps proved that the alternative was woven in the loom of any of the defendants, the case might be different. There was no such proof; and for aught they knew it might have been brought in by an enemy. Suppose such a thing had been done at the great York meeting last September: would it have been permitted to affect the principal personages then assembled without a proof of their knowledge of and participation in the introduction of that flag? Did the inscription indicate anything more than a strong feeling or an ill-selected word in the absence of any direct identity between the defendants now on trial and the particular banner? And yet this was all which was urged to show the seditious character of the meeting. There was no evidence – as at Watson's trial – of the inflammatory speech of a mad young man who recommended the people to rob a gunsmith's shop; on the contrary, all the speeches delivered were pacific.[177] Mr Hulton, indeed, thought that if the meeting was not dispersed, the town would not have been standing the next morning. Just the same right had he (Mr Holt) to say that had not the Smithfield meeting been dispersed, London would have been in flames. What right had persons to put upon speeches or upon acts any other interpretations, without proof, than their fair and

---

177    James Watson had been tried, along with Hooper, Preston and Thistlewood, on seditious charges in 1817, and was acquitted. Arthur Thistlewood's subsequent activities at the head of the Cato Street Conspiracy would bring him to the gallows on 1 May 1820.

# Fourth Day – Monday 20 March 1820.

obvious import indicates?

**Mr Holt**

The third and last charge was that of seditious riot. What was riot? He apprehended there was no such thing as riot in the abstract; the individual must be found actually doing that which tends to riot. If a multitude be even riotous, a man could not be made a rioter even if present should he be found holding no participation in the tumult that prevailed. Joseph Mills, Henry Horton and James Platt were the only witnesses who introduced Saxton's name. Mills, the police officer, spoke of him as being on the hustings, but he was not there for any unlawful purpose; he might have been there as innocently as Mr Horton, the reporter of *The New Times*, who was even locked in with the crowd, to form a barrier around the hustings. It would be clearly proved he never addressed the meeting. As well also might Mr Fitzpatrick be prosecuted for his participation in the Smithfield meeting, in the cart of which he actually was. Surely, then, the reporter of a Government print is not to be guiltless on such an occasion, and the reporter of a paper of opposite principles guilty? Saxton was nowhere found confederating with others on the occasion. Mr Scarlett said that the object of this prosecution was to inculpate not the multitude but their leaders, that the net was not to be thrown too wide to embrace those who were only casually or subordinately concerned. He again made an appeal to the jury on behalf of Saxton, and entreated them to consider him as detached from anything like guilt in this unfortunate transaction.

Mr S. BAMFORD addressed the court as follows:

**Mr Bamford**

My Lord, and gentlemen of the jury: Before I enter into a detail of the evidence which I intend to produce in my own defence, I think it necessary to notice some expressions used by the learned counsel for the prosecution in the speech which he addressed to this court on the opening of these proceedings. I allude to that part of his harangue where he said that 'Bamford was seen training a body of ten thousand men on the morning of the sixteenth'. If the brief which the learned gentleman had before him instructed him to make such assertions, so much the better; and I sincerely wish, for his own honour, that it may be so. But your Lordship and the jury cannot have failed to observe the testimony of Morris contains no such proof, and he alone has appeared against me as to the transactions which took place at Middleton previous to the procession's movement towards Manchester. Indeed the evidence of Morris states that he knows not who formed the people into section, division, and square; that they were formed, but by whom he does not pretend to say.

The learned gentleman also, in commenting upon some of the banners

# Hunt and Others.

**Mr Bamford** and their inscriptions, describes one as bearing the words 'Annual Parliaments' and 'Universal Suffrage', and then insinuates that such was accompanied by a demand, from whence he infers a design to subvert our Constitution and Government. Now the mottos upon the banner which he so erroneously described were nothing more than an avowal of what we considered, and do still consider, as our political rights. There was no such thing as a demand about it. Why should we demand that which we were going to Manchester to petition for?

The learned counsel began his speech to the jury very smoothly and very coolly, desiring them to dismiss from their minds all feelings of animosity which they might have previously imbibed against the parties accused, and – what to me appears very strange – in a few breathings afterwards he makes the above statements, so erroneous and so well calculated to prejudice. His motives for so doing I cannot tell. If his own conscience acquit him, I do willingly.

On the subject of drilling, I have in common with my neighbours heard much, seen some, and could have seen more, for it was, to use a common though a very memorable phrase, 'as notorious as the sun at noon day'. If it be not trespassing too much on the time of the court, I will endeavour to give a brief account of its origin and intention, and I am the more anxious to embrace the present opportunity from having my mouth closed when I wished to have been heard at the bar of the House of Commons at the commencement of the last session of Parliament.

In the course of the last six years, Manchester has witnessed many public meetings to all of which, with the exception of the last, great numbers of people from the surrounding towns and villages, proceeded in groups promiscuously, upon which occasion they were uniformly styled by the illiberal venal press of that place a 'mob'; a riotous, a tumultuous, a disorderly mob. They were ridiculed as illiterate, dirty and mean, having chopped hands and greasy nightcaps. They were scandalised as being drunken and disorderly, and they were denounced as being libellous and seditious, dividers of property and destroyers of social order – and was it not then very natural that these poor, insulted and vilified people should wish to rescue themselves from the unmerited imputations which were wantonly cast upon their conduct? It certainly was natural to give the lie to their enemies. To show to the nation and to the world that they were not what they had been represented to be, they determined to give one example of peace and good order such as should defy the most bitter of their accusers to criminate, and for this purpose and this alone was the drilling – so-styled – instituted. Only one witness for the prosecution has sworn to having heard amongst the drillers the word 'fire'; all the others swear only to their facing, certainly most suited to familiarise them to that species of uniformity of motion which would

# Fourth Day – Monday 20 March 1820.

**Mr Bamford**

be necessary to preserve due order and decorum in their progress to the place of meeting.

But, as to these facts, I do not tender to your Lordship and to the jury my own assertions unaccompanied by corroborating evidence. I shall produce from the papers laid before the House of Commons, relative to the internal state of the country, what I consider as a confirmation of my statement. This document is dated 5 August, which is only four days previous to the first proposed meeting at Manchester, which should have been on the ninth – so that if we suppose the drilling parties to have been in existence a week or a fortnight before the day on which this letter is dated, the ground of my argument is strengthened hereby. That military gentleman who did us the honour to stand so long before us on Saturday evening and whose services, I trow, consisted in marching with Ralph Fletcher from Bolton to Manchester and from Manchester to Bolton, talks of midnight drilling and of the parties coming to the meeting in beautiful order; the former is not, I presume, legal evidence, and of course will not appear upon your Lordship's notes. The latter confirms what I have said respecting the wish of the people to preserve the strictest decorum. Your Lordship and the jury will find, by the evidence which I shall produce, that by nine o'clock on the morning of the ever-memorable 16 August, numbers of persons assembled at Middleton; that they were formed into a kind of hollow square; and that whilst so formed I addressed them, earnestly cautioning them to be on their guard against their enemies, representing the advantage which would be taken of their numbers to create a riot by persons employed for that sole purpose; that I advised them to insult no person, but rather to suffer an insult on that day, as their enemies would be glad of a pretext to accuse them of riot and disorder; that I entreated them to bear towards everyone a spirit of good will, in token of which I distributed among them branches of laurel, emblems of purity and peace, as described by Morris and Horton; and having heard that if I went to the meeting, the police of Manchester would upon its own responsibility arrest me, I cautioned the people against offering any resistance if such an attempt should be made, as I preferred an appeal to the laws of my country to the use of force. That I insisted no sticks should be taken, and that in consequence several were left by the way; that we went in the greatest hilarity and good humour, preceded by a band of music playing several loyal and national airs; and that our fathers and mothers, our wives and children, our sisters and our sweethearts were with us. And this was the dreadful military array which the learned counsel has, in the strains of a celebrated Don, described as one vast army bearing from all points to the invasion of Manchester – poor, forlorn, defenceless Manchester! These are the soldiers, ready to fight for Mr Hunt with bare heads and with arms locked (a fighting

# Hunt and Others.

**Mr Bamford** posture, forsooth!) who terrified that immortal author of given books, Mr Francis Philips; and of these persons – O, dreadful to relate! – was composed that cordon impenetrable to everything, save the new-ground sabres of the Manchester yeomanry cavalry.

**George Swift**     GEORGE SWIFT then addressed the court in his defence. He admitted having been at the Manchester meeting, but utterly denied that he was there for any illegal purpose. He corroborated the statement in evidence of his addressing the people to be peaceable, and yet for all this he had been confined in close custody and exposed to the opprobrium of the world as guilty of a serious offence. He had no connection with the Reformers, and he left his case with the court and jury.

**Joseph Healey**     Mr JOSEPH HEALEY (commonly called the doctor) had a paper of which the following is a copy, read by the clerk of the court, as he was himself prevented from reading it by a severe cold.

## Mr Healey's defence.

'My Lord, and gentlemen of the jury. Permit me to offer a few prefatory remarks to your serious consideration. I stand here accused of a crime against the laws of my country, but I should wish to press upon your minds that just and equitable maxim – that every man is considered innocent until proved guilty by good and substantial evidence – and I therefore hope that what I shall think proper to introduce for my defence this day will be duly weighed and reflected on by you. You are sworn to well and truly try and just deliverance make of this case, to which purpose I beseech you to lay aside party feelings and interests, unrobe yourselves of all party spirit and prejudices (if you have any) and let nothing weigh in your decision but what you hear well substantiated, on oath, from creditable witnesses who are completely disinterested. In our political opinions and feelings we may perhaps differ, but as you are countrymen and Englishmen, I will not believe but that you glory in fair play – you glory in suffering every man to enjoy that privilege you would wish to enjoy, fulfilling that beautiful saying of Scripture, 'Do to others as you would wish others to do to you'. Liberality of sentiment is the greatest proof of a well cultivated mind.

Having premised thus much, I shall now come to the subject of the indictment. It is divided into such a tissue of repetition as never before occurred. We are charged with a conspiracy which is said to have commenced in July and been consummated on 16 August. At once I deny the charge altogether – neither has it, nor can it be, proved against us. If meeting my fellow countrymen to petition Parliament or the King for a

# Fourth Day – Monday 20 March 1820.

**Joseph Healey**

reform in the representation in the House of Commons be a conspiracy, then I confess I am a conspirator and am ready to bear chains, racks and dungeons for such conspiracy. But, gentlemen, I trust I shall convince you that neither I nor my fellow prisoners merit such a severe name. I am unskilled in the forms of law; it strikes me that no act or acts can be considered as a conspiracy unless such acts tended to further and mature unlawful matter, and I wish to keep this in view through this all-important trial – a trial in which the liberty of yourselves, children and country are at issue. I apprehend, if mere association and communication of ideas constitute conspiracy, then are you very conspirators, for, from distant places for one purpose, you must consult, devise, and associate – and why not, while doing so, be conspirators? Design can alone constitute criminality, and here, unless it can be shown by good and irreproachable evidence that we intended to break the peace and bring the Constitution into contempt, it is clear we have committed no crime against those existing laws of the land.

This meeting, as well as others I have attended, was called by public advertisement [which he had here read]. The document will speak for itself. You see it is for the purpose of considering the most lawful means of obtaining Reform. The day arrives -- [Here he described the meeting to consist of a promiscuous assemblage of men, women and children, with music.]

You have been told of the military array of the people; but did the laws of the land then point out in what manner the people should go to the meeting? I fearlessly say no. Then, any method was lawful. You are told of the people carrying walking sticks, but it will be proved they were very rare on that day. It was said the people had flags and devices. Were they forbidden by the then law? I say no. It is said they came with music; was that forbidden? I say no. It is said that meetings called for a lawful purpose might become unlawful by their numbers. Did the then law specify how many made a lawful meeting? I say no. St Paul has laid it down that where there is no law there is no transgression; and, thank God, the laws of my country say the same. You will think, with the great Apostle of the Gentiles, I am confident, and therefore I expect my acquittal. I am anxious to inform you that in Lancashire, where military habits are almost interwoven with the people, the scholars walk in procession with music and flags. It may be attempted to be said that the Reform we sought was not constitutional; this was a new doctrine, imported from Algiers. I apprehend the right of petition or remonstrance is a natural right, anterior to all forms of government, being planted by God in our very natures' and a right enjoyed in the most despotic states – in Constantinople as well as London. It is expressly laid down in the

# Hunt and Others.

**Joseph Healey**

fundamental laws of the land that everybody has the liberty of petitioning, and adds that all committals for it are illegal. If the people had the right of petition, they must also have a right to meet and discuss grievances. The laws of the land are conclusive for us. Would a petition for the repeal of the Septennial Law be penal? – or for the disfranchisement of Gatton, Old Sarum, et cetera?[178]

[He then referred at large to the Act of Settlement, et cetera, and said:] If this be not so, farewell reason and justice, and Duke of Richmond, Earl of Chatham, Fox, Pitt, Sir William Jones, Granville Sharp, Sheridan and thousands of other great men. I trust the meeting is now proved legal. The magistrates: I wish to impress upon you that the magistrates do not appear to have discovered the meeting to be illegal until twelve o'clock; if they knew it before, they were criminal in not giving notice of it.

[He then impeached many of the witnesses for the prosecution on account of their connection with the police and eulogized the witnesses he had to adduce, and then concluded thus:] And now, my Lord Judge, I pray you not to say anything to prejudice the minds of the jury, but leave the matter with them; and to you, gentlemen of the jury, I would suggest a word of advice, namely that the law considers you the judge in this case, and therefore you will judge for yourselves without taking any notice whatever of what may be advanced as this opinion or that opinion. I only seek to repair our old constitution, and make it a facsimile of the sentiments of the people at large.

Mr Justice BAYLEY smiled at the allusion as to what might be his charge to the jury, and turning to them, hoped they would attend to the defendant's request.

## Mr Johnson's defence.

**Joseph Johnson**

Mr JOHNSON, in his defence, said he had been induced to attend at the meeting by desire of some persons who thought he had influence over the people, and to maintain peace and order. He then asserted that what was sworn respecting himself was not true and arraigned the conduct of the police of Manchester. Mr Johnson said, not expecting the case for the prosecution to close this evening, he was rather unprepared for his defence but, conscious of his innocence, he would go forward. He was entirely unaccustomed to address such an assembly as that which he now beheld.

Mr Justice BAYLEY: If you wish to have time till tomorrow morning,

---

178 The Septennial Act 1716 extended the maximum length of a parliament to seven years. Old Sarum and Gatton were notorious rotten boroughs.

# Fourth Day – Monday 20 March 1820.

you are at liberty to postpone your defence.

Mr JOHNSON: No, my Lord, I have but little to say.

He would briefly state his connection with this meeting, and the reasons which induced him to attend it. He was requested to be present and he proceeded to the appointed place under the impression that everything would be conducted in the most quiet and peaceable manner. He went with a determination of the best kind. He knew that the people of Manchester were in a dreadful state of distress; and base men, he was convinced, were employed to work on their misery, and compel them to commit some mischievous acts. That the police of Manchester cherished this intention he entertained not the slightest doubt. The people being placed in this melancholy situation, he attended the meeting for the sole purpose of preventing them from doing anything rash or violent, however their passions might be stimulated by designing men. It was intended to have a remonstrance of the Manchester people drawn up for the purpose of being laid before the Prince Regent, so that, if possible, His Royal Highness might be induced to investigate their sufferings and to devise means for their removal. The object of that remonstrance would have been to show that they were not fairly and regularly represented in the House of Commons, and that to this non-representation their evils were entirely to be attributed. It was his decided opinion that such a proceeding was absolutely necessary. He knew that many honest men differed in opinion on this subject but, as it was a matter of opinion, he conceived he had as good a right to adhere to his sentiments as those who thought differently conceived they were entitled to maintain theirs.

Knowing that a great part of the population of Manchester laboured exceeding hard for fifteen or sixteen hours a day for which they received eight or nine shillings per week, he conceived that their situation ought to be ameliorated; and therefore he attended the meeting. He should richly deserve to have a verdict returned against him – he would consent to be found guilty – if what Slater and Willie had sworn against him was true. But he was sure the jury could never suppose that he would make such a statement as that alleged in the presence of a man he had never seen before in his life. He had serious doubts on his mind, that Mr M____, the solicitor, suborned that man, Willie, to come forward against him.[179]

Mr Justice BAYLEY interrupted the defendant. He could not suffer such gross accusations to be made in that court.

[The defendant continued.] He would prove by a gentleman of undoubted veracity that what Willie said he had declared to be a positive fact, he had, over and over again, related as a hearsay story, and one

Joseph Johnson

---

179 This, presumably, was the Henry Moore to whom Johnson had alluded in his cross-examination of Willie.

## Hunt and Others.

Joseph Johnson

which he did not believe. He should not have made these remarks against the police of Manchester if he were not acquainted with them. He had been in the habit of attending the police office and he had opposed some of their measures. In consequence, some of those connected with that establishment had taken every step to destroy his character and credit. He requested the jury to throw aside all political bias, to take leave of undue prejudice and to think for themselves. He could assure them he never stated as a fact that the men of Nottingham were to do such and such things. He always related it as a mere hearsay statement.

Mr HUNT intimated a wish, as it was then past six o'clock, to have the court adjourned till ten on Tuesday morning in order that he might examine with as much attention as possible the mass of evidence that had been adduced, before he commenced his defence.

*[The learned judge acceded to the proposition, and the court adjourned.]*

# Fifth Day – Tuesday 21 March 1820.

## Mr Hunt's defence.

Mr HUNT proceeded to address the court amidst the most profound silence and attention. He said, rising as he did, under such peculiar and multifarious difficulties, he had to entreat the indulgence of the jury, as well as that of the court while he endeavoured to lay before them, as far as his humble powers would admit, the case he had to bring forward in answer to that which had been attempted to be substantiated against him. It would not be, perhaps, intruding on their time shortly to say that when he arrived in York he was labouring under a most severe indisposition from a cold which he had recently taken, which indisposition had been day after day increased by his attendance in the court, where he had been exposed to the draught from one or two doors on his head, and thereby placed in a situation of great difficulty, and considerable danger. When his Lordship indulged him last night, by granting him an hour's further delay this morning – an indulgence which was so unfeelingly opposed by the learned counsel employed against him --

Mr Justice BAYLEY: Pray, Mr Hunt, don't use the harsh term 'unfeeling'; let us refrain from personalities.

Mr HUNT: He was in hopes that he should have been able, step by step, to read the evidence through before he came to his defence; but when he left this court last evening, he was so indisposed as to be obliged to call in an eminent medical man who recommended him by all means to abstain from any business which might cause anxiety or irritation, and to keep himself quiet as possible, or he should not be able to come into court at all. This prevented him from reading over the evidence with that care which he should otherwise have done. If, under such discouraging circumstances, he should be under the necessity of taking up much of their time, he hoped the delay would not create in their minds any prejudice against him but be attributed to the real and only cause. When he put in this claim, he did so on the score of health; he claimed not – he wanted not – to excite improper sympathy. A conscious feeling of rectitude had always dictated his motives and governed his actions and intentions and would now, he felt confident, enable him to bear up against multiplied difficulties with honour to himself, and, he trusted, with satisfaction to them.

When they heard the opening speech of the learned counsel, he was sure the jury thought they were about to try a very different question

*Henry Hunt*

# Hunt and Others.

**Henry Hunt**

from that which was brought before them. He was quite convinced they thought they were about to try some monster in human form who had been violating every principle of honour, honesty and integrity, and at the same time attempting to overturn the sacred institutions and constitution of his country. But what was the fact? When the learned counsel began by telling the jury that 'he must commence by stating his peculiar satisfaction that this case came to be tried before a special jury of the county of York. Looking to the question which was to be tried in a constitutional point of view, and on public grounds, it was exceedingly desirable that the parties accused should be arraigned before a jury that could not possibly be affected by local or personal prejudices. If he had an important cause to decide, he knew of no set of men before whom he would sooner have it discussed than before an enlightened and experienced jury of that county, the gentlemen of which had long held a high and proud character for entertaining a proper sense of public duty and of private honour. On the part, therefore, of the prosecution, as well as on that of the defendants, he was perfectly satisfied with the choice that had been made.' How could the learned counsel say this when he knew at the same moment, and the whole country knew, that he held a brief and a retainer, that a learned brother counsel also held a brief and a retainer, together with the Attorney- and Solicitor-Generals, with Mr Gurney, Mr Raine and others, to oppose with all the accumulated power of talent and industry the defendants from coming before this jury? Had the learned counsel ascertained the way in which that jury was chosen? Did he know that, when that jury was struck by the Master of the Crown Office, the sheriff stood by his side and prompted whom to select, and whom to pass over?

Mr Justice BAYLEY: The jury cannot with propriety hear such a remark.

Mr HUNT: Circumstances had come to his knowledge which he felt he was justified in adverting to. Did the learned counsel believe that any improper means were used in selecting the jury? Did he believe what was so currently reported (and which he could prove in one instance) that there had been any undue influence exercised towards the jury? Had he heard that some of them were written to by the sheriff? He had the proof that this was not a groundless statement. It could be proved that one individual declined attending in consequence of a letter written by the under-sheriff.

Mr Justice BAYLEY: If there be any just grounds for this imputation, the offence may be visited with condign punishment; but the subject cannot be introduced now as it is foreign to the issue which is to be tried.

Mr HUNT: Had it come to the knowledge of the learned counsel –

# Fifth Day – Tuesday 21 March 1820.

since the opposition that he, together with other counsel had made to the removal of this cause to York – that a tractable jury had been procured, such as would suit his purpose? Was this the cause of his altered tone? Were these the grounds of his panegyric and flattery? He had been well advised on this point, and he had no hesitation in saying that if he substantiated the facts laid before him, they would form a good ground of objection hereafter. But he had no opinion that it would be necessary to take such an objection; he had no such feeling because, if the attempt had been made, he was quite convinced that it would operate on the minds of an honest jury in his favour. The man who had endeavoured to make a tool of the jury would, he hoped, hereafter meet with his due punishment, if such an attempt had been made. He was perfectly sure, let their feelings of a political nature be whatever they might, however their minds had been prejudiced (and there was not one among them, he feared, that had not imbibed a prejudice against him and the other defendants) that they would seek to dismiss that prejudice and be guided alone by a love of justice.

He spoke of the probability of a prejudice existing because what had appeared in every newspaper throughout the country was most notorious. Even since the jury were placed in the box, one of the witnesses, a reporter to The New (the Mock) Times, had sent up a false impression of the case to London. Persons connected with the newspapers had not let the daily prints take the usual channel of conveyance, but had caused them to be sent down to themselves and placed in the very coffee room where some of the jury were taking refreshment. In those publications, he had been charged with an offence which was not in the indictment. He and the other defendants were charged not only with having endeavoured to overturn the throne, but with attempting to destroy the religion of the country itself.

But was there, he asked, any part of the charge true? Had the prosecutors dared to bring forward a single witness to prove that any one of the defendants had – on any one occasion during their whole lives – said aught against the power of the throne or the sacred dignity of our religion? There had been indeed an attempt once or twice to itch out of a witness a declaration that a person named Carlile was connected with the defendants. The learned counsel well knew what effect it would have on the public mind if he could connect the defendants with a man who had stood before the bar of public justice; and he laboured to do so. That man had received the reward of his temerity, and therefore it would be improper for him to make any observations on his case. But, knowing the effect it would have, that individual's name was introduced. In this respect the learned counsel followed the example of the public press

**Henry Hunt**

## Hunt and Others.

**Henry Hunt**

by striving to connect the reformers, and him amongst them, with that man; for he was here not wishing by evidence or by anything he should address to the jury to disavow in the slightest degree the appellation of reformer. He never professed a doctrine, private or public, which he was not ready to avow in the face of his God and of his country. He professed to be a reformer, not a leveller. He professed to be a lover of liberty, not of licentiousness. He well knew the difference between them. Sweet, lovely liberty was as pure and sacred as truth itself; while licentiousness was as dreadful and as appalling as the basest falsehood. There was as much difference between liberty and licentiousness as there was between the lovely truth and those disgraceful, black and premeditated falsehoods that had been issued against him.

Who would not have thought, when they heard the opening speech of the learned counsel – who that had read that speech (and it had been read, with all the daggers by which it was surrounded, by a vast number of persons in this county, even yet while they were proceeding with his trial) – who, he asked, having even read it, would not have thought that they had got some unheard of monster to appear before them, some low-bred villain, some despicable wretch that had led a life of rapine and murder? Would it not be supposed that the jury were called on to try men who had endeavoured to stimulate their fellow-creatures to acts of murder and desperation? What was the truth? Take even the very worst of the evidence for the prosecution – with the exception of one man, and that man bearing a high character, a high situation in life, being a magistrate of the county of Lancaster – with the exception of that man, what did the evidence prove? Except that individual, who had dared on oath to utter even a breath of slander, or to state any circumstance that implicated the defendants, or any portion of the whole of that great meeting with the smallest act of violence? But it was necessary for him not only to repel by his own assertion but also to put witnesses into that box to repel the false, the infamous misrepresentations that had been made by counsel in the opening of this case, and which the prosecutors had never dared to put a witness into the box to prove.

Mr Justice BAYLEY admonished the defendant not to use such epithets. It rested with him only to show that the accusations were false.[180]

Mr HUNT: He was charged in one instance with attending the meeting (a great crime truly) accompanied with seditious emblems and banners, and with one flag bearing a bloody dagger. Where was the

---

180 Of course, the burden of proof rested with the prosecution: Hunt was under no obligation to prove anything to be false. In fact, this comment of Mr Justice Bayley's is of doubtful provenance. It appears in the account of the trial published by Thomas Dolby, but not in the account published by Joseph Pratt.

# Fifth Day – Tuesday 21 March 1820.

dagger? Where had been the dagger? Nowhere but in the disordered, the perverted imagination of the man who gave utterance to the statement. The learned counsel smiled; but, like the story of the boy and the frogs, though it might be fun to the learned counsel, it was intended for death to him. Where was the flag? Shawcross, when examined yesterday, said that the flags, the banners, the revolutionary ensigns, the insignia of war were in York. They were, it seemed, all brought here, but none of them were produced. The prosecutors closed the case suddenly. Where was Mr Nadin? It was sworn that he had got the warrant: now, if there had been any warrant issued on that occasion, was there any living creature who heard him and who knew the tactics of the learned counsel who could believe that he would not have called Nadin forward to support the case of his clients? Where, he repeated, was the dagger? If ever such a thing appeared painted upon a flag, why did he not put a witness into the box to prove it? The learned counsel well knew the effect it would have produced – not only on the mind of the honourable judge, but also of the jury – if he had exhibited those bloody instruments to which allusion had been made. Where were the thousands of bludgeons which were shouldered on this occasion? Mr Jonathan Andrew's bludgeons: where were all these? Nowhere but in the mind of the learned counsel. Where were all the brickbats, where were all the stones, where were all the bludgeons that were hurled at the yeomanry? Mr Hulton's bricks, bludgeons and stones: where were all these? The learned counsel knew well, from the way in which that testimony was given, that there was no such thing.

The learned counsel said he knew Mr Hulton much better than he (Mr Hunt) did. The learned counsel, did, indeed, know him much better, and he gave him joy of his acquaintance. That man, placed in the box, gave a testimony of three hours' examination. And, forsooth, although he was three or four hundred yards from the hustings, he was the only person who had ever dared to swear that brickbats, bludgeons or stones were made use of; and that when the yeomanry came on the ground they were received with hissings, hootings and groanings, the flourishing of bludgeons; and that a part of the people faced about, as if to attack the cavalry. How came it that the learned counsel did not put some of Mr Hulton's brother magistrates in the box to confirm his evidence? Mr Hulton swore that nine of his brother magistrates were present when he acted. They knew that those magistrates were all in court on the first morning. Mr Hay, Mr Norris – all the magistrates were here. They were all put out of court because they came as witnesses; yet, when they heard of the examination of Mr Hulton, not a man amongst them could be found to support his testimony in any one respect. There was not a

**Henry Hunt**

# Hunt and Others.

**Henry Hunt**

magistrate in all Lancashire who would so far violate his duty and his oath as to confirm his brother magistrate. Was there no police-officers, who were in the habit of swearing hundreds of oaths every year, who would come forward and support his statement? Could not one of them be found to prop up his evidence? No; not one solitary instance. If this was a question alone relative to his (Mr Hunt's) guilt or innocence – if it were merely a question of his moral guilt – he declared to God, knowing as he did the judge that sat upon the bench – knowing his high character for honour and integrity – he would suffer the evidence to go to the jury with the certainty of an honourable acquittal.

He would point out to them – and he meant now to point out to them – that there was scarcely one item of evidence brought forward against him, that the learned counsel had not contrived to put some witness into the box immediately afterwards by whom it was contradicted. But as this was not a question whether he and his fellow-subjects were guilty or innocent, but a great national inquiry, an inquiry denied in all other places; and when he considered the great misrepresentations that had gone abroad, and the bold assertions that had been made by the counsel who opened the case – assertions which had been sent forth to the whole country, and which must prejudice this cause and the cause of all the reformers who attended the meeting at Manchester – when he saw this, there was an absolute necessity, he was driven to the necessity of calling witnesses not only to rebut the testimony given in the witness box but also to disprove all the assertions of the learned counsel. It was no part of his character either to flatter or to fawn, and if he were to attempt to make use of any panegyric – if he were to speak in praise of the learned judge --

Mr Justice BAYLEY: I request you to abstain from panegyric.

Mr HUNT: If that which he stated exceeded the common bounds of truth, it would, he knew, raise a prejudice against him in the mind of the honourable judge. He should, therefore, say nothing but that, during the whole course of these proceedings against him, the learned judge's patience had been exercised, his temper had been tried, not only by himself unintentionally --

Mr Justice BAYLEY: I should thank you not to say anything about me.

Mr HUNT: However much he might have felt disposed, in one slight word, to satisfy his own feelings, yet the hint he had got from his Lordship was quite sufficient to induce him not to allude in any part of the case to that which he wished. It would now be, perhaps, the best course for him to pursue to endeavour, after these short preliminary observations, to go through – in detail, but as briefly as the nature of the case would admit – the mass of evidence that had appeared before them. At that moment

# Fifth Day – Tuesday 21 March 1820.

to lay before them all that he was charged with, he thought, would be quite unnecessary; he would therefore call their attention to one or two prominent points.

**Henry Hunt**

This was an indictment for a conspiracy, a very fashionable mode – and a very convenient mode – of proceeding nowadays because, when a man or any body of men were charged with a conspiracy, they had no means on earth of knowing the evidence that would be brought against them. Every action of a man's life was liable to be ripped up and brought before the jury. Every act of his life that could in any possible degree be connected with the accusation might be adduced against him to show the animus – the mind – to prove his intention in any way whatsoever as connected with the case. Had the prosecutors on this occasion given any proof of bad intention? None whatsoever. The learned counsel began his opening speech with stating that he (Mr Hunt) was about to attend a public meeting at Manchester on 9 August, which meeting was declared illegal by the magistrates; that he came to Manchester notwithstanding; and that, as he passed through the country, he stopped at Stockport, where he experienced the kind and hospitable treatment of Mr Moorhouse, against whom that was alleged as an offence. The learned counsel then proceeded to state that he arrived at Manchester on the Monday.

One witness – a man of the name of Chadwick, who seemed to be a 'witness-of-all-work', for he appeared to know all that transpired – stated that he went from Manchester on the Monday to a place called White Moss, and from thence to the meeting. He trusted that this individual, who knew so much, would in future be called the witness-of-all-work. The learned counsel elicited from this witness a most immaterial fact in itself, but one which would tend to prejudice the minds of the jury against him; it was this: that he (Mr Hunt) frequently paused as he proceeded along the road and cried, 'Shout, lads! Shout!' What, was this conspiracy? No: but the learned counsel thought it would prejudice the minds of the jury against Hunt, who thus insinuated that his popularity was produced by tactics similar to those which the learned counsel made use of; but he would bring a witness before them who would set them right on this subject. He was not prepared with many witnesses to disprove some of the facts alleged against him, and which he would endeavour to overthrow; but it so happened, in this instance, that he had a servant with him – a lad who had been seven years in his service, a simple country youth – and him he would put into the box to contradict those statements and explain the circumstances to the jury. He was not a knave, but a simple country youth, and one who had attended every public meeting at which he (Mr Hunt) was present for the last seven years. The learned counsel might endeavour to get out of him what he

## Hunt and Others.

**Henry Hunt**

could, if he would condescend; and he knew that, to carry his point, the learned counsel would descend to anything; he might by the means of this witness go not merely into his (Mr Hunt's) stable or closet, but even into the inmost recesses of his bedchamber. That witness would tell the learned counsel that not only on the occasion in question but on all other occasions where a multitude surrounded him, if he saw a disposition amongst the people to ill-treat, hiss, or abuse anyone, he would cry out, 'Come, lads? Cheer, cheer; don't be ill-natured, but cheer.' And yet this act was to be tortured into an idea that he – to create his own approbation, to get some little popular applause which some men sought when they were not able to attain it – that he, who had received so much of that sort of gratulation, was so little, so contemptible a creature as to induce his friends to cheer him by giving them private whispers. He would call that witness to state the circumstances of his journey to Manchester.

When he got to Bullock Smithy, he for the first time learned that the meeting of the ninth was abandoned. He saw from the newspapers that the meeting was thought illegal – that the parties who called it had laid aside all intention of proceeding: he said 'the parties who called that meeting' for it was not called by Mr Hunt, as had been asserted. It was convened by a regular requisition, directed, as he would prove, to the boroughreeve and constables of Manchester. But when the proper authorities stated that the object was not legal, the project was given up. A public advertisement was afterwards issued which was signed by from 700 to 1,700 inhabitants, housekeepers of Manchester. Though these individuals signed a requisition – to which each of them put his name, his number, his address, and in most his occupation – in which they called upon the boroughreeve to convene a public meeting to enable the people of Manchester to assemble – for what purpose? – for the purpose of taking into consideration the propriety of adopting 'the most legal and effectual means of obtaining a reform in the Commons House of Parliament', the boroughreeve and constables, in the exercise of their discretion, thought proper to refuse their compliance to the request. The people, knowing that it was perfectly legal to meet, knowing that it was not necessary for them in the outset to apply to the civil authorities (having first paid this compliment to the boroughreeve and constables, and they having refused their assent) determined to proceed. Four hundred of them, all housekeepers, put their names and residences to an advertisement calling a public meeting for the purpose which he had just stated. This was done on 7 August, two days before he arrived in Manchester, although they had been told over and over again that it was the meeting of Mr Hunt – a meeting got up by a person who had no business, no property, no connection in Manchester. Who, after this statement, would not have

# Fifth Day – Tuesday 21 March 1820.

thought that he had sent some person down to Manchester to call this meeting in his name when, in fact, it appeared to have been called by 700 resident householders of Manchester?

Those who got up that meeting, as he would prove, agreed to ask him to attend for the purpose of presiding as chairman. For what reason? Because they not only knew that he had been at Manchester before, but that he had presided at a meeting there which had gone off with the utmost peace and quietness. They also knew that he had presided at other public meetings, and the witnesses had told them that at all the meetings he had attended (and he would frankly say he never refused to attend when he was called on by his countrymen), regularity and order had ever prevailed. It was said by the learned counsel that in attending such meetings he was actuated by vain, ambitious motives, to say the least of it. He was content to bear this so long as he could put out of the question the existence of any criminal intention. It was, it seemed, either vanity or ambition that induced him to come forward on such occasions. This, however, he could say: that he never took any underhand means to cause his countrymen to invite him, but, having been invited, he would own that he had ambition. What ambition was it? Was it an ambition to do evil? No: he followed the dictates of his heart, which led him to believe that as he had the ambition so he also had the power to do good. And when had he ever exercised that power in any other way? Did the learned counsel mean to say, after what had been declared in the witness box, after he had told them of the cordon round the hustings and declared that he had evidence to prove that the people were ready to fight and to protect him – did he mean, after all this to contend that he had abused any power which he chanced to possess? When had he exercised that power to carry any illegal purpose into effect? Where was the proof that he had on any occasion uttered an improper expression? Coming from the heart – as his speech did then, without one note to refer to – but knowing and feeling that he meant well, he could always trust himself to give utterance to his sentiments, even in the heat and agitation of such moments as those he had described. Where had his enemies traced one syllable of his exciting the people to do that which was a wrong? Where, having such power, had he exercised it against the Government? Granting that he possessed such power (and he believed that in some instances he possessed a good deal of it), still he never had been base enough to exert it for the purpose of inducing the people to act improperly. No ; he would give to his countrymen what was due to them: he would give to them the peaceable, honest, and honourable character to which they were entitled as freeborn Britons, having love and veneration for their country – having love and veneration for its authorities – having love and veneration for its laws;

**Henry Hunt**

## Hunt and Others.

**Henry Hunt**

and, with the exception of some three or four persons who had dared to speak improperly, never had he seen any number of men met together who wished any evil to the constitution, to the great authorities of the country, or who desired to remedy their supposed or real grievances by any other than legitimate means.

What could be more proper than to consider the most legal and effectual means of obtaining a reform in Parliament? He had been a teacher of that doctrine. He had, as far as had been in his power, taught it. He lost no opportunity, as far as his means extended, of teaching – what? To go burn down powder mills? To attack butchers and bakers? To wreak vengeance on those through whom the people suffered – or imagined they suffered – evils? There was no proof of the sort. If there were, did not the jury think that those who got up this prosecution (with the whole Treasury of England at their command) would have found out some person to adduce charges? No; never in the whole course of his life did he give utterance to one expression, either to the multitude or to an individual, to persuade those who were in the humble ranks of life – who are called the lower orders of society – to act with violence. He had never given to them a hint that they ought to live by any other means but by the reward of their own honest industry. What was advanced against him? There were numerous reporters, some of whom went to public meetings premeditatedly in order to catch hold of what he stated to the multitudes whom he addressed. What did the testimony on this point amount to? It amounted to this: that he had always exhorted the people to peace and quietness. All the witnesses – except one person – agreed on this: that at the meeting on 16 August he had made use of this expression: 'If anyone make a noise or commit a breach of the peace, put him down and keep him down'. Mr Roger Entwistle stated differently; and a reporter of the name of Horton, who gave his testimony as to the expression of putting down and keeping down, observed that some person said, 'That would be killing them'. When he asked that individual whether he meant to insinuate to the jury that such was his (Mr Hunt's) intention, he immediately said, 'Certainly not. I meant no such thing.'

Now, what did Mr Roger Entwistle say, who was one of Mr Scarlett's most famous witnesses? He deposed that some military appeared in Dickinson Street (where, it was proved, it was impossible for him, who was on the hustings, to see them), and that Hunt said, pointing to the military, 'There are your enemies: if they molest you, put them down, and when you have got them down, keep them down', but he would prove that the expression was not used to any portion of the constables or of the military, but to some boys – or a drunken fellow, or some person of that kind – who was creating a disturbance, and speaking of them; he

# Fifth Day – Tuesday 21 March 1820.

called out to the people to put them down, and keep them quiet. This he would be able distinctly to show.

What was next alleged against him? 'That the people marched up in battle array.' The learned counsel told them in his opening speech that instead of approaching in a peaceable manner, as a deliberate assembly would do, the people marched up with their sticks shouldered; but what did they do when they got to the hustings? What became of their wooden muskets? He asked the witnesses whether the people used them against their heads, whether they had been molested in any way. But they all answered, No. Many very respectable inhabitants of Manchester declared that they were alarmed. Mr Green, Mr Francis Philips, Mr Hardman and other individuals told the jury that the marching up of those men alarmed them greatly, although not one of them was insulted or assaulted or troubled even with a violent expression. The multitude consisted of fifty or sixty thousand persons, and yet only five cases of insult were spoken to – and some of these occurred at a distance from the town. The meeting was sworn to consist of fifty, sixty, or even seventy thousand persons, so that there was not one individual in ten thousand that had even offered a personal insult or used an improper expression. If anything could convey to their minds an idea of the peaceable, the orderly, the determined disposition of the people to be quiet, it was this very important fact which came out from all the witnesses: that no violence or insult was offered to anyone. Where was all the stamping of cudgels on the ground of which they heard so much both within and without the doors of Parliament? Where was the proof that insult was offered to every respectable man, and rudeness to every modest female? There was no such thing. It was a very good subject in Parliament, by which the public mind might be prejudiced; and it was also a very good subject for the purposes of that trial; but it unfortunately happened that there was no truth in it. What was sworn to by the host of police officers whom the prosecutors had summoned here? With all their ingenuity they could produce but five instances of impropriety. One of the people said it seemed that they would make a Moscow of Manchester. This expression was used five miles from the town, and it made no impression on the person to whom it was addressed. That person had a wife and children in Manchester, but he thought the expression a foolish one, not worth attending to, and he continued very quietly to follow his occupation. He suffered his helpless wife and children to remain in Manchester without once hastening to their assistance. Did the jury think that there was a monster in human form, who, if he had believed any such story, would not have flown to Manchester – while the people approached with slow pace – and rescued his wife and darling children from such a situation? Mr

**Henry Hunt**

# Hunt and Others.

**Henry Hunt**

Francis Philips said that he, by chance, rode out in the morning towards Stockport, and that he met a person carrying a thick stick. Eyeing this individual minutely, he shook the stick at him, which constituted insult the second. Did the man offer to use the stick? No. What did he do? He walked on. This was the statement of the author who had done more than any man to prejudice the country, who had published misrepresentations in all sorts of ways to prejudice this transaction.

Mr Justice BAYLEY: You must not indulge in such observations.

Mr HUNT: The witness, Philips, said he felt it to be imprudent to go back the same way he came; but, as soon as he possibly could, he went before the magistrates and then he stated, for the first time, what he had seen. Observing the people coming in battle array, he proceeded to the magistrates, and, together with Mr Green – a very clever man and late boroughreeve – he swore that between eleven and twelve o'clock he perceived this battle array and that he felt very much alarmed. There was Mr Hardman, who, also seeing the state of the town, proceeded at ten or eleven o'clock to the magistrates and deposed that Manchester was in imminent danger. Not one word was said as to what those gentlemen thought, or felt, or did, until a few minutes before they made their depositions; they all said they entertained no fear until that time. But up came Mr Walker, and he threw a new light upon the subject: it appeared from him that the gentlemen all met on the Sunday morning, but that they could not then agree on the form of the affidavit that was to be sworn; they met again on the Monday morning, aided by the ingenuity of Mr Walker; and at nine o'clock, before anything remarkable had occurred, they agreed on the course which they meant to pursue. Mr Philips rode out for food: he rode out to see whether he could procure anything to support that which he meant to swear. Mr Walker went another way on the same errand, and they ultimately signed that deposition which they had agreed to at nine o'clock in the morning. If Mr Walker had not been called, they would not have known one word of all this; they would have thought that the alarm had arisen from a sense of supposed danger resting on reports that were hourly coming up to the town. But it appeared that the matter was discussed on the Sunday morning, and they had not then agreed on what sort of depositions it would be necessary to swear in order to break up the meeting without being under the necessity of giving any notice, any warning to the people of their intention to disperse them by the keen edge of the newly sharpened sabres of the yeomanry, by reading the Riot Act – for that was the point under discussion on the Sunday morning. Where was the Riot Act read? The prosecutors have never brought forward a witness to prove that it had been read. If they had done so, the learned counsel well knew that the testimony of that witness would have been kicked out of court. The learned counsel was

# Fifth Day – Tuesday 21 March 1820.

perfectly aware that no Riot Act was read, and, when the contrary was asserted, it was a false and scandalous report to prejudice the public mind. He did not dare to ask Mr Hulton whether it was read or not, because he saw that he had nerve enough for anything, and would have said yes at once – although the defendants had got witnesses who were in the magistrates' house and were now here and ready to prove that no such thing took place. He, however, had made Mr Hulton swear that no Riot Act was read. He put it in this way: 'Did you or your brother magistrates caution the people? Did you go amongst them, and persuade them? Did you endeavour to do any act to make the people believe that you intended to do that which you ultimately did? Did you give them any notice of your intention, or warn them of their impending danger?' The Riot Act, they must all know, was a notice – a proclamation and a notice. If it had been read, Mr Scarlett must have known it by his brief or from those intelligent gentlemen who got up his brief. And was there a human being but must believe that if the Riot Act were read, the learned counsel would have called some witnesses to prove it? They saw what an impression the report that the Riot Act was read made upon the minds of the members of the House of Commons. It was reverberated through that house that the Reverend Mr Ethelston had sent a servant to a coroner's inquest at Manchester to say that the Riot Act was read and that, if it was necessary, he would come and prove it himself. Where was Mr Ethelston now? He was here on the first day of the trial. Where was Mr Tatton? Where was Mr Fletcher of Bolton? Where was Colonel l'Estrange? Why did not the prosecutors bring forward one of these respectable witnesses? The fact was they knew the cross-examination that Mr Hulton had gone through. They were told by their friends that he had sworn this, that, and the other, and they did not like to come into the court. Mr Hay, who was a very bold man, had gone away: he feared that the defendants would send a subpoena after him to put him into the box for the purpose of contradicting his brother magistrate. But he might have remained in perfect safety and security. He (Mr Hunt) was too old a soldier in these things to seek for his evidence. Nature had gifted him with common understanding, and he had seen a great deal too much to put an hostile witness into that box as a witness in chief. If that he could have got him into the witnesses' box as the witness of Mr Scarlett, he would have given a Jew's eye for it. But it would not do to put into that box, as his witness, a man who received for his services on that day a living worth £2,000 a year.

If Mr Hulton received a reward in proportion to his services, there was not a gift in the possession of the Crown, in the power of His Majesty's ministers, or of any of the authorities in the country, that would be equal to his deserts. Mr Hulton was the boldest man he ever saw. He understood

Henry Hunt

## Hunt and Others.

**Henry Hunt**

not only from their appearance but from report that he was addressing magistrates of the county, men walking in the higher ranks of society. He knew that when a man of character and rank was put into the witness box, his evidence had very great weight. Testimony coming from such a man as that, when put in competition with the evidence of humbler witnesses, of men moving in the lower classes of life, produced a much greater effect. Each of them might be equal in character; each of them might be equally irreproachable in conduct; but the common feelings of human nature – feelings the propriety of which he himself acknowledged – gave to the former a certain degree of influence. Such a man was supposed not only to be speaking the dictates of his conscience under the sanction of an oath, but his character as a gentleman and as a man of honour among his associates in life imparted an additional weight to his evidence. He knew that in the eye of the law it was held that an honourable man's testimony, whether in high or low life, was equal; but the principles of human nature are such that considerable influence was produced on the mind by the rank and character which a man held in society. Therefore, how much more cautious a jury ought to be in listening to what fell from an individual of that stamp if it were found that he had forgotten what was due to his character, that he was reckless of the rank of life in which he moved, and came there the bold and premeditatedly perjured man? He knew it would be difficult to take from their minds the idea of that just and honourable character which ought to belong to persons in their rank of life: feeling how incapable any one of the jury would be, even if they were not on their oath, of violating their words, he knew they would conceive others to be as nicely honourable as they were themselves. Feeling all this, he thought it necessary to bring the most unequivocal proof into court before he could induce them to believe that any man in their rank of life could stand in such a degraded situation by making a statement for which there was not the least shadow of truth. He would not put into that box any magistrate, but he would put into it such men as were connected with the higher ranks of life – men, equal in rank, equal in character, equal in education, equal in property: indeed, ten times told superior in property to Mr Hulton. If these men, having the means of judging, not being partisans, not being implicated either in the calling or the dispersion of the meeting – if these men contradicted what had been averred against him, he could not doubt of a favourable result. If he put a host of witnesses in that box who had the means of seeing and the means of knowing all that had passed, and if they decidedly contradicted this story of the bludgeons, this story of hooting and hissing, or this story of turning about and facing the military – if, instead of a shower of stones and brickbats being hurled at the military, his witnesses proved that not

# Fifth Day – Tuesday 21 March 1820.

one stone, not one brickbat, not one cudgel was opposed to them; that not one finger was lifted against those troops when they came to arrest him and his fellow prisoners: if he proved this, then, but not till then, he would demand of the jury to dismiss from their minds if they could – to draw, if it were possible, a veil over what they had heard – and to forget any impression that might have been made by Mr Hulton's testimony.

Henry Hunt

He declared, as he had said before, that if this were his individual case – if the question were, whether a verdict of guilty or innocent should be given with respect to him – he would not call a single witness, but rest his cause entirely on the contradictions which appeared in every part of the testimony, and on the almost impossibility of his having done that which had been alleged. He would have mainly relied on the extraordinary circumstance of the learned counsel's neglecting to call some one of those who were particularly employed on the day so often alluded to; which argued that they could not prove anything in support of his case. This was, however, a great public question. It was not narrowed to the point whether he should be found guilty or innocent. No: the jury had to decide by their verdict whether henceforth a particle of national liberty should be left in this country. They had, by their verdict, to decide whether, henceforth, any headstrong young man placed in the situation of a magistrate might, when he thought proper, call forth a body of military – a drunken infuriated body – and send them out against a well-intentioned meeting of Englishmen for the purpose of putting them to death. It was for the jury to decide whether this should be the law of England, or the practice of its inhabitants. With such an impression as this, he would not fail to set the question at rest, and for that purpose he would call the most unimpeachable testimony before the court, to show that the people assembled at Manchester were peaceable from the beginning to the end; that their motives were peaceable, their intentions peaceable, and their acts peaceable; that, instead of the least resistance being made to the civil or military authorities, not so much as one finger was raised against them. Let the jury visit him with their vengeance if he did not prove this to the very letter. He had been accused of misrepresentation on various public occasions. All those who had written on one side of the question had been accused of publishing gross calumnies on the magistrates and yeomanry of Manchester, but the jury had heard enough to show to their minds on which side of the question the misrepresentation existed.

He would now go through some of the witnesses he had not before touched on. First of all, he would look to the witness from Stockport, a person of the name of Lomas. He was on service on 16 August; he was out at seven o'clock in the morning, and did not come to Peterloo, or St Peter's Field, till about twelve o'clock; he swore, over and over

## Hunt and Others.

**Henry Hunt**

again, that he saw nothing on that day between the hours of seven and nearly two to attract his attention particularly. He observed the people travelling along the road going to the meeting, but he perceived nothing extraordinary; he saw no acts of violence. By and by he arrived at St Peter's Field on horseback, accoutred as a Yeomanry cavalryman. He got there, he stated, after the meeting was dispersed, and he swore that he was not there during its dispersion. He declared that he saw no person cut, that he observed no one injured, and he laughed when he was giving his evidence. He could not help laughing, it seemed, at what he had seen. Now, what did that witness come for? He came to swear the Cheshire yeomanry out of the scrape, to show that they had nothing to do with it. They carried off, indeed, some of the trophies of war, but they would not take any part in the battle. The witness disclaimed, on oath, that the Cheshire yeomanry were actively engaged in the field; but he admitted that they carried home some of the flags and banners. He said he saw nothing on the ground to induce him to draw his sword – the people had all nearly run away before the Cheshire cavalry came to the ground, and their swords were drawn before they arrived there. This was the state of things, if Lomas were to be believed – and yet, what did Mr Hulton say? He swore that he saw the Manchester yeomanry enclosed by the people, that he saw brickbats, stones and bludgeons hurled at them, and that he then called to Colonel l'Estrange to proceed to their assistance, he having two troops of Hussars, and two troops of the Cheshire yeomanry – one of them the Stockport troop – under his command; and with that force he proceeded to disperse the multitude. Lomas previously swore that the people had run away before the Cheshire yeomanry came to the ground, and he was a great deal more inclined to believe the first witness than the last.

The first expedition spoken of appeared to be that of Mr Bamford, from Middleton. Whom did they bring to prove the transactions of the Middleton division? They must all recollect 'the Mushroom Sergeant', he was sure. He merely proved that Bamford was at Middleton, that a chair was brought out to him and that he addressed a few words to the people, the latter of which – where Bamford was made to say that there would not be any disturbance until they came back, as the day was their own – he would call witnesses to prove had never been made use of. He would also prove that the use of the flags and banners was to direct to their proper division any individuals who, in the course of the day, might have strayed from their party. That witness also said that he saw the Middleton party forming in the field in broad daylight, which did not confirm the statement of the learned counsel who described the country as having been intimidated by midnight drillings. He would show to the court that the whole object of teaching those people to march was to

# Fifth Day – Tuesday 21 March 1820.

prevent them from falling into disorder when going to or returning from any meetings, they having been taunted, at former periods, for going in indiscriminate bodies. This was the case when the boroughreeve and constables of Manchester called a meeting of the inhabitants of the twenty-four townships and of the neighbouring districts in 1812 to consider of a congratulatory address to the Prince Regent on the prosperous and happy state of the country, at a time when the great body of the people were suffering from extreme distress. The call was obeyed, the whole population met in Manchester. No opposition was given to the conspiracy – for such it was – of the constituted authorities who wished the people to agree to an address the contents of which two-thirds of them knew to be false. Neither was it considered a crime to invite the neighbourhood of Manchester to oppose the Corn Law. He saw the object of the learned counsel's address to the jury when he adverted to the inscription of 'Corn Law'. He well knew that they were gentlemen living in the country, that they were landed proprietors, and that, therefore, the mention of the subject was likely to have a considerable effect on their minds. He himself had been one of the largest farmers in the country. Though represented as an outcast and one who had no visible means of support, he had landed property and was lord of the manor of Glastonbury in Somersetshire (where the principal part of his property lay), lived mostly in the country, and, in every place where he resided, he had always the honour of being acquainted with, and was respected by, the clergy of the place. He mentioned this in justice to himself, as his name had been coupled with that of Carlile. Of the religious doctrines of that man he would say a great deal if he (Carlile) were not suffering under the sentence of the law. He never approved of the theological principles which were disseminated by that man; and he now declared before God and the whole country that never in the whole course of his life did he hear or read the theological works of Thomas Paine, except at the trial of Carlile when he was waiting in the court expecting his action against Dr Stoddart to come on; and Mr Scarlett well knew that if that trial (Carlile's) had gone off, his would have been called on next; and if he were not present, the defendant would have been acquitted. He also declared, in the face of Heaven, that he never saw any of those works in the hands of the reformers. Good God! he exclaimed, was it not enough to brand the reformers with sedition, but also with renouncing a belief in their God?

[Here Mr Hunt was so much affected as to shed tears.]

In mentioning the Corn Laws, he stated that he had been a large farmer, and he opposed them on the ground that they were merely urged to support an immense load of taxation.

[Here Mr Justice Bayley observed that this had nothing to do with the

*Henry Hunt*

# Hunt and Others.

**Henry Hunt**

case.]

[Mr Hunt continued.] They (the reformers) had prayed and petitioned for reform, but their prayers were not attended to. They were yet allowed to meet and offer up their prayers to their God, and were they to be told that they were demagogues and conspirators because they had assembled to petition the Houses of Parliament for reform? The learned counsel had talked of a meeting of all the people of England assembling in one large plain; why, whoever heard of such a thing? Who had been mad enough to propose such an assemblage? It would indeed be a curious thing to see all the men, women and children of England assembled in one large plain. He should like to see what a pretty figure the learned counsel himself would cut amongst such an assembly. But could the learned counsel say that any of the defendants had advised such a wild plan? Why, then, mention it? The learned counsel had also spoken of those wild visionaries whom Hogarth had so well represented, who had cried out, 'Give us back our eleven days'. He did not know who those mad persons were; he supposed they belonged to some borough where the learned counsel himself had once cut a prominent figure – some of those mad drunken rioters whom he (Mr Scarlett) had once seen at Lewes. If Hogarth had lived in the latter time, he might have found ample matter for description in some of the scenes to which he alluded and which the learned counsel might remember. But when the learned counsel had talked of the crying out for the eleven days, he might have finished the climax and represented the defendants as calling out for their eleven days of sweet liberty which they had lost when they were confined in the prisons of the New Bailey. There, indeed, was some ground for calling out for eleven days of which they had been basely robbed.

But the learned counsel carried them to Smithfield, and here he would say a word upon another point. He would ask how it happened that the Attorney-General was not here in this most important trial? Was it that the defendant was a mere country bumpkin, and that anybody would have done against him? No: but the Attorney-General well knew that he (Mr Hunt) would have put him into the witnesses' box and have got from his own mouth that he had been consulted as to the legality of the meeting at Smithfield, and had stated it to be legal. He would have proved from his mouth that he was also consulted by the Reverend Mr Hay and his brother magistrates as to the meeting of the sixteenth, between the ninth and the sixteenth.

Mr Justice BAYLEY: That would not be evidence.

Mr HUNT: I would at least have tried the experiment, though your Lordship would probably stop me.

Mr Justice BAYLEY: I should have told the jury, if the Attorney-

# Fifth Day – Tuesday 21 March 1820.

General's opinion differed from mine, that they could not here receive that opinion as law.

Mr HUNT went on and complained that what had been stated against him in the opening speech had not been given in evidence, and he wished to remove every impression which what had fallen from the learned counsel in his opening might have made on the jury.

[He then continued:] It was attempted to connect the atrocities at White Moss with some of the parties concerned here; and for this the witness-of-all-work, Mr Chadwick, the man who, though a very material witness, never told this to the solicitor of the other side till a few days back. This was the man who wished to convey the impression that drilling was going on at White Moss at the dead hour of the night, though it was proved that the drilling was in daylight. The same was the case with respect to Murray's evidence, who on his cross-examination admitted it to have been only in the morning. Next came Haywood, whose evidence differed from that of Chadwick. Haywood remained for some time and he never heard the word 'fire', which Chadwick mentioned. When this was objected to by him (Mr Hunt), the learned counsel said he would prove that he (Mr Hunt) was closely and deeply connected with the White Moss transactions; and how was this done? By having it said that one of the men who drilled at White Moss afterwards led up a division (the Middleton division). But why did not the counsel ask whether it was Bamford who was at White Moss? This he (Mr Hunt) would show was the case. He would show that Bamford had led up the Middleton division; and, if a doubt remained on the minds of the jury, he would show that Bamford was in bed from ten on the night of Saturday until a late hour in the morning of Sunday. This would be proved by the evidence of Bamford's niece. But this witness-of-all-work would be proved to have said to some of his fellow workmen that he would swear against any one for pay.

Next came Haywood, who swore that he saw the people at Middleton go to Smedley Cottage – in order, of course, to connect Mr Hunt with what occurred at White Moss, because he (Mr Hunt) was at Smedley Cottage and the Middleton troop marched that way, and some of the Middleton troop were said to have been seen at White Moss; but why were not the men who were with Haywood called to support this testimony? Another link in this chain was that the crowd stopped before Murray's house and that they hissed; but was it proved, as asserted by Mr Scarlett in his opening speech, that he had caused the carriage to halt and gave the command to have hissings and hootings at Murray? No such thing; for one of the witnesses said the carriage was not in sight at the time, and Murray himself said he did not see the carriage.

**Henry Hunt**

# Hunt and Others.

**Henry Hunt**

Mr Justice BAYLEY: You mistake there, for Murray swore that the people in the carriage looked up.

[Mr HUNT continued.] He would bring a host of witnesses to prove every word of this to be false. He should be able to show that Murray's memory was bad on this and some other points – but if the people had shouted, was it not natural for those in the carriage to look up, when any hostility was manifested opposite Murray's house? It was not, however, proved that they had ordered it. Of Mr Murray, who swore this, the jury might judge by his testimony when they recollected how he answered to the questions which he had put to him. He (Murray) did not recollect that he had said he would rather be rowed in a boat to his own house in the blood of the Reformers than walk on the pavement. He would not, however, swear that he had not said so. He also denied, at first, his having said that if he had the command on 16 August, he would not have spared a single man. When, however, he recollected, that some of those who had heard him were present, conviction flashed on his mind; and he said he would not swear he had not said so. He could get witnesses to prove this, but it was not necessary when Murray himself would not swear he had not said so.

Then as to the shouting at the Star Inn, how was he connected with it? Did it appear that the magistrates were there at the time, or that he (Mr Hunt) had given orders to that effect? Of the Star Inn he had then known nothing, no more than he did the names of all the stars in Heaven. But this was only a part of the attempts made in the opening speech to damn his character, and he now challenged Mr Scarlett to examine his brief and see if any ground for those remarks was contained it it.

Mr Justice BAYLEY: That is a challenge which cannot be accepted here

Mr HUNT: I hope your Lordship will excuse the emotions which affect me. [Mr Hunt was at this moment in tears.] He hoped, if he did not conduct his case as he ought, he might be set right, and he would act under the direction of the learned judge, to whose opinion he would in every case bow with submission; but if he did not conduct himself in a proper manner, the jury, of course, would think of it in considering their verdict. Mr Hunt now, to show (as he observed) what unfounded statements had been made against him in the opening speech of the learned counsel, proceeded to read a part of the speech as given in a newspaper. The paper from which he should read it was The Times, and though there might be some little variations in some few places, yet The Times in this, as on all other occasions, had given the most accurate account. It stated that Mr Hunt had proceeded up the streets of Manchester surrounded by vast crowds, and at one part ordered them to halt, and which they did, and shouted, et cetera. This, he observed, was completely disproved by Dr

# Fifth Day – Tuesday 21 March 1820.

Smith and another who had not said a word about his giving directions to halt or addressed the people either opposite the Star Inn or any other place in the streets. With the evidence of Matthew Cowper he would not trouble the jury: they could judge of him by the account he had given of himself. He had defrauded his master of a sum of money fourteen years ago, and it was only within a few months that he had taken it into his head to return it. It was worthwhile to look at the description of witnesses who had been called on that day (Friday) in support of the present charge. One was Mr Matthew Cowper; the next was the mushroom sergeant, as he had called himself; and the third was an unfortunate man who had been some time confined as a lunatic. He did not object this great misfortune to the man; but it was strange that he, who had been deranged for such a time, should have been called upon when his wife was not called, who might have deposed to the same evidence; at least who was present at the time spoken of.

So then, they had this case supported by the testimony of a deserter, a lunatic, and a confessed thief. It was said, that he (Mr Hunt) had great information on these subjects: he had none but what was casually given. He had not the Treasury of England to support his case; but the things which came to his knowledge were quite notorious. The persons who saw those men in the yard sent him slips of paper, acquainting him with the facts which he elicited from the parties themselves in cross-examination. But let the jury look at the accounts given by Mr Cowper, the reporter for the *Courier* – a fit companion for the other witness, Mr Horton. These two worthies gave their accounts of what he had said on the hustings, but neither of them had said a word about his having pointed to the soldiers or constables when he said, 'If any person attempt to disturb the peace, put him down and keep him quiet'. It remained for Mr Roger Entwistle to prove this, and he had said that he (Mr Hunt) had said, pointing to the soldiers, 'There are your enemies: put them down, and when you have got them down, keep them down'. How was it that this important sentence should have escaped the attention of the other reporters who were present and who were also anxious to attend to catch at and even misrepresent all that was said?

He next came to the evidence of Platt, who had such acquaintance with the flimsies (forged notes) and who described himself as having nailed (convicted) all those persons against whom he had sworn. This Platt swore that Saxton had addressed the people – but he could not tell what he had said – and he also swore that Bamford was on the hustings, a circumstance which he (Mr Hunt) could disprove by the evidence of many witnesses, and show that at the time Bamford was in the crowd, many yards from them. Platt also swore that he saw Moorhouse on the hustings. This was most important evidence, and he begged to call the

# Hunt and Others.

**Henry Hunt**

attention of the jury to it, for it would be proved that Moorhouse was not on the hustings and that Platt himself knew that it was false at the time he swore it. Moorhouse had no more to do with this meeting than any of the gentlemen of the jury. He (Mr Hunt) did not mean to allow that any of those who had were therefore guilty – but it would be proved that Moorhouse had nothing to do with it. They might judge of this Platt by his evidence when that unfortunate transaction took place in court the other day [the shouting at a question put to Mr Hulton by Mr Hunt]. Platt was the man who came forward, and said he saw the accused man jumping up and down; and when Mr Scarlett mentioned clapping of hands, he said he saw that also; and then he added that a gentleman in the gallery could prove this; and who was that gentleman? Why, the famous Murray, a witness by trade. The jury would judge from this what sort of men those were to depend upon.

Then came the evidence of Horton, who reported for *The New Times*: The 'Mock' Times. He had said that Jones advised the people to be peaceable, and as the learned counsel said who addressed the jury for Jones (Mr Barrow), he was poor Jones indeed. The case of poor Jones was of such a nature that he fully agreed in the ridicule which that learned gentleman had thrown upon it. But, on this occasion, it fell to his lot not only to defend himself against the attacks made on him in the speech of the learned counsel opposite (Mr Scarlett), but he would also have to defend the whole case against the address of the counsel for Moorhouse (Mr Barrow). He would have to explain to the jury what that learned gentleman had taken great pains to mystify. He had, as was sometimes the practice with such counsel, taken a great deal of pains to mislead the jury.

[Mr Hunt was proceeding to comment on the speech of Mr Barrow when Mr Justice Bayley said that he had no right to act in that way. He might, if he pleased, impeach the testimony of any of the witnesses against the other defendants, but not comment on the speeches of their counsel.]

Mr Hunt submitted that if Mr Barrow had made such a defence for Moorhouse as would be prejudicial to him (Mr Hunt), he had a right to remark upon that defence as far as he was concerned. [He was then suffered to go on.] He observed that what Mr Barrow had said about the wager and the disputes between him (Mr Hunt) and the magistrates was not the case. There had been no such thing, and he would be able to establish it in evidence. In fact, when Mr Barrow read Moorhouse's own statement, it gave the lie to and completely denied the invention of the learned counsel.

He was accused of having been in Manchester nine days for the purpose,

# Fifth Day – Tuesday 21 March 1820.

as was intended to be inferred, of having a meeting on the sixteenth. It was said that he came to Manchester on the ninth; and it was added that he spoke of the proclamation of the magistrates and something about a notorious quorum and nine tailors. He had, it was true, commented on that document – the proclamation by the magistrates – which, certainly, was neither grammatical nor conveyed the meaning which it was intended to convey. He stated to the people that he was sorry the meeting had not taken place on 9 August, as he would have taken care that nothing improper should have been done there. He would prove that he said his business would not, he feared, allow him to remain in the neighbourhood over Monday to attend the meeting. What meeting? Was it one which he had called? – for this was the construction meant to be put upon it, that it was Mr Hunt's meeting. He held, however, a newspaper in his hand in which that same meeting was advertised to be held and that dated two days before the time of which he was then speaking. This notice was signed by not less than seven hundred householders of Manchester. He would prove by the evidence of his servant that he had given directions to him to be in readiness to leave that neighbourhood with him in the course of the week, and it was not till the Wednesday before the sixteenth that he told him he had been prevailed upon by his friends to remain over the Monday; and proud he was that he had so remained. Though he had been imprisoned eleven days, though he had been beaten and cruelly used, yet he would give up his very being rather than not have been present on 16 August. He would have forfeited everything rather than have been absent on that day, as he knew that it would have prevented any mischief which might have arisen if resistance were made to the cruel conduct which was practised towards the people; and he was glad that he was now present to plead the cause of those people. It was on the Wednesday he told his servant that he need not have the horse ready, and the whole of that week he remained at his friend Mr Johnson's without going two miles from it. He had had invitations from Middleton, Bury and other places to dine with several gentlemen, but he had not accepted any of them, and he now rejoiced that he had not, for he was now aware of the use which would have been made of it on the other side. The learned counsel would not have failed to torture such visits into his attending either training or some other illegal act.

Having heard in the course of the week that the magistrates had issued a warrant against him, he went on the Saturday to offer himself, if such were the case. He had been informed that it was their intention to arrest him on the hustings on the Monday, but, when he presented himself before the magistrates, he was told that they had nothing against him. It was never his practice to endeavour to fly from justice. He was once in

**Henry Hunt**

# Hunt and Others.

**Henry Hunt**

the occupation of three thousand acres of land, and if any magistrate in his neighbourhood had occasion for his presence, it was only to send him a note to that effect and he attended without delay. This was a proof that he was not afraid of his conduct, and it was a proof which he knew the jury would consider in his favour.

But how had he acted in consequence of having the meeting put off? He had, it was true, told the people to come to the meeting on the Monday, but how did he tell them to come? [Here Mr Hunt read part of the letter which was addressed to the people of Lancashire in the week before the meeting.] In it he told them to come armed with no other arms than those of a self-approving conscience, to conduct themselves in such a manner as to give their enemies no ground for opposition to them, and to do nothing which could in any degree tend to a breach of the peace. Those who were opposed to the people said that their leaders only wished to mislead them; but he invited the boroughreeve and constables to attend and, if they found that anything was wrong, to point out where it was so. That they should be heard fairly, and that if they were enabled to convince those who should be there that they were wrong in their views, they would yield to such conviction. Was this the advice which was calculated to lead the people astray? Was this conduct for which he and the other defendants were now to be accused and condemned? It was the advice he had given, and he had no regret on the occasion but for the deplorable consequences which had resulted from the conduct of others.

They had heard many respectable witnesses who said they felt alarmed; but one gentleman, the Reverend Dr Smith, did one of the most extraordinary things which could be done – he sent his scholars into the street on their way home at a time when several persons had said that the town was in danger. He would, however, bring men of equal respectability and property in Manchester – and men equally nervous, perhaps – who would prove that those alarms were unfounded.

He now came to the evidence of Jonathan Andrew, who said he saw the parties with large sticks, some of them four feet in length and shouldered like muskets – but this was not spoken to by any of the other witnesses. He, however, could bring witnesses to prove that, as far as these large sticks went, there was not a word of truth in evidence. The gentleman from *The New Times*, Mr Fitzpatrick, who had, like a second Judas, flattered to betray, and who had by appearing that day violated the principles of common honesty and committed the most wanton and unprincipled breach of confidence – what had he said? That he attended at many of the meetings where he (Mr Hunt) had presided; that he on all occasions had been peaceable at those meetings; and that, for aught he knew, the meetings had dispersed peaceably. But the testimony of the other witness from *The New Times*, who had given his evidence

# Fifth Day – Tuesday 21 March 1820.

so flippantly, he would disprove by the evidence of another reporter who was accidentally present and who had been present without any connection with the meeting or with him.

He would conclude by an observation about the locking of hands and the removal of the hustings. The locking of hands, where it did take place, was only done for the purpose of preventing the pressure of the crowd from oversetting the hustings. The hustings had, from the nature of their construction, at a former meeting been broken down, and, by a miracle almost, the people on them were saved from being hurt. The locking of arms was, then, only made to prevent the recurrence of a similar accident; but he would show that it had not taken place near that part where the constables were, and that from thence to the magistrate's house there was a free passage and that several persons had actually gone up and down by it. There was, besides, a place behind the hustings from which a passage might have been obtained without any difficulty.

[Mr Hunt proceeded to describe the peaceable and orderly conduct of the meeting at the time the yeomanry were sent, as, he observed, for the purpose of a bait to tempt the people to a breach of the peace.] The yeomanry, he observed, some of them drunk and absolutely cutting at both sides with their eyes shut, dashed amongst the crowd – among men, women, and children. Some of their horses had tumbled over the mangled heaps of those who had been trodden under feet, and they escaped with difficulty from being hurt; others endeavoured to jump over the heads of those who stood in their way, and all this time continued to attack those near them. At this time, however, there were neither brickbats nor sticks nor any other weapons thrown – nor was any resistance. made.

[He was proceeding when Mr Scarlett said that, as none of this could be offered in evidence, it ought not be stated to the jury.]

Mr Justice BAYLEY remarked that certainly the conduct of the yeomanry was not the question here, and could not be given in evidence; but the defendants might offer any evidence they possessed to show the conduct of the people in not resisting.

[Mr HUNT proceeded.] He hoped the jury would excuse this trespass on their attention; he would not, he assured them, state anything which he did not consider material to his case. It had been stated that Bamford was at the head of a party of two thousand men who were like a regular army in everything except not having uniform and arms (though he did not find that word in his notes) – and this was the army by whom it was feared that the town of Manchester would be destroyed. How were they calculated to destroy it? Where were any dark lanterns or any combustibles found? What became of the bundles of sticks and clubs which were said to have been taken from them? Where were the flags, the banners, the caps of liberty which the reporter from *The New Times*

**Henry Hunt**

## Hunt and Others.

**Henry Hunt**

described as revolutionary emblems? Where were the scythes in the shape of pikes, of which so many reports had been circulated? They had heard of caps of liberty, but let them look to the front of their hall, the pride of their county, and they would there see standing conspicuously a cap of liberty. Liberty was the boast of an Englishman, and its emblem was always held dear. It was the boast of every Englishman that he was free. He therefore respected everything which bore an emblem of his freedom. Why then should that which was approved by all in York be deemed a crime in Lancashire? If he understood the meaning of the cap of liberty, it was an emblem of a most sacred nature. In ancient Rome, if a slave had saved the life of a citizen or had performed a service to the state, he received as a reward his freedom, and, on his emancipation from slavery, he had a cap placed on his head as an emblem of his liberty. Our Saxon forefathers, when they emancipated a slave, they gave him perhaps a more appropriate emblem: they, on bestowing upon him his liberty, placed a sword by his side and a spear in his hand as the most proper appendages with which to protect and defend that blessing they had bestowed upon him. He knew that liberty was dear to every good man; it was dear to him. He had ever contended for it, and he would say, in the beautiful sentiment of the poet, 'He who contends for freedom can never be justly deemed his sovereign's foe'.[181] It was for freedom he had contended and he would ever continue to do so even at the risk of his life. He would always impress on his fellow countrymen the love of that rational liberty which had been the pride and the boast of their forefathers.

What was it which the reformers were accused of? What was it they asked for? Not for an equal distribution of property – no, but for an equal participation of rights – that was what they claimed, and they founded their claim on that great constitutional principle that no man should be taxed without his consent. He did not mean to say that each man should have a voice in the choice of a portion of those by whom the taxes were to be imposed. This was the opinion of the reformers. They might be wrong, but, if they were, let them be set right and let them be fairly convinced that their doctrines were erroneous. He had been accused of going about from place to place. He had done so, and in having done so he conceived he was doing right. He might be wrong, but his conduct was not criminal, as the law stood lately. The jury must have recollected that man who was once the representative for their county

---

181 James Thomson (1700-1748), *Edward and Eleonara*: 'He, who contends for freedom, / Can ne'er be justly deem'd his sovereign's foe: / No, 'tis the wretch that tempts him to subvert it, / The soothing slave, the traitor in the bosom, / Who best deserves that name; he is a worm / That eats out all the happiness of kingdoms.'

# Fifth Day – Tuesday 21 March 1820.

– he and others had gone about the country in the hope of being able to oppose the infamous traffic of the slave trade. They, too, might have been wrong, but their conduct was not criminal on that account. He had then advocated the common principle of the reformers – that before you could tax any man, before you could call upon him to enlist in your service, you ought to give him an equal share of political rights. If this opinion were wrong, he erred in it with Lord Raymond, with the Duke of Richmond, with Sir William Jones and other eminent men; and the Duke of Richmond, with such principles, instead of having been persecuted, was called to fill a most important situation: he was appointed Master General of the Ordnance.

Henry Hunt

Mr Justice BAYLEY said that this was not to the question.

[Mr HUNT continued.] He had only one or two observations more to make. When, in 1817, he had been called to attend those meetings, he had to present petitions from several of them – some to the Prince Regent, and others to both Houses of Parliament – but had they been kicked out and rejected as improper? It did not follow that because some rash and mad individuals had on one occasion created a riot before he came to the meeting, knowing that he (Mr Hunt) would not join in any such practice – it did not, he said, follow that this was to be attributed to the principles of the reformers. The unfortunate circumstances attending that occasion [Spa Fields, we suppose] had been attributed to him (Mr Hunt) and the death of one man laid to his charge, and by none more violently than by Dr Stoddart.[182]

Mr Justice BAYLEY: Dr Stoddart is not before this court.

Mr HUNT proceeded to show, from the speeches of Lord Sidmouth, Lord Harrowby and the Earl of Donoughmore on the Seditious Meetings Bill that at the time the Manchester meeting took place, all such meetings were considered legal; .and it was, he observed, on the ground of their being considered so that the bills were introduced, to declare they should not be so in future. The Earl of Donoughmore, in speaking of the arrest of Harrison at Smithfield, said it looked as if was intended to produce some mischief on which to ground their future measures; and the conduct of Mr Hulton in ordering the arrest of him (Mr Hunt) and others at the meeting at Manchester seemed to have been copied from this case of Harrison; for he (Mr Hulton) had said that the object was to arrest the ringleaders, as he called them, and not the poor deluded people. The learned gentleman (Mr Scarlett) would have to cross-examine some of those deluded people, and he would find them not that ignorant set of persons which he had supposed. He would find that they were not any

---

182 Editorial comment sic in transcript.

# Hunt and Others.

<sub>Henry Hunt</sub>

of those Hogarth's eleven days men, as he had called them. It appeared from the speech of Lord Harrowby on the bills to which he had just alluded that the assemblies of the people were not founded on the Bill of Rights, but on the common law and ancient practice of the constitution. It was to this point the jury should direct their intention. They should consider whether the people had acted under the sanction of the law which existed at that time.

Mr Hunt next alluded to a speech delivered on the subject of the Manchester meeting by Mr Warren, the Chief Justice of Chester, who, perhaps [continued Mr Hunt], is at this moment trying questions arising out of those transactions. In that speech Mr Warren, after a description of the meeting, observed that among other things there was a flag with the figure of a woman with a bloody dagger in her hand. Where was this banner now? What had become of it? The learned counsel, Mr Scarlett, had also talked of the bloody dagger, but had omitted the figure. He (Mr Hunt), however, believed that this bloody dagger, like the air-drawn dagger of Macbeth – 'Is that a dagger that I see before me?' – existed only in the fevered brains, the perverted imaginations, the vindictive feelings of the two learned counsel. Mr Scarlett had endeavoured to show the sanguinary temper of the meeting by mentioning a bloody dagger. This dagger was not proved to exist. Mr Hunt read the passage from Mr Scarlett's speech in *The Times* of Saturday last. What was his purpose in mentioning this? To connect them with assassination and with the Cato Street plot when he could not succeed in fixing the charge of blasphemy by making a connection with Carlile.

Mr Scarlett at the same time that he made this horrid allusion knew that his (Mr Hunt's) life was threatened by the Cato Street gang of wretches, with whose conduct he endeavoured to implicate him. Mr Hunt then complained of a paper handed about the city stating his connection with Thistlewood. These infamous calumnies had not been sold, but given away in thousands, even wrapped round parcels, to prejudice the minds of the jury.

Mr Justice BAYLEY here said that if such things were put into the hands of the jury, the parties might be punished.

Mr HUNT then went on to speak of the flags, though he said he did not well understand the law of flags; he explained why a black was used: he defended the use of the caps of liberty, and the inscriptions of the banners. The representation of Justice was even deprived of her sword that there might be no charge. She was left with her scales alone.

He concluded by expressing his regret at the imperfect manner in which he had been able to defend himself, and his entire confidence that the learned judge would supply any omissions. He called upon Mr

# Fifth Day – Tuesday 21 March 1820.

Scarlett, who would have the power of reply, to explain his allusion to the dagger. He was sure he should have a verdict of acquittal. He would produce evidence that could not be resisted. With regard to Mr Hulton --

[Here Mr Hunt paused, and Mr Justice Bayley deprecated any personalities.]

[Mr Hunt continued his speech]: -- he went over the heads of what he would prove, and called in conclusion upon Mr Scarlett to explain and reconcile if he could the contradictions of Hulton's testimony and produce the dagger – the bloody, bloody dagger.

*[The defendant here concluded his speech, which lasted from ten o'clock in the morning till a quarter before three in the afternoon. He appeared to be quite exhausted in body, but at the same time as collected in his mind as at the commencement. As he sat down there was great applause among the audience, which indecency the judge repressed in a dignified manner. It immediately ceased. The jury retired for a little at the suggestion of Mr Justice Bayley. On their return, and that of his Lordship, the evidence for the defence commenced. The following witnesses were then called.]*

[margin: Henry Hunt]

EDMUND GRUNDY, sworn and examined by Mr HUNT.

I am not in any business. I live at Pilsworth, near Bury, in Lancaster. I was a calico printer, but have retired from business. I have not made any depositions. On Tuesday 10 August, I was at Smedley Cottage. I saw you there. I recollect a conversation relative to the then-approaching meeting. You said you were returning home immediately. I endeavoured to prevail upon you to stop till the meeting of the sixteenth took place. You said you would consider of it. I think I left you then. Nothing positive was decided on at the time.

I left a printed letter for you on the next day (Wednesday). I next saw you on Saturday 14 August at Smedley Cottage. I recollect communicating to you that there was a report of a warrant being out against you, and you said it was so. In the course of the day, I waited on Mr Norris – the magistrate – in company with Johnson, the defendant. Mr Norris is, I understand, the chief acting magistrate. I told him if there was any charge against Mr Hunt, I would put in bail for any time which he chose to appoint. Mr Norris said there was no information or warrant against you, nor any intention of issuing one. I reside about seven miles and a half from Manchester; I was not in Manchester on 16 August.[183] I

[margin: Edmund Grundy]

183 At the time of the Peterloo Massacre, Grundy probably lived at Ringley – slightly closer to Manchester than Pilsworth. *Morning Chronicle*, 31 August 1819: 'Manchester, August 28: Hunt was bailed today about one o'clock. The bail are Edmund Grundy of Ringley,

# Hunt and Others.

**Edmund Grundy**

saw some persons going there, but not so many as is represented to have gone. I saw no persons armed. I have property in the neighbourhood, but nothing which occurred that day inspired me with any fears for its safety. I have several relatives and friends residing in Manchester. I saw nothing on that day which gave me any apprehensions for their safety.

*Cross-examined* by Mr SCARLETT.

I was not in court today before. I knew Mr Hunt about twelve months' since. I dined at the Spread Eagle in his company. I saw no one with Mr Hunt at Smedley Cottage on the tenth but Mr Howard, who went with me. I went to pay him a visit, but did not remain long. I only know from general report that he was there. I saw a letter posted up in the town. I was subsequently his bail.

**James Dyson**

JAMES DYSON, sworn and examined by Mr BAMFORD.

I am a weaver and reside at Middleton. I was on the Barrowfields on 16 August last, between nine and ten o'clock in the morning. There were six hundred or seven hundred people – both men, women and children.[184] I saw you there; you were walking about when first I saw you. I did not hear you say anything until you got upon a chair and addressed the people: you said, 'Friends and neighbours – those of you who wish to join in the procession will endeavour to conduct yourselves orderly and peaceably, so that you may go as comfortable as possible. If any person insult you or give you offence, take no notice of them. I make no doubt but there will be persons who will make it their business to go about in order to disturb the peace of the meeting. If you should meet with any such, endeavour to keep them as quiet as possible; if they strike you, don't strike them again, for it would serve as a pretext for dispersing the meeting. If the peace officers come to arrest me or any other person, offer them no resistance, but suffer them to take us quietly. And when you get there, endeavour to keep yourselves as select as possible, with your banners in your centre, so that if any of you should struggle or get away, you will know where to find each other by seeing your banners; and when the meeting is dissolved, keep close to your banners and leave the town as soon as possible, for if you should stay drinking or loitering in the streets, your enemies might take advantage of it; and if they could raise a disturbance, you would be taken to the New Bailey.' That is as much as I recollect; it is, to the best of my knowledge, the substance of what you said. I think I recollect something of your saying, 'I believe there will be no disturbance'.

and James Chapman of Manchester, fruiterer (formerly proprietor of the *Manchester Observer*).'

184 Sic in transcript.

# Fifth Day – Tuesday 21 March 1820.

I neither expected nor believed from the tenor of your address that any disturbance would ensue on the return of the party. I saw some few with sticks, but none with those who were not in the habit of using them. I thought to take a stick myself, having experienced the fatigue before, but I was prevented. I took one to Barrowfields and there I lent it to a man named John Barlow, who was also going to Manchester. The procession had not gone more than a quarter of a mile before he returned it to me again; and, this being observed, several cried out, 'No sticks shall go with us'. They said it had been agreed that no sticks should go. I said one stick could not make much difference, and they said I was as well able to go as they were and I must leave it behind, and so I sent it home with my father in law.

**James Dyson**

I went to Manchester with the procession. I saw nothing on the way but peace and good order. We walked four abreast. There was no disagreement on the way. Saw no insult offered to anyone; there were some jeering words used, but nothing worth notice; they were used to the bystanders who were looking on. We went in this order to St Peter's Field. You led the party up, and got upon the hustings yourself. This was before Mr Hunt's arrival; I saw him arrive. You were then standing near me, about forty yards from the hustings. You did not go upon the hustings afterwards, to my knowledge. When Mr Hunt arrived, I removed about fifteen yards from the hustings and I saw you no more that day. I did not see you upon the hustings after that period.

*Cross-examined* by Serjeant HULLOCK.

I can't tell where Bamford went after I left him. We were not joined by any party before we left the ground. The Rochdale people passed us, but we met and joined with them in the town. About half the meeting were men. I cannot exactly say how many persons joined in the procession – perhaps a thousand. Some persons had laurel. I had none. I know not whether those who wore laurel were officers; those who were in front wore it. There was no one in particular to give the word of command. I don't know that Bamford was commander-in-chief on that day. I was not a sergeant. There were men by the side to keep order, and when the step was lost it was recovered again by their calling out, 'Left, right'.

When we met the Rochdale party, they fell in behind us. I do not know how many persons were in the Rochdale procession. Perhaps there was not much difference between their numbers and ours. It was said to be agreed upon that no sticks should go.

We had two banners that day, one of which was left on St Peter's Field. Upon a green flag we had the words 'Parliaments Annual, Suffrage Universal'. Upon a blue one we had 'Liberty and Fraternity, Unity and

# Hunt and Others.

James Dyson

Strength'. We never had been mustered before, to my knowledge. On a Sunday morning, a few weeks before, a party of Middleton people marched down through the town, and I went by the side of them. After going through the town, they dispersed. It was said they had assembled on the Tandle Hill. It was after six o'clock when I met them. They were not all Middleton people. I might have remained near an hour on the hill, looking at what was going forward. There were several men drilling, as it is called. I never was drilled in my life. I marched to Manchester as others did. Bamford was not present on that day. There was two thousand or three thousand persons assembled. I think this was on the Sunday week before the meeting of the sixteenth; but I will not swear it. There were women and children present. The women were not drilling. I never saw a drilling party before.

The Rochdale party had banners, but I do not recollect the inscriptions upon them. We did not go from Middleton to St Peter's Field by the nearest road. I do not know the reason why we went round. We had music on that day; we had a drum – they do not use it in church music unless at oratorios. We have sacred music, sometimes, in church at Middleton; we also have bassoons and clarinets, et cetera, occasionally on Sundays. The bassoon, in our party, belonged to the man who played it; the drum belonged to a man who keeps a farm.

We left Middleton about ten o'clock. On arriving at St Peter's Field, I saw many flags and banners on the hustings; ours were taken to the hustings, but Mr Bamford ordered them back again. We joined the other parties on the ground – our line was broken, and every man went where he liked. I never heard Mr Hunt speak before that day. I was not at the meeting in January. I did not write down Mr Bamford's speech; I took it from memory; I suppose it has been in my head ever since I made a deposition to Mr Pearson, and I then saw it.

Mr Serjeant HULLOCK: How long is it since you saw your deposition? — How long? Why, you seem to want to know the time particularly. I saw it about the middle of the week before last, at Samuel Bamford's house. After the words, 'If they strike you, don't strike again,' were the words, 'for it would serve as a pretext for dispersing the meeting'.

Go on. — Must I go on?

Yes – you seem to have forgotten it. You had better begin again. — No, no; but you seem to hurry one on like. [Witness went on to repeat the speech, nearly in the same words as before; but not precisely in the same order as before.] I cannot exactly recollect the words Bamford put to me.

*Re-examined* by Mr BAMFORD.

I know Thomas Ogden, a musician; he did play in church, but I don't

# Fifth Day – Tuesday 21 March 1820.

*James Dyson*

know whether he does so at present. I know Thomas Fitton: he and Ogden played with our party.

[To questions by the judge.] My wife did not go with me on that day, but the wives of several of the party accompanied their husbands. There were several hundreds of women with our party and the Rochdale party; I saw many of them in Manchester: several boys also accompanied us; I saw several on the ground that I knew. I saw no Middleton women on St Peter's Field that I recollect. It appeared that the women did not wish to press so far into the crowd as I did. The women who accompanied us were relations of the men who marched in the procession. It is customary at our wakes and rush-carts in Lancashire to have banners and music. The rush-carts are held of a Saturday, and on the following Monday the men walk in procession, but they do not keep the step.

[Mr Justice BAYLEY asked an explanation of the term rush-carts. Mr Bamford said that it is an annual custom to have a cart on which rushes are neatly placed; this cart is drawn by young men decorated with ribbons and preceded by young women, music, et cetera.]

JOHN BARLOW, sworn and examined by Mr BAMFORD.

*John Barlow*

I am a weaver residing at Middleton; I am a married man. I recollect the people assembling in the Barrowfields on 16 August. You addressed them. You commenced by calling them 'friends and neighbours'. [The only difference between this witness and last, respecting Bamford's speech, was that the latter heard him (Bamford) exhort the people to proceed to Manchester as in the performance of a solemn duty.] I went to the meeting with you. I saw no one insulted by the way, nor on St Peter's Field. I saw you on the ground. When we got in the field you went upon the hustings, remained there about five minutes, and then came down again and stood not far from me, opening an avenue between the people. I saw Mr Hunt arrive – at that time you were not upon the hustings. You stood near me. You were not upon the hustings while Mr Hunt remained. I stood at about fifty yards from the hustings. The Middleton party had two banners.

*Cross-examined* by Mr Serjeant CROSS.

I have no knowledge of any committee. We did not meet the day before the meeting of the sixteenth. I had no connection with any meeting. I had nothing to do with the Oldham party before that day. I was once on the Tandle Hill – it was on the Sunday but one before the meeting. I went there between six and seven in the morning. There might be six hundred or eight hundred persons present, or perhaps more. They were what I call being in companies when I saw them, possibly about thirty in each

# Hunt and Others.

**John Barlow**

company. I do not know how many companies there were. I do not think there were a hundred companies – perhaps there might have been eighty. Those who passed me had companies. I heard the words 'march' and 'halt'. I waited until they were dismissed, which was about eight o'clock. Before that they were all in one line and stood two deep. I do not know who gave the command when they formed in line. I did not know any of the leaders. I do not know whether the man who gave the command was in our party to Manchester on the sixteenth.

I heard of drilling and I went to Tandle Hill out of curiosity. I rather doubted that there was any drilling before I saw it. They had no sticks. I have been in the local militia and have seen soldiers drilled. The drilling there was the same as marching and halting. I did not see much countermarching. I fell into the ranks at Middleton. I cannot say who the man was that formed the hollow square. I have never seen him since. When the word of command was given, I had no occasion to move.

I heard from rumour that there was to be a muster on the Barrowfields on the sixteenth. I live there. I saw Bamford before. I saw him mount the chair, and tell us how to conduct ourselves. I do not know that he assumed the command; those who were not commanders got laurel, as well as those who were. I got none. Those who went to the chair got some. We got no instructions from anyone but Bamford. The man by whom the square was formed did not mount the chair. I took no notice of him. I do not know who formed us into line again. I understood that we were to meet several other divisions at Manchester. I do not recollect Bamford's saying that if there was to be anything to do, it would be after we got back. He cautioned us against going into public houses. I did not take my wife with me.

I must have gone to Manchester on an errand, even had there been no procession on that day. We halted at Harbour Hay, and after that we did not halt till we got upon the ground. We joined those whom we found there, and remained stationary.

*Re-examined* by Mr BAMFORD.

Barrowfield is a public place. There were two hundred or three hundred women and children standing by as spectators on the morning of the sixteenth. There were many spectators on Tandle Hill. The training was quite public. There appeared to be no secrecy. As we came back from it, we came by the high road.

The people who were on the hill marched through Middleton. We proceeded a mile and a half at least on the public highway. It was between eight or nine in the morning. There were many women and children attending the party to Manchester on the sixteenth. I knew some of them

# Fifth Day – Tuesday 21 March 1820.

to be related to persons in the procession; it seemed to be a pleasure to them. I never before appeared in a court of justice to give evidence.

[To questions by the judge.] I did not see any of the women in Manchester, but I saw them near the town. I had no thoughts about taking my wife there; she had something to do at home. She did not express a wish to go.

John Barlow

WILLIAM KENDALL,[185] sworn and examined by Mr BAMFORD.

Before I quitted my house, I left my wife and child there with my son at home.[186] I saw nothing particular in the movements of the people except their passing to and fro. I saw no bludgeons among them, but a few old persons walking with common walking sticks. I saw them from an eminence from which I could watch them. They went on with a deal of women and children, and seemed very joyful. I saw no symptoms of alarm on the road. I am no reformer. I don't profess to be one of any political knowledge, though I am a member of the Loyal Orange.

William Kendall

*Cross-examined* by Mr LITTLEDALE.

I knew a good many of them; they were doing no harm at Middleton, and marched off regular. Women, some by the side of them and others after them, joined in the procession.

JAMES FRANKLAND, sworn and examined by Mr BAMFORD.

I reside in Middleton, and am a clogger and leather-cutter, and farm a little by keeping a few cows. I have eight children and a wife. I remember the people assembling in Middleton on 16 August and afterwards going on. I looked after them. They were on the way to Manchester. I heard the substance of what you said, which was that they would be conducted to Manchester in a body as they were, and, when they got to the place where the meeting was to be held, they would remain in a company by themselves, and not intermix with others, and return in a body also when this meeting was over without straggling in the multitude. You also recommended them not to mind any insult, nor be induced to resent it if offered. The people were all quite peaceable. I do not belong to any body of reformers, nor did I go to Manchester with the procession, though I had a son eighteen years of age who went. I knew of his going, and gave no orders to prevent him. I believe he marched in the procession and did

James Frankland

---

185 According to the *Evening Mail* (24 March 1820), a shopkeeper; according to the *Oxford University and City Herald* (25 March 1820), of Middleton. Surname also given as Kendal and Kenyon.

186 Sic in transcript.

# Hunt and Others.

**James Frankland**

not apprehend any danger or riot, or I should not have allowed him to go.

*Cross-examined* by Mr SCARLETT.

I know Mr Bamford for a great many years, but I did not know who was to take the command of the party. My son did not tell me he was to go. I saw him in the procession, and it was mentioned in the family he meant to go. There have been several public meetings of the Reformers in our neighbourhood, but my son is not one of them. I know nothing of private meetings. I don't know whether my son took either refreshment or money in his pockets for the march to Manchester.

JOHN TURNER, sworn and examined by Mr BAMFORD.

**John Turner**

A tailor and draper at Middleton. Recollected the procession there on the morning of 16 August, and its music and banners. He saw a number of women and children among them. I saw no large sticks, but a few old men carried their common walking sticks. I was no ways alarmed while they passed, as I had no occasion to be alarmed. I saw none drunk or riotous. I am not a reformer. I gave never a penny to the concern, nor ever did I see Mr Hunt in my life, unless I see him in this court, and yet I don't know him. I felt no alarm for Manchester by any means.

Mr Serjeant HULLOCK: Well, then, you have had the pleasure of seeing Mr Hunt by coming to York.

**Mary Lees**

MARY LEES said she resided at Middleton and had five children. Her husband was a plumber and glazier. Recollected the procession passing her house on 16 August. She was then standing with her children at the door and was afterwards assisting the mistress of the public house opposite in filling liquor for a great many who called as they passed. They all seemed quiet and cheerful. They paid for what they got. These people came from Rochdale with a great number of women, both young and old. I heard them drink several toasts, and among the rest 'God save the King' which, though not a common toast, is made use of by the country people. I saw many of the people return in the evening, while I was again called upon to assist at the public house. They many of them burst into tears, and others remained silent.

*Cross-examined* by Mr Serjeant HULLOCK.

'God save the King' was not a common toast. 'Hunt for ever!' was often heard; but she did not know whether this was good or bad.

[In answer to questions from the court, she said:] She saw Middleton women go with the procession and return back again in the evening. She did not know whether they were relatives of the men who went, but they

# Fifth Day – Tuesday 21 March 1820.

(the women) were persons of good character.

**Mary Lees**

ELIZABETH SHEPPARD, sworn and examined by Mr BAMFORD.

I live at Middleton. I am fifteen years of age, and am the daughter of a publican. I live with John Buckley now. I went to Manchester on 16 August. I went with Ellis Hulton, of my own age. I went in the ranks with women. There were many from Middleton. I walked before the men. I heard no singing. I saw Bamford's wife on the way. She went all the way. I saw at her Manchester on St Peter's Field. I was close to the hustings. Bamford's wife was about two yards off when I saw her. My mother did not know of my going.

**Elizabeth Sheppard**

*Cross-examined* by Mr Serjeant CROSS.

I know nothing about a meeting of female reformers that morning. Nobody desired me to go to Manchester: I went with the procession a little and a little farther till I came to Manchester: I marched with women. Bamford's wife was in the first rank, and myself in the second. I never heard anybody say all must go that can today.

MARY YATES, sworn and examined.

I have six children. I went to Manchester on 16 August: I walked before the men. There were a great many women. There were children – many of other people's, but none of mine. I saw Bamford's wife on the way. We walked arm-and-arm together. I recollect no songs. I saw Mrs Bamford at Manchester. We stood a considerable distance, twenty yards, behind the hustings. We remained on the ground between a quarter and half an hour before Mr Hunt came. Mrs Bamford retired before Mr Hunt arrived as she could not bear the pressure. I remained and heard Mr Hunt, but could not tell the words.

**Mary Yates**

Mr Hunt, when the soldiers were coming, took off his hat and desired the people to give them three cheers. I heard no hiss or groan at the soldiers. I joined in the cheers. I was not the least alarmed, and gave cheers myself, thinking they were to protect us. I saw no clubs or cudgels brandished at the soldiers. I thought they were coming as friends. There were many women in the crowd. I moved from my situation when the soldiers came. I saw no resistance to the soldiers from the first to the last. We all moved on the approach of the soldiers. I fell down among the people, and remained some time. My husband was on the field.

*Cross-examined* by Mr SCARLETT.

I thought the soldiers were come to calm the uneasiness that might arise by the presence of so many people. I heard the words, 'Give them

## Hunt and Others.

**Mary Yates**

three cheers!' The noise made was a shout of rejoicing; I huzza-ed as well as the rest. We were all very comfortable together. The women sometimes shouted as well as the men. We walked sometimes three abreast, and sometimes more. I would not have gone if I expected to see such a sight. Mrs Bamford went also. She was going when I came to her. I do not belong to any society of female reformers. If one should be made, very likely I shall be one. I don't know of any female reform society in Manchester.

[By THE COURT]: I would not have gone to the meeting if I thought there was any danger.

> *[This woman's evidence closed the business of the day, and at nearly seven o'clock the court adjourned till nine o'clock.]*

# Sixth Day – Wednesday 22 March 1820.

*[At nine o'clock, the judge and some of the parties entered the court. The jury was called over and one of them, an infirm elderly gentleman, not at first appearing to his name, the court delayed proceedings for him. He mentioned on his return that he had been exceedingly indisposed.]*

WILLIAM ELSON, sworn.

I reside at Chadderton. I am a farmer. I was at Middleton on 16 August; there was a great assembly of people there, many women and children among them. I saw no bludgeons, only walking sticks in the hands of the old people. Bamford addressed the meeting. I recollect what he said. He got up on a chair and advised the people, whatever was done on that day, to be peaceable, and not to molest any person upon the road nor at the place where the meeting was to be held. He was well aware that there would be bad persons among them and desired them to take care of them. If any person insult you, said he, show no resistance whatever; and if any person offered to come to take him or any of those who are called leaders, never let it disturb you. Let them take us, said Bamford, for what we have in view is a reform, and let us pursue it peaceably. Soon after that, he broke pieces of laurel and gave a number of men each a piece to hold in their hand, and charged them if they saw anything amiss among the people to order them to be peaceable. I went with the meeting accompanied by three children of mine, two boys and a girl. I did not join the procession except in narrow places where I could not keep out of it. My daughter is seventeen years of age, my sons fourteen and thirteen.

I went to Manchester and was on St Peter's Field. The procession was peaceable on the road, except a little altercation between two laurel-men. I lost my children in the crowd in St Peter's Field. I was not uneasy about them as I knew they were acquainted with Manchester. I had no fear till I saw the yeomanry coming. My reason for allowing the children to go was that they pressed the request both from their mother and me.

*Cross-examined* by Mr SCARLETT.

I was not afraid in the crowd – nobody was. I heard Bamford say, 'If anybody should take me, or anybody called leaders, do not interrupt them'. I do not know the leaders. I know not the committee. I do not know that Bamford was a leader. I did not hear Bamford press people to go, saying, 'The greater number, the better'. Bamford gave the laurel

# Hunt and Others.

**William Elson**

sprigs to ten or a dozen of people. I know not the purpose of the sprigs of laurel. The persons were in the square, and Bamford went early round to give the laurel. I have known Bamford many years. I know nothing of Bamford's being in a committee. I have heard Bamford read papers. I know he went to London two or three years ago. I was told it was for reform. I have heard Bamford read the *Manchester Observer* in his own house. I never practise reading newspapers. I have seen Knight but should not know him again by sight. I cannot say that I ever saw Knight at Middleton. I never saw him in Bamford's company. I attended a reform meeting some years back. I was not at the reform meeting of January last. I cannot say how long before the meeting I heard Bamford reading the *Manchester Observer*; nor do I remember that he read any advertisement calling the meeting.

[Examined by THE COURT.] I should not have allowed my children to go to the meeting had I apprehended any disturbance or riot; nor would I have gone myself had I entertained such a fear. There was nothing on the road that induced me to think there would be any disturbance; everything was peaceable and orderly. I had no other motive but curiosity in going to the meeting. I am a farmer, and have fourteen acres of land with four cows.

**Edmund Newton**

EDMUND NEWTON, sworn and examined by Mr BAMFORD.

I live at Mills Hill in the parish of Chadderton. I am a cotton-weaver. I was at Middleton on 16 August last. I went from home that morning about eight o'clock, in company with three other men. When I set out I had a stick with me; I did not take my stick with me to Middleton; I left it behind because one of the men said it was desired nobody should take any weapon of any description or any stick with them. Nobody did take any weapon. I heard of no intention of taking weapons. I took my stick merely to assist me on the road. I always take a stick when I go to Manchester.

*Cross-examined* by Mr Serjeant HULLOCK.

I do not know who desired sticks not to be taken. We had only three sticks when we set out, and as we had heard that it was desired we should not take them, we left them at a friend's house. I never was at a drill meeting, but I have seen people marching. I was never at Tandle Hill nor White Moss at a drilling. I saw people marching to town. I cannot tell when. I think there might be about twenty people. I was at five hundred yards' distance. It was about six o'clock in the evening, and nearly dark. I never saw drilling before and am not sure if this party was then drilling. I heard of the meeting of 16 August from report. I do not read

# Sixth Day – Wednesday 22 March 1820.

**Edmund Newton**

the *Manchester Observer* regularly. I was at the meeting when Mr Hunt was at Manchester before, and heard him make a speech. I did not stay dinner in Manchester.

[To a question, 'Do not you always dine?' witness replied:] We sometimes dine, and when we cannot get a dinner, we take twopennyworth of cheese and bread. I heard Mr Bamford speak at Middleton, exhorting the people to go peaceably and quietly. Both women and children accompanied the procession; my wife and children were not there. The sticks which we took with us and left by the way were common walking sticks.

[Examined by THE COURT.] I went to hear what was to be said, and with no other intention. I had no expectation that the people who went from Middleton would behave riotously or tumultuously. There was nothing in the deportment of the procession that could alarm the passengers on the road.

**Jacob Dakin**

JACOB DAKIN, sworn and examined by Mr BAMFORD.[187]

I reside at Middleton. I am a calico printer. I am in the employ of D. Burton and Sons, and have been for some years. I saw the procession of 16 August about halfway between Middleton and Manchester. I saw banners. I saw instruments of music. I saw women, children, old men and old women. I saw no sticks but walking sticks. The people seemed to be good-humoured and cheerful. They were very quiet.

*Cross-examined* by Mr Serjeant CROSS.

I did not go to Manchester with the procession. I never was at a meeting in my life.

Mr Serjeant CROSS: Do you remember a procession that paid Mr Burton's premises a visit? — Yes, I do. I remember that procession that made Mr Burton a visit; they were at first quiet, but they afterwards attacked the factory of Messrs Burton. There was firing from the factory. One of the houses belonging to one of the partners was burnt down.

[The learned judge said to Mr Serjeant Cross, who was going on with this examination, that he doubted whether it was evidence.

Mr BAMFORD said that as the learned gentleman had made the allusion to this transaction, he wished to re-examine the witness to show that reform was not then common, that this was a Luddite attack, and that Mr Burton was obliged then to guard his premises by an armed force. The examination of the witness accordingly continued.]

---

187  Surname also given as 'Deakin' and 'Daykin'.

# Hunt and Others.

**Jacob Dakin**

*Re-examined* by Mr BAMFORD.

These outrages happened more than four years ago; reform was not then so much talked of as now. He said this was in 1812. The premises were not now guarded, as they were then, by an armed force – nor had they been exposed to danger since. No works were stopped on 16 August. Instead of requiring an armed force (as then), there was only one constable in Middleton called James Lees, and whose wife had been called for the defence yesterday. There are no soldiers quartered in Middleton now.

**Lucy Morville**

LUCY MORVILLE, sworn and examined by Mr BAMFORD.

I am a widow woman residing at Middleton. I am thirty-nine years of age. [The witness appeared much older, and excited a smile at her declaration of age.] I was at Manchester on 16 August. I went in a company of twenty; I walked by the side of the procession. I have three children – a daughter married, and two boys that live with me. The two boys, one of nine and the other of twelve years of age, went to Manchester with the procession. I took the youngest boy by the hand, meeting him on the way, and went on with him. I met my eldest boy near Manchester, turning towards Smedley Cottage, and took him likewise by the hand, stopping with both till Mr Hunt came from the cottage. I then went to St Peter's Field, a nearer road than the procession, with my two boys. I did not go near the hustings, having my two boys with me. I stood beside a body of men formed in a line who refused to let me pass them. A man said when I attempted to pass, 'You cannot pass that way; the line is composed of sworn-in constables'. I stood there till Mr Hunt came on the ground. I saw a man in black clothes riding off from the body of the people. The constables smiled at this, and one of them said, 'I should wish the start to begin just now'.

[The learned judge here said he could not hear evidence as to what the constables did or said. The conduct of the meeting was only now in question, and not that of the constables except so far as it produced an effect upon the meeting. The learned judge then asked the witness if the special constable received any provocation from the meeting.]

Witness: No, not the least.

Mr Justice BAYLEY: Did you say anything when you heard the person speaking of the start? — Yes, I said nobody wished to create disturbance or kick up the start but themselves.

[Further examined by Mr BAMFORD.] I saw the yeomanry cavalry come on the ground, led by the man in black who rode off from the meeting. I then made the best of my way off with my children when they came on the ground. I thought then that there was danger. I saw

# Sixth Day – Wednesday 22 March 1820.

them passing on, but did not see them in the crowd. I saw no resistance offered.

<small>Lucy Morville</small>

JOHN HAMPSHIRE, sworn and examined by Mr HOLT.

<small>John Hampshire</small>

I live seventeen miles from the town of Manchester. I know Saxton; I saw him on 16 August. I called on him about twelve o'clock. I went to give him an order about printing some bills, and found him at home. I remained with him about an hour. I dined with him that day. I had only seen him once before. I left the house a little after one o'clock. I left it with Saxton. We went to the *Manchester Observer* office. Saxton had some situation in the Observer office. He was a reporter to that paper. I stayed a short time with him there and saw him preparing paper and pencils to write notes at a public meeting.

I went to the meeting. I went onwards, but the crowd pressed and I got sick rather. Some person, seeing this, said I had better get on the hustings, and I was handed up. I saw Saxton there on the hustings after I had mounted some minutes. I did not see him before Mr Hunt arrived. I saw him writing on the hustings. Saxton did not address the multitude in my hearing. I must have heard him had he spoken, as he was down in the cart body as a reporter. I stayed till the dispersion of the meeting.

[When the witness had been examined, Mr HUNT said:] I am going to call some witnesses in the regular order followed by the prosecution. As the learned counsel marched in the division, we must follow them, and trace their conduct.

John Hampshire, being recalled and examined by the court, said he saw no disposition in the crowd to resist the military. Mr Hunt neither made resistance nor encouraged the crowd to make resistance. I heard a military officer say, 'You, chairman – come down this moment'. Mr Hunt's reply was, 'Very well, sir,' and he got down off the hustings.

JOHN SMITH, sworn and examined by Mr HUNT.

<small>John Smith</small>

I am concerned in the *Liverpool Mercury*. I attended on 16 August to report to that paper. I have made no deposition before. [On this the witness was desired by Mr Hunt to proceed, and give a narrative of what he had observed. He did so for some time, but the greatest part of his evidence was drawn from him by the questions of the learned judge.]

Previous to twelve o'clock, he said I observed various bodies proceeding towards the meeting from different avenues. I was struck with the orderly manner in which they advanced and in which they gave way to carts, carriages, and passengers. I stood on the ground at St Peter's Field, and heard the conversation of different persons in the crowd as to the objects of the meeting. I expressed my supposition that

# Hunt and Others.

**John Smith**

those around me were all friendly to Parliamentary reform. They all said yes. I replied, 'Peaceably so, I hope'. They rejoined, 'Nothing but peace and freedom do we seek'. Between twelve and one, the meeting kept increasing considerably, and I heard a band of music playing what I thought, from the beat of the drum, to be the tune of 'God Save the King'. The beat of the drum in that tune is peculiar. I observed that the persons nearer the band than I was were uncovered at that moment, and I asked a person nearer the band if it was 'God Save the King', and was answered, 'Yes' – when I said, 'I am happy to hear it'.

I was stationed twenty-five yards from the left corner of the hustings, rather in advance. I considered the meeting as complete when Mr Hunt arrived, and thought it the finest sight I had ever seen, and was gratified with the good order of the whole. I heard Mr Hunt's speech: he congratulated the people that the effect of the postponement of the previously intended meeting was the increasing of the numbers of the present; he made some observations respecting a placard which had been exhibited, of which I do not distinctly recollect the bearing; he thanked them for proposing him as their chairman, and hoped every person would keep the strictest order. He added: if any person shall be seen attempting to disturb the peace, those who were near him must put him down and keep him quiet. In a short time, the cavalry arrived. I was astonished at the circumstance, as well as those around me; but the general feeling was that they came to preserve the peace: the people gave three cheers, which appeared to me to be in accordance with that feeling. The military returned the cheers. There was then a pause, and the cavalry, after this pause, advanced rather hastily towards the hustings. I saw no resistance: the cavalry advanced quicker than I could have supposed it possible through so dense a crowd. A general cry was raised around me – 'What is to be done?' – and the general answer to that question was that the cavalry must be bringing some magistrate to listen whether any seditious expressions were to be used. We were sure all would be quiet still. In no case whatever did I see any attempt to resist, nor any encouragement to resistance given by Mr Hunt or any other person either by word, look, or gesture. I saw no sticks lifted up against the military. I saw no brickbats or stones thrown till the close of the dispersion, when I saw one stone thrown. If any stones or brickbats had been thrown, or any sticks raised in defiance of the military, I must have seen it. My eyes and countenance were in a direction towards the military. Up to the moment of their reaching the hustings, I did not feel, nor did those around me express, any alarm till the military appeared. I saw the people on the hustings seized. No resistance was made by them. After clearing the hustings, the horsemen diverged round the hustings, and the crowd dispersed, shrieking and weeping.

# Sixth Day – Wednesday 22 March 1820.

[Examined again by Mr HUNT.] I am more than six feet high, and therefore was enabled to see all that took place. I saw a great many women and children in the field and spoke to several of them. They appeared many of them respectable and clean dressed, as if they came to a holiday feast. I saw many old people, a few at the head of each company; being on the field early, I saw nearly all the parties come up. The elderly persons had sticks – perhaps a dozen at the head of each company – I mean walking sticks. The marching parties had very rarely any sticks. I did not observe the party with the black flag. I think it was on the field when I arrived, but did not remark it particularly. I saw no particular party marching into the field with long thick sticks shouldered as muskets. This is quite new to me. It could not have escaped me. Had it occurred, I, as a reporter, must have noticed it. May I make one observation? I thought the few sticks at the head of the divisions were properly employed in keeping away the boys, who would otherwise have impeded the procession. I remained on the plain till the crowd was dispersed. I neither heard any offensive expressions uttered nor saw any acts of violence committed by the people from the time of their assembling to their complete dispersion: good humour was in every countenance. I saw no alarm in the respectable persons of the town who attended the meeting either expressed in their countenances or conduct. I thought many appeared to be inhabitants of Manchester from their dress and conversation. I arrived in Manchester the preceding night; and neither during the Sunday night preceding nor the Monday morning did I see any expression of alarm. I was on 'Change and in several other places, and I heard it was the general understanding that no interference would take place, and that all would go off quietly.[188] I saw not the slightest apprehension of danger. All seemed to act on the understanding that the authorities would not interfere.

Mr HUNT: Did you hear me say, when the soldiers appeared, pointing to them, 'There are your enemies; if they molest you, put them down, and, having got them down, keep them down?' — No. I conceive it impossible that anything of the kind could have been said. I must have heard it, if it had been said; and if I had heard it, I must have noticed it. The passage of Mr Hunt's speech about putting down disturbers

John Smith

---

188 Smith places himself at the Manchester Cotton Exchange. The expression 'on 'Change' is familiar – although it relates to London, rather than Manchester, and to financial commodities, rather than cotton – from Dickens's *A Christmas Carol* ('Marley was dead: to begin with. There is no doubt whatever about that. The register of his burial was signed by the clergyman, the clerk, the undertaker, and the chief mourner. Scrooge signed it: and Scrooge's name was good upon 'Change for anything he chose to put his hand to. Old Marley was dead as a door-nail.')

# Hunt and Others.

**John Smith**

was uttered before the military arrived on the field. I saw the cavalry arrive at the meeting. I did not hear the crowd hoot and hiss, nor see them brandish their cudgels. The feeling was of a different description. The cheering with which they were received was of the same kind as that with which Mr Hunt was received when he arrived. I joined in this compliment to the military, though I did not join in the previous cheer to Mr Hunt, whom I did not know at that time.

*Cross-examined* by Mr SCARLETT.

Witness: I meant the cheers as a compliment to the military.

Mr SCARLETT: Are you in the habit of complimenting the military? — Yes, when they deserve compliments.

Are you the J. Smith invited, in this requisition, to attend the meeting? [The learned counsel held in his hand, and read from, a *Manchester Observer*.] — I am.

Do you know any of the other parties invited along with you? — Yes, some.

Do you know Major Cartwright? — No.

Do you know Mr Wooler? — No. I did not know him then.

Do you know Mr Crompton? — Yes, I have the honour of his friendship.

[The learned counsel then asked the witness regarding other names which it is not material to mention.] I attended as connected with the paper to which I belong. I did not go on the hustings because, as I had been invited, I might have been expected to speak, which I had declined doing previously.

Mr SCARLETT: Are you in the habit of praising the military, that you joined so cordially in the shout? — I do not know to what you allude; I will praise them when they deserve it. I am not editor of the *Liverpool Mercury*. I am junior editor and have been concerned in it ten years. My sentiments are well known, I hope. I attended a meeting at Wigan, a considerable time before. It was in the summer of 1816. I spoke there in a debating room.

[The witness was here questioned about an inflammatory speech of Knight's at the Wigan meeting, reported in the same number of the *Manchester Observer* in which the requisition for the Manchester meeting appeared, but said that he had not seen that speech as he copied into his paper only paragraphs from the *Manchester Observer*, and frequently did not read it through. The passage was of an inflammatory nature, and need not here be repeated. The learned judge interfered and suggested it was not evidence unless the questions were intended to affect the credibility of the witness. Mr Scarlett then proceeded to examine the witness regarding Mr Hunt's observation about the placard, as showing

# Sixth Day – Wednesday 22 March 1820.

his disrespect for the magistrates.] I understood Mr Hunt alluded to a placard but I do not recollect what he said. It was not, certainly, to recommend the placard to the meeting, but I did not consider that he spoke against the magistrates. I could not help laughing at the placard myself as I saw it on the walls: it was so ungrammatical. I daresay Mr Hunt might have used the word 'enemies'; it is a term commonly used in a political sense, as 'political enemies', or 'enemies to the liberties of the country.' I most decidedly did not hear Mr Hunt say, 'There are your enemies: put them down,' et cetera. He, I daresay, did use the words, 'Put those down who disturb the meeting,' or words to this effect. I think nothing could be more criminal than to disturb the meeting. I would have collared any man near me if he had disturbed the meeting.

John Smith

I did say, when I saw them coming on the ground, 'I hope you are friends to parliamentary reform, and peaceably so'. I said this because I was confident they would be peaceable. I had heard the persons who had attended reform meetings described by the press as outrageous, and I was glad to find them so orderly here, for I never saw a more orderly meeting in my life.

I never knew of any training. I had heard of various things on this subject to which I did not attach much credit. I saw the people coming in regular order – not keeping the step, but in lines – which I considered very proper, in order to keep regularity. I should have felt confidence rather than alarm at an appearance of men walking in such order as to betoken previous concert, and particularly as on this occasion. I saw good humour beaming on every countenance. I have seen in Liverpool large bodies of men walking together in rank as public convenience dictates it, to prevent confusion. I swear solemnly that on the Exchange at Manchester that day I heard no one expression of alarm, but then I left it before eleven o'clock. I received no letter to attend the meeting, but in a letter addressed to Mr Thomas Smith, he was requested to bring himself and another.

*Re-examined* by Mr HUNT.

The Exchange at Manchester opens before breakfast hour and is much thronged between eight and eleven o'clock. When the cavalry came to the meeting I was looking towards you (Mr Hunt). I saw a placard posted up on the day of the meeting, cautioning the people to keep their children and servants at home. I cannot say whether it was to that Mr Hunt applied the words, 'Signed by some obscure individual, Jack Long or Tom Short'. I cannot say whether it had any other signature than that of the printer. I remember I saw, on Monday, one placard which cautioned the people to abstain from the meeting 'this day', though it was dated

# Hunt and Others.

**John Smith**

on Monday, and it struck me as singular. I did not conceive, certainly, that what Mr Hunt said was meant as disrespectful to the authority of the magistrates. I saw at the meeting several women, children and boys, and several of the women very decent and orderly. Indeed, I looked upon this as a sort of guarantee for the peaceable conduct of the men as to any heated expression, for I consider the presence of the ladies always chastens the company. I certainly do not think the appearance of those women merited the term of 'profligate Amazons'. I saw the woman on the dicky of the carriage in which Mr Hunt rode and I did not consider her to have deserved that appellation. I considered her as the wife or the daughter of some person in the carriage, who had consented to carry the flag in honour of the meeting.

**James Stott**

JAMES STOTT, sworn and examined by Mr HUNT.

I reside at Pendleton, near Manchester parish; I am a land-surveyor; I have some property in the neighbourhood. I saw some people going down our road – they were not parties, but were marching promiscuously. I saw nothing in the conduct of any of the parties that caused alarm in my mind. I went to the meeting – it was about one o'clock when I got on the field. I am a married man and have six children. I saw nothing to excite my fears for their safety. The people were standing promiscuously till Mr Hunt came. There was a great crowd consisting of men, women and children. I then saw nothing to excite my fears for the town or my family, either from the numbers or behaviour of those present. I waited until you (Hunt) arrived, and there was great cheering. I did not see persons there with large staves, four and a half feet long, shouldered as muskets. I saw no such thing. I was situated in the front of the hustings, looking towards the Windmill. I was about sixty to eighty yards distant from the hustings at the first. I got nearer afterwards, perhaps to within a dozen or fifteen yards. I did not hear distinctly what Mr Hunt said, so as to relate it. While I was there I did not hear the people make use of any violent expressions or commit any violent act. I saw a great many respectable-looking persons walking about and a great many decently-dressed females. Some of them were inhabitants of Manchester and some were not. I never heard any of them express any apprehensions for their personal safety or for the safety of the town.

I saw the yeomanry arrive on the field. On their arrival they were cheered. The cheering was as great as when Mr Hunt came on. I did not hear any groaning or hissing, nor see any brandishing of cudgels at the soldiers; I believe I should have observed anything of that kind if it had taken place. I saw no act of defiance to them. When the yeomanry first came in, I saw two of them galloping along. I never saw any resistance

# Sixth Day – Wednesday 22 March 1820.

made to them or any encouragement given to them to make resistance.

[Witness was going on when Mr Justice BAYLEY said, 'You must not tell us of any act done by the soldiers; you may say what was done by the people'.] My Lord, I was not going to speak to that. I saw, when the two men who had advanced could not get on, they fell back to their party. I saw no advantage taken of the two men who were separated from the rest. I heard several express their fears that the soldiers were going to attack the people, and many began to move off. The soldiers then cheered, and the people cheered the soldiers. I was then looking more towards the yeomanry than the stage. The people did not go away then. My impression was that the soldiers came to protect the people, and to keep the peace.

Soon after, the soldiers proceeded towards the hustings. They galloped towards it as well as they could. I saw them nearly arrive at the hustings. I saw no such thing as throwing brickbats, bludgeons or sticks. In their way, they cut at the people, and galloped on them. The people kept running away as fast as they could, and made no resistance whatever.

*Cross-examined* by Serjeant HULLOCK.

The hustings were about one hundred yards from Buxton's house. I never attended any meeting of the kind but this. I went to Liverpool to meet Mr Cobbett, intending to dine with him. I did dine with him, but did not carry an address to him; nor did I invite him to come to Manchester. This was in November last.

[Mr Hunt objected to this evidence, and Mr Justice Bayley allowed the objection.]

[By the court, at the request of Johnson.] I have often been in conversation with Johnson, and never heard him say anything disrespectful of the government.

JOHN HAMPSHIRE, recalled and examined by Mr HUNT.

I was on the hustings from the time Mr Hunt arrived until after he was arrested. I never heard anything to this effect from Mr Hunt: 'There are your enemies – put them down, and when you get them down, keep them down'. I was on the hustings. I saw the military arrive. They first stopped to form, and then charged towards the hustings. My whole attention was bent upon the military after the charge commenced. During their progress, I did not see the least resistance on the part of the people.

*Cross-examined* by Mr SCARLETT.

I did not see anybody carry any papers on the hustings. There were writing-papers like these [pointing to the books of the reporters]. I saw

James Stott

John Hampshire

# Hunt and Others.

| | |
|---|---|
| John Hampshire | no printed papers. |
| John Shuttleworth | JOHN SHUTTLEWORTH, sworn and examined by Mr HUNT. |

I am a merchant residing at Manchester. I recollect being at the Exchange about eleven o'clock on 16 August. I witnessed several parties pass the Exchange to go to St Peter's Field. They were marching with considerable regularity, in the form of a procession, and conducted themselves in an extremely orderly and decorous manner.

I observed that several of the parties had banners or flags with inscriptions upon them. Many of the inscriptions merely stated the district from which the parties to which they were attached came. Some of the inscriptions had reference to questions of political interest. My attention was directed to the Lees, Saddleworth and Mossley division. In a consequence of the black flag, my attention was particularly directed to that party. I conceived they conducted themselves in a strictly orderly manner. I cannot speak as to the number of sticks in that party, but I can speak as to the average of sticks in the whole body. In consequence of the observations which had been made as to the number of sticks carried at previous meetings at Manchester, I determined to count as accurately as I could the proportion on this occasion. I did so in several hundreds; until, indeed, I thought I had a fair average; and the result left no doubt on my mind that there was not one stick to ten persons. I speak only of those, however, who were walking in procession. Those who were walking on the sides did not come under my notice. The sticks were walking sticks such as are usually carried by country persons. I certainly did not perceive men with large staves, four and a half feet long and shouldered as soldiers shoulder their muskets. If any persons had been conducting themselves in such a manner with such weapons, I think I must have observed them. It is, however, necessary to state, that there was a crowd round the black flag, and the parties there I could not so distinctly see as the remainder of the procession. Certainly nothing objectionable took place in my presence. There were several gentlemen standing where I was at the same time, and were equally favourably situated for observation. I did not hear a single expression indicating alarm or fear in that quarter. The only objection that was made to any part of the procession was applied to the black flag. I was at St Peter's Field a little before twelve. I assuredly did not see anything in the conduct or manner of the parties assembled on that occasion so as to excite alarm for the safety of the town.

Mr HUNT: Was there anything in their conduct, manner or language that could fairly excite alarm in any rational mind? — Nothing, according to my construction of the tendency of such circumstances. On arriving at

# Sixth Day – Wednesday 22 March 1820.

**John Shuttleworth**

St Peter's Field, I passed through the line of constables which extended from the house in which were the magistrates, and took my station about thirty or thirty-five yards from Buxton's house, on the elevated ground at the top of Windmill Street. This situation was at an angle, but by no means halfway from Buxton's house. I was about eight yards from the hustings. I saw several parties at a distance.

Mr HUNT: Did anything you saw of these parties excite your fear for the safety of the town of Manchester? — No. I was upon an elevated situation and could command a view of the whole area. When the different parties arrived, they were received with cheers and congratulations by the others. It appeared to me that those who came to the ground in procession had a way made for them to the hustings. I remained till past one o'clock, when it was understood that you [to Mr Hunt] and those who were with you were coming. I then took my station behind the hustings, about fifteen yards from them. When you arrived, you were loudly cheered; the cheers were loud, and of long continuance.

I could hear what you said. When you were called to the chair, you called to order and made some remarks on the necessity of keeping silence, in order that those at the extremity of the meeting might have as favourable an opportunity as possible for persons in their situation. You still exhorted them to be peaceable, when some trifling disturbance took place in the rear of the hustings; and that was the only part of the meeting from which any noise proceeded. Mr Hunt appeared to me to turn round, and he stated that they must conduct themselves with the greatest order and propriety; yet he did not wish to compromise the right of every Englishman to interfere to prevent disturbance, and if parties in that direction would persist in attempting to breed a riot (these were his words), he trusted they would put them down and keep them down – and he turned towards the place from which the noise came. Where I stood was a large posse of special constables, many of whom seemed anxious to hear Mr Hunt; and when this appeal of Mr Hunt's succeeded in occasioning tranquillity, many of them exclaimed, 'Well done, Hunt; that's right'.

Immediately after, some companies of a foot regiment marched round the corner of Cooper Street into Dickinson Street and faced there, fronting the meeting. This occasioned some disorder in that part of the meeting which was in sight of the station they took. Mr Hunt, observing the disorder, said something about its being a trick and desired the people to give three cheers. This was complied with.

Mr HUNT: Did I at this time, pointing to the soldiers, say, 'There are your enemies; put them down, and keep them down?' — Assuredly not. On the contrary, I had my doubts whether any person on the hustings could see Dickinson Street. It seemed to me that your object was only to

# Hunt and Others.

**John Shuttleworth**

restore tranquillity, and it had that effect. There was a very considerable body of constables near this place. I stood near the Windmill public house. It appeared to me quite practicable to have communicated with the hustings from that part. There was some little change of situation among the people who were stationed in that part, but it did not appear to me anything that could cut off the communication.

Mr HUNT: Then it did not appear to you that a dense body, a phalanx of reformers, ten or fifteen deep, surrounded the hustings? — In the rear of the hustings, certainly, there was not. I saw the yeomanry cavalry arrive near Buxton's house. Up to that time I had seen nothing in the meeting or elsewhere that day to excite my fears for the safety of the town. I had not seen any respectable persons that day, at this time, who expressed such fears. To the best of my recollection, you [to Mr Hunt] desired the cavalry to be received with cheers, and they were so.

Mr HUNT: Did the people, instead of complying with my request, assail the cavalry with groanings, hissing and hooting? — I heard nothing of the kind. If they had done it near where I was, I must have heard it. The people turned round, but I saw no brandishing of cudgels. I saw no act of insult or violence offered to the military on that occasion.

Mr HUNT: What followed this? — While the people were cheering, I moved from where I stood to a few yards from the left flank of the yeomanry, and while I was doing this the yeomanry shouted and flourished their swords in the air. This seemed to excite considerable agitation and there was a confused noise for a few moments, and many of the special constables reaching from Buxton's house towards the hustings fell back along with the people near them, so as (it appeared to me) to leave an open space of about fifty yards. When this was done, the cavalry proceeded at a quick pace towards the hustings and, when they came to the space comparatively open, those in front appeared to gallop. Their progress seemed to be checked by the dense crowd, and this appeared to me to cause in them considerable confusion. I did not observe any of them separated from the rest. They appeared in one circular mass. The people did nothing to resist them. I saw them go on the hustings. I saw not a stone, brickbat or bludgeon hurled at them. As soon as they got up to the husting, I left the ground.

*Cross-examined* by Mr Serjeant CROSS.

I never knew Mr Hunt before. I occasionally saw the *Manchester Observer*. I do not take it in. I did not know of Mr Hunt's having been at a meeting in London. I heard of his having been at a meeting at Spa Fields. This did not make me afraid that he should preside at Manchester. I do not know whether that was the reason for his having been invited to

# Sixth Day – Wednesday 22 March 1820.

Manchester.  **John Shuttleworth**

The meeting was the largest I ever saw. There were several persons in Manchester capable of presiding at a meeting. I have no acquaintance with the parties who arranged former meetings of this kind at Manchester. The only meetings I am connected with or attend to are those at the Exchange, the parish meetings, or at the police office. I was not at the former meeting in Manchester, nor had I anything to do with it. I saw Mr J. Smith, the editor of the *Liverpool Mercury*, at the Exchange on the sixteenth, and shook hands with him. It certainly was a subject of congratulation among the many parties there that the meeting was not to be interfered with. A rumour had prevailed on Saturday and Sunday that there would be no interference, or most certainly I should not have gone to it. I had heard of drillings in the neighbourhood before this and I was not afraid, because I understood those drillings took place only for the purpose of proceeding to the meeting with more regularity. I had never seen such a notice as this posted up: 'that the people should take the advice of Mr Cobbett and keep a memorandum book, and note down every act of oppression and violence against them that they might be remembered at a future day'

[Mr Hunt objected to this, but the counsel for the prosecution contended that it was necessary in order to show what ground of fear and alarm had existed on the sixteenth. His Lordship held that it ought to be admitted, not as connecting it with the prisoners, but to show what impression it might have made on the mind of witness.]

I was [witness continued] not aware of any circumstances before the meeting which excited my fears for the safety of the town. I apprehend that whatever fears were excited were made in consequence of the threats of violence on the part of those who were known to be connected with the magistrates; and also the notorious fact that the swords of the cavalry were sharpened shortly before this. It appeared to me that all the fears of others were excited lest the magistrates should interfere with and disturb the meeting. I had heard of no confederacies or combinations of radical reformers. I do not know what you mean by combinations and confederacies. The only association I knew of was the Reform Union. I heard of no associations that excited alarm. There were no manifest symptoms of alarm amongst my neighbours.

I saw the people marching to the town. They appeared very much pleased. I am not aware of any persons being alarmed. I was not aware that there had been a meeting at the police office of what you call 'the respectable inhabitants' until some days subsequently. I counted the sticks so as to satisfy my own mind. Less than every tenth man, I think, carried a stick. The walk of those whom I saw pass the Exchange was

# Hunt and Others.

**John Shuttleworth** a lounging, sauntering walk. This description applied to all except the Rochdale division. The magistrates, I understand, were at the house of Mr Buxton. I was not there. I am a member of the Manchester committee for the relief of the sufferers on 16 August.

As the bodies came up from the country, they assembled round the hustings. Speaking from recollection, I do not think Mr Hunt, in addressing the people, used the word 'enemies'.

*Re-examined* by Mr HUNT.

I am a member of the committee for the relief of those who were wounded and injured by the forcible dispersion of the people on the sixteenth. I was actuated, in becoming a member of that committee, by feelings of humanity; for I cautiously abstained from all political interference. It was clear from what I saw and the information I received in conversation that an immense amount of human suffering was occasioned by the dispersion of the meeting; and therefore, from feelings of humanity, in order to alleviate that suffering, I became a member of the committee.

Mr Hunt here put a question relative to the cause which gave rise to the drillings previous to 16 August

Mr Justice Bayley would not allow the question as it went, like several other of the questions put by the defendant, to injure his cause.

Mr Hunt persisted in the question.

Mr Justice BAYLEY: I wish, Mr Scarlett, that you could change places with me.

Mr HUNT: God forbid, my Lord!

[Re-examination continued.] Witness understood that the people practised marching for a short time before the meeting in order that they might be able to preserve order in proceeding to and returning from it. I saw nothing whatsoever in the conduct of the people to excite alarm or terror. I heard that a great body of people had assembled at a former meeting at Manchester at which you presided. The proceedings were then regular and peaceable, and the assembly dispersed quietly. I heard of no violence or tumult having taken place on that occasion.

I well remember a meeting convened by the boroughreeve and constables of Manchester a few years ago to consider of an address to the Prince Regent. I believe it was a meeting of the people of Manchester and of the adjoining districts. I was present at it. The meeting was broken up somewhat suddenly, and rioting and breaking of windows took place. The windows of the Exchange were broken. I don't believe the people marched in regularly, but I have no doubt that individuals came in from the country. At that meeting I think there were at least fifty thousand

# Sixth Day – Wednesday 22 March 1820.

persons. The meeting was called by public advertisement, by the municipal authorities.

**John Shuttleworth**

There was a very large procession in Manchester on proclaiming the peace. I joined the procession. I do not know that Mr F. Philips was present, but it is probable he was. Many of the labouring classes joined the procession. We walked three or four abreast. The shop windows in St Anne's Square, in Market Street and along the whole line of the procession were shut. There were far more windows shut on the day when peace was proclaimed than on 16 August. There were many women and children in St Peter's Field.

JOHN TYAS, sworn and examined by Mr HUNT.

**John Tyas**

I am a reporter to *The Times* newspaper. I attended at Manchester in August last in consequence of a public-meeting that was to be held there. I arrived at Manchester on Friday before the time appointed for the first meeting, which was fixed for the ninth. I remained until after the meeting of the sixteenth. I met you for the first time (except casually at public meetings) in a room at the New Bailey. I only sent up one report to London; another gentleman came down to Manchester and relieved me. I recollect sending an article relative to something that occurred at the police office previously to the sixteenth. It was entitled, 'Another Bounce of the Orator's'.

I had heard much conversation about the meeting of the sixteenth. I went to the ground about eight o'clock. I was on the alert, the paper to which I belonged always giving the most voluminous accounts of things of this kind. There were very few people on the ground when I arrived. I have given in no deposition on this subject; neither have I been examined by your solicitor. I refused to be examined by anyone. I saw the people marching in St Peter's Field. They came with flags, banners and music, and walked as the electors of York did the other day after the election, with something of a military step. If I had not heard of this trial, I should not have considered that there was the slightest difference between the march of the one party and of the other.

I have the notes which I took on the spot, and those which I afterwards wrote down in the New Bailey prison. About half past eleven, the first body of reformers arrived on the ground with two banners each, surmounted by a cap of liberty. They marched into the centre of the field and, from what I observed, a cart was brought to them, but I am not sure. It might have been there before. I saw other parties arrive. They behaved very peaceably and orderly. I did not see them take up their position in a military manner. I am in the habit of attending public meetings, and I saw nothing in the proceeding of the reformers different from what I had

# Hunt and Others.

**John Tyas**

seen on various other occasions. The first party of course, as was always the case, procured the best situation. Perhaps the conduct of the people was more regular than what had observed at other popular meetings. I recollect the black flag coming into the field. It belonged to the Mossley and Saddleworth Union. I remember, when the parties approached the hustings: 'God Save the King' and 'Rule, Britannia!' were played. I did not see the parties take up any particular position. The divisions all went towards the hustings. Most of the people in the divisions had sticks, but they were merely walking sticks. I did not observe any person marching up in military array, as it was called, shouldering staves four feet and a half long and as thick as a man's wrist. I was induced to remark that circumstance particularly because I saw it stated in the *Courier*, prior to 9 August, that the people who escorted you into Manchester were armed with staves that might be converted into pike-handles. If, therefore, such a circumstance occurred, it would have attracted my attention.

I saw no act committed by any of the parties which excited the slightest apprehension in my mind for the safety of the town. Their conduct was quite the reverse of riotous or disorderly. I had several conversations with different persons belonging to the reform party who said they only wished a restoration of their rights, and, above everything else, were desirous to preserve order and tranquillity. I felt it my duty as a reporter to a public newspaper to relate all I saw and to endeavour to ascertain the truth of the reports I had heard. I saw nothing in the conduct of these people that was violent or irregular. There were a great number of women and children present. Many of them marched in ranks, like the men. I saw two female parties, in particular, who came in at the head of divisions. They appeared to be dressed in their best clothes on the occasion. If I, in my capacity of reporter, had perceived anything calculated to excite alarm or apprehension, I should, as an Englishman, have thought it my duty to inform the proper authorities. Before Mr Hunt arrived, I saw a crowd round a waggon, and a young man addressing the people.

As I was very ill, and unable to make my way through the crowd, which was dense, I determined to meet you. I met you at the Exchange. The people were huzza-ing. I requested that you would get me a place on the hustings as a reporter, which you promised to do, telling me to keep close to the carriage. You said you would have given me a place in it if it had not been full. I saw no attempt to conceal any part of the proceedings. I took hold of the carriage door and went on with it. I did not see you, when the carriage arrived opposite the Star Inn, stand up in it and order the people to hiss and hoot. The carriage did stop there, but I think that was occasioned by the people not getting on before. You might have got up in the carriage, but you gave no orders to hiss or hoot. There were, however, hissing and hooting at the Star Inn, and

# Sixth Day – Wednesday 22 March 1820.

afterwards opposite to the police office. I did not see you take any part in it. There was a stoppage near the police office and Mr Moorhouse, who was on the other side of the way, in the crowd, was hailed by you and accommodated with a seat in the coach. When the coach arrived on the field, the bands struck up 'See the Conquering Hero Comes', and the people formed in two lines to let the coach pass. You were received with loud cheering, and appeared to 'bear your blushing honours' meekly.[189]

John Tyas

I recollect your getting on the waggon. There was a black flag at the further corner of the waggon from the house in which the magistrates met, and you said, 'It is very foolish', or words to that effect. I recollect your complaining that the hustings were so erected that you had to speak against the wind. After you got on the hustings, I ascended with many other persons. I did not know them. Several females also got on the hustings through the barouche. They did not come in the barouche, but I believe were handed through it to the hustings in consequence of the great pressure. I saw several banners in the middle of the crowd and many women amongst the multitude. The crowd was more dense and jammed together than any I ever observed before or since. The first circumstance that took place after you arrived was the election of a chairman, and Mr Johnson proposed you. The crowd was rendered dense, I believe, from the anxiety to get near the hustings. There was nothing of a military appearance in the crowd. I could not perceive from the waggon, though immediately over the people, that their arms were locked. I saw nothing to keep them from the hustings. I heard you complain of the pressure of the crowd who were constantly pressing against the waggon, lest the hustings should be overturned. The people were close up to the hustings, all the way round. There was no vacant space around, preserved by a body of people with their arms locked. It was impossible for a vacant space of five or six yards round the hustings to have escaped my attention. I remark at all public meetings that people near the hustings take their hats off, and I did not observe it more particularly at this meeting than any other.

[Mr Tyas here read his notes of the proceedings which took place after he arrived on the hustings, commencing with the election of Mr Hunt as chairman and terminating with his capture, which have already been published.]

When Mr Hunt came to that part of his speech where he spoke of 'Jack Short and Tom Long' as having signed a paper cautioning the people from attending, the yeomanry appeared, and considerable alarm was manifested at the extremity of the crowd. The cavalry advanced, as far as

---

189  *Henry VIII*, Act 3 Scene 2.

# Hunt and Others.

**John Tyas**

I could judge, at a quick trot, and formed near Mr Buxton's house, where the magistrates were. I do not know when they drew their swords, but I perceived by their flourishing that they were drawn. Mr Hunt, as I collect from my notes, ordered the people to give three cheers, which they did. My opinion was that the cheers were given for the purpose of showing the military that they were not-daunted by their unwelcome presence.

The cavalry advanced and Mr Hunt told the people it was a mere trick to disturb them, but he trusted they would all stand firm. He scarcely had said these words when the Manchester yeomanry rode into the mob, who opened for them in the most peaceable manner. The cavalry directed their course to the hustings, and, when they arrived there, took a number of individuals into custody. I recollect an officer went up to you with his sword in his hand and desired you to surrender. You said you would not surrender to a military officer, but if any peace officer came up, you would surrender. No peace officer had presented himself to the hustings before that. Nadin then came, as it appeared to me, from under the waggon. He said he had information on oath against you. You immediately surrendered, after first desiring the people to be quiet.

I saw no resistance made by the people to the yeomanry as they advanced towards the hustings. The people got out of their way as fast as they could. My eyes were directed to their progress from the time they left Mr Buxton's till they reached the hustings. I saw no stones, brickbats and bludgeons hurled at them as they advanced to the hustings. I cannot speak of your turning pale or manifesting alarm because your back was towards me. You certainly incited no one to resistance. If brickbats, stones, cudgels and bludgeons had been hurled in the air in any great quantity, I must have seen them. I saw no such thing.

I don't recollect having seen any foot soldiers from the hustings before the yeomanry appeared. If there were any soldiers present and you had pointed at them and said, 'There are your enemies: if they molest you, put them down and, having put them down, keep them down,' I must have heard you. Nothing of the sort occurred. I can say positively that nothing of the kind happened. When the yeomanry appeared, you desired the people to cheer, and they did. Those cheers were of the same kind as were given when you first ascended the hustings, but perhaps louder. The multitude did not hiss, hoot or groan at them. I only heard cheering – which would prevent hisses from being distinguished. If there had been groaning, hissing and hooting at the extremity of the crowd, the cheering of those round the hustings would prevent me from hearing it.

I saw no sticks flourished by the people as the cavalry approached. Had they been flourished, I must have seen it. I was looking towards the magistrates' house. I saw the special constables using their staves.

# Sixth Day – Wednesday 22 March 1820.

They beat the people with them, and of course raised them in the air. That was after the yeomanry had arrived at the hustings; the constables were then in the rear of the yeomanry. I do not know that the constables were beating those who escaped from the yeomanry. They were striking those around them. If there had been a general resistance on the part of the people when the yeomanry came up, I must have seen it. There was no such thing.

*Examined* by Mr BARROW.

I am son of the late Mr Tyas, an eminent Proctor in the City of London. It was a little after one when I saw Mr Moorhouse in the street. He was hailed by Mr Hunt. Mr Johnson and Mr Hunt went on the hustings together. I do not know whether or not Moorhouse got on the hustings. I did not see any person at work on the hustings.

*Cross-examined* by Mr SCARLETT.

As the cavalry advanced towards the hustings, the people made way for them as fast as they could. The constables were behind the cavalry and were striking persons between the cavalry and them. From the time the cavalry arrived until Mr Hunt was taken occupied about five or six minutes. I was taken into custody. I meant to have followed Mr Hunt to the New Bailey, as he was the great source of attraction – but, seeing the yeomanry strike several persons, I looked out for a constable, and placed myself under his protection. I was, however, apprehended.

I took a note of several of the inscriptions on the banners. [Here the witness spoke of the several inscriptions on the flags, as they have already been stated.] There were two bands of female reformers. The ladies from Royton had a flag with the extraordinary inscription, 'Let us die like men, and not be sold like slaves'. There were many caps of liberty, and the inscription generally was, 'Hunt and Liberty'. Mr Hunt told me at the Exchange that there was no room in the carriage for me, but room was found for Moorhouse. Carlile, whom I have since seen in London, was in the carriage; I believe Knight was also in it. I don't recollect any hissing after we left the avenue leading to the police office. I recollect every symptom of popular disapprobation being manifested as the crowd passed the Star Inn and the police office. The magistrates had their headquarters at the Star Inn. I am not sufficiently acquainted with the streets of Manchester to know whether the procession advanced to the hustings by the most direct road. The people appeared to me to go up to the hustings and place themselves promiscuously round it.

I think, when Mr Johnson and Mr Hunt told the people to cheer, the cheer was greater than that which was given to Mr Hunt. I think the

John Tyas

# Hunt and Others.

**John Tyas**

cheer seemed to intimate, 'We have met for a fixed purpose to petition for reform, and your presence shall not prevent us'. In one sense, it was a cheer of defiance, but not in another. I do not think it was meant to intimate that they would resist the yeomanry, but that they had met to do what they conceived to be their duty without transgressing the law, and they would not be intimidated. In this latter sense, it might be considered a cheer of defiance.

I think there were about eighty thousand persons present, but it was a very difficult point to decide on. As the divisions advanced, most of those who composed them had walking sticks, I did not observe them carry the sticks on their shoulders – they used them for walking. I arrived in Manchester on the sixth. I saw Mr Hunt on the ninth, coming down the street called Piccadilly and by the Exchange, but I did not hear him make his speech. I knew nothing of the meeting but by public advertisement – nothing of the plans or arrangements of their committee.

*Re-examined* by Mr HUNT.

The report I sent to *The Times* appeared in that paper, except that some parts (which were stale, owing to the delay) were struck out, and that some remarks (in which I reflected strongly on the conduct of the yeomanry) were softened down. I saw no such thing as a bloody dagger at the meeting. When the military appeared, there certainly did seem a disposition in some part of the crowd to run away. The cheer ordered by Mr Hunt was recommended by him [Hunt] to restore confidence to those who were running away. I heard Mr Hunt say to some persons on the hustings, 'We will give them three cheers to re-assure them', or to that effect; but this was not said publicly to the people. There was not, as far as I could discover, any resistance whatsoever offered to the yeomanry. It did not strike me that the people wished to close in on the military for the purpose of cutting them off; but when the military had passed, the people were pressed in and, to prevent the pressure made in giving way, rushed back to their former places. This was, as I suppose, not a voluntary rush, but a rush occasioned by the pressure. The people at the outskirts continued going away when the yeomanry came, but I did not observe the general flight until the yeomanry began to cut the flags and banners.

On Mr Hunt's arrest, the people were flying in every direction. I was struck at myself twice on the hustings, and I was not resisting. I never heard you [to Mr Hunt] desire or urge the people to resist, but, on the contrary, you desired the people not to resist. A part of the crowd might have hissed without my having heard them. I heard none. I should think, from their very peaceable conduct, that there was none.

# Sixth Day – Wednesday 22 March 1820.

**John Tyas**

[By THE COURT.] When I passed by the Star, I did not see either Mr Hunt or Mr Johnson do anything which could have produced the hissing. I don't recollect that they did anything to put a stop to it. Nothing was said or done by either of them to encourage or produce hissing at the police officers, nor did I see them do anything to prevent it. The hissing was general as far as I could observe. It was of no very long duration. Mr Hunt had desired the people to observe tranquillity at several times. I think the carriage of Mr Hunt was stopped without any direction. It was frequently stopped by the crowd not getting on. They [Hunt and Johnson] certainly gave no orders to have the carriage stopped at the places mentioned. The address of Mr Hunt – not to resist – was to the people at large. The words were, 'By all means do not resist'. In short, he was perpetually addressing them on this point, and very earnestly. He desired them at various times not to resist. He said, 'If they want me, let me go.' This was before the military had got to the hustings. Words to this effect he repeated several times.

[By Mr JOHNSON.] I think I did see you put your hand to the people to restrain them from hissing at the police, but I cannot swear to it.

*[At the conclusion of this examination, the court adjourned.]*

# Seventh Day – Thursday 23 March 1820.

*The moment the court was opened this morning, both the galleries and the body of the court were crowded to excess. At nine o'clock, Mr Justice Bayley entered the court.*

*Mr Hunt – having, with the other defendants, taken his seat at the table – proceeded to call witnesses.*

*The first person called was John Earnshaw, a member of the Society of Friends. Mr Hunt submitted that he had a right to examine this witness upon his affirmation as to what he had seen on 16 August.*

*Mr Justice Bayley said that Quakers were, by the 7th and 8th William III, chapter 34, precluded from giving evidence in criminal prosecutions otherwise than upon oath.[190] The learned judge cited several cases where the evidence of Quakers had been refused. He mentioned also an instance where a rule for a criminal information had been discharged on the ground of its having been obtained upon the affirmation of a Quaker.*

*Mr Hunt said that he would not press the point against his Lordship's opinion, particularly as he had other witnesses to prove the same facts. He then proceeded to call other witnesses.*

JOHN BRETTARGH, sworn and examined by Mr HUNT.

John Brettargh

I am a wharfinger and reside at Pendleton, near Manchester. On 16 August, I was in company with Mr Earnshaw and Mr Bancroft (two members of the Society of Friends) in a room overlooking the meeting. I went to Manchester on that day to collect money; business was going on as usual. I went up to the New Cross, where a great crowd of people was assembled. There were no shops shut up then; business was going on as usual at New Cross. This was about ten o'clock. There were great crowds there; they were forming into line. I conversed with several persons on the subject of the meeting, but no one expressed any alarm for the safety of the town. I felt no alarm myself; if I had, I should have stopped my teams. I had two teams at work on that day, and they carted as great a quantity of coals as on any other day.

I suppose the people formed into line for the purpose of getting through the streets with more ease. I saw several parties come into town;

---

190 The Quakers Act (1695) – the seventh and eighth year of the reign of William and Mary – forbade Quakers 'to give Evidence in any Criminal Causes or serve on any Juries or beare any Office or Place of Profitt in the Government'.

# Hunt and Others.

**John Brettargh**

there were many women and children with them. The women were tidily dressed, apparently in their holiday clothes. I saw one party headed by several females walking in procession. At Shudehill I saw the Bury party; they also had numbers of women and children with them. I saw the black flag borne by the Lees and Saddleworth party. They had not large bludgeons or cudgels in their hands – they had some common walking sticks. If they had staves four or five feet long and as thick as my wrist, shouldered like muskets, I most assuredly must have seen them; but I did not see any such thing. The Bury party were walking quietly along when I saw them. I saw no ill conduct or acts of violence committed by any of them.

I went to the meeting about twelve o'clock in order to witness the proceedings. I was on the second floor of a house about thirty yards from the hustings. I had a complete view of the hustings and of the whole field. I went to the room by the invitation of Mr Bancroft, who had taken it in order to see the meeting. I saw several of the parties arrive. I saw nothing in their appearance different from those I have already mentioned. They had flags and bands of music. I heard 'God Save the King' and 'Rule, Britannia!' played. They were received with loud approbation. It did not strike me as a disloyal meeting. I saw no symptoms of disloyalty amongst them.

I don't belong to any of the unions for reform. I observed, when they were all assembled, that it was the grandest sight I ever saw in my life, and so I think yet. I saw a double line of constables directly under me. Many of them were persons whom I knew to be special constables. I saw no acts of violence or any insult offered to them. I saw Nadin come down the line and go up again towards Buxton's before you came. There was no insult or violence offered to him.

I saw you arrive; you were received with cheers. The people took off their hats when they cheered. When 'God Save the King' was played, all the people that I supposed belonged to the meeting took off their hats; but the constables did not take off their hats.

Mr HUNT: That is a curious fact, my Lord.

Witness [continuing]: I heard part of what you said when you got upon the hustings, but not distinctly. I was between the hustings and the magistrates' house. After you addressed the people, there was some disturbance behind the hustings. You turned round and, extending your hand, said, 'If anyone create any disturbance, put him down and keep him down'. This appeared to be addressed to someone belonging to the hustings. I did not hear you say, pointing to the military, 'There are your enemies: if they molest you, put them down and keep them down'. It was impossible, as the soldiers had not arrived at the time.

# Seventh Day – Thursday 23 March 1820.

**John Brettargh**

I saw the military come up at the corner of Dickinson Street. This caused some confusion, and the people in the outskirts began to run. You cheered in order to keep them together, and the effect of it was that the people stood still again. Then the cavalry came in and formed opposite the house where, as I since understood, the magistrates were. They put themselves in line, and cheered. I saw nothing done by any of the crowd to resist them. I never took my eyes off the cavalry till they got round the hustings. They advanced at either a canter or a gallop; they came as fast as they could. There were not any stones or bricks thrown at them, nor any sticks thrown at or lifted up against them. I could see all that passed as well as I can see this court now.

*Cross-examined* by Mr SCARLETT.

I have lived in Pendleton thirty-four years. I lived in London about nine years since. I have men to go with my carts. I shook a handkerchief out of the window when Mr Hunt arrived. I joined in the shout. I cannot say whether there was any difference between the shout given when Mr Hunt arrived and that given on the arrival of the cavalry. I have heard people say there were 150,000 persons present.

I gave a pound note towards Mr Hunt's election for Preston before I left Manchester. This was the only subscription in which I joined.[191]

*Re-examined* by Mr HUNT.

I never saw you before you arrived in the carriage.

**Henry Andrews**

HENRY ANDREWS, sworn and examined by Mr HUNT.

I have been your servant seven years. I have been at many meetings. I accompanied you to the three meetings at Spa Fields, London, to the public meetings at Bristol, Bath, the county meetings in Wells, Wiltshire and Salisbury, and the public meetings at Westminster. I have heard that you are a freeman of Bristol. I know that you have property in Bath; you have houses, a large yard, and out-premises there. You are Lord of the Manor of Glastonbury in Somersetshire and have a farm there. I perambulated the bounds there for you. You also have farms in Wiltshire and Hampshire. I know you are a Liveryman of London. When you attended the Westminster meeting, you resided there. I accompanied you to the Manchester meeting, as well as to all the others which you have attended. I never saw any riot or breach of the peace committed by

---

191   Parliament had been dissolved on 29 February 1820, and a general election was ongoing. Hunt was running on a reform ticket in Preston, but he did not win the seat, finishing fourth.

## Hunt and Others.

Henry Andrews

any of the persons composing those meetings. The meeting on Brandon Hill, Bristol, was surrounded by horse-soldiers. The people and yourself cheered them, both in going to and coming from the meeting. This did not appear to give any offence to the soldiers. I recollect meeting some of the Horse Guards on our return from one of the Spa Fields meetings; they were cheered. There was also some hissing. You did not hiss. You rose in the gig and told the people not to hiss the soldiers, but to cheer them; this was done, and the soldiers passed quietly on. We met a second party of soldiers, and the same thing occurred. There were no lives lost. I was with you at the second Spa Fields meeting. There had been a riot before we arrived. We arrived at Spa Fields about twelve o'clock. The rioters were gone then.

I accompanied you to Bullock Smithy in August last. When you heard that the meeting was put off, you said you would return. You went to Stockport, and the next morning you went to Manchester. I walked before the gig. In Manchester you addressed the people. You said you must return, and the people said, 'No, no, wait to the sixteenth'. I recollect this as I wanted to go back myself. I left a wife and family behind me; besides, I had lost my linen in the way down. We returned to Mr Johnson's.

Next day, you came into the stable and said you would remain till the sixteenth. I remember your speaking about your political horse, Bob. Bob is now dead and buried at Preston. I saw his grave. It was said that he was poisoned at Lancaster Assizes. I know you have had large farms at Enford, where you were born. You were always called the poor man's friend.

Mr HUNT: My Lord, I call this witness to character.

Mr SCARLETT: This is reversing the thing. It was usual to call the master to the character of the servant.

HENRY ANDREWS [continuing]: I never heard you urge any meeting to acts of violence. You were called the poor man's friend, as you said that if a poor man worked hard all the week, he ought to have enough to support a family. You were generally visited by Squire Wigmore and Mr Hutchins, the clergyman of the parish. I never saw you or any of your company intoxicated in my life. My fellow-servant (a female) has lived upwards of six years with you.

*Cross-examined* by Mr Serjeant HULLOCK.

My fellow-servant is not here to give my master a character; he can say as much for me as I have said for him. I do not know my master has any property at Manchester. I remember hearing that Mr Beckwith's shop was broken open and some guns stolen on the day of one of the Spa

# Seventh Day – Thursday 23 March 1820.

Fields meetings; I heard a man was shot in the shop. This was before he went to the meeting. Mr Hunt was chairman at that meeting. I did not see Watson there; I cannot say that I knew him at the time. I never saw Thistlewood and Dr Watson in company with Mr Hunt.

**Henry Andrews**

I knew no other person at the meeting but Mr Hunt. I did not accompany Mr Hunt to London after his liberation from Lancaster gaol. I was not at the dinner given after his entry into town. We came to Mr Moorhouse's house from Bullock Smithy. My master remained all night. I cannot say that Knight was there when we went. I first saw Knight at Smedley Cottage. I do not know Mr Carlile. I can't say whether he was at Smedley Cottage or not. I was not with Mr Hunt when his action against Dr Stoddart was expected to come on at Guildhall, London. I was in the country, at Middleton Cottage.

I was never at Blackheath with my master. I have heard of his having been a brewer at Bristol. I believe Mr Hunt is a lodger when in London. When he lodged in Norfolk Street, Strand, he had three rooms and a kitchen. I have not been in town with him lately.

Whilst we remained at Manchester we were at Johnson's house. I knew that Mr Grundy called on Mr Hunt because I held his horse. I saw Mr Hunt and Mr Johnson go in a carriage to the meeting on 16 August. I believe Knight also was in the carriage. There was a fourth person, but I do not know who he was. I never saw him before or since. My master breakfasted with Mr Johnson that morning. I do not know whose carriage it was. Mr Johnson does not keep a barouche.

*Re-examined* by Mr HUNT.

I never in my life sat down with you to dinner. I never professed to meddle with politics. I have enough to do in minding my business.

Mr HUNT: No, it is quite enough that the master should be a politician.

[To questions by the judge.] When my master said that a poor man who worked from Monday morning to Saturday night ought to get enough to support his family, I did not understand him to insinuate that people so working did not get enough.

EDWARD BAINES, JUN., sworn and examined by Mr HUNT.

**Edward Baines**

I have not made any depositions. I am connected with the *Leeds Mercury*. I have not read any newspaper containing the evidence given on this trial. I have cautiously abstained from doing so.

I attended the meeting on 16 August for the purpose of giving a report of the business. I was upon the hustings that day. I arrived on the field at twelve o'clock. I saw the different parties come up in ranks, arm in arm; they were received as they advanced to the hustings, each with three

# Hunt and Others.

**Edward Baines**

times three cheers. They did not take up their stations in a very regular manner; they all got as close to the hustings as they could. Nothing particular struck me but that they came in bodies; some attended with music and banners. I do not recollect any of the tunes played.

I took particular notice of their sticks; my attention was, from previous information, particularly drawn to this point. I saw nothing in their hands but common walking sticks; many had them, but I cannot say the proportion. I did not notice a greater proportion of sticks than is usual among country people at races, or on other such occasions. I saw no long staves shouldered like muskets, nor anything resembling them. I looked at all the parties as they came on the ground but I saw no such thing. If such a circumstance as this occurred, I, attending as a reporter, must, I think, have noticed it.

I advanced to the hustings (or cart) about half past twelve and remained in that situation till one o'clock, when another cart arrived with boards. When the hustings were formed, I mounted them. There was no removal after the first erection of the hustings. One or two young men from the hustings frequently recommended order as the parties arrived, and the order was observed as perfectly as, under such circumstances, it could be. About one o'clock a subscription was raised to get those who came from a distance some ale, but they afterwards resolved to have nothing but water, and a can of water was sent for.

About one, you arrived, followed by a very large procession. On mounting the hustings you appeared out of temper at the situation in which they were placed. Among those who came upon the hustings were a number of girls, dressed uniformly in white. They appeared on an average to be about twenty-two or twenty-three years of age: I think there were twelve or fourteen in number. I think the reason of their being on the hustings was to avoid the pressure of the crowd, which was very great at the time. One or two women had fainted from the pressure. An attempt was now made by those nearest the hustings to push themselves back, in order to avoid pressing against them: they partially succeeded. To the best of my knowledge, while Mr Hunt was speaking, the crowd was close to the hustings. After a few minutes you began your speech. I took notes of that speech in shorthand; I had some difficulty in doing so. [Here witness produced his notes, and also a copy of what he had written from them.]

The speech commenced thus: 'Friends and fellow countrymen, I must beg your indulgence for a short time, and beg that you will keep silence. I hope you will exercise the all-powerful right of the people in an orderly manner.' [Here witness said that the words 'orderly manner' were not in his notes.]. I wrote it a few hours after from memory; that was usual with reporters.

# Seventh Day – Thursday 23 March 1820.

[He proceeded to read:] 'And any man that wants to breed a disturbance, let him be instantly put down. For the honour you have done me by inviting me to preside at your meeting, I return you my thanks, and all I have to beg of you is that you will indulge me with your patient attention. It is impossible that, with the most patient attention, we shall be able to make ourselves heard by the whole of this immense assembly. It is useless for me to attempt to relate to you the proceedings of the last week or ten days in this town and neighbourhood; you well know them, and the cause of the meeting appointed for last Monday being prevented. It is therefore useless for me to say one word on that subject – only to observe that those who put us down and prevented us from meeting on Monday last by their malignant exertions have produced a twofold number today. It will be perceived, that in calling this new meeting, our enemies, who flattered themselves they had gained a victory, have sustained a greater defeat. There have been two or three placards posted up last week with the names of one or two insignificant individuals attached to them – one Tom Long or Jack Short, a printer --'

**Edward Baines**

At that moment, I observed the cavalry come on the ground at a rapid pace, from the direction of St Peter's Church. They were in considerable disorder. They had not then come into the crowd. They drew up in front of Mr Buxton's house, the foremost of them being opposite to it.

I have omitted one circumstance which occurred before the cavalry arrived. Mr Hunt stopped in the middle of his speech – for what reason I do not know – and directed the people to give three cheers; he turned round and said to those near him, 'There is some disturbance in the outskirts. 'Tis only to rally them, that is all.' As the cavalry approached Mr Buxton's house, Mr Hunt said, 'You see they are in disorder. This is a trick.' The cavalry, after halting about three minutes, brandished their swords and advanced. I saw no attempt made to resist them, nor did I hear any encouragement given to do so. My eyes were directed towards the cavalry till they began to advance to the hustings. When they had got about ten yards into the crowd, I turned away. I saw no stones or brickbats thrown, nor any sticks lifted up against them. I should think the hustings were sixty or seventy yards from Mr Buxton's house. When the cavalry were within about thirty yards of the hustings, I turned away.

In about half a minute they arrived at the hustings. Mr Hunt, stretching out his arm, cried, 'Be firm!' His face was then in the direction of the cavalry. The words were addressed to the whole crowd. No application had been made, to my knowledge, for the cavalry to pass through. I had no knowledge of the purpose for which the cavalry advanced, nor have I any reason to suppose Mr Hunt had. There was a large body of special constables near the cavalry, but they remained stationary. I saw no constables accompanying the cavalry.

## Hunt and Others.

**Edward Baines**

I heard nothing from Mr Hunt after the words, 'Be firm,' but the words, 'Give three cheers'. These words were repeated, as were the words, 'Be firm'. I think the last direction to give three cheers was when the cavalry first arrived. I left the hustings when the cavalry had advanced about ten yards into the crowd. I got off at the back of the hustings and went through the people to the distance of about four yards, in the opposite direction from Mr Buxton's house. By that time I saw a trumpeter on a piebald horse wheeling his horse to the back of the hustings; the crowd, as if by one impulse, moved back. I was carried about thirty yards back; I then got upon a cart, and looked towards the hustings. I saw no resistance made to the military.

Mr HUNT: Did you not see something done by the cavalry which, according to your impression, was calculated to cause resistance on the part of the people?

Mr Scarlett objected to this question.

Mr Justice BAYLEY: I can't allow the witness to answer that question, and for this reason: because the jury would be trying the question from prejudice, and not from the evidence. I have thought much upon it and I am of opinion that the question ought not to be asked.

Mr HUNT: My Lord, I think I have a right to show the nature of the attack made upon the people.

Mr Justice BAYLEY: I am of a different opinion. I have taken a note of your observations, and you shall have all the benefit arising from it.

EDWARD BAINES, jun. [continuing]: When I got off the hustings, I met with no impediment but from the density of the crowd. The trumpeter was about two yards from the hustings and an equal distance from me when I saw him. He was between me and the hustings. He had been enabled to come round through the crowd. In that quarter (the back part and side), there was no locking of arms near the hustings. I cannot say how they were at a distance. I did not see a cordon of locked arms eight or ten deep round the hustings. I did not see any people locked arm in arm. I think it was not possible to see whether any persons had their arms locked at a distance of four yards. I can't say whether or not they were locked arm in arm close in front of the hustings.

I saw the whole of the people form round the hustings as they came up. I perceived no difference between the manner of their forming and that usual at other meetings. I have attended public meetings at Leeds, York and elsewhere. I did not hear anyone direct the people to lock arm in arm in order to keep the cavalry from coming amongst them. It was not possible to see from Mr Buxton's house whether the people were locked arm in arm or not. I saw nothing warlike in the meeting. The people had not the appearance of disciplined troops ready to protect Hunt or to fight

# Seventh Day – Thursday 23 March 1820.

for him, as occasion offered. I saw no infantry. My impression was that the cheers were cheers of conscious innocence, confidently relying on the protection of the laws.

**Edward Baines**

You did not point to the soldiery and say to the people, 'Your enemies are among you; if they attempt to no molest you, get them down and keep them down'. I stood near you and I think I must have heard the words, had you used them. I heard nothing like those words. I did not hear you say, when the cavalry arrived, 'They are only a few soldiers, very few, and we are a host against them'. If any such words were used, I must have heard them. When you bid the people be firm, you used no gesture or action or other expression to induce them to resist. My impression was, that you merely wished the people to stand, and to prevent danger from their running away.

Mr Scarlett objected to any questions respecting witness's impressions of what was said.

Mr Justice Bayley said the witness had a right to give his impressions of what he had seen and heard.

Mr HUNT: My Lord, I--

Mr Justice BAYLEY: Mr Hunt, I have decided in your favour.

Mr HUNT: My Lord, I shall waive the question with respect to this and all other witnesses, and perhaps it will be for your Lordship's convenience, provided Mr Scarlett will consent to expunge from the evidence the impressions of Messrs Green, Hardman, et cetera.

Mr SCARLETT: That is different. Those are impressions with respect to the meeting.

[To questions by the Judge.] When the words, 'Be firm' were used, the people stood perfectly still. I saw no sticks lifted up or stones thrown. The people did not put themselves in any posture, either of offence or defence. All eyes were bent on the cavalry. It was very possible for those nearest the cavalry either to have rushed upon them or struck them. It did not appear that the words used by Mr Hunt were for the purpose of inducing the people to put themselves in a posture of offence or defence.

By Mr HUNT: When you used the words, 'Be firm', you stretched out your arms, with your hands open and the palms down.

*Cross-examined* by Mr SCARLETT.

I do not know whether Mr Hunt had his hat on or not. I only saw the left hand. I do not know what he had in his right hand. I was induced to notice the sticks from having heard that the radical reformers came to their meetings armed with clubs and cudgels. I have no recollection of having seen a letter of Mr Hunt to the people of Manchester inviting them to come to the meeting armed with no other weapon than a self-

# Hunt and Others.

**Edward Baines**

approving conscience.

[To questions by Mr Barrow.] I did not see Jones on the hustings.

[To questions by Dr Healey.] I saw you on the hustings; you desired the people to be quiet.

[To questions by the judge.] I took notice of the places from which the parties came, as they were mentioned on the banners.

**Thomas Schofield**

THOMAS SCHOFIELD, sworn and examined by Mr HUNT.

I reside at Shelderslow, near Manchester. I was at Lees on 16 August. I saw about forty or fifty men assemble on that morning; they had nothing in their hands more than common walking sticks used in the country. I went to Oldham that morning. I saw a large assembly of people on Bent Green. I left them there and proceeded to Manchester on my business. I am a cotton carder.

I found that business was going on as usual at Manchester. It was half past eleven when I got down to the infirmary. I heard no fears expressed of the consequences of the meeting. At the top of Mosley Street, I saw the Stockport people pass. They consisted of men, women, boys and girls, all walking in procession. There were many of the women walking arm in arm with the men in the procession. They did not look to me as if they were going to commit any act of violence. Some appeared rather decent, and others not. They appeared to be a people sadly torn down and in distress. I dare say they had on the best clothes they could muster.

The shops were all open the same as they are on any other day, for anything I saw. I saw the Oldham, Royton, Lees, Saddleworth and Mossley parties pass the Exchange door, and looking through the windows. [Mr Hunt here observed that the Exchange was a large building where the gentlemen of the town go to read the papers and transact business.] The gentlemen seemed laughing at the flags. There was no symptom of alarm manifested. The people passed by in a peaceable and orderly manner. I saw no insult offered to anyone. I saw no uncommon number of sticks with the people. I did not join the procession. I saw nothing to alarm me.

I went to St Peter's Field. I saw some peace officers, but did not know them to be such until they began to use their bludgeons. I saw the cavalry come upon the ground. They formed in front of Mr Buxton's house. I saw no resistance on the part of the people.

[To questions by the judge.] I saw no resistance on the part of the people.

[To questions by Mr Hunt.] I was near the hustings, but not so near as that the cavalry could reach me with the cuts of their sabres. I saw no insult or abuse whatever offered to the cavalry or constables. The people appeared to get out of the way as fast as they could, to let the cavalry

# Seventh Day – Thursday 23 March 1820.

pass. I was nearer to the hustings than to Mr Buxton's house. I kept my eyes on the yeomanry as well as I could till they got up to the hustings. I am five feet ten inches high. I could see very well over the people. I saw no brickbats or stones thrown, nor sticks lifted up against the cavalry. The people were so jammed and crowded together, that they could not do so, even had they been inclined.

Mr SCARLETT: You may go, my friend. I have no questions to ask you.

ROBERT HARROP, sworn and examined by Mr HUNT.

I live at Lees and manage a spinning concern for my father. I recollect directions having been given to buy linen to make a flag – some white bleached cambric was bought. It was to make a flag to go to the Manchester meeting. Directions were given to have inscriptions and devices put upon it and they were put on accordingly, but it would not answer because, when the painter began to letter it in black, the lettering was seen through, and it prevented the reading. We determined to have it of some other colour, and the painter having no paint but the black with which he was painting the letters, we agreed that the flag should be painted black, and that the inscriptions and devices should be painted white. This was the sole cause of the white flag being made a black one. It was never pointed out to us – nor had we any idea – that a black flag was more offensive than a white one.

I did not see the procession go off to Manchester. I did not go with them. I went by myself. I saw the parties in Manchester. I did not see any of my townswomen with them. There were women with the Stockport party. I saw no large sticks or staves either with our own or either of the other parties. If any of my own townspeople had come armed in this way, I should have noticed it.

I went to the meeting. I saw nothing in the course of the morning which created any alarm in my mind for the safety of the town; the shops were all open, and business going on as usual. I was at the Exchange. There were many of the townspeople there. I heard no expression of alarm by any of them. I did not see any act of violence or any insult offered to the gentlemen on the Exchange, or to anyone else, by any of the parties. I saw the cavalry go to the hustings.

[To questions by the judge.] I did not see the people do anything to resist the cavalry. I was at the extremity of the meeting and had to look across the people. I was not in a situation to see whether any resistance was offered near the hustings. I saw no resistance during the whole of the day. Some of the cavalry came near where I was, but there appeared no disposition to resist them. I could not see any clubs with the people

*Thomas Schofield*

*Robert Harrop*

# Hunt and Others.

**Robert Harrop**

near me.

*Cross-examined* by Mr SCARLETT.

I did not put on the flag the words, 'No boroughmongering', 'Unite and be free', 'Saddleworth, Lees and Mossley Union' on one side; and on the other, 'Taxation without representation is unjust and tyrannical', 'Equal representation or death'. There was a hand holding the scales of justice, and the word 'Justice' under it. On the other there were two hands clasped, and the word 'Love' under them. [Here the flag was produced: it was about six feet long by three or four broad.]. That is the flag; the women, I think, put the white fringe upon it. I selected some of the mottos.

Mr SCARLETT: Did Doctor Healey choose any of the mottos? — No. Because he seems to have a parental fondness for it.

Mr HUNT: I perceive there is a piece cut out of the flag. I hope it won't be said the bloody dagger was upon that piece. — No. There was not a bloody dagger on the flag.

Dr HEALEY: I was afraid you would not produce the flag, Mr Scarlett, and so I have brought a model of it. [Here the doctor produced a small model of the flag with the inscriptions, et cetera. It was fastened to a stick, suspended from a pole, as hanging signs are over shop doors or windows.]

Mr Scarlett observed that the word death was in small letters on the model, but on the flag itself the letters were large.

Mr HUNT: My Lord, the model is done from memory. — [The witness.] I am quite sure there was no bloody dagger painted upon it.

Are you quite sure that there was no bloody dagger on the flag, as described by Mr Scarlett? — I am sure there was not.

Mr SCARLETT: I shall explain that by-and-by.

**William Nicholson**

WILLIAM NICHOLSON, sworn and examined by Mr HUNT.

I live at Lees. I am a printer. I was not called upon to paint a flag before 16 August. I went to Manchester on that day, but not with the Lees party. I saw them near the Exchange at Manchester; they had a black flag; I saw part of it painted.

I saw no difference in the appearance of Manchester on that day, save in one instance: I saw a public house with the windows shut. I went in with some friends and called for a quart of beer. A female servant said they could not give it as they had received orders from the magistrates not to sell any on that day; however, she would ask her mistress. She afterwards returned and we got two quarts of beer.

I saw a procession pass. A waggon broke through it without molestation,

# Seventh Day – Thursday 23 March 1820.

as did also several gentlemen. I took notice of their sticks: I think about one to four had sticks; they were for the most part switch sticks. The procession was headed by about thirty or forty females rather poorly attired. They walked four abreast. I saw people pass along without taking any notice of the procession, which surprised me. I heard no one express any alarm at the entrance of the people into town.

Mr HUNT: Were you on St Peter's Field? — I beg your pardon, sir. I have made a digression; I must go back to the Exchange, if you please.

Sir, I wish to bring you as shortly as I can to the evidence. You had better let me question you. Were you on St Peter's Field? — I was.

Did you see me arrive? — I beg your pardon, sir. Are you Mr Hunt?

Yes. Did you see me arrive on the field? — Oh, I beg your pardon, sir; I had not the pleasure of knowing you before. Yes, I saw you arrive. I had heard of your great reputation for oratory, and so I was anxious to get near the hustings in order to hear you and judge for myself. I saw the soldiers advance, but not a single person offered them the least opposition; in fact, the people were so dense that it was impossible to get out of the way. I did not see Dr Healey advance with his party, but I was too busily employed looking at the people in the Exchange. They seemed anxious to see the procession pass, but they positively betrayed no symptoms of alarm. I saw one yeoman pass the Exchange, and nobody insult him. I saw both Wylde and Dr Healey on the hustings and heard the latter say, 'Be peaceable; take care you are not thrown into confusion'. He lived at Lees, and had a considerable property there, with his father.

When the cavalry had advanced beyond the hustings he saw some sticks thrown; this was after the arrest.

[The court held that this evidence was not necessary.]

*Cross-examined* by Mr Serjeant HULLOCK.

We are booksellers, but never sell any of the 'trash' publications, as they are called – that is, Cobbett, Wooler, and such like. We never sold Hunt's Speeches; do not know whether they are trash.

[This witness excited considerable laughter from the didactic manner in which he delivered his evidence. At one time Mr Hunt was north-east of him, at another south-west. Sometimes he saw his back, sometimes his front; at other times the wind was in his favour, as well as against him. The witness himself, being a cheerful, good-natured man, heartily joined in the laugh, which the gravity of the court could not occasionally resist.]

JOHN HULLEY, sworn and examined by Mr HUNT.

Was a woollen-clothier residing in Mossley, and went to the Manchester

**William Nicholson**

**John Hulley**

# Hunt and Others.

**John Hulley**

meeting with his mother and wife. The former was sixty-five years of age.

There was no appearance at Manchester of alarm. The shops were at business, and the people following their usual occupations. He saw the different processions enter and in a peaceable, quiet, and orderly manner, without offering the slightest insult to anybody. He took his goods into Manchester and went round as usual to his customers. He had not the slightest fear about his property on that day. His customers did not appear to be alarmed about the meeting; they were carrying on their trade as usual, and expressed no apprehensions about the people. Witness went to the meeting with his wife; and his mother, after she transacted some business of her own, was to have joined them. He saw no insult offered by any of the people at the meeting to anybody.

Did you see any violence committed by any person else?

Mr Justice BAYLEY: No, don't ask that question. It is obvious to what he alludes. I have other reasons for not wishing that their case should be investigated or prejudiced here.

Mr Hunt had no wish to press any question upon a witness which his Lordship considered irregular.

WITNESS: He saw Mr Buxton's house as well as the hustings, and could see plainly what occurred in the line between them. He saw the cavalry come from Buxton's to the hustings. There was no resistance whatever offered to the cavalry by the meeting. He did not hear any of the cavalry say what they wanted at the hustings. He was nearer to the cavalry than the people on the hustings, and if any of the latter heard any of the cavalry say what they wanted, he must have heard it also. He did not know the object of the cavalry to be to enable the constables to get up to serve a warrant. If any such communication of their object had been loudly made, situated as he was, he must have heard it as soon at least as anybody on the hustings could.

**Nancy Prestwich**

NANCY PRESTWICH, sworn and examined.

Was mother of the last witness, and went to Manchester on 16 August, and walked there – thought it was ten miles distant. She saw a dozen or so of her own townswomen (from Mossley) and a number of others at the meeting. Though she was sixty-five years of age, she walked out towards Smedley Cottage after her walk into Manchester – and they formed her there at the head of the line, as commander of about two hundred or three hundred women. She knew St Peter's Field, and got there before Mr Hunt came. She wanted relief, and went and got a gill of beer when she met Mr Hunt. As she was coming back to the ground, the cavalrymen were coming there; she stopped there. Neither herself

# Seventh Day – Thursday 23 March 1820.

nor any of the two hundred or three hundred women offered to take the cavalry prisoners. She went with peace, and joined in the shout when Mr Hunt arrived, before she got her gill of beer.

**Nancy Prestwich**

When the cavalrymen came up, she heard shouting, but did not join in it, not knowing what it was for. The people of Manchester did not seem alarmed about the meeting. If she had had any apprehension of riot she certainly should not have gone there.

*Cross-examined* by Mr SCARLETT.

Mr Scarlett said it did not follow that because strangers entering the town had no apprehensions of riot, therefore the inhabitants in the town should be also free from alarm. He here freely confessed, that he did not mean to charge Mr Hunt with intending to excite the people at the instant to actual tumult. It was quite enough to show that the effect of his proceeding was intimidation.

Mr Justice BAYLEY: Then it may so happen, perhaps, that your object is not sufficiently stated in the indictment.

Mr Scarlett thought intimidation would be quite enough.

Mr Justice BAYLEY: I would not for the world mislead the jury. If I can hold the scales of justice equally balanced, then I shall do my duty.

Mr Scarlett could not see Mr Hunt's object in putting a number of the questions he had put. The only effect was to occupy a large portion of time.

Mr Hunt was surprised at this observation. The prosecution occupied four days – not quite as much was yet given for the defence, and yet the learned gentleman complained.

Mr Scarlett said that three quarters of the time during the prosecution was taken up in cross-examinations.

Mr HUNT: Yes, and very necessary ones.

Mr SCARLETT: We have shown that a strong alarm was felt in Manchester.

Mr HUNT: We have shown the reverse.

Mr Justice BAYLEY: I must leave that to the jury.

Mr Scarlett repeated that it signified little what was the feeling of those who came in from the country; it was the people in the town whose feelings were to be principally considered.

Mr Justice BAYLEY: There are two questions: first, whether there was actual terror in any considerable portion of the inhabitants; secondly, whether there were any accompanying circumstances in the meeting so as to excite reasonable grounds for apprehension of the consequences. These two points I shall submit to the jury.

[Cross-examination resumed.] They were all women; no man came to

# Hunt and Others.

**Nancy Prestwich**

put them in order. She went to look at the great man and see what was going on. She had nothing to do with the flags.

*Re-examined* by Mr HUNT.

I carried no sword. We had good intentions – that we had. [A laugh.]

**Robert Wood**

ROBERT WOOD, sworn and examined.

Is a chemist and druggist in Manchester, residing near New Cross. He observed the Oldham and Saddleworth people enter the town on 16 August, and saw nothing particular in their conduct. Men, women and children passed altogether quite peaceable. He did not shut up his shop until evening, when the Magistrates ordered the doors to be closed. He saw no cause whatever for alarm. The people had no appearance of an invading army. Some few had common walking sticks; he saw no large staves whatever. He went to St Peter's Field about twelve o'clock, and certainly heard no alarm expressed by any inhabitant.

Mr Serjeant CROSS: Ten thousand may have no fear, and yet twenty thousand others may.

Mr HUNT: Yes, but if ten thousand have no fear, it is clear that they were free from the apprehension.

[Examination resumed.] Witness (Mr Wood) with Dr Earnshaw of the Society of Friends attempted to pass up to a window of a house to overlook the area, but were prevented by constables. They, however, at length got to the window and had a complete view of the hustings and the whole line between it and Mr Buxton's house. He saw many divisions of the people come up to the field. Some played 'God Save the King' and 'Rule, Britannia!' and those near the music took off their hats, he supposed, on account of the tunes. He saw no insult whatever offered by the people. He saw Mr Hunt arrive on the ground amidst loud cheering. [He then described Mr Hunt's speech, as before described by other witnesses.]

While the speech was going on there seemed to be some slight disturbance towards Deansgate, and he heard Mr Hunt say he had no doubt people would be sent among them to create a disturbance; that if any such appeared, they should put them down and keep them down. Where the disturbance was, the place was exactly opposite Dickinson Street. It was some time before the soldiers came that Mr Hunt desired the meeting to keep down their enemies. The observation could not possibly have been meant for the soldiers, who were not at the time on the spot.

He saw the yeomanry advance at a quick pace round Brown's cottage and form in a line opposite Mr Buxton's house. He afterwards saw them

# Seventh Day – Thursday 23 March 1820.

during their progress to the hustings and did not see the least resistance opposed to them by the people. He saw no brickbats, sticks, or stones flung at them as they advanced; if such had been thrown, he must have seen them. The place where the yeomanry charged was opposite his window. He saw no sticks held up against them; some constables held up their staves. The cavalry were within twenty yards of where he stood, and he did not hear them say what they wanted at the hustings. The staves appeared to be held up by the constables to protect themselves from the swords of the cavalry.

Mr Justice BAYLEY: That must not be asked.

[Examination resumed.] He was in the window with Dr Earnshaw and Mr Bancroft (two of the Society of Friends). They were family men and expressed no apprehension for the safety of their families. He saw no resistance offered to the cavalry except from the density of the crowd; the people could not get out of the way.

Mr HUNT: How did they get up to the hustings if the crowd could not get away?

Mr Justice BAYLEY: Do not ask that.

[Examination resumed.] Witness said a passage was kept up nearly to the hustings by the constables; he saw Mr Nadin and others pass it. If a person from his window said that a constable wanted to get up, it must have been heard. Nadin was frequently within hearing of Mr Hunt; he (Nadin) was never disturbed whilst walking up and down through a cordon of constables. He did not see a cordon of people around the hustings. From what witness saw, Nadin, he thought, might have passed up to the hustings; he (witness) could certainly have got there.

The people stood about the hustings in the ordinary way. He was in a second floor, and much nearer the hustings than Buxton's house; about eighty-five yards nearer. If bludgeons were thrown, he must have seen them; he saw no appearance of disciplined troops in the crowd, ready to fight for Hunt if occasion offered (the words of a witness for the prosecution). He did not hear Mr Hunt say they (the soldiers) were very few, and the meeting a host against them. He merely heard him propose to give them three cheers. When the soldiers came, many at the skirts of the crowd began to run away. The cheers restored peace, and the people came back.

JOHN ROCKLIFFE, sworn.

Lived near Lees, and was a master cotton-spinner. Was at Manchester on 16 August and saw business going on there as usual, without any symptoms of alarm or any shops shut. Mr Peel's works were going on, and the people were looking out for the procession rather with the

*Robert Wood*

*John Rockliffe*

# Hunt and Others.

**John Rockliffe**

appearance of cheerfulness than of alarm.

Witness was afterwards at the meeting, which he described as being of the most peaceable description. In the streets he saw many respectable ladies – like those in court – walking in the streets, free from alarm and insult. Indeed, as he passed along High Street, he felt astonished at the indifference of the people.

The first time he saw the yeomanry, they were drawn in line before Mr Buxton's house, brandishing their swords. Witness was from a dozen to twenty yards before the hustings; saw the yeomanry approach; they went quite close to him. The crowd made no opposition whatever to them, or he thought he must have seen them. Nothing at all was thrown at them, or he must have seen the missiles, for he saw the whole space made by the cavalry to the hustings, and saw them coming. He watched them the way they went; he did not look whether the crowd closed in behind them. When the cavalry came through, everybody strove to make the best of his way off.

**Mary Jones**

MARY JONES, sworn.

She was the wife of a fustian-cutter residing in Windmill Street, near St Peter's Field. She was at home on 16 August last, and would never forget that day. She then described the arrival of the different parties of the crowd, and also of the yeomanry cavalry. She saw no person whatever insulted by, or alarmed at, the crowd. She saw the whole of the approach of cavalry to the hustings and no opposition was made to them by any of the crowd; if it had been made in any manner, she must have seen it. The people fled when the yeomanry came up to the hustings; a great many could not get away. Many near her door were so pressed as to throw down an iron railing, and a woman was there killed.

**John Lees**

JOHN LEES, sworn.

He lived at Crompton, was a master-manufacturer, and went to see the meeting. He saw the crowds advancing to Manchester: they consisted of men, women and children. A few had walking sticks, but no other weapons. He then described that he saw the people afterwards on the field from the front window of the Windmill public house, almost immediately at the back of the hustings. The meeting was most peaceable; they fled when the yeomanry came and made not the smallest resistance, or he must have seen it. He saw Nadin on the day, walking up and down in the line of the hustings. Heard nobody call out and make way to have a warrant executed. He did not hear the smallest notice given to the people of the approach of the cavalry, nor of any warrant being about to be served.

# Seventh Day – Thursday 23 March 1820.

Mr Scarlett observed that many of Mr Hunt's questions today were founded on a misapprehension of Mr Hulton's testimony.

Mr Hunt denied this and said he wanted to show that neither Nadin nor any other person had attempted to execute a warrant; if they had, there would have been no resistance. He was under no misapprehension respecting Mr Hulton's evidence. That gentleman had represented Nadin's telling him he could not execute the warrant without military aid, and he (Mr Hunt) wished to show that there was no necessity for such assistance.

Mr Justice BAYLEY: I must ultimately tell the jury that there is no evidence from Nadin to justify the employment of the yeomanry to support the civil power in the execution of a warrant.

JOHN FELL, sworn and examined.

I am a grocer in Manchester. I saw the people come up to the field on 16 August. They were as peaceable as this court. Some had a few common walking sticks, but no staves. He corroborated in all its parts the evidence already given of the quiet demeanour of the meeting, from beginning to end. He saw many magistrates in the first floor of Mr Buxton's house when the cavalry advanced: among them were Mr Hay, Mr Fletcher and Mr Wright, and he saw them in York since this trial commenced. He saw a tall gentleman call from the window for the boroughreeve, and soon after he saw Mr Nadin called. The latter went to the range of constables. The yeomanry came up just as they were cheered by the populace, and returned that cheer; witness heard the word 'Forward' given from the window, or the officer at their head – he could not say which.

They then advanced, sword in hand, though not the slightest opposition was offered to them and the people were making away as fast as they could. The crowd did not close in upon the cavalry as they advanced, nor brandish sticks, nor hoot, nor anything of the kind. He had no apprehensions for the town when he heard of the meeting and saw it. The yeomanry could not have been closed in upon for they were supported by the regular cavalry, then by the Cheshire, and last by two pieces of flying artillery.

MARY BRYAN, sworn and examined.[192]

She resided at Manchester in Lad Lane, and was at the meeting of 16 August; she remained on the field until Mr Hunt was taken from the hustings. She stood upon a rising ground near the Windmill public house. She saw all the processions come upon the field with flags and music and

---

192 Surname also given as 'Briant'. Age given in the *Morning Post* (25 March 1820) as fifty-four, and address as Lad Lane, Hollywell Buildings.

# Hunt and Others.

**Mary Bryan**

felt no alarm at all for the safety of herself or of the town. She also saw the cavalry come upon the ground and advance towards the hustings. The special constables fell back to admit them in. She heard the people cheer the soldiers, but did not hear the soldiers return it. Did not hear the people hiss or groan at the soldiers. Saw no bricks or stones thrown, or sticks held up at the soldiers. Some few old people had walking sticks. Did not see anyone offend the soldiers in any way. Saw the people running away from the soldiers. [This witness was not *cross-examined*.]

**Joseph Watson**

JOSEPH WATSON, sworn and examined by Mr HUNT.

I reside at Oldham. I overtook and passed an Oldham party as they were going to Manchester on 16 August. They were going along quietly. I saw no acts of violence. I saw a few walking sticks; there were not many who had them. None of them had long staves shouldered like muskets.

I observed Dr Healey amongst them. I walked with him. He and two others walked a little before the rest. I walked near two miles with him. The whole party seemed in the best humour. The party halted near New Cross for a time. They made room on the road for horses and gigs as they passed on the road. They were walking in procession, by which means they were enabled to make more room for passengers than if they had been walking indiscriminately. There were many females with the party. They did not look like an army going to invade a town. The procession marched in the same order as the Benefit and other societies do. I did not go to the meeting until the dispersion had commenced. I was not under any apprehension for the safety of the town, nor did I conceive there was any danger.

*Cross-examined* by Mr Serjeant HULLOCK.

I did not intend to speak at the meeting. I never pretended to be a maker of speeches. Properly speaking, I never addressed the people. I might have read something to them, but I never made an extempore speech. I perhaps read a string of resolutions. I suppose I was styled chairman on that occasion. It was near Rochdale, on 16 August 1818. It was the first and last time I was placed in such a situation. There were near one thousand persons present. I do not recollect many dissentient voices to the resolutions.

Mr Justice Bayley objected to this mode of examination. They had a right to ask witness as to every act of his life connected with the proceedings before the court, but no other.

[Cross-examination continued.] I know Mr Knight. I was at a meeting where he was present. It was in the latter end of July, between the twentieth and twenty-eighth; I think it was the twenty-sixth. Knight was

# Seventh Day – Thursday 23 March 1820.

not the chairman of the meeting. I heard him speak at it. I do not recollect his having made any allusion to the meeting of 16 August.

After passing the meeting, I came up and walked with Dr Healey. He seemed in spirits; he did not tell me what the resolutions were; I don't think he knew himself. I heard him advise the people to be orderly, and not to offer any insult. That advice arose out of another circumstance. It was understood that the party was going to Manchester. I will swear that, to the best of my knowledge, he did not tell me about the business of the meeting.

Mr Serjeant HULLOCK: Do you mean to swear that he did not tell you what the business was to be? — Did you mean to ask me, sir, whether he told me what the object of the meeting was?

That is exactly what I was endeavouring to ask you. — I swear, to the best of my knowledge, he did not. We talked about the weather and various other things.

*[The Court adjourned at a quarter past six.]*

# Eighth Day – Friday 24 March 1820.

*The court met at the usual hour of 9.00 am, and the evidence for the defence continued. The examinations today were directed to disprove the terror said by the prosecution to have been felt at the assembling of the meeting of 16 August. The principal witnesses whose depositions were taken are most respectable merchants, manufacturers and other inhabitants of Manchester.*

ROBERT WRIGHT, sworn and examined by Mr HUNT.

I live at Hollywood, about five miles from Manchester. I am a hat manufacturer. I remember going to Manchester on 16 August last. My house is about a mile from the main road between Lees and Manchester. I went to see the procession. I saw the Oldham, the Royton and Saddleworth divisions; they were perfectly peaceable, and walking in a kind of order. They had a considerable number of women and children mixed with them. I saw no large sticks or bludgeons; they made use of no improper language; they neither insulted nor assaulted any person. This was the procession which had the black flag.

I took my horse and rode to Manchester to see the meeting. I did not go in any of the processions, nor have I any connection with those called reformers. I reside in the neighbourhood of Mr Duncough. I saw nothing that created alarm for my person or property, though I am a man of considerable property. I am a married man; I have a wife and family; I left them to go and see the meeting. It was assembled when I arrived; I arrived on the field near one o'clock.

I was there half an hour before Mr Hunt came on the field. I took up my station in the field near the line of constables in the space between the hustings and Mr Buxton's house. I observed the conduct of the people; they appeared perfectly peaceable; I saw none of them armed with large staves or sticks shouldered as a soldier shoulders his musket. I did not observe one large staff; the ground on which I stood was high, and I could see all the crowd, but I saw no large sticks or staves shouldered. I remained, and saw the military come on the ground.

[Examined by THE COURT.] I saw them advance towards the crowd. The crowd cheered when they came on the field at Mr Buxton's house; the military cheered again. I heard no groaning, hooting or hissing when the military advanced. I saw nothing done by the crowd as the military advanced that indicated resistance; I heard nothing said on the hustings

# Hunt and Others.

**Robert Wright**

encouraging resistance. I was within forty yards of the hustings, and could hear what was said. I saw nothing thrown at the military; I saw no sticks held up in opposition to them or in defiance of them.

I saw nothing that created any alarm for the safety of the town or of my property. When the military arrived on the ground, the people cheered, and the military cheered again. There was a little panic in the outskirts of the crowd as the military approached. I heard a cry of, 'Be firm!' and I thought it was intended to allay the fears of the people, lest some accident should occur in their running away. The sudden running away would create danger.

There was a panic when the military approached, and the cheers from the multitude rather re-assured me. I saw the infantry arrive in Dickinson Street. I did not hear Mr Hunt say, turning to them, 'There are your enemies: put them down and, having got them down, keep them down'. In the advance of the yeomanry to the hustings, they passed within one yard of me. During their progress from Mr Buxton's house to the hustings, I kept my eye upon them. There were neither large stones, brickbats, cudgels nor bludgeons hurled at them. When the cavalry passed, I did not see the people close in again. The people endeavoured to make their escape and did not press on the yeomanry.

I heard no expression of alarm at the appearance of the meeting before the military arrived. I heard no request made by the constables, at the time of the approach of the military, to have room to serve a warrant. I did not hear them state why they were proceeding to the hustings. I remained near the line of special constables all the time. I was on the field till the dispersion of the meeting.

*Cross-examined* by Mr SCARLETT.

I thought the military, as they advanced, were going to take somebody on the hustings. I saw the constables near them. I was about forty yards at first from the hustings, and I retreated about twenty or thirty yards nearer Buxton's house. When I had my face towards the hustings, the line of constables was on the left. The crowd was very thick towards the hustings.

I attended the meeting of January. I was at no meeting of blanketeers.

Mr SCARLETT: How did you receive notice of the meeting? — I saw it in the papers.

The *Manchester Observer*? — Yes.

Do you take in that paper? — No.

Did you see it at the village, or in what house did you see it?

[The court objected to this as no evidence.]

What number of the *Manchester Observer* did you see? — I saw the

# Eighth Day – Friday 24 March 1820.

Saturday's paper before the meeting. I observed in it the requisition and the signatures of persons requested to attend the meeting. I went to the meeting as a spectator. I expected Mr Hunt to speak. I did not know Carlile, nor had I heard or read at that time that he was indicted for blasphemy. I say this on the best of my recollection. I cannot recollect now that I had heard then that he was under prosecution.

**Robert Wright**

I did not see the *Manchester Observer* regularly. I cannot recollect that I had read in that paper an account of the Smithfield meeting. I attended the meeting in January at which Mr Hunt presided, but I was not at the dinner after it.

I knew there was to be a meeting on the ninth. I had heard it spoken of, and I had likewise heard that it was put off.

I know the defendant Johnson. I have known him about a year.

Mr SCARLETT: Where did you see him first? — I cannot recollect. I pass his shop in going to market, and sometimes call in. I have read in his shop the newspaper: never much. I never saw any paper but the *Manchester Observer* in his shop. I never heard him read it in his shop.

On your solemn oath, did you not hear him read the *Manchester Observer*? — Yes, I will swear that I cannot recollect that I did. I have been often in Mr Johnson's shop, but I do not recollect how often. I heard of Cobbett's arrival at Liverpool, but do not recollect that I read it in a newspaper.

Did Johnson ask you to attend the meeting of 16 August? — I think he did.

Had you then heard that Carlile had opened a shop to sell Paine's works called The Temple of Reason and the Office of The Republican and Deist? — I have seen so in the papers.

Did you ever read Tom Paine? — Never a word of it.

When Johnson asked you to attend the meeting, had you heard of the resolutions of Smithfield? — I cannot recollect that I had. I have no knowledge of those resolutions. I cannot recollect that I was to attend the meeting of the ninth, which was postponed. I live at Hollywood. I had heard it reported that people were drilling. I never saw any drilling party in my neighbourhood. I cannot say how long before the meeting I heard of drilling.

*Re-examined* by Mr HUNT.

Johnson never was at my house in his life. We are not on visiting terms. I never was at Johnson's house in Smedley in my life. His shop is in the public street, in Shudehill, and it was there I saw him. I called for the purpose of hearing the news.

Did you ever see in his shop *The Age of Reason*, or any of the

# Hunt and Others.

**Robert Wright**

theological works of Paine? — I never did.

Are these works sold in Johnson's shop? — No.

[Questioned by THE COURT.] What is Johnson? — A brushmaker. If I saw a newspaper lying on the table, I used to take it up and read it a little, but I never saw the works of Paine. It was a current report that there was to be a meeting on 9 August. It was likewise a current report that it was put off, and to take place on the sixteenth. I would have attended that meeting whether I had seen Johnson or not.

Mr HUNT: Did Johnson invite you to attend that meeting, or take any part in the proceedings? — I cannot recollect that he did.

[Examined by THE COURT.] I would not have attended if I had had any reason to apprehend anything illegal, riotous or tumultuous at that meeting.

[By JOHNSON.] Did witness become acquainted with me through a friend called Mr Gee? — Yes. The first time I went to his shop was with Mr Gee. I never heard from Johnson that drilling was going on, nor have I heard so in Johnson's hearing. I have heard that the drilling was confined to marching, and I had no reason to suppose that it went beyond marching. I never heard Johnson say anything seditious in my life.

**Sidney Walker**

SIDNEY WALKER, sworn and examined by Mr HUNT.[193]

I am a lieutenant in the Bengal native infantry. I am returned from India about two years. I was at Manchester on 16 August last; my family resides there – it consists of my mother, my sister and her family, and a brother.

I observed the processions on 16 August. The people were perfectly peaceable and orderly. I went to the meeting afterwards. I saw the processions pass through Deansgate at the bottom of St Peter's Street. I saw nothing before one o'clock in the conduct of the people calculated to excite fears in the respectable people of Manchester. Neither my mother nor my sister nor any of my relatives nor anybody else that I know of expressed fears for the safety of the town.

I saw the cavalry on the field, but not at Mr Buxton's. I was on the Deansgate side of the hustings, Mr Buxton's house being on the opposite side. Neither in the field nor in the course of the day did I observe any

---

193 *Liverpool Mercury*, 14 July 1826: 'Died, on 16 March last, on his passage home, on board the Honourable Company's ship Princess Charlotte of Wales, Captain Sidney Walker, aged thirty-two, of the 7th Regiment Bengal Native Infantry'. A subsequent lawsuit for the deceased's estate identified him as 'Sidney Walker of Gartside Street, Manchester, Lancashire, and afterwards of Lyons Inn, London, but late on board the East India Company merchant ship Princess Charlotte of Wales, captain in Bengal Regiment of Native Infantry'.

# Eighth Day – Friday 24 March 1820.

act of violence committed by the people. I saw one or two going to fight among themselves (who were prevented by those around them, who would not allow a riot to be created). I heard no threat made to any respectable person.

**Sidney Walker**

*Cross-examined* by Mr Serjeant HULLOCK.

I am out of the army. I am not on pay as I have been absent two years and a half, two years being the longest absence allowed. I am to retire from the army. I am now a student in the Inner Temple. I arrived at Manchester two days before the meeting and heard of the meeting by common report; and I came from the country, where I was at my sister's, about a mile from Manchester, to see it. My mother lives about four hundred or five hundred yards from St Peter's Field.

I am a member of no political society. I only knew that Mr Hunt was to attend. I knew none of the other parties. I did not know that Carlile was to attend the meeting.

Mr Hunt objected to questions about Carlile, as he was not one of the defendants.

Mr Justice Bayley said the question was legitimate, as Carlile's name was found in the requisition among those invited to attend the meeting.

Mr HUNT: But none of the defendants' names are among the requisitionists.

Mr Serjeant HULLOCK: Do you know Mr Wooler? — Yes, I do.

Where is his shop? — In Fleet Street.

Is not Carlile's shop likewise in Fleet Street, and called the office of The Republican and Deist? — Yes

Did you know Mr Hunt before? — No.

Had you seen him before? — Yes.

Where? — At the Crown and Anchor tavern.

When, or on what occasion? — After the death of Sir Samuel Romilly.

Who presided at that meeting? — Sir F. Burdett.

Did you see any other political characters there?

Mr Hunt objected to this question: he saw no reason why all the persons that he ever met with should be dragged forward in court.

[The examination of the witness proceeded.] I was not at Guildhall on Carlile's trial. I never saw Mr Hunt at any other place before 16 August except at the Crown and Anchor.

I remember seeing the procession coming into Manchester. The divisions marched in order. I do not know whether they kept the step or not. I cannot judge of the numbers. It was said that there were between 50,000 and 100,000, but I could not judge how many. I heard Mr Hunt's address. I saw the carriage of Mr Hunt at a distance coming to the field.

# Hunt and Others.

**Sidney Walker**

*Re-examined* by Mr HUNT.

The persons assembled were not in military order. They certainly were not so; for, as a military man, I might then have computed their numbers. I should have done so, had they been in lines.

I had not heard that Carlile was convicted of any crime before 16 August. I never heard that Mr Wooler had been convicted of any crime. I heard he had been tried. I never saw you in company with Carlile or Wooler. I never saw Carlile in my life.

The two houses where I slept the two nights after my arrival were my mother's, in Manchester, and my sister's, two miles off. I thought the people in the field in a very unmilitary order, and not like disciplined troops. I saw none with large sticks shouldered as soldiers shoulder their muskets.

Mr HUNT: Did the people round the hustings appear like disciplined troops, ready to defend and protect me if any molestation was offered? — No, certainly they did not appear ready to fight, for they had no arms.

[Examined by THE COURT.] As a military man, I did not, from the appearance of the procession, think that the people must have been drilled. It did not strike me that they must have been drilled, either from the sound of their feet or from any other circumstance. To the best of my belief they did not look up like soldiers. Their ranks were at some paces distance, so far were they from being locked up.

**William Thelwall**

WILLIAM THELWALL, sworn and examined by Mr HUNT.

I am a builder; I reside at Manchester. I was there on 16 August last. I live about two hundred yards from the place of meeting. I have a wife and family. I live in Lloyd Street.

I saw some of the processions coming into Manchester on the sixteenth; they came peaceably, in the same manner as they walk at club feasts. I was employed that day about my own business. I felt no alarm, from what I heard or saw for the safety of the town or of my family. I have considerable property in Lloyd Street. Nothing that I heard or saw induced me to believe that my property was in the slightest danger. I was not much out of the house till about twelve o'clock. None of my neighbours or any other person expressed alarm.

I saw processions come in like benefit clubs. There was nothing to distinguish them. Some had walking sticks. They were accompanied by females and children. There was no closing of shops, locking of doors or barricading of premises before eight o'clock.

I went to the meeting about half past twelve. I was in the outer part, adjoining my own house. I saw great numbers of Manchester people there, my townsmen and neighbours. None of them expressed any

# Eighth Day – Friday 24 March 1820.

consternation or alarm before the soldiers came on the field. I did not see the black flag. I saw no body of men with large sticks shouldered like muskets. I was in the northern corner of the field, at the angle opposite to Buxton's house. I stood upon some timber and commanded a view of the meeting. I saw the cavalry arrive and form in front of Buxton's house. I saw them move towards the hustings.

[Examined by THE COURT.] I saw no attempt to oppose the military. I heard no groanings, hootings or hissings at them. I saw neither stones, sticks nor brickbats thrown at them or thrown in the air as they passed. I saw no sticks held up at them. I was in a situation to have seen it if anything of that kind had occurred, although I was at a considerable distance.

**William Thelwall**

*Cross-examined* by Mr Serjeant CROSS.

I was stationed at the corner of the field lower down than the Quakers' meeting house. I knew Mr Johnson. I did not know him till within three days of 16 August. I saw Mr Hunt before at the other meeting in January. I heard of an additional number of special constables being sworn in, and of an additional military force brought into the neighbourhood. I heard of a meeting of the justices on the Saturday or Sunday before. I considered them not expressions of alarm, but precautionary measures. I heard no expressions of alarm for the peace and safety of the town on account of the people assembling. I heard of the postponement of the meeting of the ninth. I did not understand that members of parliament were to be elected at that meeting, though I had heard of what took place at Birmingham.

[The learned counsel here handed a paper addressed to the inhabitants of Manchester, dated Smedley Cottage, 11 August, and the witness was asked if he had read it.]

*Re-examined* by Mr HUNT.

I cannot swear I saw this paper before the meeting. It might be after it.

ROBERT GRUNDY, sworn and examined by Mr HUNT.

[Before he proceeded, he begged to know from the learned judge if he could demand his expenses. He was an unwilling witness; he had been here for nine days, and had received nothing.

The judge said he had no power in a criminal case to direct the payment of expenses.

Mr Hunt said he would contribute his share. We have a great number of witnesses, said he, and those who can support themselves are the last paid.

**Robert Grundy**

# Hunt and Others.

**Robert Grundy**

Witness said he acquiesced and was examined.]

I am a woollen-manufacturer. I reside in Salford. I attended the meeting of 16 August. I saw some of the processions going to the meeting. I went to the field at half past eleven. I was a special constable on that occasion. I remained till between half past one and two o'clock.

Mr HUNT: Be so kind as to state what you saw, as I have no deposition. — I came to the field at half past eleven, and remained till you (Mr Hunt) came. I remained till the cavalry came. I saw the persons march up in procession. I was not in the line of the special constables all the time. I sometimes was. I was about fifteen or twenty yards from the hustings. I cannot speak precisely as to distance. I went to Mr Buxton's house when the cavalry made their appearance and had partially dispersed the meeting.

The processions came regularly with colours and music. They made no particular impressions on my mind at the moment. They created no terror or alarm in my mind. They had no offensive weapons, neither clubs nor staves shouldered like muskets. Some of them had walking sticks such as people usually carry to places of public resort. I saw no insult or violence offered to any persons whatever. I was surrounded by a thick multitude. The persons round me were aware that we were special constables. Some of the constables showed their staves. I perceived no insult offered to them.

[Examined by THE COURT.] No opposition was made to the cavalry on their advance. I saw nothing done to intimidate the cavalry. They were neither hooted at, hissed at nor groaned at. They were received with three cheers. I saw neither stones, sticks nor brickbats thrown at them, or thrown up in the air as they passed. I did not keep my eye on the cavalry all the time they were advancing. I endeavoured to get to the extremity of the meeting, to the right of them.

[Examined by Mr HUNT.] From what I saw of the meeting, I was not at all apprehensive for the safety of the town or of my own person. I was not alarmed till I saw the cavalry, for this reason: that I had heard the magistrates were not to interfere, directly or indirectly, with the meeting. I felt no alarm at the result, if they did not interfere. I saw the yeomanry come up. I then endeavoured to get away, as did those about me.

Mr Hunt asked if the witness was alarmed at the military. The witness was not allowed to answer the question, as the conduct of the meeting was alone under inquiry.

*Cross-examined* by Mr SCARLETT.

The special constables are generally persons of respectability. I have been one for two years. I often heard of drillings before the meeting,

# Eighth Day – Friday 24 March 1820.

but I felt no alarm. The bodies marched in regular order to the meeting. They came in sections. By sections I mean a number of persons abreast. I saw several bodies enter after I came to the field. They marched something like a file of soldiers. I perceived no leaders or conductors of the procession. I perceived no persons who had any marks of distinction like bits of laurel. I think they marched like people that had been drilled. I was not sufficiently near them to say whether they were drilled. They marched in more regular order than people usually observe in walking through the streets. I certainly thought they would not have walked in this way without some instruction. The impression on my mind was that they had received some instructions. As to drilling, I know nothing.

**Robert Grundy**

The number assembled I cannot tell; but I never saw such a meeting. They marched peaceably along. When they arrived on the ground, they got round the hustings. I will give you my reason for being satisfied and not alarmed as to the result: it was because I had heard that the magistrates intended to let the meeting pass off quietly.

Mr SCARLETT: Supposing that at that meeting speeches had been delivered of an inflammatory nature by various speakers, and in ridicule and contempt of the local magistrates, would you have considered the town safe with such a meeting? — I should conceive that speeches of that kind would have at all times a bad effect certainly; but I never heard any such in my life, and therefore cannot be a judge.

Mr Scarlett then read an extract from the *Manchester Observer*. It went on thus: 'The farce of petitioning is over; a million and a half have petitioned for reform. The greater part of these were rejected, and none have been attended to; and should the people ever again stoop to anything in the shape of petition, they will deserve what they now suffer for their dastardly conduct; but we are confident that the spirit of the country will never again condescend to pray to those whom the people themselves ought to delegate. The most determined men in the country are in the ranks of reformers. The clans of corruption, where can they find such writers --?'

Mr Scarlett had read thus far, when Mr Hunt objected to this extract. It might be the speech of the learned gentleman himself for aught he knew. It was as much his as any of the defendants.

The judge said that the prosecutors had a right to suppose that any speech, however bad, was delivered at the meeting for the purpose of asking whether, in the opinion of the witness, such a speech in such a meeting would have produced danger to the town.

His Lordship having taken the whole of the extract into his notes, it was read to witness. It went on to ask, where could the clans of corruption find such writers as Cobbett and Wooler, and such determined men as

# Hunt and Others.

**Robert Grundy**

Wolseley and others? It then alluded to what it described as the state of the country: burdened with taxes, with crowds of black cattle, the bishops, and a pampered soldiery ready to give a bullet when the people asked for bread.

Mr SCARLETT: Now, suppose such a speech as this had been delivered at the meeting, would you consider the town safe? — I should consider the speech as very improper, but I can't say positively that I am competent to answer the question. I am no politician.

Well, I shall put it in another way. Were many of the meeting of the working classes? — Yes, the great portion of them appeared to be so.

And had been complaining of distress before this? — Yes, I dare say.

And perhaps exasperated at that distress? — I dare say some of them felt so.

Then in a meeting of such numbers as you have described, and under such circumstances, would you have thought it safe to the town of Manchester to have such a speech delivered as I have read? — I should think it would be improper, and would irritate them.

Suppose such a resolution as this had been proposed. [Here the learned gentleman read one of the resolutions which were proposed and carried at the Smithfield meeting, where Mr Hunt presided. Its substance was that after 1 January 1820, the people should not conceive themselves bound in justice or equity to obey any act of that body calling itself the House of Commons, except it proceeded from a full and fair representation of the people.] Suppose such a resolution as this had been passed, would you have considered it dangerous? — I think it would be likely to produce irritation. I am not sufficiently acquainted with the dispositions of the people to know. Many of them were suffering, certainly. I am not aware that any such speeches or resolutions were made or circulated.

But, if it were so, would you have considered it dangerous? — That would depend on the degree of irritation which existed among the people.

But would not this be calculated to produce irritation? — I have said so.

Did the appearance of the parties coming to the field show to you a previous arrangement? — I should think there was such.

You say you never saw such a meeting before. Am I to understand you, then, to say that such a meeting coming in large bodies from a distance of ten or eleven miles would not be dangerous? — I should think where there were greatest numbers there would be the greatest danger at all times, but the character of that meeting appeared peaceable. I never said, to my knowledge, that such a meeting was dangerous and ought to be dispersed. I do not know Mr Carlile.

*Re-examined* by Mr HUNT.

# Eighth Day – Friday 24 March 1820.

I have heard there was a public meeting in Smithfield at which you presided.

**Robert Grundy**

Mr HUNT: Suppose that such a resolution as that you have heard was proposed and passed at Smithfield without producing ill effect, have you any reason to suppose that it would have produced a worse effect in Manchester than in London? — I have no reason to suppose so, except that perhaps the people of Manchester might have taken a greater interest in the question than in London, and that might have produced a different effect.

Have you ever heard that the resolutions passed in London produced any bad effect? [This was not answered.]

What reason have you to suppose that a stronger feeling existed on this subject in Manchester than in London? — Because Manchester is a manufacturing district, and many persons are out of work there.

Suppose such a speech as you have heard had been read at Wigan, have you any reason to suppose it would have produced at Wigan a worse effect than at Manchester? — I have no reason to suppose so; both are in manufacturing counties.

Suppose that a public man, of great talents and of high legal knowledge, had made such a speech as this. [Mr Hunt had in his hand a volume of Dolby's Parliamentary Register, and was proceeding to read an extract from a speech of Mr Scarlett's on the question of the Manchester affair when he was interrupted by Mr Serjeant Cross, who objected to the extract being read, or to any question on it being put to the witness.]

Mr HUNT: It is not one of your speeches, Mr Cross. I dare say I shall never have to select from any of your speeches in Parliament.

Mr Justice BAYLEY: I must have no observations of this sort.

Mr HUNT: My Lord, I am here supposing a case of a speech delivered somewhere, in which advice is given to the whole nation to demand an enquiry into the proceedings at Manchester, and I wish to ask the witness whether, if such a speech were delivered at the meeting, would he have considered it dangerous?

Mr Justice BAYLEY: I think you have a right so to do.

Mr Scarlett observed that Mr Hunt was here putting a report of a speech in Parliament as evidence, which ought not to be received.

Mr Hunt denied that he offered this as a speech delivered in Parliament, as evidence; and observed, that what Mr Scarlett had said was a falsehood.

Mr Justice BAYLEY: Mr Hunt, I must tell you that if you do not conduct your case with decency, I must act with the firmness that belongs to my situation here. Your observation is highly improper. I can make allowance for feelings on such occasions, but your conduct in this is highly improper. Mr Scarlett is going to object to the question you

# Hunt and Others.

Robert Grundy

propose. I shall hear what he has to offer, and then you shall be heard in reply.

Mr Scarlett objected to the extract being read or any question founded upon it. It was not a speech addressed to any public meeting. It purported to be the report of a speech delivered in the House of Commons, and could not be made the subject of examination here.

Mr Justice BAYLEY: I shall allow the question to be put and the extract read on the same ground that I allowed you to put the question respecting the extract from the paper – that is, that supposing such words had been used, what might be their effect on the meeting?

Mr HUNT: I hope your Lordship will allow me to answer the observations of the learned counsel.

Mr Justice BAYLEY: I shall not decide the point until I hear you reply.

Mr SCARLETT: The defendants are accused of conspiring to excite disaffection in the minds of His Majesty's subjects, and if I can show that speeches to that effect, and spoken by one of them, were in circulation before the meeting, then I have the right to do so. But this does not give Mr Hunt a right to introduce speeches foreign to the question.

Mr Serjeant CROSS: And we propose further to show that the speech (that mentioned in the *Observer*) was delivered by one of the defendants at a former meeting.

Mr Hunt was about to reply when Mr Justice Bayley wished to see the book from which the extract was intended to be given. It was handed to his Lordship, who, having read it, showed it to the counsel for the prosecution.

Mr Hunt, after a moment, proceeded to answer the objections offered. He began by apologizing to his Lordship for the indiscretion into which he had fallen, and assured him that, though he might have been betrayed into improper warmth, it did not proceed from any disrespect towards his Lordship. With regard to one question argued by the learned counsel on the speech in the *Manchester Observer*, it went on the supposition that such a speech had been delivered, and he wished to infer that a bad effect might have been produced by it. Now he submitted that only a part of that paper (the *Observer*) was proved, and anything which appeared in another part of it ought not to be adduced against him unless it bore directly on the matter before the court.

He begged to refer his Lordship to the case of the King v. Perry. There it was attempted to bring some matters in another part of the paper (in which the alleged libel was) against the defendant; but it was held that no other parts of it could be adduced except they bore directly on the matter charged. The extract to which he was willing to call the attention of the witness he only supposed to be a speech delivered somewhere,

# Eighth Day – Friday 24 March 1820.

and he had, he maintained, a right to ask whether such words, addressed to the whole nation, and advising them to demand an inquiry, would be dangerous if delivered at the Manchester meeting.

**Robert Grundy**

Mr SCARLETT: I appeal to your Lordship whether this is evidence which can apply to the present case. It is my business to show, if I can, the irritation which might be excited by improper speeches delivered to large bodies of men, but the speech now offered was not delivered where such feelings of discontent could be excited. I do not mean to deny or disavow any expression contained in that speech; but I ask, is it decent in a court of justice to offer that which occurred in Parliament and which could not be published without a breach of privilege? No judge could allow, or jury receive as evidence, a report of what occurs in Parliament. If I had published my speech, and that it contained anything of a seditious nature, I might be indicted for it; but a report of what passed there is not evidence, and I submit that what cannot be proved ought not to be supposed. I again repeat that I do not, and shall not, disavow what is said in that speech, and I have no personal objection to its being quoted; but, standing here as I do, I am bound to oppose it.

Mr HUNT: I hope your Lordship will not think that I offer this as a speech in Parliament.

Mr Justice BAYLEY: If Mr Hunt had put this extract as a speech delivered in Parliament and asked an opinion of the witness on it, that certainly could not be allowed. But here the case is different. The question is whether such and such speeches, if addressed to the meeting on the sixteenth, would have produced danger to the town of Manchester. The speech is only a supposed thing, and the question asked is as to the effect which such words, if used, might have been likely to produce. It is in that sense alone that I could allow the question to be put; and it was on the ground that the language of the former extract was from Mr Scarlett's own imagination that I allowed it to be read. But Mr Hunt, in putting this question, might use the same words that were used in Parliament on another occasion; and, as a man, I might know that they were a report of something that passed there: but as a lawyer, and in the discharge of my duty here, I cannot refuse them. It is a matter of delicacy, and I myself would rather the question were not put; but still I think the defendant has a right to put it.

Mr HUNT: Your Lordship has now allowed me to put the question, but I should not be doing justice to my own feelings if I were to put it after what has just fallen from your Lordship; I shall therefore, my Lord, waive it.[194]

# Hunt and Others.

**Robert Grundy**

[Re-examination continued by Mr HUNT.] Do you not think that the public notice and advertisements of the meeting might have brought the separate parties into Manchester, without a previous communication between them? — It is possible, certainly; but I should suppose the way they came was arranged. I saw nothing in their manner that day, nothing in the deportment of the people different from other public occasions except in their being in procession. I have seen benefit societies. They are very frequently attended with banners and flags. I have seen the proclamation of peace. I have seen the people walk abreast, but not in such numbers as on the day of the meeting of the sixteenth.

[By THE COURT.] Do you mean by 'previous arrangements' the time or the manner? — I mean both, my Lord.

Without any meeting of delegates, do you think the arrangement might have taken place as you saw it? — I should not think it absolutely necessary that there should have been previous arrangements between the several places to come as they did, but it is probable there was.

**Thomas Rothwell**

THOMAS ROTHWELL, sworn and examined by Mr HUNT.

I am a tanner and live at Cheetham, about a mile and a half from Manchester. I saw the people go to Manchester. I live near to Mr Heath (a witness for the prosecution). I saw the Bury division move on five abreast, and they went peaceably. I heard no violent expression from them. There were women and children, some of twelve years old, with them. They walked five abreast as well as the men. There were a great number of women. I can't say how many. They were in the proportion of eight men to one woman or child. There were children of both sorts (boys and girls). I heard them say they were going to hear Mr Hunt. I saw nothing in their manner or conduct to excite the least fear in me for my person or property.

I have known Mr Johnson seven years. I never heard him say that he ever intended to overturn the government.

*Cross-examined* by Mr LITTLEDALE.

---

194 The following is the debated extract from Mr Scarlett's speech: 'The people meet to petition. The magistrates issue a warrant to arrest certain individuals and, that being executed, the yeomanry disperse the crowd at the edge of the sabre. Three days afterwards the thanks of the Prince Regent were given both to the civil and military authorities; and what was the unavoidable inference but that opinions, however absurd or preposterous, were to be put down by the bayonet, and that ministers intended to act on a system of military coercion? Did not this demand inquiry? Did not this call upon the whole nation to insist that inquiry should be instituted?' (*Dolby's Parliamentary Register*, Second Session, page 43.)

# Eighth Day – Friday 24 March 1820.

There might be about three thousand persons in the Bury party. Bury is about nine miles from Manchester.

*Thomas Rothwell*

JOSEPH SCHOFIELD, sworn and examined by Mr HUNT.

*Joseph Schofield*

I reside at Hollinwood, near Manchester. I am not in business.

I saw one of the parties going to Manchester on the sixteenth. I think the party was from Oldham. I saw the black flag with them. I observed their conduct as they passed along. It was peaceable, orderly, and quiet. I did not go to Manchester that day. I received no insult from the party. Few of them had sticks, and these were common walking sticks. None of them had large staves shouldered as soldiers do their muskets. I felt no alarm and saw nothing to excite it. I never heard anything said about making a Moscow of Manchester.

SAMUEL SLACK, sworn and examined by Mr HUNT.

*Samuel Slack*

I live at Manchester, in Windmill Street. I was at home on 16 August last. I was confined the greater part of the forenoon in my warehouse in Oldham Street. I saw several processions pass Oldham Street. I went home to see the meeting. I did not think my property in any danger. My house was in that situation that I could look over the whole of the area (St Peter's). I was in an upper room where I could see the whole of what passed. I was about thirty yards from the hustings and had a view of Mr Buxton's house. I saw no procession enter the field but that which came with the carriage. The others had previously arrived.

I was busy that morning; business went on as usual. I did not see any person shut up shop and give up business that day. I did not see or hear any person who expressed any alarm for the safety of the town that day. I saw no persons march by with large clubs or staves. I saw walking sticks – common walking sticks. Saw no persons in the fields with staves shouldered as muskets, nor did I see anything in the field before the military arrived which excited in me or in those about me any alarm. I went from my own house to within eight or nine yards of the hustings; if I had wished to have gone to the hustings, I saw nothing to prevent me except that the press was uncommonly great – that's all.

My intention in going to the hustings was to hear the speeches. I remained till I heard a man on the top of a house say that the cavalry was coming. I had seen all the meetings there before and saw nothing in this different from the others except that this was larger. I had seen three or four meetings before, and they met and dispersed peaceably. I did not see the dispersion of the blanket meeting.

When I heard that the military were coming, I made the best of my way to my own house. I heard some people say, 'Stand still!' and that

# Hunt and Others.

**Samuel Slack**

the military would not hurt them. When I got to my window, the cavalry had got upon the field and were ranged parallel with Mr Buxton's house. They were cheering the soldiers, and in a short time the cavalry cheered in return. They flourished their swords and charged down towards the hustings.

[By THE COURT.] At the time the cavalry arrived on the ground, was anything done to oppose or resist them? — I did not see anything to resist them, except that the crowd was dense. I saw nothing done to resist them. There was no hooting, hissing and groaning at the cavalry. I did not see any stones or brickbats or sticks thrown at them or thrown up in the air. I was looking that way. I saw no sticks held up at any time in defiance of the military. I could not see over the hustings, but I could see a wing of each of the cavalry.

*Cross-examined* by Mr Serjeant HULLOCK.

I saw several meetings before. I went as a spectator, from curiosity. This was the largest I ever saw. I don't mean to say that the former meetings had come in procession. There might be ten thousand or fifteen thousand, but I cannot say exactly. I am in the service of M'Farlane and Barbaud, shippers at Manchester. It was their property which was in Oldham Street. Neither of my masters are here today. We have only one in Manchester.

*Re-examined* by Mr HUNT.

I did not hear my master or anybody else express any fear for their property. If we had been afraid, we should have shut up the warehouse and gone home: we did so the next day.

How were you employed from the time you went to the meeting till four o'clock in the afternoon? — Why, in the beginning of the afternoon we were assisting the wounded.

**John Molineux**

JOHN MOLINEUX, sworn and examined by Mr HUNT.[195]

---

195 *Saunders's News-Letter*, 30 July 1819, reporting the Manchester Quarter Sessions: 'At these sessions, five indictments have been found against James Wroe, the editor of the newspaper called the *Manchester Observer*, for various libels upon the constituted authorities of the country. ... The first is for a seditious libel against the government and constitution of the country; the second and third are of the like nature; the fourth is for a libel on the whole body of the clergy, without regard to their denomination, so as to affect religion generally; and the fifth is for a libel on the administration of justice. Wroe has already been apprehended upon a Bench warrant upon two of the indictments, and has found bail: his own recognizance in £500 in each case, with two sureties in £250 each. The sureties in one case were Joseph Johnson of Smedley, brush-maker, £250; and John Molineux of Strangeways, tin-plate worker, £250.'

# Eighth Day – Friday 24 March 1820.

**John Molineux**

I live in Market Street, Manchester. I am a lamp manufacturer and tin-plate worker. Market Street, though a narrow street, is one of the principal streets and great thoroughfares of Manchester. I left my shop about eleven o'clock. The street was crowded several times in the day, but I did not see any processions go through it. I did not shut up my shop in consequence of what I saw. I know Mr Styan, the gunsmith. He is my next door neighbour. I did not observe his shop shut when I went to the meeting at eleven o'clock. I did not then observe any shops shut up about me. I left my wife's sister to take care of the shop. If I had apprehended any danger, I would not have left my shop at all.

I returned to my shop before twelve. I saw no necessity then of shutting up my windows. When I returned from the meeting, it was by the way of Back King Street. I saw no shops shut up except the toy-shop and the saddler's shop at the end of the street. I went again there at twelve. I met my daughter on the ground. She expressed a wish to go, and went with her uncle. My daughter is sixteen years of age. I remained on the field till the meeting was dispersed. My daughter remained with me and my brother in law. I saw the military arrive.

[By THE COURT.] I was in a situation to see them from the time they arrived in front of Mr Buxton's. In the course of that day I saw nothing calculated to create in my mind, or the mind of anybody with whom I conversed, any alarm. I heard no alarm expressed. No opposition was made to the military that I saw. There was no groaning or hooting or hissing at them. I perceived nothing done to intimidate them. I saw no stones or sticks or brickbats thrown at them or thrown up in the air.

*Cross-examined* by Mr Serjeant CROSS.

I was at the meeting before, of a similar kind. It was when Mr Hunt was there. I believe Mr Hunt presided on that occasion. I do not remember Johnson on the hustings. I dined with Mr Hunt and others that day at the Spread Eagle. There were speeches and toasts. I heard a toast given 'to the immortal memory of Thomas Paine'. Mr Hunt was then in the chair.

Mr Justice BAYLEY: Is this evidence?

Mr Sergeant Cross and Mr Scarlett submitted that it was evidence if it showed that Mr Hunt had, by speeches or toasts, incited to disloyalty or disaffection.

Mr Justice Bayley said he would allow them to put any question as to the character of the witness. The witness had admitted that he was present when an improper toast was given – but then this was at a dinner in January, and it did not follow that because a man was disloyal in January, he should also be disloyal in August.

Mr Scarlett observed that similar evidence was allowed in the case of

# Hunt and Others.

**John Molineux**

Horne Tooke and Hardy.[196]

Mr Hunt replied that that was part of the case, and did not refer to any time previously to the particular acts charged. He (Mr Hunt) had been invited to the dinner, and anything which fell from him there or which was said by others could not, he submitted, be now urged as evidence against him unless it could be shown that it tended to produce the conspiracy charged.

After some long and desultory observation on both sides, Mr Justice Bayley, who had in the meantime looked into the case of Horne Tooke, decided that the question was one which ought not to be put. It was not, he conceived, proper to bring any act of the defendants against them now which occurred before the period of the present charge. If an indictment were preferred against a man for perjury, it would not be admissible evidence to say that up to the period of the alleged crime he had been in the constant habit of not telling the truth.

It was then contended by the counsel for the prosecution that the question ought to be put, as it might affect the character of the party.

Mr Justice Bayley admitted it might, in another shape; but though it would be legal in another manner, yet having got at it in an illegal way now, he held that it could not be received. As the defendant had given evidence of character, it was competent to the prosecutors to give also general evidence of character, but not in this way. The question was not admitted.

[Examination continued.] Mr Hunt was in the chair at that meeting. I do not remember Johnson, Knight, Bamford, or Moorhouse being present. I believe Mr Hunt made a speech after dinner. I did not hear him say that he would be amongst them soon again. I had no expectation of the kind. He was, I believe, called on to take the chair by the committee. I was not one of the committee. I was not at Johnson's house before 16 August last. I never was there in my life. I attended the meeting on 16 August. I cannot say I disapproved of the objects of that meeting.

**Isaac Wood**

ISAAC WOOD, sworn and examined by Mr HUNT.

I live in Back Queen Street, Manchester. I am a tanner. My residence is about two hundred yards from the place where the meeting was held. I have a wife and eight children. I was in Manchester on 16 August last. I went to the country on Saturday, the fourteenth, and returned about one o'clock on the Monday. I did not find on my return that anything had stopped my business.

I waited at the meeting for a few minutes. There were a great number of persons assembled together. I then went home to my family, but I did

---

196  Treason trials of 1794.

# Eighth Day – Friday 24 March 1820.

not do so on account of any alarm I felt from witnessing the meeting. I saw nothing to excite alarm. I went home, as usual, to my dinner. I did not find my wife and family in a state of consternation. None of them expressed any alarm to me. I have no reason to suppose that they felt apprehension or alarm on account of my absence. I returned to the meeting, which was not then dispersed. The cavalry had just come to the ground. I was opposite the end of the Quakers' meeting house. I saw a part of the cavalry come in. They advanced towards the hustings and no resistance was made to them by the crowd. They went up close to the hustings and surrounded them. I was in a situation where I must have seen any opposition made by the people to the military, had resistance taken place. I saw the cavalry from the time they were seventy yards from the hustings until they came quite close to them. They were not, that I know of, hissed, hooted or groaned at. I saw nothing thrown at or lifted up against them. If any stones, brickbats or sticks had been hurled in the air, I was in a situation to have seen them

*Cross-examined* by Mr LITTLEDALE.

I have been acquainted with Mr Johnson for a short time. I am one of his bail. I am not bail for any of the other defendants.

*Re-examined* by Mr HUNT.

I have been in the volunteers at Manchester. I was in a corps who clothed and armed themselves, but I left it about two years before it was disbanded. I was connected with it for seven years. I entered about the year 1802. It was a rifle corps.

Mr Hunt here expressed a desire, that, as so much evidence had been given in proof of certain facts, it would be well if the learned judge were to state to the jury that those facts were fully proved, and that there was no need to call further evidence to them.

Mr Justice BAYLEY: I cannot at this moment suggest anything to the jury.

MR JAMES SCHOLEFIELD, sworn and examined by Mr HUNT.[197]

I am a dissenting minister and live at a place called Hulme, near Manchester. I was at Manchester on 16 August last. I came in on business. I saw several of the processions coming into Manchester. I went there

---

197 Scholefield was the minister of Christ Church, Hulme. Paul A. Pickering and Alex Tyrrell identify 'Scholefield' as 'the spelling that he favoured' – ahead of 'Schofield' and 'Scholfield' – in their article, "'In the thickest of the fight": The Reverend James Scholefield (1790-1855) and the Bible Christians of Manchester and Salford" (*Albion*, Volume 26, Issue 3, Fall 1994, pp. 461-482).

# Hunt and Others.

**James Scholefield**

to attend professional business. There were many women and children with the parties.

Mr Justice BAYLEY: That fact appears to be sufficiently proved.

Mr SCARLETT: It is not only proved that women and children were present, but even their proportion was spoken to.

[Examination continued.] I saw the people going to St Peter's Field. The processions exhibited the utmost regularity, jocularity and good humour. I saw no person insulted. I was situated between the house where the magistrates were and the hustings. I was in an elevated situation which commanded the whole meeting. I observed a double row of special constables about ten yards before me. They extended from Mr Buxton's house to the hustings. I was informed that the magistrates were at Mr Buxton's house, and I was near enough to see some of them through the window.

I was there when you arrived on the field. After you had arrived and got on the hustings, a board was exhibited bearing in large characters the words, 'Order! Order!' As far as I could perceive, every disposition was shown by the people to obey that direction. There was no interruption by talking or otherwise. The different divisions had bands, which played the air generally called 'Rule, Britannia!' and the national anthem of 'God Save the King'. When the latter was played, the people, for the most part, took off their hats.

I felt no alarm, nor did I hear any person express alarm at the meeting. I was highly gratified to see so numerous an assembly behaving in so peaceable a manner. I saw the military arrive; I perceived no opposition to have been manifested towards them. I saw nothing held up except the hats of the people. As the cavalry advanced, the people held up their hats as a sort of guard against the cutting of the swords. The people were fleeing away as fast as they could. There were no brickbats, stones or sticks hurled against them. They passed within ten yards of me. The people attempted to disperse immediately, but the crowd was so intense that they could not.

*Cross-examined* by Mr SCARLETT.

When the cavalry advanced, the people at the extremity of the crowd fled, but those immediately contiguous to the hustings closed in. Some of the constables followed the cavalry; others were mixed with the crowd, and could not get out. I preach at a church called Christ Church. I never saw so large a congregation at one time before. Though my voice is good, I could not have made all the people at the meeting hear me. I could have made upwards of twenty thousand of the people hear me.

I think the meeting was a pleasant and friendly one. There were eighty

# Eighth Day – Friday 24 March 1820.

thousand persons present. I was highly gratified at the sight of a meeting so numerous and so peaceable. I did not disapprove of the meeting – I approved of it 'as a people'. I could not approve of the meeting particularly, unless I knew the intentions with which it was called. I saw the placards convening the meeting.

James Scholefield

I saw several flags. One of them had two hands united, and the word 'Union' written under them. I saw another inscribed, 'No Corn Laws'. I also saw a flag on which were the words, 'Annual Parliaments, Universal Suffrage, and Vote by Ballot'. I did not consider those banners as pointing out the objects for which the meeting was convened. They only spoke the sentiments of those who carried them – that universal suffrage, annual parliaments and vote by ballot would be agreeable to them. I should approve of a meeting called for the purpose of inculcating doctrines of this kind, if they were beneficial to the people.

I have written for several newspapers, but not particularly for the *Manchester Observer*. I am not a hired writer. I wrote two pieces for the *Manchester Observer*. Those pieces were not of a political nature, farther than the Scripture connected them with politics. The Scripture does not make use of the words 'Annual Parliaments' and 'Universal Suffrage'. The Scripture may, in many points of view, be connected with politics. One of the articles I wrote was (I believe) before, the other since the meeting. I did not sign my name to either of the essays. There was no particular title to either of them. One of the articles probably may be 'A letter to the subscribers of the Manchester declaration'. Several letters were written on that subject. My address was to the ministers – to the ministers of the Four Evangelists – I mean to the clergymen who had signed the declaration in support of the police of Manchester. I wrote to disapprove of murder – to express my opinion that a minister ought not to approve of murder. I did not condemn the clergy. I would not condemn any one. I wished to convince. I blamed the clergy. The Scriptures were my guide. The declaration was signed by many of the clergy of the Church of England. It was not signed by the majority of the dissenting ministers. I am not attached to any sect in particular. I and my flock conform ourselves to the Scriptures and act according to them. We are denominated 'Bible Christians'.

I did not know that Mr Carlile was to be present on 16 August. I am not acquainted with that gentleman. I saw two or three of my congregation present at the meeting. They were not on the hustings.

*Re-examined* by Mr HUNT.

I believe my two letters were written after 16 August. One of them went to condemn the conduct of the magistrates who had signed a

# Hunt and Others.

James Scholefield

declaration in favour of the conduct of the police of Manchester on 16 August. I cannot speak positively as to the time when I wrote the articles. They were signed with the initial 'S'. My first letter contained a disproval of the prominent part which some of the clergy had taken in political matters.

Thomas Brooks

THOMAS BROOKS, sworn and examined by Mr HUNT.

I live at Stockport and am a pattern-drawer. I was at Manchester on 16 August last. I was on Mr Moorhouse's coach at the Bulkeley Arms, and saw a great number of people pass by. Moorhouse was present with me most part of the time.

I went to Manchester in company with Moorhouse. We passed the people about a mile from Stockport. They were not walking regularly, but in an indiscriminate manner. There were women and children amongst the crowd. I saw no bludgeons with the people. Some of them had walking sticks. The people passed us at the watering-place where the coach stopped. All was quiet and peaceable. We passed the people again before they got to Manchester, at Hardy Green Bridge. We proceeded straight to the White Bear, situated in a street called Piccadilly. The Ashton people were in sight when we approached the White Bear. Hardy Green is about a mile from the White Bear.

I know Mrs Moorhouse. The coach overtook her on the road, about a mile and a half from Stockport. She was taken into the coach. She was then pregnant. The horses were taken from the coach at the White Bear, and the people wanted him to go on to the meeting with the coach – which, he said, he was willing to do if he were paid. The coach did not, however, proceed to the ground, Mr Moorhouse being afraid that people would climb on the roof and break it down.

I went to the field soon after one o'clock. Moorhouse was not with me. I saw him come to the field in a carriage. I was then taking some refreshment in Deansgate. The carriage in which you were got within five or six yards of the hustings. I did not see Moorhouse quit the coach or go upon the hustings. I was the person who handed down the chair to enable you and the others to get up on the hustings. I was very near the hustings and if Moorhouse was on them, I must have seen him. I was between the carriage and the hustings, about a yard from them.

I saw no people locked arm-in-arm round the hustings. I saw nothing but a great crowd. I stood near the hustings till the cavalry appeared.

*Cross-examined* by Mr Serjeant HULLOCK.

I went to Manchester by the coach, in order to attend the meeting. Mr Moorhouse was on the roof with me and other passengers. He did not tell

# Eighth Day – Friday 24 March 1820.

me what was to be done at the meeting. We had no conversation of any moment. I did not ask Mr Moorhouse what the resolutions were to be.

**Thomas Brooks**

I knew that Mr Hunt had been at Mr Moorhouse's. I saw him standing near the door. I saw Mr Hunt and Mr Moorhouse going to Manchester on Monday 9 August. I have attended very few meetings. I was present at one that was held in January, at which, I believe, Mr Hunt presided. The Stockport division were mustering at a place called Sandy Brow, at Stockport. I was present at one meeting there. I never saw Moorhouse at any of the meetings at Sandy Brow.

When I passed through Stockport in the morning, there might be about eighty or a hundred persons assembled. We passed the Ashton division on the road. The people were walking in a straggling way, not at all like military. Mrs Saxton and some others were in Mr Hunt's carriage.

I do not know Carlile and cannot say whether he was there or not. The people made way promiscuously to admit the carriage to pass. Hunt and Johnson got on the hustings, but I lost sight of Moorhouse.

WILLIAM BROOKS, sworn and examined.

**William Brooks**

Was son of last witness, and corroborated his father's evidence that Mr Moorhouse was not on the hustings on 16 August; he was with him in the Windmill public house when the cavalry advanced to the hustings.

JOHN HOBSON, JUN., sworn and examined.

**John Hobson**

Was not in any profession; resided at Heath Green, three miles from Manchester. Was not acquainted with many of the inhabitants. Was in a house in Windmill Street, overlooking the meeting of 16 August. He was with his uncle and friend. The house in which he was, was exactly behind the hustings.

He saw the meeting assemble, and conducted most peaceably; he had no apprehension whatever respecting the safety of the town. He saw the soldiers advance to the hustings. There was no disposition whatever to resist them on the part of the people; quite the contrary. There were no stones, brickbats or clubs thrown in the air as the yeomanry approached. He did not meet that morning a single individual who had the slightest apprehension of that meeting.

*Cross-examined.*

He went to the meeting with his uncle who had come over from Liverpool, and had never been at a meeting before.

JOSEPH BARRETT, sworn and examined.

**Joseph Barrett**

Resided at Newton Heath, where he was a manufacturer and employed

# Hunt and Others.

**Joseph Barrett**

from one to two hundred men. They had a warehouse also in the market place at Manchester. He was there on 16 August in company with the last witness, whose testimony he distinctly corroborated in every part respecting the peaceable demeanour of Mr Hunt and the meeting up to the time of their violent dispersion by the military, to whom not the smallest opposition was made. There were no sticks, brickbats nor stones flung about, nor was there any hooting. He did not see Mr Hunt point to any persons and say, 'There are your enemies: get them down, and keep them down'. No such thing occurred, or he must have heard it.

*Cross-examined.*

Did not recollect any subscription for blanketeers. He was not concerned in any Reform Club.

**Jonathan Hobson**

JONATHAN HOBSON, sworn and examined by Mr HUNT.

Was with the two last witnesses at Manchester; also related the same description of what had occurred there on 16 August. He stated that he resided at Liverpool where he was a merchant; he also had a house and a third of a warehouse at Manchester.

He overlooked the whole field where the meeting assembled from the window of a house directly behind the hustings. He went there out of mere curiosity and got into the house as he did not wish to stand in a crowd. He saw no bludgeons whatever among the people; there were some common walking sticks and about a dozen white wands not thicker than his finger. He saw the line of special constables reaching from Mr Buxton's house nearly – but not quite up – to the hustings. The people were more compact near the hustings than those at a distance. The circle next the hustings had their arms in each other prior to Mr Hunt's coming. After that, he did not think they remained linked together. It was impossible for him to see whether more than one row was linked. A small space was kept open about two yards in front of the hustings, but he could not say whether it remained so after Mr Hunt came; he thought not.

The crowd was perfectly quiet, except when they gave occasional shouts. There were two persons said something to the meeting before Mr Hunt came, but he could not hear what they said, though he heard Mr Hunt. No military (infantry) made their appearance in Dickinson Street while Mr Hunt was speaking. He heard him say something about keeping down whoever disturbed the meeting, but no such expressions could have been addressed to the military, for no soldier was then in sight. He considered the words thrown out to anybody who would venture to be riotous. He heard Mr Hunt exhort the meeting to be quiet and defeat the

# Eighth Day – Friday 24 March 1820.

wishes of their enemies, and not to call out, 'Silence!'

You then said if anybody was there to disturb the peace of the meeting, they were to put him down and keep him down. He saw the cavalry arrive, and saw nothing done by the people to them like intimidation or resistance; nothing whatever was thrown at them. There was a great shout on their approach – a shout (as he thought) of welcome, like that on Mr Hunt's approach. He recollected the music playing up some tunes, particularly 'See, the Conquering Hero Comes'. He heard Mr Hunt say no such words as, 'They' – the military – 'are few, very few; and we are a host against them'.

The people were round the hustings just as they would be anywhere else in a crowd. They (the crowd) exhibited no appearance of disciplined troops; he observed a great many women mixed with the crowd and apparently dressed in their best clothes. The greatest part of them were near the hustings. He saw no defiance whatever hurled against the cavalry. If any sticks had been brandished or stones thrown, he must have seen them – no such thing took place. He saw nothing till the cavalry arrived which occasioned in his mind the least apprehension for the safety of the town. Until then he saw nothing at all calculated to excite fear in any rational mind.

*Cross-examined.*

The house in which he was, was about the same distance from the hustings as Mr Buxton's was. What occurred near the latter, unless spoken very loud, he could not hear. The line of the constables extended to nearly ten yards of the hustings. There was still a very thick crowd between there and the hustings. It was after two persons said something from the hustings, before Mr Hunt came, that the front row before the hustings – but not to the back – locked arms. They opened to admit Mr Hunt. He could see the crowd.

WILLIAM BURNS, sworn and examined.

Had something to do in making the ornament for the Bury flag; he made a piece of tin in the form of a fleur de lis and was to paint it yellow, but, not having much time on his hands, he painted it red. It came to him on the Saturday evening late and, not liking to paint it on Sunday, and having no yellow paint by him at the moment, he used the red. This was the only reason.

JOHN SMITH, sworn and examined.

Was a cotton merchant at Manchester. Remembered 16 August, and was on that day in a house that overlooked St Peter's Field. The house

# Hunt and Others.

**John Smith** was in Mount Street and in the same row as Mr Buxton's.

He then described the assembling of the meeting, their orderly and peaceable demeanour. He also saw the military arrive, and said there was not the slightest resistance opposed to them. He saw nothing in the conduct of the meeting to excite in the mind any apprehension for the safety of the town.

He saw the yeomanry form in front of Mr Buxton's house, for he was in the next house but one to it. He heard no hissing or groaning until the dispersion took place. There was some cheering before the cavalry advanced to the hustings.

*Cross-examined.*

Was a partner in the cotton firm. He remembered the placards convening the meeting. He did not approve of annual parliaments and universal suffrage.

**Thomas William Sanderson** THOMAS WILLIAM SANDERSON, sworn and examined.

He was a merchant in the firm of Sanderson and Co. at Manchester. Their house of business was at Manchester, but his private residence was twelve miles distant from the town. He generally came into Manchester once or twice a week in his own carriage. He was there on 16 August and saw the meeting assembled. He transacted his ordinary business during the whole of the day.

He went to St Peter's Field about twelve o'clock. He went there out of curiosity, and most certainly not as a radical reformer. He went to get an affidavit which it was necessary should be sworn before a magistrate. For that purpose, he went to Mr Buxton's house. He saw nobody that day in apparent alarm in consequence of that meeting until its dispersion took place by the military.

*Cross-examined* by Mr Serjeant CROSS.

He merely entered Manchester on that morning, and of course could not state what the feeling was there on the previous day. While he was getting his affidavit sworn, he did not learn of any alarm among the magistrates; he was with them getting his private business done about five minutes; he was not a stranger among the magistrates, for he knew Mr Fletcher.

He did not approve of the object of the meeting; he disapproved of the manner in which the meeting was brought together; he had seen large meetings before, but never meetings formed of large bodies marching like that. He knew country people went in bodies to a racecourse. He did not like to see people brought together in large bodies from the country.

# Eighth Day – Friday 24 March 1820.

From the then temper of the people, however, he did not see anything inconsistent with the safety of the town in the congregating of a hundred thousand people in Manchester. From the temper of the people, he apprehended no outrage. The labouring classes were quiet, though some discontents prevailed. But he judged of their temper from what he saw of them on the particular day.

His private house in the country was situated in the midst of a very populous number of labouring people: they were then quiet and contented. There certainly did prevail a discontent at Manchester among the working people, in consequence of their not being able to earn sufficient for their subsistence. He repeated, however, that he saw no danger from the bringing together of a multitude in Manchester. He did not think danger likely to accrue from assembling a hundred thousand of the labouring people at Manchester; he certainly disapproved of the bringing people from the country in this manner because it led to idleness and possibly to danger, but that was a mere supposition of his. He was not a radical reformer; he did not understand the term 'radical'.

Mr Serjeant CROSS: No, nor I.

Witness: He might be a reformer; every man was to a certain extent a reformer. He had not the slightest knowledge of Mr Hunt, but he was an enemy to violent measures of any kind. He was a man of very large property.

Mr HUNT: You do not know what a radical reformer means? — No.

If you heard it meant, as was insinuated in the famous speech of a learned counsel, a pistol loaded with nine bullets, would you believe it?

Mr Justice Bayley laughed, and prevented the witness from giving any answer. It being now half past seven o'clock, the trial was adjourned until nine o'clock tomorrow morning.

Mr Hunt said that he had a number of witnesses remaining to give similar evidence to that which he had already laid before the court. He felt very indisposed to occupy the court unnecessarily, but the moment he had got a hint that sufficient had been shown, he would stop.

Mr Justice BAYLEY: You must be entirely governed in your case by your own discretion. It would be unbecoming in me to drop one word which would have the effect of inducing you to withhold a single witness whose testimony you may think material.

Mr HUNT said he had already sent home eighty-three witnesses from a conviction that those already examined had said quite enough, touching the same points to which he meant to call them.

One of the jury having intimated some desire to know the probable duration of the remainder of the trial, Mr Pearson, who has been indefatigably occupied as solicitor for the defendants, said that they

*Thomas William Sanderson*

# Hunt and Others.

Thomas William Sanderson

meant only to call four more witnesses as to facts, and two to impeach the character of some of the witnesses for the prosecution. He thought – unless the cross-examinations were very protracted – the testimony of these witnesses would not occupy more than three hours.

Mr Justice BAYLEY: Then I apprehend, gentlemen, we shall have a speech from the learned counsel in reply, and it will remain afterwards for me to direct your attention to some leading points which may guide you in your coming to due consideration of the whole circumstances of the case.

*[Adjourned.]*

# Ninth Day – Saturday 25 March 1820.

*On Mr Justice Bayley entering the court, the deputy sheriff requested any gentleman of the jury present would hand to his Lordship the letter by which they were summoned. Several Jurors immediately handed over the letters they received on being summoned – they were all alike.*

*The judge read the letter, which merely intimated to the special jurors that they were summoned but did not use a single syllable beyond this mere intimation. His Lordship, on reading this letter, remarked that he saw nothing of irregularity whatever in it. Such an intimation was by no means unusual when there was hardly time enough to have the special jury reduced and the regular distringas issued. There was nothing in any manner irregular in this letter.*

EDMUND DARLEY, sworn and examined by Mr HUNT.

I reside in Manchester. I am a builder. I have known John Willie, a butcher, from two to three years. From what has come to my knowledge, I most certainly would not believe him on his oath.

*Cross-examined* by Mr SCARLETT.

I have lived in Manchester twenty years. I never saw Willie examined in a court of justice. I was at the meeting on 16 August. I never was at a public meeting before or since; I went out of curiosity.

[By THE JUDGE:] My reason for not believing him is that he has within the last few months frequently deceived me.

WILLIAM PHILLIPS, sworn and examined by Mr HUNT.

I live in Salford, Manchester. I am a butcher. I know John Willie; he has been a butcher, but he is now out of business. I have known him several years. From what I know of his character, I would not believe him on his oath.

*Cross-examined* by Mr Serjeant HULLOCK.

I have lived in Salford nearly all my life. I left Manchester on Wednesday night. I did not before that see any account of the progress of the trial. I did not see an account of the witnesses examined. I did not know that Willie was examined until I came to York.

I was not at the meeting on 16 August. I was not one of those who cheered Mr Hunt on his going home last night. I came to speak of Willie's

# Hunt and Others.

**William Phillips**

character. I have got my subpoena here. I never saw Willie examined in a court of justice in my life. He was in jail in Lancaster and took the benefit of the Insolvent Act. I was asked if I knew Willie, and I said yes, and then I got a subpoena.

**Rev. John Gough Roberts**

THE REV. JOHN GOUGH ROBERTS, sworn and examined by Mr HUNT.

I reside at Manchester. I am a dissenting minister. I reside in Mosley Street. I was at home the greater part of the day on 16 August. I saw several parties pass my house. I went over the ground before you arrived, and I afterwards saw you in the marketplace with a party attending you. I afterwards went to my own house.

I was not at the meeting, but I went to the ground after it was dispersed. I could see a part of the meeting from my dressing room window. When in the town, I saw nothing which excited fear in my mind.

**Michael Heaviside**

MICHAEL HEAVISIDE, sworn and examined by Mr HUNT.

I am a general dealer in Manchester. I buy goods and finish them. I have a warehouse in Palace Street but I reside in Boundary Street. I have a wife and four children. My warehouse was open as usual on 16 August. The business of the town appeared, upon the whole, to go on as usual; there was occasionally a shop shut up.

In my way home I went to the meeting. I was there when you arrived. The meeting appeared to be a peaceable one; I saw nothing to the contrary. I remained until the yeomanry arrived. Up to the period of the arrival of the troops, I saw nothing which excited in my mind any fears for the safety of my person, my family or my property.

*Cross-examined* by Mr LITTLEDALE.

I saw nothing of the processions as they entered the town.

**Rev. Mr. Robert Hindmarsh**

THE REV. MR ROBERT HINDMARSH, sworn and examined by Mr HUNT.[198]

I am a dissenting minister and reside at Salford. I was in Manchester on 16 August last. I saw several parties pass on to the meeting on that day. They appeared to me to be perfectly peaceable and quiet.

I was upon St Peter's Field near an hour and a half; I made it a point to observe what was the character and complexion of the meeting and therefore I traversed every part of it. I went there merely as a spectator.

---

198 Hindmarsh, an early Swedenborgian, was the minister at the New Jerusalem Temple in Salford.

# Ninth Day – Saturday 25 March 1820.

**Rev. Mr. Robert Hindmarsh**

I considered, in the first place, that I was perfectly secure under the protection of the laws while the people remained in a state of tranquillity; I therefore thought I might remain upon the ground with safety. I saw nothing upon the ground which altered this impression. I everywhere heard congratulations on the peaceable complexion and character of the meeting, and every one hoped it would terminate quietly.

In the course of my perambulation, I went near the house in which the magistrates were. I saw a double line of constables leading to the hustings. The crowd were close to the constables. I saw no disposition in the people to insult them. The line of constables reached a considerable way into the crowd.

I remained upon the field until the cavalry arrived. I saw nothing before their arrival which excited any fears for the safety of person or property or the safety of the town. I had not the least idea of any such thing. I saw nothing which, in my judgement, could excite the fears of any rational, temperate, sober-minded man.

I am not a radical reformer. I never associated myself with any party in the state. I do not consider myself a political character. In consequence of what I had heard about the reformers, I went to the meeting. I wished to satisfy myself of the state of society. I thought the people appeared peaceful and cheerful in a remarkable degree. I should not, from what I saw, expect the crowd to follow bad advice. I think they were not disposed to acts of violence. I have lived nine years in Manchester and the neighbourhood.

I saw the cavalry arrive. I was then removing from the field. I was perhaps fifty yards from Mr Buxton's house. I saw a general bustle, and on looking round I saw the cavalry come up at a smart pace towards Mr Buxton's. I saw them go the hustings. From the first to the last, I saw nothing done either to intimidate or insult or oppose the military. If any hissing, hooting, groaning or brandishing of cudgels took place on their arrival, I think I must have seen it; but there was no such thing within my hearing and sight. I kept my eye on the cavalry until I found it necessary to provide for my own safety. I saw no stones, brickbats or sticks hurled in the air or at the cavalry.

*Cross-examined* by Mr SCARLETT.

I was standing near the Quakers' meeting house. There was a great crowd between me and the hustings. I went to inspect the meeting and – partly – to see Mr Hunt, whom I had not seen before. I have kept aloof from all parties for forty years.

I had nothing to do with the banners; they were, I think characteristic of the meeting. I consider 'Equal Representation or Death' to be nearly the

# Hunt and Others.

**Rev. Mr. Robert Hindmarsh**

same as 'Liberty or Death' – I mean that equal representation is essential to liberty. I think there was no intention of a breach of the peace on that day. I did not suppose that any of the banners were intended to be acted upon on that day; as to any future results, I am incapable of judging.

Mr SCARLETT: I ask you if you thought it safe to have the doctrine of 'equal representation or death' preached to the people? — I do not think the safety of the town was endangered by it upon that occasion.

Did you see a flag with the inscription, 'Let us die like men, and not be sold like slaves'? — No.

We will assume it to have been there, and now I ask you if it ought to have been held up to the people? — I consider it to be a general sentiment that, on many occasions in public life after Members of Parliament are elected, the voters are sold like slaves I think the preaching of such an opinion in public is safe. I do not know that I am qualified to say whether the people were sold like slaves. It is the duty of every man to preach what he believes true. I think that that doctrine, if used on the sixteenth, would not be productive of danger.

So that if a man thought representation itself was a tyranny, and that every man ought to have a personal vote in the making of laws, he has a right to preach it? — I did not say that. When I spoke of preaching what a man believed to be true, I spoke as a preacher and not as a politician. I do not conceive it expedient that a man should publicly inculcate everything he believes, but when people assemble to state and consider their grievances, they have a right to go the length of saying as their opinion that they are sold like slaves. I think the people have the same liberty of speech as is exercised by the House of Commons in doing business. They have a right to express their opinions, provided it is done consistently with the law and the peace of society. Sometimes an individual is not so good a judge of political matters as his neighbour. I think toleration in religion and politics should be equal. I think every man has a right to indulge his own thoughts consistently with the peace of society.

But who is to judge of the peace of society? — The proper functionaries.

Who are the proper functionaries? — The magistrates.

Had you any curiosity to see Carlile? — No. I do not know him. I did not see his name on a placard – or, if I did, I have forgotten it.

*Re-examined* by Mr HUNT.

If I had seen a placard – signed by seven hundred persons – calling a public meeting to consider of a reform in Parliament, I should not have called such a meeting either improper or illegal.

Mr Justice BAYLEY: Witness cannot judge of the illegality of the

# Ninth Day – Saturday 25 March 1820.

meeting.

Mr HUNT: Had anyone delivered an inflammatory speech exciting the meeting to acts of violence, I should consider it immoral and illegal. [To the witness.] Had you heard that a man had in a certain speech in a particular place – which speech was afterwards circulated by the public press – recommended the whole nation to insist on the performance of a particular act, should you think it illegal? — Witness: — Yes, if it was recommended to be done by violence. My understanding of the people being sold like slaves is when the voters sell their votes, and that the member returned disposes of the liberties of the people without consulting their interests. This I take to be selling the people. This, I think, is matter for the discussion of a public meeting. I did not hear the speakers. I think the meeting was dispersed before they went into the question.

*Rev. Mr. Robert Hindmarsh*

JOHN ROBINSON, sworn and examined by Mr HUNT.

I am a merchant residing in Manchester. I was there on 16 August. The people were nearly all assembled when I went to the meeting; I went at a quarter before one. I had previously been about my usual avocations. I was not out of my counting house until I went to the meeting. Persons called upon me that morning about business as usual.

I was in a situation on the ground to see the meeting. I was within thirty yards of Buxton's house when the cavalry arrived; they passed me as they formed. I was within thirty yards of them; I did not see any of the people offer any insult or violence to them. When they arrived, I was in a situation to see the conduct of the people nearest to them. When they came up I found some difficulty in getting out of their way. I did not see the people hiss, hoot, groan or brandish their cudgels at the cavalry as they advanced. I think if a man had put his hand above his head, I must have seen it. If there had been hissing or groaning, I must have heard it, unless it happened while I was falling back: in that case it might have happened without my knowledge. I saw the cavalry advance towards the hustings.

[By THE JUDGE:] While they were advancing, nothing was done to intimidate, oppose or insult them.

[By Mr Hunt:] I saw nothing on that day which excited my fears for the safety of myself or my family. If I had, I should not have gone to the meeting.

*John Robinson*

*Cross-examined* by Mr Serjeant CROSS.

I went to the meeting through curiosity. I do not think I could see better from Buxton's house than from where I stood.

# Hunt and Others.

**Henry Hunt**  Mr HUNT: My Lord, this closes our case.

## Prosecutor's reply

**Mr Scarlett**  Mr SCARLETT commenced his reply for the prosecution. The time had now arrived when it became him to address the jury on the evidence produced in this tedious but most important case, and neither on his own account nor on theirs would he take up more of their time (on which there had been so large a demand already) than he should feel to be necessary, and commanded by the most imperious duty. He need scarcely remind them that a counsel, in conducting a cause like the present, carries about with him no personal views – that he acts not from personal motives; that he is a minister of justice – that, in the observations which he finds it necessary to make, he acts on public principle – and that it is neither just nor candid to suspect him of any sinister intentions or to impute to him any improper motives while he performs what his conscience dictates and his office demands. He premised this because, in conducting this reply, he would endeavour with boldness to unmask the hypocrisy of the defence which they had heard, and show that four-fifths of the mass of evidence which had occupied their attention and exercised their patience for the last four days had no more to do with the issue now to be tried than with any other public transaction or any other meeting which the defendant had attended.

Before, however, he entered on this, he must make a few observations of a personal nature. He must show the manner, tone and temper observed by the defendant that they might be able to decide whether, in a court of justice, that system of intimidation and violence is to be acted upon which had been attempted – and with but too much success – in the town of Manchester. Fatal, indeed, would be the result, and melancholy the day, if that spirit of disorder and intimidation which had been manifested out of doors should ever find its way into a court of justice, and if this court should be converted into a hustings where the voice and decision of the jury should be demanded on grounds of popular fear or popular favour. He hoped he should not see that day; but, if he did, entertaining as he did the solemn conviction that the dearest rights and privileges of the people depended upon the calm, orderly and dignified administration of justice, he would struggle to prevent its approach. He therefore craved their indulgence while he proceeded to lay before them the observations which he had to make in this important cause, without any regard to popular favour or to popular clamour which he should despise himself if he did not despise.

He called upon them to attend to him while he made a few remarks on

# Ninth Day – Saturday 25 March 1820.

**Mr Scarlett**

what was not immediately connected with the case but was forced upon him by the conduct of one of the defendants (Mr Hunt). That defendant, on opening his speech for his defence, had chosen to say that, after the close of the evidence for the prosecution and the hearing of counsel for the other defendants, when he (Mr Hunt) asked that the court might meet an hour later on the following day to allow him to prepare himself for addressing the jury, labouring as he did under infirmity of body and anxiety of mind, the request was unfeelingly opposed by 'that man' ('pointing to me,' said the learned counsel). Nothing could be more untrue than the insinuation here made. The jury would recollect that when the defendant applied to the court to meet an hour later on the Tuesday, he (Mr Hunt) did it upon the ground not that he was indisposed, but that he might have a little more time for going through the great mass of evidence which had been taken in the case: he (Mr Scarlett) opposed the request because he did not think it necessary for the defendant's preparation. Sunday had intervened, during which he had time to examine the evidence of the previous week; and only three witnesses had been heard on the Monday, whose evidence it was easy to review. But he (Mr Scarlett) was accused of being unfeeling, as having opposed the request when made on the ground of ill-health, and this was done that it might go forth to the country that he acted on unfeeling and persecuting principles. If the defendant had applied for a little time on account of indisposition, he (Mr Scarlett) hoped that he was too well known in this place to be suspected of any wish to oppose it. He objected to the favour because he thought it was asked in order that an audience like that, whose feelings of zeal for the defendant his Lordship could scarcely check on a previous day, might be again collected to applaud him.

The next personal remark to which he would allude was that which had been made by the defendant on the expression of satisfaction which he (the learned counsel) had uttered in his opening speech that the cause was to be tried by a Yorkshire jury. He accused him (Mr Scarlett) of expressing that satisfaction while he knew that he had a retainer to oppose a change in the place of trial from Lancaster to York. The defendant knew that this was not true at the time he uttered it, but he thought that the statement would prejudice him (Mr Scarlett) in the opinion of the jury, and therefore he resolved to make it. He would now tell them the truth and briefly explain to them the real state of the facts. The defendant had applied on the last day of Term to have the venue altered from Lancaster to York. When he (Mr Scarlett) entered the court on that day, he had no knowledge that such an application was to be made; so far was he from being engaged to oppose it. He (Mr Scarlett) heard his honourable friends the Attorney- and Solicitor-

# Hunt and Others.

Mr Scarlett  General say that the object of the defendants was only delay, that they could never be brought to agree on coming to York, and that the trial would be postponed; but he (Mr Scarlett) did not speak a word or utter a syllable upon the subject. His (Mr Scarlett's) private friends well knew his sentiments, and were well aware that he was pleased with the change of place for the trial, and that what the defendant said was totally untrue. And he must do his learned friends the Attorney- and Solicitor-General the justice to mention to the jury what in his candour and gratitude the defendant had concealed: that so far were they from any desire of taking an undue advantage of him after the court had decided upon the change, that they had actually lengthened his recognizances, the recognizances of the defendants having been forfeited.

Mr Hunt here interrupted the learned counsel and denied that the recognizances had been forfeited or that he had received any favour from the law-officers of the Crown.

Mr Justice Bayley said that they had been forfeited – that the record was sent down too late.

[Mr Scarlett continued.] He mentioned these things not to defend himself (for he required no defence from such a charge coming from such a quarter, and that in a place where he was known), but to show the temper with which the defendant conducted himself. He had gone on to say that he (Mr Scarlett) wished a brief in the cause against the magistrates; but that he (Mr Hunt) could not get any counsel to bring forward their conduct properly in the Court of King's Bench. Now, in answer, he would say that if Mr Hunt had wished to bring the cause before the Court of King's Bench, there was not a counsel who would have objected to undertake it, or would not have lent him all the assistance in their power. But, instead of applying to any gentleman of the bar who, according to the rules of court and the regular administration of justice, must conduct such proceedings, he thought of making the application himself, though he was aware he could not be heard.

Mr Hunt again interrupted the learned counsel, declaring that he could not allow such mis-statements to pass uncontradicted. At the time he made the application to the Court of King's Bench, he was not aware that he was prevented by any rule of court from arguing the case for himself. Neither was it true that he had made no application to gentlemen of the Bar; he had applied to the Attorney-General, who had declined, and that the learned counsel (Mr Scarlett) well knew.

Mr SCARLETT: I do not know it, nor do I now believe it. The defendant, instead of making an application where it would have been heard, was determined to show his own powers and came into court while he knew he could not be listened to.

# Ninth Day – Saturday 25 March 1820.

Mr Hunt again declared the observation was untrue, and repeated that he had applied without success to the Attorney-General.

**Mr Scarlett**

Mr Scarlett said that if such an application was made, it was a mere application of impertinence. The defendant well knew that the Attorney-General never came into the Court of King's Bench unless called there to perform an official duty. Now, with regard to the third personal attack which had been made by the defendant, he did not think it necessary to animadvert on it, as the question had been already set at rest by his Lordship. The defendant had unjustifiably brought forward a charge against the under-sheriff in calling the jury, preparing himself, no doubt, for styling them, in case they brought in a verdict of guilty, a 'packed jury'. The defendant was most unfortunate in the number of his enemies; he was at war with all juries, with all magistrates, with all constables, with all peace-officers, with all authorities, with all the House of Lords and all the House of Commons. In proceeding with his personal attacks, he (Mr Hunt) had stated that he (Mr Scarlett) had invented part of the charges against him, and that the bloody dagger of which he (Mr Scarlett) had spoken only existed in his distorted imagination. If the Lord of the Manor of Glastonbury, who was so highly respected in his neighbourhood and who always enjoyed the intimacy of the clergyman of the parish, had imbibed from his society any portion of justice or candour, he might have supposed, in the first instance, that he (Mr Scarlett) would not have invented this charge but that it was in the brief put into his hands. The least degree of reflection would have convinced him that such a charge, unsupported either by the instructions in his brief or the testimony of his witnesses, would have been most injurious to his cause. But, to show that the bloody dagger was not the creation of his fancy, he would read the part of the brief from which he obtained the statement regarding it. [The learned counsel then read a sentence to the effect stated.] The statement was not indeed supported by the witnesses, as no dagger was painted on the banner, but the mistake admitted of easy explanation. The standard alluded to had not indeed a dagger painted upon it, but the top of the staff was pointed like a dagger, as had been stated by one of the witnesses, and painted red. He would leave the defendant all the advantage which might arise from this correction, which he did not think very material.

The next thing that he (Mr Scarlett) was charged with doing contrary to truth and justice was to connect him (Mr Hunt) with Carlile. It seemed that he (Mr Scarlett) was so incensed against the defendant that he must prosecute him in all ways; that he must invent charges when he could not find them; and that, forsooth, he must make him not only hostile to the throne but to the sacred institutions of religion. And then the gentleman, who, among his oratorical figures, had tears at command on the mention

# Hunt and Others.

Mr Scarlett  of this charge, shed a tear of sorrow and mortification, declaring that he, on the contrary, so far from being connected with Carlile, held his principles in detestation; that he disliked them so much that, if Carlile was not suffering already the infliction of the laws, he would have expressed what he felt at his temerity in attacking the sacred doctrines of religion. Then he stated his belief that his hated name was introduced to the jury to prejudice his cause; that the reformers were friendly to religion, and God forbid that he should associate with infidels. But let the jury see what was the real state of the case, and consider the absurdity of this hypocritical cant. What had been proved in the case? Mr Hunt had put into the box a witness (his most respectable witness) of the name of Tyas who said that Carlile and the defendant were in the carriage and proceeded to the hustings together.

He (Mr Scarlett) came now to a part of the defendant's speech which was more to the subject, and to facts of which he could not deny that he (Mr Hunt) made a proper use, for he was willing to allow him merit where he deserved it. The defendant had asked why the magistrates were not called, and he was entitled to take the benefit of the absence of their testimony until the reason of it was explained. He (Mr Scarlett) would now state the reasons which would give the jury a clue to the whole case. Whether the magistrates on that day acted discreetly or indiscreetly on exercising their authority to disperse the meeting – whether the constables told them what was true or false, or behaved with moderation or violence – whether the yeomanry did right or wrong in approaching the hustings, or in their conduct afterwards had nothing more to do with the cause than whether Mr Hunt is Lord of the Manor of Glastonbury, or is visited at Middleton Cottage by Squire Wigmore and the clergyman of the parish. On the first day, the solicitor for the Crown, not being aware of the course of examination or how the learned Judge would direct the proceedings, had summoned the magistrates as witnesses and had them in attendance. He (Mr Scarlett) thought from the beginning that their evidence would not be required and, on opening the case, he had studiously abstained from that part of the transactions of the day which related to them. He had accordingly resolved not to examine evidence as to anything which happened after the military appeared on the field. In this he was confirmed by the learned judge. The inquiry into the conduct of the magistrates had no more to do with the inquiry now pending into the conduct of the meeting than any two events whatever: the former inquiry might be instituted in another shape, and he did not wish to distract or prejudice the minds of the jury by mixing them together. If the jury were trying the magistrates, they would be trying a more important cause than the present, and which, being connected with a deeper interest,

# Ninth Day – Saturday 25 March 1820.

**Mr Scarlett**

would, if brought into view on the present trial, only tend to prejudice the public mind. This was his justification for not calling the magistrates. His lordship concurred in his opinion, and the jury would observe that the examination was always broken off or interrupted when it came to involve them. Whatever, therefore, had been said, or whatever the jury had heard regarding the conduct of the magistracy and the yeomanry, ought to be dismissed from their minds and ought not to influence their decision. The charge on the record was to be tried in the same manner as if no magistrate, no constable, no yeoman had appeared on the field during the day. If the meeting was in its original formation and concoction an illegal meeting, it was immaterial to this issue whether it went through all its proceedings and dispersed of its own accord, without any act of violence, or was dispersed by the military, or in its dispersion committed acts of violence. What might have been the result of the meeting was not now the question. The legality of it is a point to be determined entirely distinct from any result which might have happened.

The appearance of the yeomanry on the field is merely a circumstance which, by the mode in which they were received, might determine the character of the meeting. Whether the yeomanry attacked the crowd, or the crowd attacked the yeomanry, or whether there was no attack from either had nothing to do with the question; the original formation and character of the meeting itself was the only point at issue. Though the motives of the law in declaring meetings illegal were grounded on the apprehended result of violence and riot, it was not necessary that that result should be consummated to constitute its illegality: but the motives of the law were wise; for who could say what could be the consequences of such meetings? What power could restrain their violence, or repress their excesses? Was it safe, was it reasonable that one man should be allowed to assume the power of commanding eighty or a hundred thousand people? and did the jury think that Mr Hunt, whatever were his powers of oratory over a mob, should assemble fifty thousand people, or that he should carry them about like a wild beast muzzled, to be let loose or not as he should think proper? Could he, or could any man, however transcendent his influence over the minds of the people, be sure that he could always command them when they were excited or calm their tumult, like the sage of the poet, (Virgil), by a look, by a word, or by the waving of his hand? The defendant did not possess that power: nor did any man, and therefore the law had wisely declared that such meetings, creating such alarm and tending to such dangers, ought not to be permitted.

Having said thus much, he would now come to consider how the last three days had been occupied. They had been occupied in hearing

## Hunt and Others.

Mr Scarlett    evidence foreign to the question. In a crowd of eighty thousand people, a question as to the conduct of persons in one part of the people was not to be decided by what was observed at another. Was a witness to be proved perjured because he stated what occurred in one part of the multitude, and which was not seen at another? Of the four hundred of the Spa Fields rioters who went to attack the Tower, three hundred would swear there was no violence intended. Besides, did anyone deny many things that the defendants endeavoured to prove? Did anyone deny that the leaders of the party inculcated order? Did any one of the witnesses for the Crown deny that Mr Hunt inculcated order? Or did any witness but one attribute to him any design of assaulting the military under the title of 'enemies' of the meeting? Yet all the witnesses called for the last two or three days for the defence only established negatives by assertions that had never been contradicted.

[Mr Scarlett then said he would read for the jury a part of one of his (Hunt's) speeches, on a former occasion.]

Mr HUNT: My Lord, I submit this cannot be read as a speech.

Mr Scarlett said he would only read it as a part of his (Mr Scarlett's) own speech, and the jury would see from it what sort of defence a man who was charged for the unlawful assembling of a mob was predetermined to make. He would suppose Mr Hunt to say, 'This is the mode in which I shall defend myself'. 'Let them,' said Mr Hunt at the meeting in Smithfield, 'bring their spies and informers to give evidence against me. I have fifty thousand of you before me whom I can call in my defence, and if I only bring thirty a day it will take three years and a half to try me, which no judge or jury can stand'. So it was here: witnesses were brought for several successive days to prove what was not material to the case. His Lordship had tried several riots --

Mr Justice BAYLEY: No, I have not, Mr Scarlett.

Mr Scarlett had thought so from the long experience of the learned judge; but he (Mr Scarlett) had witnessed many such trials, and he had never seen a large body of the rioters themselves called to prove that there was no riot. But if, instead of forty witnesses, the defendant had called four thousand, what would their evidence amount to? They might have said that they had gone to the meeting, some with their wives and some with their daughters; but he would show by and by that this was no ground of defence, and he would also show that the whole of the defence was one of craft. It had been stated to the jury that the meeting of the sixteenth had been called by several hundred resident householders of Manchester. Was that proved? Did any of the friends of the doctor (Healey) give any proof of this? Why not call some of those householders? Did Mr Hunt think that the jury were to be caught by such

# Ninth Day – Saturday 25 March 1820.

Mr Scarlett

chaff as this? Why not call them? Did the jury think that this would not have been done by Mr Hunt, or his legal adviser would not have called some of those people, if it was thought they could stand the fire of cross-examination? But no; there was not one single tittle of proof that the meeting had been so called. This, he maintained, was the best negative evidence that could be produced that no such thing had been done.

There was one subject to which the defendant had not alluded and which, if the trial had lasted for twenty-four days, would have been buried in oblivion, and the jury would not have heard about it except from the notes of the learned judge. It was that many days before the intended meeting of 9 August there had been military training going on in the neighbourhood. Was not that calculated to create alarm in the minds of the magistrates at Manchester? Could anything be more natural than that such a circumstance was calculated to create alarm?

But mark, gentleman of the jury: the defendants have not brought forward a single witness who had been of the drilling parties --

Mr HUNT: Yes, we brought one.

[Mr Scarlett observed that the jury saw the effrontery as well as craft with which the defendant conducted his defence; but he would expose both before he sat down, in spite of those interruptions.]

Mr SCARLETT [resuming]: But, as he was observing, not a single man had been called to account for this drilling and show its object was innocent, if such was the case. No one was put into the box to contradict the evidence of Chadwick, of which he would speak more presently. What then was the inference which the jury were to draw? Was it that eighty thousand men were assembled in the manner described, and that no one was called to say why they had been so disciplined – to state that the object was innocent, if so it was? They had not dared to offer a word of evidence on this point.

So much for this part of the case for the present. Bamford – and when he mentioned the name of this defendant, he could not but express his regret at the situation in which he saw him now placed – he (Mr Scarlett) admired his talents, and the respectful manner in which he had conducted himself in the course of his defence; and probably others as well as himself were sorry that he was not found in better company. But Bamford had told the jury – and Healey said the same, and it was frequently repeated by Mr Hunt – that they had assembled to look for their political rights, though they admitted that some honest men differed from them on this point. It was assured by them that annual parliaments and universal suffrage were the rights of the people of this country. This was not the tribunal before which the question of parliamentary reform could be discussed. Whatever might be the opinions of the jury (or his

# Hunt and Others.

Mr Scarlett  own) on this question was not material to the case, but this he would say: that if a man held such opinions ever so honestly, they were not such as ought to be dictated to parliament, and those who did so were not only wrong, but the very worst enemies to reform, annual parliaments and universal suffrage, and the political rights of the people. Surely, the political rights of the people were only such as were established by the laws and the constitution of the country: but it was said that these were the natural rights. Why, a man, upon this principle, had as much natural right to be a king, or to be a peer, as to be a member of the House of Commons. He should be glad to learn in what page of the Book of Nature this right was to be found; whether any of the defendants could point it out? This doctrine was not only advocated as the rights of the people, but as material to the safety of the kingdom. The gentlemen of the jury knew, for it was a matter of historic record, that the origin of the House of Commons was an emanation from the power of the King; and in progress of time it grew to what it now was – a balance of power between the King and the people, a balance formed upon the wisest plan which human ingenuity could devise; and so it would continue unless it was attacked by the rude hand of revolution. But at no one period of our history were such things known as annual parliaments and universal suffrage. In the early history of parliament, it was a fact that one member was named by the King, the other by the sheriff; and, in the towns, members were elected by the King's bailiff, or by some others under his authority. It had gradually improved to its present mode of election; but this it was sought to destroy by one of those measures which were destructive in themselves, and, if good, were too sudden to last.

If any man preached at a public meeting the doctrine that annual parliaments and universal suffrage ought to be the law of the country, he might as well say that there should be no representation at all, but that every measure which was to operate as a law should be put separately to parishes, and let them decide; and had any man a right to say that the doctrine of universal suffrage should prevail, that every man should give his opinion upon every law, or that death should be the alternative if such doctrine were not allowed? Suppose that Mr Hunt could prevail upon Bamford or any other of the defendants that the opinions of the 'immortal Paine' were correct: he might with the same justice say, 'no king, or death', or 'no republic, or death'. He might, it is true, hold his opinions of those different modes of government, but he had no right to say at a public meeting that we should have such government or none at all. As well might Carlile say that reason should be the law and that we should have no religion. If such were his opinion, he might say that human beings perished like the beasts of the field; that man ceased to

# Ninth Day – Saturday 25 March 1820.

exist at all when he ceased to exist in this world; that the universe had no soul; that the heavenly bodies had no arrangement; that salvation was a fable, and the Bible a fabrication, invented by the rich to keep down the poor, and that therefore it should no longer be believed. Such might be his (Carlile's) opinions; but had he a right to preach those opinions at a public meeting?

**Mr Scarlett**

Having mentioned the name of Carlile, he would ask who was it that had invited him to this meeting – this man who had been notorious as the salesman of the Deist and the Republican? Was it his fame and the knowledge of his principles which produced him a seat in the coach with the Lord of the Manor of Glastonbury and the cultivator of five thousand acres? Had Mr Hunt told them what brought Carlile to the meeting? Was there any man who would lay his hand to his heart and say that it was not the approval of his principles which had brought him thither? Good God! to what a state of society must we have come, when we found that the man who could neither read his own language nor any other, the man who had embraced and published such principles, was taken by the hand and introduced to the people of Manchester – probably, for aught they knew, as the colleague of Mr Hunt – if the meeting of 9 August had taken place? He asked what other conclusion could be drawn from the presence of Carlile at the meeting of the sixteenth; and if the people were deluded into the principles of that man – if the thirty witnesses a day, of whom mention had been made, had imbibed such principles – what would become of the sanctity of an oath, and what credit could be due to such witnesses? What, then, would become of the demagogue who should persuade them to take their religion from this man, and their politics from Mr Hunt?

He would now come to look at the case which had been laid before them, and view that case as they (the jury) had heard it; he considered himself as fully entitled to their verdict as he ever was by any evidence which he ever produced in any case. They (the counsel for the prosecution) charged the defendants with a conspiracy to excite discontent; they charged them with assembling in a formidable and menacing manner, and with an unlawful meeting. This was the substance of the indictment. Let them now look at the proofs which have been offered; and would anyone say that they had not been sufficient to support that indictment? At a meeting which was held in Smithfield, before the close of parliament, the last summer – a meeting at which Mr Hunt presided – certain resolutions were agreed to. Those resolutions were handed to Mr Fitzpatrick, the last witness whom he had called. He (Mr Scarlett) had not read those resolutions before, because he did not know whether they could be proved: he had only alluded to the substance of them. The jury had heard Mr Hunt say that if

# Hunt and Others.

Mr Scarlett     no heads were broken, no houses demolished at any of those meetings, therefore they were lawful. This he denied: that circumstance could not constitute legality, and he would show that, whether their result were peaceable or otherwise, the object was a delusion of the people – not a reform in Parliament, but a destruction of the government of the country.

He would read some of these resolutions to the jury. The first was a declaration that every man born in the British dominions was a freeman. This he (Mr Scarlett) admitted; every man in this country was undoubtedly a freeman; there was no country in which more freedom was enjoyed; there was no country in which such a spectacle as that they now witnessed could be produced – where a cause, carried on, he would admit, with all the support of government – was left to the decision of such a judge and such a jury. Looking to the government of other countries and of other times, they would find no such scene as the present. It was well known that the Roman consuls could put to death any man who should disturb the laws, and in cases of emergency a dictator was appointed, with the power of life and death over all the people: but what country was it, ancient or modern, where, as was the case with this nation, the administration of the laws and the very government itself were placed in the hands of the people?

The next resolution declared that it was expedient that a code of laws should be provided. But why provide a code of laws? Had we not a code already – a code of laws which we were bound to obey, and which could not be altered in a body except by violence? But it seemed a provisional administration was to be appointed. Why a provisional administration? He supposed: until Mr Hunt should frame this code of laws.

The next resolution was that every man in the kingdom had a right to a voice in the making of those laws: of course, that a lunatic had a right – a lunatic who Mr Hunt had twitted the other day on his misfortunes, and who, though, according to Mr Hunt, he was not competent to give evidence against him, ought to have an equal voice in the making of a law. That the man who lived by the labour of his hands and who could not be supposed from his station in life to have the necessary knowledge was to have an equal voice with the highest authority in the land in the making of laws – such were the doctrines inculcated at Smithfield.

The resolutions went on. The next was that, in order to raise a fund for supporting such a system of government, every man should pay his proportion of taxes. He did not know whether this resolution met with the applause that Mr Fitzpatrick stated had been given to others; at least, it was not so marked. He (Mr Scarlett), however, denied that the consent of every man was necessary for the imposition of a tax.

The next resolution stated the House of Commons was not formed as

# Ninth Day – Saturday 25 March 1820.

**Mr Scarlett**

it ought. That might be true: its construction might not be the best, but their own government had within itself the means of removing those grievances which might arise, and no person should presume to inculcate on the people their removal by force.

To the next resolutions, he begged to call the particular attention of the jury; they were, in substance, that after 1 January 1820, no man was bound in equity to obey any act of that body calling itself the House of Commons unless it was chosen by a large proportion of the people; that books should be opened in every parish for the purpose of enrolling the names of all those men who were of sound mind and proper age, and who should have a voice in choosing representatives. An address was then agreed to, founded upon those resolutions, calling upon his Royal Highness the Prince Regent to order the issue of writs for the election of members under those circumstances, and that the parliament so chosen should assemble in the January next; so that here the authority of the House of Commons was to be at an end. These daring and traitorous resolutions, and the address founded on them, were published. Daring, indeed, they were, for he could state, as long as he had been acquainted with the law, he had never known so much daring suffered to pass unpunished. Mr Fitzpatrick had told them how the resolutions were passed; they were not put separately. Mr Hunt pulled them printed from his pocket and they were carried en masse, deliberation being wholly out of the question. After this, they were printed in all the newspapers and circulated throughout the country, so that it appeared as if the whole people of London had embraced and published such sentiments. This was soon known at Manchester, and it was also known that at Birmingham the people had proceeded to elect a legislatorial attorney. Accordingly it was found that the people at Manchester were to be induced to follow the example, and for that purpose a notice of a meeting was publicly announced, at which the unrepresented inhabitants were also to choose a representative of their own and to adopt Major Cartwright's plan of reform. Henry Hunt was announced as the chairman. The boroughreeve or constables were not mentioned – they would not do, but Mr Hunt was to preside: Sir Charles Wolseley, Pearson the lawyer, Godfrey Higgins, Esq, Wooler, and others were to be present. And here again he should observe that not one of those whose names were said to be affixed to this notice had been called to prove that they had signed it; and this began the head of this charge against Mr Hunt. What did he dare to do? The boroughreeve and constables were advised to attend. To preside? No: to attend and listen to what was to be brought forward. They, as became them, advised the people to abstain at their peril from such a meeting – a phrase which the jury had heard so much commented upon as not

# Hunt and Others.

**Mr Scarlett** correct, but which he maintained was justifiable according to the idiom of our language and might be found in several writers, though perhaps it was not as precisely correct as the strict rule of that language admitted.

What then had happened after this notice of the boroughreeve and constables? Mr Hunt came down from London.

[Mr Hunt here interfered, and said he had not come from London on that occasion.]

[Mr Scarlett continued.] Well, he had dropped from the clouds, or come from Coventry.

Mr HUNT: My Lord, is this in evidence?

Mr Justice BAYLEY: How can it be in evidence? It was only used as a figure of speech.

[Mr SCARLETT proceeded.] The jury would observe the impertinence of the defendant. It was of a piece with the rest of his conduct. If he would not have it that he came from Coventry, he (Mr Scarlett) would say he had dropped from the clouds, or arose out of the earth. At all events, he was found at Bullock Smithy before 9 August; there he met with Mr Moorhouse, and proceeded with him to Stockport; from thence he proceeded to Manchester, and what was his conduct there? Was it to excite respect for the magistrates? No; on the contrary, it was proved by three witnesses that his language had a different tendency; that not only was his language disrespectful, but even was calculated to excite resistance to the magistrates, if necessary. His own servant, who had been called to give him a character, did not disprove this fact. What did he (Hunt) say? He was sorry that, in obedience to the magistrates, the meeting had been put off; and alluding to the notice to that effect he observed that as it took nine tailors to make a man, so it took nine magistrates to frame this notice. After this, he invited the people to attend at the meeting on Monday. The learned counsel then went on to state that nothing more appeared of Mr Hunt till 16 August except his ridiculous bravado before the magistrates on the Saturday preceding that day; and that he was only known in the interim as being at Johnson's, and by his intentions with respect to the meeting.

What those intentions were he should show from the letter which Mr Hunt had read as part of his speech, but which he had not dared to offer in evidence. That letter, which he had addressed to the people at Manchester, he would now read from the shorthand writer's notes. But he should first observe, that at the time it was written, drilling was going on in the neighbourhood of Manchester, and that a disposition was evinced in the people to come armed to the meeting. This he was aware of, but he wished to prevent the too-sudden explosion until his troops were regularly prepared. The letter said, 'Come, then, my friends

# Ninth Day – Saturday 25 March 1820.

– come to the meeting armed with no other arms'. Who told him that they intended to come with any arms? Who had told him that they had intended to come at all? Could anybody doubt, who read this letter, that it had been intended by previous consultation to come with arms, but that he then wished them to come without them? He had put it to them in this way: to 'come armed with no other arms than a self-approving conscience'. And how could he have known that they intended to come otherwise, except by previous consultation? Indeed this was proved, for it appeared that by one of the parties it was agreed to go without sticks. This was the result of the order given by one individual who on this occasion combined sentiments of fear with those of policy, and who did not wish for an explosion (in his presence, at least) till everything was in readiness; till, perhaps, the other great manufacturing towns in the kingdom were prepared to act in concert with those at Manchester. If the jury had seen the printed paper, they might, for aught he knew, have found the word 'armed' in italics. What could be his object but to keep his people quiet until the proper occasion offered, and to preach peace and good order to them?

**Mr Scarlett**

The letter then proceeded to invite the boroughreeve and constables to attend the meeting to hear his reasons; but he used no reasoning in London, nor at any of the meetings elsewhere he attended. There was no reasoning in any of his speeches except in that which the jury had heard on a part of the present evidence.

The letter proceeded: 'They say your leaders...' What leaders? Who were they? Was it Carlile, or Knight, or Smith of Liverpool? God forbid that he should say anything against Mr Smith: whatever might be his (Mr Smith's) opinions, he did not mean to condemn his evidence; he had acted properly in not accepting the invitation to attend as a speaker. But who are the leaders who were here pointed out? Was the invitation to the boroughreeve and constables to come and discuss political questions with Mr Hunt and the other defendants, and to let Mr Moorhouse decide? No such thing. The letter said it was in this way they treated the magistrates. Yes, indeed, it was, and they would have been exposed to insult and derision. Looking at these circumstances, he stated now, and he would state it anywhere: whatever his opinion might be as to the result, if the magistrates had not felt alarmed for the safety of the town, and taken precautions accordingly, they should have been dismissed from their functions as traitors to their duty.

See what had been done on the night of 15 August. Chadwick went to White Moss at twelve o'clock, where he saw large bands of men training by regular leaders. They had no arms, it was true; but the word 'fire' was given, at which there was a regular clapping of hands. Why was not

# Hunt and Others.

Mr Scarlett somebody called to contradict this, if it could be contradicted, instead of wasting four days in proving what was unnecessary? The evidence of Shawcross, Heywood and Murray was not in contradiction to that of Chadwick. They spoke only as to marching, and it was not necessary to give the word 'fire' in marching. Chadwick also saw Murray on the ground and heard him called a spy. The jury had heard Murray himself describe the ill-treatment he had received: they obliged him to abjure his allegiance and administered the form of an oath to that effect, after which he was let off with two additional blows. They had heard that one man, who acted as a leader and formed the party into a square for the purpose of reading a letter which had been received from Manchester, was afterwards seen heading a party to the meeting. It next appeared that the procession to the meeting, in which Mr Hunt was, had stopped before Murray's door, for the purpose of hooting and hissing, and some of them cried out, 'No White Moss humbugs'. Mr Hunt might say he had no control over them; but could he be suffered to blow hot and cold? He who at one time boasted of such control at another denied he had any. He (Mr Scarlett) did not mean to say that it was the intention of Mr Hunt to commit a riot there, but did not the circumstance show the connection between the White Moss training and 16 August? The hissing before Murray's door was proved by the respectable testimony of Mr Tyas and of Dr Smith; but Mr Tyas went further, and he (Mr Scarlett) was glad that Mr Tyas had been produced for he had understood, since he came to York, that he was a respectable young gentleman who had distinguished himself considerably at the University of Cambridge. Mr Tyas's evidence proved the hissing near the police office. Did that show respect to the magistrates? Hissing and obedience were quite different; Mr Hunt knew it as well as any man. What could be inferred from this hissing but a disposition hostile to those magistrates?

The learned counsel then proceeded to state the training at Tandle Hill and the circumstance of Bamford's giving directions to his division, on setting out for Manchester, to keep order, and of his having distributed laurel leaves to the leaders. Why was it necessary to command them to be orderly unless they had a disposition to be otherwise? The defendants have also graced their cause by the evidence of Mr James Scholefield, the dissenting clergyman. He would say nothing more of him than asking whether he could be believed on his oath, he who could not recollect whether he had written for the *Manchester Observer* or not, or what he had written? He (Mr Scarlett) had called seventeen witnesses, respectable men, men of property in Manchester, who all proved that they felt alarmed for the state of the town; indeed, their acts had proved their alarm, for they had taken precautions to guard against the apprehended

# Ninth Day – Saturday 25 March 1820.

**Mr Scarlett**

mischief. Bamford himself seemed to have the same feeling, by the orders which he had given to keep quiet. He meant not to charge them with any disturbance: they were quiet in consequence of commands from headquarters. He did not mean to charge the defendants with expressions – 'We shall have a Moscow', and such like. No doubt the object of their leaders on that day was to keep them peaceable: 'Good friends! Sweet friends! Let me not stir you up to any sudden flood of mutiny.'[199] These might have been his words; but, like another Anthony, he held up to them the garment of the constitution, and pointed to its stabs. His object was not to produce a riot then, but to show to those whom he designated as enemies that the people had power to trample on them if they pleased, and to destroy Manchester, but that it was not proper to exercise it then without looking to the result.

He (Mr Scarlett) gave credit to the feelings of those who conceived that Manchester was in danger if that meeting continued together. It was of no use to say that the leader did not intend they should act. Lord G. Gordon, at the head of ten thousand persons over whom he had influence, was not able to restrain them, and he was only acquitted of high treason from his peaceable intentions. So would Mr Hunt now be, if he had been indicted for high treason. Would it be said that Mr Hunt could have controlled the meeting of the sixteenth if they had broken out into acts of violence? Why then should not danger have been feared? The Lord Mayor of London was prosecuted for not having dispersed the Gordon mob, even before any riot had been committed. It was unnecessary for him to say more on this point. His only object was to vindicate the character of that high-spirited magistrate, Mr Hulton, than whom a more charitable and amiable man did not exist in the county where he lived.

The evidence of Mr Hulton was quite natural for a man standing where he had. He had not sworn that sticks and stones were thrown at the cavalry, but that it appeared to him they were raised up. It appeared, however, from the evidence of Mr Hulton and others, that the crowd had closed upon the cavalry, and it was then natural for a person in Mr Hulton's situation to feel alarmed for their safety. The circumstance of women and children being among the meeting did not disprove the present charge. Women and children had mixed in Lord George Gordon's meeting; but that was proved to be illegal, and so must every meeting be which was calculated to inspire terror and alarm in his Majesty's peaceable subjects. It was laid down by Mr Serjeant Hawkins, in his Pleas of the Crown, that to constitute an illegal meeting an act of riot or violence was not necessary. Any meeting calculated to intimidate

---

199  A near-miss for a quotation from Shakespeare's *Julius Caesar*, Act 3, Scene 2.

# Hunt and Others.

**Mr Scarlett** was illegal. They had heard from Bamford that to train men it was not necessary to have his Majesty's commission. He admitted this; but then it depended upon the object for which they were trained. Why had not the defendant shown that the object here was lawful?[200] And here he should observe that one of the greatest causes for alarm was the mystery with which these trainings were conducted. It had been said that the meeting assembled to discuss certain political questions. If those people meant to pass resolutions, it was evident that they could not be discussed by them. Which, he should be glad to know, of those industrious weavers and cotton-spinners who attended the meeting were fit to decide on such questions as these? Was it to be supposed that political science, as it had been called, could be considered by an assembly of fifty thousand persons? He would, in Mr Hunt's own language, give a description of the meeting; and he would then ask of the jury whether, on his own showing, he did not mean to inspire the peaceable inhabitants with alarm, to fill the magistrates and local authorities with fear, and to hold up to scorn all those public functionaries which the law had appointed to administer the justice of the country. Did not Mr Hunt state to the people that it was 'a tremendous meeting'? Did not two of the witnesses prove that he used this expression? It was indeed a tremendous meeting, and its consequences would be fearfully tremendous if the verdict of the jury sanctioned it as a legal one.

Mr Hunt returned thanks to the people for the honour which they had conferred on him in calling him to the chair, and observed 'that it was impossible he could make himself heard by every member of the tremendous meeting he there saw before him'. He (Mr Scarlett) verily believed that at that moment there was in the mind of Mr Hunt a mixture of fear and vanity. 'It was useless,' he proceeded to say, 'for him to call to their minds the circumstances which had taken place for the last ten days in the town'. It was evident from this that he was privy to those circumstances, and knew them well. He next observed 'that the efforts of those who attempted to put them down by the most malignant exertions were the means of making them meet that day in twofold numbers'. What was this but to say, 'You were prevented from meeting on 9 August to proceed to the election of a member to represent you in Parliament – I deny the right of the magistrates to prevent you. But now you have met on the sixteenth, and their malignant exertions have had the effect of making you meet in a twofold number. I don't advise you to resist the constituted authorities; but show your firmness, and I will meet you again in fourfold

---

200   It was not the defendant's responsibility to prove that his actions were lawful; it was the prosecutor's responsibility to show that they were not lawful.

# Ninth Day – Saturday 25 March 1820.

**Mr Scarlett**

numbers. At present, you are raw and undisciplined troops, and fly at the sight of a red coat; but stand firm, manoeuvre in the very face of the magistrates and of the army, and you must succeed. We must persevere, since the former meeting was adjourned, or postponed.' Mr Hunt was for two hours examining a respectable gentleman from Manchester, to show that he had not, in speaking of the projected meeting of 9 August, made use of the word 'adjourned', but that he had adopted the word 'postponed'. The evidence, however, proved that he had used both these words. 'The meeting,' continued Mr Hunt, 'was put off. Who put it off? The magistrates, who showed by their conduct that they had sustained a defeat.' This sentence was, it seems, followed by loud and long applause. When the cavalry appeared and drew their swords, Hunt and Johnson told the people to give three cheers. Those cheers were explained by Mr Tyas, in his evidence, as being intended to show that they were not daunted by the unwelcome presence of the military, although another witness had declared that it was meant for a cheer of approbation.

The legality of the meeting, at common law, was to be decided by the circumstances connected with it. Mr Hunt had defended it as a meeting no less legal than an assembly of citizens in Palace Yard. But who could ever contend that all the people of England might meet there? The meetings in Palace Yard were of a description that was well known to the Constitution. The meeting at Manchester, on the other hand, was convened by some secret committee, assisted by Mr Hunt. It was not a county meeting nor a town meeting, but a meeting of every person who might be pleased to attend. It was, in fact, calling on all those who had any grievance, real or imaginary, to come forward, while Mr Hunt preached his political doctrines to them. The broad question for the jury to decide was, whether this was or was not a lawful assembly. To that point he hoped they would give their most serious consideration. They were to say whether they thought it was lawful to assemble in such a form and with such banners as had been described.

As to the designs of those who thus assembled, they had no evidence; they were left to conjecture. If Mr Hunt and those who met on 16 August designed to pass any such resolutions as those that were agreed to in London, that design alone made such a meeting illegal, and formed a very grave and serious ground of offence. Mr Hunt had not called before them any person to show what resolutions he meant to propose; the jury had no information of what was the object of the meeting. It was, therefore, only to be judged of by circumstance: by the mode, for instance, in which the people were assembled. He contended then – and he called on the jury to come to the same conclusion – that the intention of Mr Hunt was either to call on the people to meet for the election of a member to serve

# Hunt and Others.

**Mr Scarlett** in Parliament, as had been done at Birmingham, and of which purpose notice had been given on 9 August, or else to pass such resolutions as were agreed to at Smithfield in the month of July. If they were of opinion that the parties had either object in view, then the meeting was clearly illegal. But even independent of that, if the mode of assembling, if the vastness of the numbers, if the system of organization which appeared – if these circumstances, taken together, conspired to impress terror on the minds of peaceable men, it was an unlawful meeting.

The next matter for their consideration would be the part which each of the defendants took in the transaction. With respect to Mr Hunt, no doubt whatsoever could be entertained. He appeared to be the grand mover of the whole machine. With respect to Johnson, they found him with Mr Hunt at the hustings, and there proposing him as chairman. A very remarkable conversation which took place with Johnson was also detailed by two of the witnesses. Evidence was, however, given by two persons who declared that they would not believe the witness Willie on his oath. But how did the fact stand? Slater, one of the witnesses, was a publican, and Willie a butcher, a total stranger to Johnson. Johnson happened to go to Slater's while Willie was there, and the conversation turned on the business of the approaching 16 August. Had anyone contradicted the fact that such a conversation had taken place? No; but two persons, a butcher and a builder, were sent for express from Manchester, who stated that they did not believe Willie on his oath. Willie swore that he had a certain conversation with Johnson, and, having mentioned it to some person, it came to the ears of the magistrates, who sent for him. It appeared that he was watched, and, as he returned from the magistrates, Johnson sent a servant after him, to call him into his shop. Where was that servant? Why was not he produced? The witness was, however, corroborated by Johnson himself, for he asked Willie whether he had not said so-and-so, which showed that there must have been a meeting between them. It was quite plain, from this circumstance, that Willie was watched by Johnson, and it thus appeared that there were some individuals who kept spies and informers in their pay, as well as those who were more commonly blamed for employing such instruments. Willie's evidence sufficiently proved that Johnson had a previous knowledge of the meeting, and that he had said they would bring such numbers together as would enable them to set at naught any soldiers that might be brought against them.

Moorhouse, it also appeared, was with Mr Hunt; he had gone to Smedley Cottage and had also accompanied Mr Hunt to the hustings. At the Stockport meeting he told the people to attend at Manchester on the sixteenth, and to bring with them as many of their friends as they could. Moorhouse, on the morning of the sixteenth, set out with his coach

# Ninth Day – Saturday 25 March 1820.

from Stockport, and in the midst of this eight-mile stage he stopped and watered his horses for half an hour. Was not the object of this delay to wait for the procession, and to arrive regularly with it? Moorhouse went on and was hailed by Mr Hunt opposite the Exchange. He got into the barouche and they approached the hustings in the same carriage. Moorhouse, he therefore argued, was a principal party in this design. It would be for the jury to consider whether he was not the person who chiefly incited the Stockport people to attend the meeting.

He next came to Wylde, whom they found directing the people to lock arm-in-arm round the hustings. Dr Healey, it appeared, was also there. 'But,' said the doctor, 'where there is no law, there can be no transgression'. It would be a very good thing for the doctor if there were no law. He seemed to think it would be proper to allow men to march to public meetings as they pleased, to hear what they pleased, and to deliver any sentiments they liked. Fortunately, however, there were laws connected with points of that kind. Well, they found the doctor arranging a body of people and marching with them to the ground. He appeared to be intimately connected with 'the black flag' as he produced a facsimile of it, 'in little'. He (Mr Scarlett) in consequence produced the original; and if the defendants had put in a facsimile of their caps of liberty, he would have exhibited some of the real ones. They had heard much of the cap of liberty. It had been, since the French Revolution, a revolutionary emblem. The mischiefs that had been hatched, engendered and perfected under the ensign of the cap of liberty had converted it into an emblem of disaffection. It was no longer the cap of liberty; it had degenerated into a badge of licentiousness.

With respect to Saxton, as it was stated that he was a reporter and attended the meeting in that capacity, that would be a fair ground for the jury to give a verdict in his favour. I beg leave, therefore, to dismiss him from your attention altogether.

The defendant Knight, it was proved, was in the carriage with Mr Hunt and proceeded with him to the hustings.

He had now merely to call their attention to the particular points which they had to consider. First, whether the assembly was an unlawful one; and, next, what part the respective individuals took in it. He would be perfectly at his ease when he had discharged his duty on this occasion. As to consequences, he feared none, except indeed the verdict of a British jury asserting that such a meeting was lawful. He trusted the jury would discharge from their minds any idea of the public impression which their verdict might produce, and only consider how they best might execute the great duty they had to perform. Much had been said in favour of great public meetings: but some of those who spoke most in praise of

*Mr Scarlett*

# Hunt and Others.

Mr Scarlett them seemed to wish to press the system to boundless licentiousness. If such were to be the practice, if great bodies of people were to be congregated together from all quarters, it would be better to give up the power rather than retain it, when it threatened perilous consequences to their persons and properties. The great Roman historian had described a state of things somewhat similar when he depicted the people of Rome, on the accession of Augustus, becoming the willing instruments of their own slavery – 'ac novis ex rebus aucti, tuta et praesentia quam vetera et periculosa mallent'.[201] Why had they done so? Because they well recollected the strife and misery to which they had been exposed by the licentious dispute of contending factions at former periods of their history. He hoped the jury would, by their conscientious verdict this day, save their country from so lamentable a trial. When the verdict of a jury sanctioned and preserved the laws, those who pronounced that verdict did the most essential service to the interests of society in general by showing that the laws of a country were sufficient to maintain the peace and adequate to the punishment of those who attempted to infringe them. On the other hand, if, in consequence of certain topics which were unfortunately connected with this question, the jury should be induced to give a verdict finding this to have been a lawful assembly, he would hang down his head in sorrow, for he should begin to fear that the law was not sufficient to preserve the public peace. He was, however, of opinion that the law as it now existed was powerful enough to repress disorder. He hoped the jury, by their verdict, would show that it was, and that no twelve Englishmen would be found to say that such a meeting, assembled under such circumstances and in such a manner, was or ought to be tolerated by law.

## Judge's charge.

Mr Justice Bayley   Mr Justice Bayley, after a short pause, proceeded to address the jury. They had now, he said, at length arrived at the end of this most important case, and it became necessary for him to offer to them such observations, in summing up, as the circumstances appeared to him to demand. He would, as accurately as he could, lay down to them the law which was applicable to the case; and he would make such remarks on the evidence as, in the discharge of his duty, he might deem proper in order to point out for their consideration the grounds on which they were to proceed in forming their judgement. He would be as brief as possible in adverting to the merits of both sides of the question. And, in the first place, he

---

201   Tacitus, Annals (1,2).

# Ninth Day – Saturday 25 March 1820.

earnestly entreated of them to dismiss entirely from their minds every feeling connected with political or party question and not to take into consideration what the consequences of their verdict might be, but merely to consider what verdict, according to the evidence, they were bound to give.

**Mr Justice Bayley**

With respect to the observations he should make to them on this subject, it was their duty to weigh them maturely, but not to adopt them unless they met with their perfect concurrence. He would, in this case, lay entirely out of the question the conduct of the military and the magistrates. The great point for consideration was the conduct of the crowd on this occasion: and as the acts of the magistrates, of the military and of the constables might create a prejudice in their minds, he had cautiously abstained from suffering them to be investigated or entertained in the course of the trial. The propriety of the conduct of the individuals to whom he alluded could not then be discussed, and the jury must not suffer their minds, in any respect, to be influenced by the consideration how far their verdict would operate either in favour of or in prejudice to the magistrates, constables or military employed on the occasion in question. It was with a view to prevent a prejudice of that kind that he had, in the course of the trial (not, he hoped, inconsistently with the situation which he held), desired the defendant not to put a question which, in point of law, he was entitled to do. He saw the way in which that question was propounded and embodied in the case, and he perceived that it could not serve the defendant. He therefore thought it was his duty to prevent the question being persevered in. For this reason, and for this reason only, he desired the defendant not to press the question.

He was quite sure that, in this case, as in all others, the Jury would give to the defendants every fair credit which, on a proper consideration of the evidence, they might appear entitled to receive. If the case justly admitted of doubt, they would give to the defendants the benefit of that doubt, and pronounce, with respect to them, a verdict of acquittal. He hoped and trusted, and was indeed satisfied, that if the evidence imperiously called on them to come to a different conclusion, they would come, boldly and fearlessly, to that conclusion. His idea was that the inquiry should be conducted in such a way, as, if possible, to give even the defendants themselves satisfaction as to the mode in which it was carried on, so that if a verdict of guilty were recorded against them, they might have an opportunity of saying that their trial was an impartial one.

After these very few preliminary observations, he should proceed to point out to the jury the nature of the present indictment. It contained a charge of conspiracy; it contained a charge of unlawful assembly; it

# Hunt and Others.

**Mr Justice Bayley**

contained a charge of riot. But on the subject of the charge of riot, he would not propound to them any observations, because he conceived that the consideration of the other charges alone remained for them. The circumstances of the conspiracy, as they were stated in the indictment, were these: the indictment set forth 'That the defendants conspired to meet, and to cause and procure other persons to meet, for the purpose of disturbing the public peace, and the common tranquillity of the King and realm'. This was one count; and it would be for the jury to say, whether any conspiracy was made out, so as to authorize them to find a verdict of guilty. The count further charged that the defendants met together for the purpose of raising and exciting discontent and disaffection in the minds of the subjects of our Lord the King, and also to incite them to contempt and hatred of the government and constitution as by law established. Therefore there were here three heads of charge: first, that of a seditious meeting, to disturb the public peace; a second purpose was to raise and excite discontent and disaffection in the minds of the subjects of the King; and the third purpose was to incite the subjects of the King to contempt and hatred of the government and constitution of the realm as by law established.

The unlawful assembling was stated to be with two different views; and if the existence of either one or the other of those views were made out in evidence, it would be sufficient to warrant a conviction. The first view charged was that the defendants, by themselves and also with various other persons, unlawfully, maliciously and seditiously did assemble, for the purpose of raising and exciting discontent and disaffection in the minds of the liege subjects of the King; and, second, with a view to excite contempt and hatred of the government and constitution, as by law established. Therefore, the meeting, which in the first instance was charged as a conspiracy to disturb the public peace, was, in the next place, described to be an assembling for the specific purposes which he had stated.

Another count set forth 'That the defendants met and assembled, together with divers others, to a very great number, in a threatening and menacing manner, with sticks and other offensive weapons, and with divers seditious ensigns and flags on which there were various inflammatory inscriptions and devices, to the great terror of the peaceable subjects of our Lord the King'. One of the purposes, therefore, to effect which they were charged with unlawfully assembling, was to excite discontent and disaffection in the minds of his Majesty's subjects; and, secondly, they were charged with meeting in a menacing manner and in military array in order to effect that illegal object.

On the subject of unlawful assemblies, he would quote what Mr Serjeant

# Ninth Day – Saturday 25 March 1820.

Hawkins, perhaps the best writer on the question, stated as necessarily constituting an unlawful assembly. He said 'any meeting whatever, of a great number of people, with such circumstances of terror as cannot but endanger the public peace, and raise fears and jealousies among the King's subjects, seems properly to be called an unlawful assembly; where, for instance, those great numbers having some grievance to complain of, met armed together for the purpose of discussing the best way of ridding themselves of that grievance; because, under these circumstances, no one can say what may be the event of such a meeting'. Mr Sergeant Hawkins's opinion then, was, that a great number of people, meeting under such circumstances as cannot but endanger the public peace and raise fears and jealousies among the King's subjects, was an unlawful assembly. And he adduced, as an exemplification of his opinion, persons meeting together armed, in a warlike manner. That, however, was not essentially necessary to constitute an unlawful assembly. Taking all the circumstances together, if a meeting 'endangered the public peace', and tended to 'raise fears and jealousies among his Majesty's subjects', it was an unlawful assembly, although the people did not appear armed. Therefore, one of the questions the jury would have to decide was whether the meeting now under consideration consisted of such numbers of people, and was called together under such circumstances, as could not but endanger the public peace. It might be, that, in a very large assembly, there were many persons entirely innocent of any improper object. They might meet for what was a strictly lawful purpose; and yet there might, in that meeting, be many other persons illegally assembled who might wish to make the innocent parties the instruments in their hands for effecting their unlawful purposes.

Now, he had no difficulty in stating that, in all cases of unlawful assembly, they were to look to the purpose for which the people met, the manner in which they came, and the means which they were using to effect their proposed object. All these were circumstances which the jury were bound to take into consideration. He had no hesitation in stating to them that it was not because a meeting was composed of sixty thousand persons, or because it was a body containing women and children, that therefore it was an unlawful assembly. That number of persons might meet under such circumstances as were not calculated to raise terrors, fears or jealousies in the minds of the people in the neighbourhood. But, in an assembly so constituted, and met for a perfectly legal purpose, if any individuals introduced themselves illegally in order to give to that meeting an undue direction, which would produce terror in the minds of his Majesty's subjects, although fifty-nine thousand persons out of a meeting of sixty thousand were completely innocent, yet there might be

**Mr Justice Bayley**

# Hunt and Others.

**Mr Justice Bayley**

twelve or twenty illegally met there, and those twelve or twenty would be liable to be tried on the ground of having illegally assembled. It followed that although a meeting might be perfectly legal as to the great bulk of the people attending it, yet if any persons by a plan among themselves introduced objects new to that meeting (by placards or any other means), which objects were likely to give to the meeting a direction not before contemplated, so as to produce alarm or to endanger the public peace and strike terror into his Majesty's subjects, those persons were liable to be indicted for illegally assembling together.

The case as it was stated by Mr Serjeant Hawkins seemed to contemplate the event of immediate danger resulting from the meeting. He, however, was not prepared in his own mind to say that the appearance of immediate danger was necessary to constitute this offence. If in the results the jury were satisfied that, from such an assemblage, accompanied by the circumstances he would by-and-by point out to them, terror must have been inflicted on the minds of his Majesty's subjects, leading to an apprehension of immediate danger, they would give a verdict against those who occasioned that apprehension. On the other hand, if, from the peaceable demeanour of the people at the time and the association of women and children on the ground, the meeting was not sufficient to produce a feeling of immediate danger – though it might of future danger – he would recommend it to the jury to find a special verdict. If they found a special verdict, he would call on them to state whether they thought the circumstances attending the meeting were such as were calculated to produce immediate danger. If they thought not, they would then find that the persons met under such circumstances as were not likely to inspire the fear and terror of immediate mischief, but which were calculated to create a fear and terror of distant danger.

With respect to the subject of conspiracy, it was necessary to observe that the defendants were not liable to be found guilty – although they were seeking the same end – if the jury were not of opinion that they were acting in pursuance of one common design, with the privity of all. It might be that, in a case of this kind, twelve or twenty persons might go to a meeting, each of them intending to sow sedition: yet, if each person intended to sow that sedition from the mere motive and impulse of his own mind, and not in common with the other parties, they could not be found guilty of conspiracy. To prove conspiracy, there was no necessity to show the absolute meeting together of the parties accused. If the circumstances were such as to induce the jury to believe that they could not have occurred without the previous concert and combination of the parties accused, it was sufficient. If the circumstances were of such a nature as to imply that there must have been a previous plan, that

# Ninth Day – Saturday 25 March 1820.

would warrant conviction for conspiracy. If, in this case, the jury should be of opinion that these persons could not have come together in the way described – generally speaking, with a regular step, and approaching a particular place, at the exact time they did – if they believed they could not come in that way in the common order of circumstances without a previous meeting between the parties, that was sufficient evidence of a preconcerted plan. But if the jury were of opinion that they might have met together by accident, without previous arrangement, then the charge of conspiracy must be dismissed from their minds. A party expressing an intention to go to this or any other meeting might induce other persons who heard of it through him to attend also, without any previous design. They could only implicate, in the offence of conspiracy, those persons who the evidence showed either actually were, or from circumstances must have been, parties to the formation of the original plan. Those who joined in a plan, though at a late period of the transaction, could not be distinguished from those with whom it originated, because they in fact agreed to all that had previously been done and thus became conspirators. In considering the matter of conspiracy, they must look to the case of each defendant and see with which of the other defendants he conspired. It might be that, as to the conspiracy charged in this case, they would be of opinion that one, and one alone, of the present defendants, together with divers other persons not named, had formed the plan: it would subject the defendant, and him alone, to be found guilty of the charge. The fact of assembling did not stand on the same ground; because, if in such a meeting as that, twelve persons assembled for unlawful purpose (that was, to give an improper direction to the proceedings of those who were legally and properly met), those twelve might be found guilty of illegally assemblings, though there was no previous conspiracy.

**Mr Justice Bayley**

In deciding this case, they would take all the attending circumstances into consideration. One of these circumstances was the appearance of the parties as if they had been drilled. With respect to banners bearing inscriptions, their illegality did not extend to every man present at the meeting, but only to those particular persons who adopted those banners, and the sentiments inscribed on them; or who, with a full knowledge of their existence, gave perfect confidence and co-operation to the meeting. So also in the case of drilling. It could only affect those who knew that drilling was practised for illegal purposes. If he knew that persons were drilled for the purpose of overawing his Majesty's subjects and bearing arms, and he attended a meeting of that kind and gave it his confidence, then he was guilty of attending illegally. But if, on the other hand, he was present at a drill-meeting, not being aware that it was assembled for illegal purposes, the law considered him innocent, because he was not

# Hunt and Others.

Mr Justice Bayley — privy to the fact which alone rendered the thing illegal.

As to the point whether a specific assembly was likely to produce terror, future or immediate, the fact might be proved in two ways: by showing, on the one hand, that terror was actually produced; or, on the other, by proving the absence of all terror. To show whether terror was or was not produced, he would state the testimony on both sides in this case. They would find in the evidence on the part of the prosecution a great deal which imported that no apprehension of immediate danger existed; and the circumstance of women and children being present would be worthy of their consideration in that respect. It was admitted that an attempt was made to keep the peace at the meeting. But this might have been done in order to forward future objects. It might have been hoped, that, by this means, the prepared seed would be sown, while those who pursued this course would wait till the time of harvest to reap the benefit of it.

Having made these observations, which he deemed it necessary to do, in order to enable them to arrive at a correct conclusion and at a proper understanding of the evidence, he would now point out to them what the nature of that evidence was. The learned judge then proceeded to recapitulate the voluminous evidence adduced in the course of this interesting trial, briefly commenting on it as he went on. He observed that a meeting of sixty thousand persons, if they all came to a certain point with a common knowledge of what was to be done, might create terror. With respect to the banners, he again observed that those only who showed that they were favourable to any motto inscribed on them (by carrying or immediately marching under them) could be considered as liable to any penalty which the illegal nature of any of the inscriptions might warrant. It was given, he observed, in evidence that Moorhouse was a religious man, and constantly read the Bible to his family – a fact stated to induce the inference that he would not be guilty of an illegal or immoral act. It was also stated that Mrs Moorhouse, though in the family way, went through the crowd; and it was not likely, if danger had been apprehended, that her husband would have permitted her to attend. With respect to persons walking in the military step, to which several witnesses had sworn, it could not affect the persons charged unless they were proved to have been cognizant of the fact. With respect to the inscription, 'Equal Representation or Death', if it meant that those who adhered to such a standard would lose their lives unless they procured what they deemed 'equal representation', it amounted to sedition: but if, as Mr Hunt explained it, the inscription merely meant that if they could not procure 'equal representation' they would be starved to death, it would not come within the character of sedition. Again, the inscription of 'No Corn Laws' left the jury to consider whether the meaning of it was

# Ninth Day – Saturday 25 March 1820.

that the corn laws were so oppressive that every means, legal or illegal, were to be taken in order to get rid of them; or whether it was a mere expression of disapprobation. In the former case, it would certainly be sedition; in the latter, it would not.

**Mr Justice Bayley**

As to the cap of liberty, it was one of the insignia of the Crown, and when the King went to Parliament an officer of state always bore it before him. It did not, therefore, of necessity, mean anything seditious. With respect to the stoppage of business occasioned by the meeting, it was positively sworn by a great mass of evidence for the defendants that it was not at all interrupted; and, certainly, if any interruption of business had taken place, in a great town like Manchester, it would have been easy to have called evidence to that fact.

[When his lordship had come to the testimony of Chadwick, reading the evidence at length, Mr Scarlett suggested that, if all parties would agree, the reading of the evidence might be very much abridged. All the parties agreed. His Lordship then said he would read the evidence and if he omitted anything material he begged it might be suggested, and he would read it.]

Mr BAMFORD: I leave it entirely to your Lordship's judgement. You have had a great deal of trouble.

Mr Justice BAYLEY: I grudge no trouble; you have a right to my services.

[His Lordship then continued to sum up.] He said the phrase sworn to by one of the witnesses as having been used by a person going to the meeting – namely, that they would 'make a Moscow of Manchester' – seemed to be inconsistent with the general intention expressed by the reformers on that day. There was every reason to believe that Mr Entwistle was mistaken in the expression of Mr Hunt about their enemies, as applied to the soldiers. With regard to the shout set up when the military appeared, it might be the shout of consciousness of innocence and a determination to remain on that consciousness, or it might be the shout of intimidation. Its nature was to be determined by the circumstances in which it was uttered. There was no other witness that spoke to threatening expressions but Mr Francis Philips. The multitude round the hustings appeared to this witness disciplined troops, ready to protect Mr Hunt in case of any molestation. If he had a false impression in this case, he might in another, and there seemed to be no evidence that the multitude were ready to fight, as the majority of them had no arms, the most of them being even without sticks.

The learned judge, having proceeded through the evidence given on the first three days, and the hour having arrived at which the court usually adjourned, said to the jury that he would desist, and adjourn the

# Hunt and Others.

**Mr Justice Bayley**
court if he fatigued them. No answer being returned, he continued for another hour, when an intimation was given that, as the business could not terminate today, it might be convenient to adjourn now (at half past seven.) This was assented to by the learned judge, and the court was adjourned till Monday at nine o'clock. Mr Hunt, before the court broke up, intimated a wish to the jury that they would in the interval abstain from conversing with others on the subject of this trial and also from reading the newspapers, which had been filled with libels on him during the last week. His Lordship expressed a confidence that the jury would attend to the wish now expressed; but if Mr Hunt was anxious to secure it under the sanction of an oath, he would put the book into their hands and swear them on both points. Mr Hunt thought this unnecessary. After what had fallen from his Lordship, he was sure they would attend to their duty.

*The court then adjourned till Monday at nine o'clock.*

# Tenth Day – Monday 27 March 1820.

*The utmost anxiety was manifested to obtain early admission to the court this morning as it was generally known the judge meant to conclude his charge early in the day. At eight o'clock, every part of the court was occupied. Precisely at nine o'clock, Mr Justice Bayley entered. All the defendants soon after took their seats. The learned judge throughout the day seemed oppressed with indisposition, and repeatedly took medicine.*

His LORDSHIP, in his commencement this morning, said that he had on Saturday night advanced so far in his charge as the evidence of Shawcross, who merely produced the placards. The learned judge then proceeded to detail the remaining evidence for the prosecution with respect to the part taken by Mr Hunt at the Smithfield meeting, the resolutions of which, on 21 July, his Lordship read seriatim; the jury were, from a consideration of the tone and temper of those resolutions, to form a judgement of the disposition of the individual who recommended them. He commented with severity upon that one which pointed out that the people were absolved from any obedience to the laws, except on such conditions as was therein expressed, from and after 1 January 1820. How far such resolutions were consistent or inconsistent with due subordination to the law, he left it to the jury to consider; as well as how far they were or were not calculated to bring his Majesty's government into hatred and contempt.

The next evidence was that which related to Bamford, and it only showed that he recommended peace and order; still, he was identified with the placards, if they thought them illegal. If a meeting for considering a reform in Parliament be illegal, he is an offender; but it was his Lordship's duty to tell them that it was not. There was no illegality in carrying sticks unless they were for an unlawful purpose; nor banners, unless their tenor was such as to excite suspicion of the objects of those who carried them there or concurred in bringing them there with an evil intention. As to numbers, they alone did not make a meeting illegal unless attended with such circumstances as did actually excite terror, or were reasonably calculated to excite terror. Such circumstances were forbade by the law. They had truly heard that where there was no law, there was no transgression. If the meeting was innocently intended, then the law was not violation.

You then come, observed his Lordship, to Dr Healey's admonitory remark to me to take care and not in anything I say prejudice your minds

Mr Justice Bayley

# Hunt and Others.

**Mr Justice Bayley**

against him. If I do, gentlemen, discard any expression of mine having such a tendency altogether from your minds. I mean to do my duty with integrity to the best of my poor judgement: if I err, and err with intention, then, gentlemen, there is that power to which I am awfully responsible.[202] Between the Crown on the one hand and my country on the other, I shall do, I hope, equal justice. The defendants, I trust, shall suffer no undue prejudice at my hands: my conscience will uphold me in what I have to say to you; and he who will sit in judgement upon all our poor acts will have to say what motive dictated them. I have now closed my observations upon the evidence for the prosecution and, before I sum up that for the defence, I wish to state that I have made a summary of it which will bring its leading points with less fatigue to your minds. If, however, I omit anything material for any of the defendants, or as I go on, shall miss one, touching upon any fact in their favour, then it will be only necessary to remind me of the omission, and I shall read in detail the part to which my attention shall be called.

Mr HUNT: Probably you will allow us, my Lord, to avail ourselves of your kind permission, as you go on, without deeming our interruption obtrusive.

Mr Justice BAYLEY: Yes, Mr Hunt, I not only allow you but desire you promptly as I go on to call my attention as you may please.

The learned judge then resumed his charge and said that, with respect to Bamford, all that had been proved in his speech was a recommendation to peace and order. There were no sticks in his group, save a few sticks carried by old men; there were women and boys in the throng; and it was for the jury to consider whether Bamford and these people, carrying their wives and daughters with them to such a crowd, meant to create on that day riot, tumult and disorder. With such an intention, nothing was less likely than that they would carry to the scene those who were the dearest objects of their affection. According to the evidence for Bamford, the people in his party, so far from being tumultuous, were peaceable and joyful; and the drilling, as it was called, so far from being illegal and nocturnal, was open and innocent, the only object being merely to enable the people to attend the meeting as conveniently for each other and the public as it was possible. The learned judge then enumerated the names of the witnesses who swore the parties on 16 August went to the meeting in the utmost peace and conducted themselves while there with equal tranquillity. There was no act of violence, according to these witnesses, committed by them; no violation of peace which would bring them under the reprehension of the law.

---

202  'Awfully' sic in both Dolby and Pratt's accounts of the trial.

# Tenth Day – Monday 27 March 1820.

So far in favour of Bamford. With respect to Saxton, the Crown had abandoned the case. In behalf of Mr Hunt, three different propositions were established in his favour by the witnesses produced in his defence. First, that the procession moved to the field in the utmost order – that all the exhortations to the people were in the spirit of peace, and that they imbibed and adopted that spirit in every respect. There was no insult, no offence given, except some few loose expressions only implicating the individuals using them and not fairly attributable to the bulk of the people. There were none saw sticks thrown, nor bludgeons, nor brickbats; no panic in Manchester; all was tranquil and free from apprehension up to the moment the military arrived on the ground. It was admitted that the people shouted when the cavalry came: some said this was in defiance, but, for the defendants, a different construction was put upon the act, and that it merely signified their confidence in being legally assembled, and their determination to remain in the discharge of what they considered a justifiable duty without fear of interruption. If the object were legal, and the means of effecting that object legal, then the people had undoubtedly a right to remain while so conducting themselves, and there was no proper reason why they should be disturbed. Under such circumstances the people had a right to stand firm.

**Mr Justice Bayley**

It was also deposed that besides the promiscuous group of women and children who came into Manchester, there were many other (to all appearance) respectable females who walked to and fro among the multitude without seeming to apprehend any danger from their situation. There was also in evidence that marks of respect were paid to loyal tunes, that not the slightest indication of disturbance took place, and that no stones, brickbats or sticks were flung up in the air during the day, nor hooting nor hissing at the cavalry. The learned judge then enumerated the witnesses who spoke to the peaceable character of the meeting. As to the drilling, if it were only intended to promote regularity and convenience at the meeting, then it was not illegal. He thought they might put out of their consideration that the words 'these are your enemies' were addressed by Mr Hunt to the soldiers in Dickinson Street, for that must have been a mistake; such an expression could not have occurred, according to the witnesses for the defence, or they must have heard it. This was the summary of the evidence for Mr Hunt.

[Mr Hunt suggested that, when he saw the black flag, he expressed his opinion to those around him that it was very foolish. The learned judge assented that it was in evidence Mr Hunt made that remark.]

The learned judge then proceeded to notice the cross-examination of the witnesses for the defence. With respect to the animadversion cast upon the use which Mr Scarlett made of Carlile's name in his opening

# Hunt and Others.

**Mr Justice Bayley**

speech, it was in evidence that Carlile was on the hustings. The allusion to him was therefore justifiable, and not, as Mr Hunt had said, an unwarrantable calumny. It happened, as it often did, that the opening speech did contain matter, which, though justifiably introduced, was not subsequently proved in evidence. When the learned judge touched upon the evidence given by the dissenting ministers, he applauded the observations made by them that they abstained from any interference in party politics. In their ministry 'charity thinketh no ill', and as teachers of the Gospel it became them to remain aloof from the angry politics of the day.

With respect to Moorhouse, it was in evidence from the witnesses called in his defence that he did not mount the hustings – that he was not in the carriage until after the hissing took place at the Star Inn and the police office, and therefore not responsible for those acts of contempt towards the magistracy, if they were intended as such; and it ought also to be borne in mind that one witness had an indistinct recollection that Johnson attempted to stop these expressions of popular displeasure by a motion of his hand. The evidence of Mr Tyas was very important to show the apparently pacific demeanour of Mr Hunt, for he deposed to his repeated and continued exhortations to peace when the cavalry came on the ground and while they were advancing to the hustings; that he used the words, 'By all means be quiet; don't resist. If they want me, let me go at once.' Then as to the panic: it would seem that in so populous a place as Manchester, if that panic at the congregation of such a meeting was any way general, a multitude of witnesses could be brought to state the fact, and that it would not be left on the part of the prosecution to depend upon the evidence which had been produced. Of this, however, the jury were alone the competent judges.

Of the general character of Mr Hunt's life, he must also remind them – they had the testimony of one of his domestics, who proved that his master was always in the habit of visiting the clergyman and the squire of his neighbourhood; that he has seen his company often, and never remembers any man riotous or intoxicated in his house; but, on the contrary, the utmost regularity and sobriety. He added that he had often heard his master's doctrines, but never any which had the smallest tendency to encourage the working classes to look for support to any other means than the fruits of their own industry. He had heard him say that he thought the sober and industrious man who worked from Monday morning to Saturday night ought to be able to earn a livelihood for himself and family.

A placard had been put in which was represented as being one of those in pursuance of which the meeting of 16 August was convened; it

# Tenth Day – Monday 27 March 1820.

represented the meeting to be called 'to consider the most lawful means of procuring a Reform in the Commons House of Parliament'. Such a meeting for such a purpose had certainly nothing illegal in its mode of convocation, unless in its accompanying circumstances it assumed a different character, and did either actually excite terror or became calculated, by its appearance, to inspire such a sensation in the mind of a rational person. The question, then, in the first place, was, was this meeting, or was it not, legally convened? Secondly, was it, or was it not, peaceable? If it were not so, a third question arose as to the persons who became criminal by their conduct. The meeting may be illegal in the first instance; circumstances may make it so in its subsequent conduct: but in either case there may be a number attending it whose intentions were perfectly innocent. It was the province of the jury to ascertain and arrange this distinction if the evidence bore them out in forming it; and by the evidence could they only ascertain and fix that point. A meeting to recommend a reform in Parliament was clearly legal, unless from its numbers and the subsequent misdirecting of them it assumed a different character. If the manner made the meeting illegal, then those only who countenanced that manner, and who went to promote it, incurred the displeasure of the law. With a view to consider that point, they must scan the evidence minutely as it affected each of the defendants. It must be clear that the manner, the numbers, the banners, the apparent military step had an evident tendency to produce terror, and then the individuals who had so produced the terror, or who knowing it, attended to add to its effect by the demonstration of their numbers, must be specifically designated just as the evidence, and nothing but the evidence, shall warrant their designation. If this terror be in this particular case excited, its existence or effect must be made out previous to the dispersion of the mob. It was suggested, on the part of the Crown, that it was not intended to produce the mischief at the exact time the meeting assembled; perhaps not on that day, but to have a prospective operation; that the public pulse was only to be felt on that day, and the full panic only prepared for a future. To judge of the legality of the motives which actuated the principal personages on that day was the arduous task entrusted to the jury, and they were to form their opinion upon the impressions which the evidence produced upon their minds.

With respect to the numbers composing the meeting, they were so great as to warrant anybody in rationally concluding that deliberation was not their object – that was actually impossible. One of the counts in the indictment charged the defendants with conspiring to bring together a meeting to raise disaffection and discontent in the minds of his Majesty's subjects and to incite a hatred and contempt of the laws and constituted

**Mr Justice Bayley**

## Hunt and Others.

Mr Justice Bayley

authorities of the realm as by law established. In the first place, for what was this meeting called? They had heard that it was by seven hundred of the respectable householders of Manchester, and for the purpose set forth in the placard: namely, Parliamentary Reform. What was intended to be proposed at that meeting? Where are the Resolutions? Which of the seven hundred respectable inhabitants was called to state the precise object of the meeting? They were therefore left so far in the dark as to the purposes of the meeting. It was no evidence before them that, on 23 July, Mr Hunt attended a meeting at Smithfield, where certain resolutions were proposed and adopted, which they had read in evidence. It was for the jury to say whether such resolutions were or were not calculated to excite disaffection. Did Mr Hunt mean to tender resolutions of the same import at Manchester? He must, one would imagine, have conversed upon the resolutions intended to be proposed there; he has brought no evidence to rebut the presumption, if the jury thought it fairly to arise, that he meant to pursue the same course at Manchester which he had just before pursued in Smithfield. If they thought that were his object, and that then the Smithfield resolutions were to be repeated at Manchester, then, quo ad, Mr Hunt's attendance at the meeting was illegal; but this did not implicate the other defendants, unless they were knowingly and wilfully assisting and co-operating for the same purpose.

The learned judge said he would next call the attention of the jury to the inscriptions upon the flags, and again remind them that such as were illegal could only affect those who carried them or who followed them, assenting to their meaning and character; to such only could the flags apply. They would see from a perusal of the inscriptions whether any end and which of them bore any similitude to the resolutions of the Smithfield meeting already adverted to. One of them (the Stockport) bore the inscription, 'Annual Parliaments, Universal Suffrage, Voting by Ballot'. If these inscriptions were merely to express an opinion in favour of such doctrines, and merely an opinion without meaning to act upon it illegally, then they were not guilty of a criminal intention. The same observation applied to the inscription 'No Corn Laws'. Many opinions prevailed respecting these laws and there was no illegality in expressing them provided the intention was not to intimidate or overawe the legislature. 'No Boroughmongers.' That phrase had certainly a reference to one of the Smithfield resolutions. 'Unite and be Free.' If that merely recommended harmony as essential to the enjoyment of freedom, it was harmless; if it meant to insinuate a unity of effort to promote an object inconsistent with the spirit of law, then it is criminal. 'Equal Representation or Death.' The same observation there again applied. It might be harmless with the meaning attached to it by one

# Tenth Day – Monday 27 March 1820.

of the defendants; but if it held out the alternative of risking life for the attainment of a particular object, then it was for them to say whether it was not a criminal allusion.

'Taxation without Representation is Unjust.' If by that it is meant to inculcate the opinion that it is criminal and unjust to levy taxes upon any man who has not a direct share by a vote in returning a representative to Parliament, then it was for the jury to say whether such an insinuation had not a tendency to excite in the minds of the King's subjects a hatred and contempt of the constituted authorities of the realm. There never was a time in the history of this country when every individual had a vote in the election of members to serve in Parliament. Every member who was elected was certainly considered not the representative alone of the place from which he was sent, but of the people of the country at large. He was not only bound to take care of the particular interests of his constituents but also of the general safety and prosperity of the kingdom at large. No copyholders, as such, had a vote; no leaseholder for a term of years, as such, had a vote. In all counties, towns, cities and boroughs, there were always a vast number of persons who had no votes, and had they a right, without incurring the responsibility of an illegal offence, to say that because the law conferred upon them no votes, that therefore they were illegally and unconstitutionally taxed? He entreated the jury, however, not to make applications to any of the mottoes which could in the result affect any of the defendants without feeling the full conviction that they were warranted in the application by the fair reason of the thing.

Another motto was 'Labour is the Source of Wealth'. That was a true inscription, and long may labour continue to be the source of wealth in this country, and long may the inheritance which it is so prosperously found to bequeath rest on the safe protection and stability of the law.

The learned judge recapitulated many of the leading points of his charge with respect to Mr Hunt; they had evidence of his being at Smedley Cottage on the eve of the intended meeting at Manchester on 9 August, that he had that day expressed himself in terms not very respectful of the local magistracy; he was not indeed found at Oldham, at Lees, or at Bury: he was at Manchester, and had given no evidence respecting the resolutions which it was meant to propose at the meeting that had been broken up.

Mr HUNT: May I submit, my Lord, that the resolutions intended to be proposed at that meeting were snatched by Nadin out of Knight's hand when the yeomanry came up to the hustings? We have since made every effort to obtain them, but without effect, and have served an order on the prosecutor to produce them – an order which your Lordship sees has been disregarded.

**Mr Justice Bayley**

# Hunt and Others.

**Mr Justice Bayley**  Mr Justice Bayley then resumed his charge. He said that with reference to Johnson, it appeared he had gone from Bullock Smithy to Manchester with Mr Hunt; he had appeared with him on the hustings, whether according to a previous concert, and for an illegal object, the jury, according to their construction of the evidence, must decide. As to the case of Moorhouse, there was evidence of still less participation. He was not on the hustings, if the evidence adduced on his behalf were to be credited. Wherever there appeared doubt of criminality of intention, should they decide upon fixing on any of the parties the guilt of any of the counts in the indictment, the safer course for the jury to pursue would be to record a verdict of acquittal. Swift was on the hustings, but there was no proof of his being criminally engaged there, and for an illegal purpose, if his witnesses' statements were correct.

Against Healey there was the black flag, if they inferred any criminality from that emblem. The inscription it bore was as follows: 'No Boroughmongers; Unite and be Free; Equal Representation or Death; Saddleworth, Lees, and Mossley Union; No Corn Laws; Taxation without Representation is Unjust and Tyrannical.' If these devices were, he repeated, calculated from their nature to excite in the minds of the people hatred and contempt of the authorities of the state, then they were certainly illegal, and the parties bearing them and concurring in them amenable to the law for their conduct.

With respect to Bamford, who carried the Middleton flag, nothing could be more decent than his conduct throughout the whole of the day. If the account given by the witnesses he adduced be a correct description of it, he was everywhere described as recommending peace and order. Then came the flags with the mottoes 'Unity and Strength', 'Liberty or Death'. Now these were, like the others, innocent or culpable according to the meaning affixed to them by those who brought and concurred in bringing them into the field. If that unity and strength would overawe the laws was the meaning attached, then it was an illegal emblem. Another party was led up by Wylde, but what their banners were did not appear in evidence. Jones merely put up the hustings, and whatever else he had done appeared, according to the evidence, as of little importance; he recommended what everybody would wish to see adopted: namely, union and harmony.

[The learned judge was then once more about to revert to the Smithfield resolutions when Mr Hunt begged leave, with great deference, to submit to his Lordship whether a chairman who merely received such Resolutions at the moment of the meeting and possibly without his concurrence in their formation ought to be held so strictly responsible for their contents.]

Mr Justice BAYLEY: The law imposes upon a man so acting the

# Tenth Day – Monday 27 March 1820.

responsibility to which I allude. I have in my charge, Mr Hunt, done fairly by you in putting to the jury those circumstances which may bear in your favour, as well as those which may have a contrary operation. I have done so, I hope, impartially; I know conscientiously: and I solemnly declare that if this were to be the last moment of my life, I should charge as I have now charged.

Mr Justice Bayley

The learned judge then proceeded to refer to the evidence and to enforce upon the minds of the jury that the main question they had to try was whether the meeting was, or was not, according to its manner, calculated to produce terror either in the manner in which it was formed, or in the circumstances that ensued before its dispersion. If they thought it was so constituted or conducted, then the parties with that view attending it were criminal, and the jury would specially record the species of criminality they attributed to them. The learned judge concluded thus: You, I have no doubt, have considered throughout this arduous trial, and with patient attention weighed the evidence on both sides. Between the defendants and the public, I know you will impartially and justly judge, laying aside, as I implore you to do, all considerations of party or prejudice which may prevail elsewhere, and give your verdict – as you upon your solemn oaths are bound to do – upon the evidence alone. I have only one observation more, and I peremptorily require attention to it out of respect to the court and out of deference to the laws: when your verdict is given, be it one of Guilty or Not Guilty, I require that no symptom of approbation or disapprobation shall be uttered within these walls; any such demonstration of feeling is a high contempt of this court, and calculated to subvert the principles on which juries should always act. If a judge or jury should ever act on the popular effect which any particular decision may create or travel out of the evidence before them to form their opinion, their conduct would not only be highly erroneous, but most criminal. Find no defendant guilty, gentlemen, whose guilt is not in your minds clearly established by the evidence; find no defendant innocent if you think the evidence establishes his guilt: wherever a doubt arises, the defendant ought to have the benefit of it.

## Verdict.

At a quarter past twelve o'clock, the learned judge closed his charge and the jury retired.

Shortly before five o'clock, the jury returned into the box. The foreman held a paper in his hand, and said the jury had agreed upon their verdict, which he read as follows:

Moorhouse, Jones, Wylde, Swift, Saxton: Not Guilty.

# Hunt and Others.

Henry Hunt, Joseph Johnson, John Knight, Joseph Healey and Samuel Bamford: Guilty of assembling with unlawful banners an unlawful assembly, for the purpose of moving and inciting the liege subjects of our Sovereign Lord the King to contempt and hatred of the government and constitution of the realm, as by law established, and attending at the same.

Mr Justice BAYLEY: Do you mean that they themselves intended to incite?

The FOREMAN: Yes.

Mr LITTLEDALE: This verdict must be taken on the fourth count.

Mr Justice BAYLEY: Let the verdict be so recorded. You find, gentlemen, on such counts as the words of your verdict are applicable to? You do not mean to find that they created terror, or incited it in the minds of the liege subjects of the King?

The FOREMAN: We meant, my Lord, to find on the first count, omitting a few words.

The learned judge then requested they would retire and look over the counts of the indictment again, and say to which count they meant to apply their verdict. The jury withdrew for a few minutes, and returned with a verdict of Guilty generally on the fourth count, and Not Guilty upon the remaining counts.[203]

Mr Justice BAYLEY: I take it for granted the defendants are still under recognizance.

Mr HUNT: We are, my Lord.

Mr Justice BAYLEY: Then let them now additionally, in court, enter into their own recognizances to keep the peace and good behaviour for six months: Mr Hunt in the sum of £2,000; Mr Johnson of £1,000;

---

[203] The fourth count of the indictment: 'And the [grand] Jurors aforesaid upon their oath as aforesaid, do further present the said Henry Hunt, John Knight, Joseph Johnson, John Thacker Saxton, James Moorhouse, Joseph Healey, Samuel Bamford, Robt. Jones, George Swift, and Robt. Wilde, being malicious, seditious, disaffected and ill-disposed persons, and unlawfully, and maliciously, intending and devising to disturb and molest the peace and common tranquility [sic] of our Sovereign Lord the King, of these Realms, and unlawfully, and maliciously aforesaid, heretofore, to wit, on the 16th day of August in the 59th year of the Reign of our Sovereign Lord the King, &c., with force and arms at Manchester aforesaid, in the county aforesaid, unlawfully, maliciously, and seditiously, did meet and assemble themselves together with divers other persons, whose names are to the Jurors unknown, to a large number, to wit, to the number of sixty thousand and more, for the purpose of raising and exciting discontent and disaffection in the minds of the liege subjects of our said Lord the King, and for the purpose of moving and exciting the liege subjects of our said Lord the King to hatred and contempt of the Government and Constitution of the Realm, as by Law established, in contempt of our said Lord the King and his Laws, to the evil example of all others, and against the Peace of our said Lord the King, his Crown and Dignity.'

# Tenth Day – Monday 27 March 1820.

Bamford and Healey, £500 each.

The parties immediately entered into their several recognizances.

Mr HUNT: What is meant by good behaviour, My Lord? It is a very indefinite term.

Mr Justice BAYLEY: The law defines it, sir.

Mr HUNT: I always, my Lord, wish to show good behaviour to the law.

Mr Justice BAYLEY: Then you have only to continue to show to it the good behaviour you observed in court during this trial.

Mr HUNT: I hope I shall always do so, my Lord; in anything that fell from me, it was far from my intention to give any offence to the court.

Mr Justice BAYLEY: You gave me no offence, Mr Hunt.

Mr HUNT: I never shall, I hope, my Lord. I have to thank your Lordship much for your patience during this long trial.

Mr Justice BAYLEY: You owe me no thanks for doing that which was my duty, nor in what I say to you do I do more than state a fact; I do not mean a civil expression.

Mr HUNT: If I move the Court of Kings Bench for a new trial, I suppose, my Lord, the defendants who are acquitted need not attend, though the indictment charges a conspiracy?

Mr Justice BAYLEY: I can't advise, but there was a case in Surrey – I forget the name. I'll recollect it directly.

His Lordship then turned round to the jury and said they had his best thanks for the patient attention they had bestowed upon this arduous trial. He was very much obliged to them. Then facing the body of the court, his Lordship added, 'I very much approve of the conduct of the court at the time the verdict was given in,' alluding, we presume, to the universal silence which prevailed at the time.

It was near six o'clock before the court broke up. Mr Hunt was cheered as he went home to his lodgings. He maintained, to the last, his wonted composure, and there was a calmness and respectful decorum in his manner at the close of the trial which excited much sympathy for his situation.

# Appendix.

# APPENDIX I.

## Proceedings in the Court of King's Bench, on Mr Hunt's Application for a new Trial.[204]

---

On Wednesday 26 April, 1820, Mr Hunt attended in Court, and stated to the Lord Chief Justice that he had several grounds of objection to the trial at York, and he now applied to his Lordship for a rule to show cause why a new trial should be granted to the defendants. These objections were briefly as follows:

First: That evidence had been rejected which ought to have been received.

Secondly: That evidence had been received which ought to have been rejected.

Thirdly: That evidence had been received of the training, drilling, and an assault at White Moss.

Fourthly: That evidence of the flags and banners had been received, which was not the best, as they themselves ought to have been produced.

Fifthly and lastly: That the judge has misdirected the jury.

These objections the Lord Chief Justice deemed sufficient to call upon Mr Justice Bayley for the production of his notes, which were so voluminous that the learned judge was several days in going through them. At length, on Friday 5 May, he concluded the evidence, and stated the leading features of his charge to the jury at York.

Mr Hunt was then heard in support of his objections. In the course of his arguments very long discussions frequently arose, and it was not until late on Saturday 6 May that he concluded. The judges deferred giving their opinions until the following Monday.

On this day, 8 May, the Court delivered its judgement *scriatim*:–

The Lord Chief Justice Abbott said he would deliver his opinion with as much brevity as possible.

The first point (he said) is the rejection of evidence as to the supposed misconduct of the military in the dispersion of the meeting, which evidence I think decidedly irrelevant to the matter in issue. The matter in issue was the intention and object of the meeting. I am, therefore, of opinion that such evidence was properly rejected.

The second point is as to the admission of the Smithfield Resolutions, to which the

---

204  Abstracted from *An Impartial Report of the Proceedings in the Cause of the King versus Henry Hunt and Others for a Conspiracy* (Manchester: Joseph Pratt, 1820).

# Hunt and Others.

objection is two-fold: first, that the best evidence was not produced, and secondly, that no evidence was admissible on the subject. As one of the defendants had been chairman of the meeting at which those resolutions were passed, I think that evidence was relevant to the matter in issue, and therefore admissible.

On the third objection, the Lord Chief Justice remarked that the question before the jury was the general behaviour of the persons who composed the assembly, as in all cases of riot and conspiracy; and next, how the particular charge was connected with that general character. Now, the evidence of the drilling and training, and the assault on an individual, was unquestionably evidence both as to the general character of the meeting and as far as affected the particular defendant who came from that place.

With respect to the last point, he did not think it necessary to produce the flags and banners, and that the inscriptions on those flags were more in character of speeches, uttering the sentiments of the meeting, rather than writings.

As to the alleged misdirection of the judge, he thought that the whole evidence was properly left to the jury, who had come to a conclusion warranted by that evidence.

Therefore, he was of opinion that the rule should be refused.

Mr Justice Holroyd and Mr Justice Best very briefly expressed their concurrence in his Lordship's opinion.

Mr Justice Bayley went over the same grounds, and concluded by stating that he persisted in the same opinion which he held on the trial.

The Attorney-General prayed the judgment of the court on the defendants, who requested time and obtained leave to send to Manchester for affidavits in mitigation.

They were directed to appear in court on the following Saturday, which they did, and stating that their affidavits had not arrived, farther time was allowed them until 15 May.

On Monday 15 May, the day appointed, they appeared in court and put in a number of affidavits, after which Mr Hunt addressed the court at considerable length, more in behalf of the other defendants than himself. In the course of this address, he said that it gave him great pleasure to perceive that Mr Knight was not brought up for judgement. He therefore supposed there was no intention of punishing him any farther. The Lord Chief Justice said in reply, 'Knight's case is not before us, Mr Hunt'.

After a few observations from the Court on some parts of his (Mr Hunt's) speech, Mr Justice BAYLEY pronounced upon the defendants the following

SENTENCE:

Henry Hunt to be imprisoned in Ilchester Gaol for the term of two years and six

# Appendix I.

months, and to find sureties for his good behaviour for five years, himself in One Thousand Pounds and two sureties in Five Hundred Pounds each.

Joseph Johnson, Joseph Healey, and Samuel Bamford to be imprisoned in Lincoln Gaol for one year, and at the expiration of that time each to enter into sureties for his good behaviour during five years, himself in Two Hundred Pounds and two sureties in One Hundred Pounds each.

Mr Hunt was then given into the custody of the tipstaff, and the keeper of the house of correction removed the other defendants.

# INDEX.

Abbott, Lord Chief Justice, 327-8
Abingdon Jail, 24
Andrew, Jonathan: evidence at trial, 119-21; as witness, 140, 190
Andrews, Henry: evidence at trial, 231-3; as witness, 173-4, 189, 296
annual parliaments, 58-9, 158, 271, 291-2
anti-Corn Law movement, 3
Ardwick Bridge 'conspiracy' (1817), 26
Ardwick Green, 70, 94
Ashton-under-Lyne: weaver strike (1818), 6; contingent to St Peter's Field, 137, 272, 273
Ashworth, John (Oldham engineer): evidence at trial, 86
Ashworth, John (special constable): killed at Peterloo, 86 & n, 126
assembly, lawful and unlawful, 49-51, 96, 157, 193-4, 289, 299-300, 306-8, 309-10
assizes, 29n
Attorney-General *see* Gifford, Sir Robert

Bagguley, John, 5 & n, 6-7
Baines, Edward, 6
Baines, Edwards, Jun: evidence at trial, 233-8
Bamford, Jemima ('Mima'), 22-3, 24, 26, 203
**BAMFORD, SAMUEL:** brief biography, 22-5; forms Middleton Hampden Club, 3; arrested and detained (1817), 10, 24, 26, 36; involved with *Manchester Observer*, 36; heads Middleton contingent, 56, 81-2, 161, 185, 191, 196, 199, 200, 205-6, 298-9; on the hustings, 118, 187, 197, 199; eyewitness account of massacre, 16; arrested, 17; charged and bailed, 18; journey to York, 30; trial (*see* trial, York Castle); speech in defence, 159-62; judge's summary of evidence concerning, 313, 314, 320; convicted, 322; bound over, 322-3; sentenced, 329; sent to Lincoln Castle, 33; later life, 24; as poet, 10, 23, 24; prison writings, 10, 24; 'A Song of Slaughter', 23; 'A View from Tandle Hill', 24n; 'Lines, Addressed To My Wife From The King's Bench Prison, May 15th, 1820', 24; 'To Liberty!', 10; 'Touch Him!', 23; *Account of the Arrest of Samuel Bamford*, 10, 24;
*Passages in the Life of a Radical*, 23-4
banners *see* flags, banners and ensigns
Barlow, John (Middleton weaver), 197; evidence at trial, 199-201
Barlow, John (publican in Deansgate): evidence at trial, 99
Barrett, Joseph: evidence at trial, 273-4
Barrow, Mr: cross-examinations (Thomas Fidler, 61-2; Henry Lomas, 63; Michael Bentley, 66; Mary Cadman, 67; Samuel Morton, 68; Roger Entwistle, 92-3; Matthew Cowper, 101; Joseph Mills, 108; Henry Horton, 111; Jonathan Andrew, 120; Thomas Hardman, 121; Joseph Green, 123-4; John Ellis, 125; William Hulton, 129); speech for the defence, 150-5; speech decried by Hunt, 188; examinations (John Tyas, 225)
Barrowfields ground, Middleton, 56, 82, 196, 199, 200, 205-6
Bay Horse public house, Manchester, 143-7
Bayley, Mr Justice: deprecates personalities and angry discussion, 142-3, 167, 170, 178, 195; quells disturbance in court, 130; questions witnesses, 133, 199, 208; rulings on evidence and legal process, 85, 96, 105-6, 128, 140, 143, 150-1, 156-7, 168, 188, 191, 229, 242, 245, 261-3, 279; rulings on objections, 54, 65, 71-2, 75, 122-3, 237; summing up, 243, 304-21; requests clarification of verdict, 321; sets bail, 322-33; at appeal hearing, 328-9; pronounces sentence, 328-9
Beckwith's gun shop, Spa Fields: attack on (1816), 232-3
Bellingham, John, 93n, 145-6, 146n
Bentley, Michael: evidence at trial, 65-6
Best, Mr Justice, 328
Birley, Mr J (Francis Philips's companion), 94, 95
Birmingham Hampden Club, 3
*Black Dwarf* (radical journal), 19, 33n
'black flag' of Saddleworth *see under* flags, banners and ensigns
Blackburn Female Reform Society, 7, 19, 25
Blackley, near Manchester, 74
Blanketeers' March (1817), 5, 26, 124, 220-1

## Index.

Blasphemous and Seditious Libels Act, 12–13
bludgeons *see* sticks and other 'weapons'
Bob (Hunt's horse), 19 & n, 71, 232
Brandon Hill, Bristol, 232
Brandreth, Jeremiah, 5–6
Brayshaw, Joseph, 7–8
Brettargh, John: evidence at trial, 229–31
brickbats *see* sticks and other 'weapons'
Bridle, William, 34
Brooks, Thomas: evidence at trial, 272–3
Brooks, William: evidence at trial, 273
Bruce, Lord, 36
Bryan, Mary: evidence at trial, 247–8
Bullock Smithy, near Stockport, 52, 61–2, 151, 174
Burdett, Sir Francis, 4 & n, 17n, 34n, 255
Burke, Edmund, 32n
Burnley, 25
Burns, William: evidence at trial, 275
Burtons weaving factory, Middleton: Luddite arson (1812), 207–8
Bury: contingent to St Peter's Field, 230, 264–5, 275
Bush, Michael, 15, 16
Buxton's house, St Peter's Field, 88, 92, 126, 134–5, 247

Cadman, Mary: evidence at trial, 66–7
*Caledonian Mercury*, 14n, 28n, 32, 93n
Carlile, Richard: bookseller, 253, 255; invited to attend meeting (16 August 1819), 255, 293; journey to St Peter's Field, 72, 225; arrives at St Peter's Field, 127; connection with Peterloo reformers, 169–70, 194, 287–8, 292–3, 315–16; prosecuted for blasphemy and seditious libel, 35n, 183, 253; *Peterloo Massacre (or Battle of Peterloo)*, 20
*Carlisle Patriot*, 75n, 78n
Cartwright, Major John, 3 & n, 21, 26, 212, 295
Cartwright, William, 145 & n
Castle, John, 4
Castlereagh, Lord, 12, 26, 145
Cato Street Conspiracy (1820), 5 & n, 6, 35, 158n, 194
Catterall, John, 74, 75n
censorship of the press, 8
Chadderton: contingent to St Peter's Field, 84
Chadwick, John: evidence at trial, 70–4; as witness, 173, 185, 297–8

Chapman, Thomas, 30n; stands bail for Hunt, 196n; conversation with James Murray, 77
Chartism, 9
Cheshire Yeomanry, 63–5, 96, 129, 182
Chippindale, William, 85, 86
Clifford, Henry, 36
Clifford's Tower, York, 31
Cobbett, William, 21 & n, 27 & n, 215, 219, 241, 253
coinage acts, 3
Coldbath Fields Prison, 4n, 34n
Collier, John, 155
conspiracy, charge of, 48, 156, 173, 305–6, 308–10
conspiracy theory, 9 & n
Corn Laws, 3 & n, 58, 157, 183, 318
Corresponding Societies Act (1799), 12
Courts Act (1971), 29n
Cowper, Matthew: background and character, 102–3, 124, 187; communications with Henry Horton, 117; evidence at trial, 100–3; as witness, 187
Crompton: contingent to St Peter's Field, 84
Cross, Mr Serjeant: examinations (Henry Lomas, 62–3; Samuel Morton, 67–8; John Shawcross, 77–8; William Morris, 81–2; Joseph Travis, 84–5; Joseph Slater, 145–6); re-examinations (Joseph Slater, 147); cross-examinations (John Barlow, 199–200; Elizabeth Sheppard, 203; Jacob Dakin, 207; John Shuttleworth, 218–20; William Thelwall, 257; Samuel Slack, 266; John Molineux, 267–8; Thomas William Sanderson, 276–8; John Robinson, 283)
crowd, the, 10
Crown and Anchor, Strand, 255
Cruikshank, George, 10; *Britons Strike Home*, 20; *Poor John Bull*, 8; 'The Belle Alliance', 7n
cudgels *see* sticks and other 'weapons'
'curse', of female reformers, 28 & n

Dakin, Jacob: evidence at trial, 207–8
Darley, Edmund: evidence at trial, 279
Dawes and Fogg (Bolton brewers), 102
death penalty for high treason, 6n, 35–6
Debtors' Prison, York, 31
Dickens, Charles, *A Christmas Carol*, 211n
Donoughmore, Earl of, 193
drilling, 141, 160–1, 182–3, 219, 254, 291, 309, 314; on Tandle Hill, 198, 199–200,

# Index.

206, 298; at White Moss, 54, 71–4, 76, 78, 297–8; Unlawful Drilling Act (1819), 12
Drummond, Samuel, 5 & n, 6–7
Duncough, James: evidence at trial, 88–90
Duncough's weaving mill: arson attack (1812), 88, 89 & n, 147
Dynes, Mr (from Ipswich), 33n
Dyson, James: evidence at trial, 196–9

Earnshaw, John, 229, 244, 245
Eaton, John: evidence at trial, 83–4
Edwards, George, 5n
election by ballot, 59, 271, 292
Ellis, John, 121, 123, 124; evidence at trial, 125–6
Ellis, Parson, 25
Elson, William: evidence at trial, 205–6
ensigns *see* flags, banners and ensigns
Entwistle, Roger: fails to appear when first called, 88; evidence at trial, 90–3; as witness, 140, 152, 176–7, 187, 311; suicide, 93n
Erskine, Thomas, 35 & n
Ethelston, Rev. Charles, 48, 179
*Evening Mail,* 119n
Exchange *see* Manchester Cotton Exchange

Failsworth, near Manchester, 87
Fell, John: evidence at trial, 247
Female Prison, York, 31
female reform societies, 7 & n, 14 & n, 15 & n, 19, 20, 25, 28, 29, 204, 225
Fidler, Thomas: evidence at trial, 61–2
Fielden, John, 25n
Fielding, Jeremiah: evidence at trial, 87
Fildes, Mrs Mary, 15 & n, 20
Fildes, William, 1
Fitton, William, 25–6 & n
Fitzpatrick, Michael, 118; at Smithfield meeting, 148, 149; evidence at trial, 148–50; as witness, 190–1, 294, 295
flags, banners, and ensigns: banned by law at meetings, 12; 'black flag' of Saddleworth, 14 & n, 26, 60, 86, 92, 103, 106, 216, 239, 240; Bury flag, 275; confiscated by cavalry, 64, 157; dagger motif, 60, 86, 109, 170–1, 194, 240, 287; inscriptions, 8, 14, 57–9, 101, 158, 240, 271, 281–2, 310–11, 318–19, 320; Oldham flag, 14 & n; Peterloo commemoration flags, 20; Royton red flags, 14, 225

Fletcher. Colonel Ralph, 48, 84, 161, 179, 247, 276
Frankland, James: evidence at trial, 201–2
free-born Englishmen, liberties of, 8
French Revolution, 10

Gagging Acts, 11–12
Gardner, John, 23
Gaunt, Elizabeth, 15n, 18
Gee, Mr (friend of Johnson), 254
George III, King: assassination attempt on, 35n
Gifford, Sir Robert (Attorney-General), 184–5, 286–7, 328
Gillray, James, 10
Glorious Revolution (1688), 8
Gordon Riots (1780), 299
Green, Joseph, 140; evidence at trial, 123–5; as witness, 177
Gregorian calendar, adoption of (1752), 59
Grey, Earl of, 6
Grundy, Edmund, 233; stands bail for Hunt, 195n; evidence at trial, 195–6
Grundy, Robert: witness expenses, 257–8; evidence at trial, 257–64

*habeas corpus,* suspension of, 2 & n, 3, 5, 27
Hadfield, James, 35n
Halifax, 8, 20; *see also* Skircoat Moor
Hampden, John, 3n
Hampden Clubs, 3 & n, 9–10, 12, 26, 27
Hampshire, John: evidence at trial, 209, 215–16
Hardman, Thomas, 125; evidence at trial, 121–3; as witness, 177, 178
Hardy, Thomas, 12n, 35, 36, 267–8
Hargreaves, Sarah, 15n
Harrison, 'Parson' Joseph, 63, 70, 149, 193
Harrop, Robert: evidence at trial, 239–40
Harrowby, Lord, 193, 194
Hastings, Warren, impeachment trial, 32 & n
Hawkins, William, *A Treatise of the Pleas of the Crown,* 299, 306–7, 308
Hay, Rev. William, 48, 122, 171–2, 179, 184, 247
Healey, Elizabeth, 14, 27
**HEALEY, JOSEPH:** brief biography, 26–7; at meeting with Johnson, 249; alleged threats against, 109; with Oldham contingent, 56, 248; with Saddleworth and Lees contingents, 85; and black flag, 106, 240;

333

# Index.

at Failsworth, 87; arrives at St Peter's Field, 57, 106, 107–8, 118; on the hustings, 119, 238, 241; trial (*see* trial, York Castle); speech in defence, 162–4; courtroom manner criticised, 32; part played in transaction, 303; judge's summary of evidence concerning, 320; convicted, 322; bound over, 322–3; sentenced, 329; sent to Lincoln Castle, 33

Heath, James: evidence at trial, 87

Heaviside, Michael: evidence at trial, 280

*Hertford and Ware Patriot*, 29

Heywood, John: trial for assault on, 79n; evidence at Hunt trial, 78–9; as witness, 185, 298

Higgins, Godfrey, 295

high treason, punishment for, 6n, 35–6

Hillier, James, 34

Hindmarsh, Rev. Mr Robert: evidence at trial, 280–3

Hobhouse, John Cam, 17 & n

Hobsbawm, Eric, 4

Hobson, John: evidence at trial, 273

Hobson, Jonathan: evidence at trial, 274–5

Hogarth, William, *An Election Entertainment*, 59, 184

Hollinwood, near Manchester, 88, 91

Holroyd, Mr Justice, 328

Holt, Mr: cross-examinations (Samuel Morton, 68; Joseph Mills, 108–9; Henry Horton, 111–12); speech for the defence, 156–9; examinations (John Hampshire, 209)

Hone, William, 35

Horsfall, William, 143 & n, 145 & n, 147

Horton, Henry, 124, 150; characterisation of Mary Waterworth, 15n, 114; evidence at trial, 109–18; as witness, 153, 159, 176, 187, 188

Horton, William, 124

Howard, Mr (dining companion of Edmund Grundy), 196

Huffman, Mr (Preston radical), 19

Hulley, John: evidence at trial, 241–2

Hullock, Mr Serjeant: examinations (Thomas Fidler, 61; Michael Bentley, 65; James Murray, 74–6; Francis Philips, 93–5; John Barlow, 99; Edmond Simpson, 100; Joseph Mills, 106–7; James Platt, 118; Joseph Green, 123; John Willie, 143); re-examinations (Thomas Fidler, 62; Michael Bentley, 66; Joseph Green, 125; John Willie, 144–5); cross-examinations (James Dyson, 197–8; Mary Lees, 202–3; Edmund Newton, 206–7; James Stott, 215; Henry Andrews, 232–3; William Nicholson, 241; Joseph Watson, 248–9; Sidney Walker, 255; Thomas Brooks, 272–3; William Phillips, 279–80)

Hulton, William: evidence at trial, 126–36; denounced by Hobhouse, 17n; denounced by Hunt, 171–2, 179–81, 182, 193, 195, 247; as witness, 158, 299

**HUNT, HENRY:**

**Before Peterloo:** property and land ownership, 231; first imprisonment, 36; as 'gentleman radical' and 'poor man's friend', 21, 232; talent for public speaking, 21; at Spa Fields meeting (1816), 4, 22, 150, 193, 218, 232; at Bristol meeting (1816), 232; religious views, 7; at first Manchester meeting (18 January, 1819), 220, 253; dines at Spread Eagle, Hanging Ditch, 77, 196, 267–8; at Smithfield meeting (21 July 1819), 7, 22, 52, 135, 148–9, 260, 290, 318; invited to speak at second Manchester meeting (August 2, 1819), 10, 13; mail intercepted, 13; at Bullock Smithy, 52, 61–2, 174; at Stockport, 52, 62–3, 65, 151–2, 154, 173, 233; travels to Manchester, 52–3, 67, 70–1, 152; prohibited from holding meeting (9 August, 1819), 13, 53, 71, 142, 147–8; reproaches magistrates, 53, 67, 70, 71, 189, 296

**Peterloo:** new meeting convened for 16 August, 13, 53, 67, 174–5, 189, 190; 'come to the meeting armed' exhortation, 190, 237–8, 296–7; at Smedley Cottage, 53, 79, 185, 189, 195, 208, 233, 319; presents himself before magistrates, 189–90, 195; journey to St Peter's Field, 56–7, 67–8, 72, 74, 97–8, 99, 100, 186–7, 222–3, 227, 233; outside Murray's house, 56, 76, 185–6; outside Star Inn, 56–7, 97–8, 186–7, 222, 227; arrives at St Peter's Field, 1, 15–16, 66, 127, 131, 223; on the hustings, 16, 90, 91, 142, 210, 217–18, 223–4, 225–6, 274–5; addresses crowd, 101, 110–11, 234–5; 'put them down' exhortation, 66, 90, 91, 110, 113, 138, 176–7, 211–12, 224, 230, 237, 274; arrested, 17, 114, 116–17, 209, 224; rescued from assault by Nadin,

# Index.

115–16; at Mr Buxton's house, 88, 134; bailed, 195n; imprisoned, 18; indicted, 18; celebratory procession across Lancashire, 18–19; presented with liberty cap at Blackburn, 19; triumphal return to London, 19; prospective parliamentary candidate for Preston (1820), 30, 231 & n; journey to York, 30; 'butchers of Peterloo' speech at Manchester, 30

**Trial and after:** (*see* trial, York Castle); request for delayed start, 166, 285; speech in defence, 167–95; charge against under-sheriff in calling jury, 168–9, 279, 287; seeks to comment on Mr Barrow's speech, 188; seeks to introduce Scarlett's Commons speech as evidence, 261–3; courtroom manner criticised, 32; part played in transaction, 302; judge's summary of evidence concerning, 315, 316, 318, 319; convicted, 322; bound over, 322–3; applies for new trial, 327–8; sentenced, 328–9; sent to Ilchester Gaol, 33–4; legal battles over his Breakfast Powder, 33–4; prison reform, 34; self-presentation and vanity, 21–2; trademark white top hat, 1, 28n; *A Peep into a Prison*, 34

Hussars, 15th, 6, 116, 129, 133, 182

Ilchester Gaol, 33, 34
Illuminati conspiracy, 9 & n
insurrection, fear of in upper and middle classes, 9

Jenkinson, Robert *see* Liverpool, Robert Jenkinson, 2nd Earl of
**JOHNSON, JOSEPH:** brief biography, 27; radical journalism, 8n, 28; co-founder of Patriotic Union Society, 25, 27; London bookseller, 253–4; surety for James Wroe, 266n; invites Hunt to address Manchester meeting (August 2 1819), 13; seditious talk at Bay Horse public house, 143–7; with Hunt at Stockport, 52, 63, 65; in Manchester (August 9), 67, 70–1; at Smedley Cottage, 53, 189, 233; journey to St Peter's Field, 67–8, 72, 76; at Star Inn, 227; arrives at St Peter's Field, 56, 66, 127; on the hustings, 66, 101, 119, 138, 223, 225–6; arrested, 114, 117; bailed, 269; trial (*see* trial, York Castle); speech in defence, 164–6; character references, 215, 264; part played in transaction, 301, 302; judge's summary of evidence concerning, 320; convicted, 322; bound over, 322–3; sentenced, 329; sent to Lincoln Castle, 33

Johnston, John, 5 & n, 6–7
Jones, Mary: evidence at trial, 246
**JONES, ROBERT:** brief biography, 28; prepares hustings, 101, 111, 120, 121; addresses crowd, 57, 109, 111, 121, 124, 125; arrested, 114; trial (*see* trial, York Castle); speeches in defence, 150–1, 153, 188; courtroom manner, 28n; judge's summary of evidence concerning, 320; acquitted, 321

Kay, David, 79n
Kendall, William: evidence at trial, 201
Kitchen, Mrs Alice, 7
**KNIGHT, JOHN:** brief biography, 25–6; itinerant orator, 51; forms Manchester Hampden Club, 27; inflammatory speech at Wigan (1816), 212; chairman of Blackburn Female Reform Society, 7, 25; involved with *Manchester Observer*, 28; speaks at meeting (26 July 1819), 248–9; refuses to help Jemima Bamford, 26; not seen in Bamford's company, 206; with Hunt at Smedley Cottage, 53, 233; journey to St Peter's Field, 72, 225; prepares hustings, 57; on the hustings, 101, 319; eyewitness account of Peterloo massacre, 16; radical journalism, 8n; trial (*see* trial, York Castle); part played in transaction, 303; convicted, 25, 322; sent to Lancaster Gaol, 33; case not before Court of King's Bench (15 May 1820), 328

Lancaster Castle and Gaol, 18, 33, 70, 75n, 78, 79n, 280
*Lancaster Gazette*, 20
lawful assembly *see* assembly, lawful and unlawful
*Leeds Mercury*, 6, 89n, 233
Lees: contingent to St Peter's Field, 26, 85, 118, 137, 216, 230, 238, 240
Lees, James, 208
Lees, John (Peterloo victim), 17n, 29
Lees, John (witness at Peterloo): evidence at trial, 246–7
Lees, Mary: evidence at trial, 202–3

# Index.

L'Estrange, Colonel Guy, 48, 128-9, 132, 133, 134
liberty cap: in antiquity, 192; as symbol of radical revolution, 10-11, 14 & n, 303; in façade at York Assize Court, 30, 86; insignia of the Crown, 311; presented to reformers, 7, 19
Lincoln Castle, 24, 27, 33
Littledale, Mr: examinations (Mary Cadman, 66-7; James Standering, 70; John Heywood, 78; John Eaton, 83; John Ashworth, 86; Jeremiah Fielding, 87; James Duncough, 88; Thomas Hardman, 121); re-examinations (Thomas Hardman, 123; John Shawcross, 147); cross-examinations (William Kendall, 201; Thomas Rothwell, 264-5; Isaac Wood, 269; Michael Heaviside, 280)
Liverpool, Robert Jenkinson, 2nd Earl of, 2, 6
*Liverpool Mercury,* 93n, 209, 212, 254n
Lomas, Henry: evidence at trial, 62-5; as witness, 181-2; death, 62n
London Corresponding Society, 3, 12 & n
Luddite activity, 5, 88, 89, 143 & n, 147, 207-8
Ludlam, Isaac, 6

magistrates *see* Manchester magistrates
Manchester and Salford Yeomanry: arrival and advance to hustings, 1, 128-9, 132-3, 135, 182, 214-15, 217-18, 223-5, 230-1, 235-7, 244-6, 251-2, 270, 281; massacre and dispersal of crowd, 1, 16, 29, 37, 191; praised by Prince Regent, 20, 264n; conduct not under examination at trial, 96, 105-6, 191, 242, 245, 289, 305; satirised in print, 20; *see also* Cheshire Yeomanry
Manchester Cotton Exchange, 211 & n, 213, 216, 219, 220, 238, 239, 241
Manchester Female Reformers, 15 & n, 28, 29
Manchester Grammar School, 97n, 98
Manchester Hampden Club, 27
Manchester magistrates: prohibit meeting (9 August, 1819), 13, 53, 71, 147-8; reproached by Hunt, 53, 67, 70, 71, 189, 296; learn of reformers' activities, 53-4, 55; Hunt presents himself before, 189-90, 195; assemble at Star Inn, Deansgate, 56, 126, 225; hissed at by parties en route to St Peter's Field, 56-7, 97-8, 186-7, 222; adjourn to Mr Buxton's house, 126; warned of growing fear and alarm, 123, 131-2, 139-41, 142, 178; observe assembly, 126-7, 130-1; and reading of Riot Act, 178-9; issue warrant for arrests, 61, 128, 131-2, 135; request military assistance, 128-9, 132; order advance of Hussars, 129, 133-4, 135; seating at trial, 31; ordered out of court, 48, 171; Hunt derides at trial, 171-2; conduct not under examination at trial, 288-9, 305; *see also* Hulton, William
*Manchester Observer:* publication, 7n, 27, 28, 36, 209; distribution, 147, 252; radical agenda, 91, 206, 212, 253, 259-60; articles by James Scholefield, 271; prosecution for libel, 266n; closure, 7n
Manchester Patriotic Union, 10, 13, 25, 27
Marshalsea Prison, 4 & n
mass platform, 6-7, 9, 10, 21, 22
Mather, Ruth, 15
Meagher, Edward, 29, 77
Metropolitan and Central Committee, 16-17
Middleton: contingent to St Peter's Field, 14, 56, 81-4, 161-2, 182, 185, 191-2, 196-8, 200, 201-3, 205, 206-7, 208, 298-9
Middleton Hampden Club, 3
Mills, Joseph: evidence at trial, 106-9
Milne, Mr (assistant to Solicitor of the Treasury), 73, 85, 117, 147
Molineux, John: surety for James Wroe, 266n; evidence at trial, 266-8
Montgomery, Peter, 119n
Moore, Henry, 143, 165 & n
**MOORHOUSE, JAMES:** coach proprietor, 28, 61, 63, 93; family man, 67, 152; at Bullock Smithy, 52, 61-2, 151; with Hunt at Stockport, 52, 62-3, 151-2, 154, 173, 233; travels to Manchester, 70-1, 273; journey to St Peter's Field, 90, 91, 93, 223, 225, 272-3; arrives at St Peter's Field, 56, 66, 127; possibly on the hustings, 119, 187-8, 272, 273; arrested, 155; trial (*see* trial, York Castle); speech in defence, 150-5; his account of events, 153-5; part played in transaction, 302-3; judge's summary of evidence concerning, 310, 316, 320; acquitted, 321
Moorhouse, Mrs, 272, 310
*Morning Post,* 34, 102
Morris, William (the 'Mushroom Sergeant'): evidence at trial, 81-3; testimony refuted by Bamford, 159-60; as witness, 182

# Index.

Morton, Samuel: insolvent debtor, 70; evidence at trial, 67–70
Morville, Lucy: evidence at trial, 208–9
Moscow, 'make a Moscow of Manchester' threat, 86, 106, 177, 265, 299, 311
Mossley, 138; contingent to St Peter's Field, 86, 118, 137, 216, 238
Murray, James: assaulted at White Moss, 54, 72, 74–5 & n; hissed at by Hunt's party, 56, 68, 76, 185–6; opinion of reformers, 77; evidence at trial, 74–7; as witness, 185–6, 188, 298
music *see* songs and music

Nadin, Joseph: hated by local radicals, 24; intelligence network, 76, 87, 107, 119 & n; at Peterloo, 66, 97, 133, 230, 245; issued warrants, 128, 131; requests military assistance to execute warrants, 128, 247; makes arrests, 114, 117, 224; confiscates resolutions, 319; rescues Hunt from assault, 115–16; not called to give evidence, 157–8, 171; in song, 11 & n
Napoleonic Wars: political and economic effects, 2–3
New Bailey, Salford, 17, 19n, 24, 28, 114, 155, 221
New Cross, Manchester, 229, 248
*New Times, The,* 112, 113–16, 117, 148, 149, 169
*Newcastle Courant,* 5n
Newspaper and Stamp Duties Act, 13
Newton, Edmund: evidence at trial, 206–7
Nicholson, William: evidence at trial, 240–1; cheerful and good-natured witness, 241
'nine tailors' expression, 53 & n, 67, 70, 71, 189, 296
Norris, James, 76–7, 103, 139, 147, 171, 195
Nottingham, 6, 166

Oldham, 138; radical meetings, 25; Hampden Club, 26; contingent to St Peter's Field, 14, 56, 84, 122, 123, 137, 238, 244, 248, 251, 265; *see also* Tandle Hill
Oldham Female Reformers, 14 & n
Oldham Political Union, 25–6
Oliver the Spy (William J. Oliver), 6
'on 'Change' expression, 211n
oratory, political, 3
Owen, Richard, 131, 132

Paine, Thomas, 7n, 35, 183, 253–4
Pearson, Mr (solicitor), 47, 198, 277–8, 295
Pentrich Rising (1817), 5–6, 35
Perceval, Spencer, assassination, 93n, 145–6, 146n
Peterloo: original meeting cancelled (9 August 1819), 13, 53, 147–8, 174; new meeting convened, 13, 53, 67, 174–5, 189, 190; size of crowd, 15–16, 100; arrival and advance of cavalry (*see under* Manchester and Salford Yeomanry); arrests, 17–18, 61, 114, 116–17, 131–2, 209, 210, 224; massacre, 1, 16, 29, 37, 191; panic of crowd, 114–15, 126, 226; fatalities, 16–17, 27, 29, 86 & n, 126; principal eyewitness accounts (Edward Baines, 233–7; Samuel Bamford, 16; Michael Bentley, 65–6; John Brettargh, 229–31; James Duncough, 89–90; Roger Entwistle, 90–2; Henry Horton, 114–17; William Hulton, 126–31, 132–5; Henry Lomas, 63–5; Francis Philips, 96–7; John Shuttleworth, 216–18; John Smith, 209–11; John Tyas, 15, 221–5; John Walker, 137–8, 141–2); relief fund/ committee, 17, 76, 220; material culture, 14, 37 (*see also* flags, banners and ensigns; liberty cap; sticks and other 'weapons'); responses to, 18–20; attempts to explain and justify violence, 20n, 37; anniversary commemorations, 29; significance and importance, 1, 37
petitioning, 3, 5n
Philips, Francis: witnesses assassination of Spencer Perceval, 93n; publishes account of Peterloo affair, 95–6; evidence at trial, 93–7; as witness, 140, 162, 177, 178, 221
Phillips, William: evidence at trial, 279–80
placards, 78, 147–8, 212–13
Platt, James: inveigler of forgers, 118–19 & n; arrests Moorhouse, 155; evidence at trial, 118–19; as witness, 159, 187–8
political satire and caricature, 7n, 8, 10, 20, 22, 59
Poole, Robert, 5n, 9
*Poor John Bull: The Free-Born Englishman Deprived of His Seven Senses by the Six New Acts?* (print), 8
press: censorship fears, 8; laws relating to, 12–13; *see also* titles of specific newspapers
Preston (parliamentary constituency), general election (1920), 30, 231 & n

337

# Index.

Prestwich, Nancy: evidence at trial, 242–4
Prince Regent (*later* George IV), 4, 5, 20, 165, 193, 264n, 295
prison reform movement, 34 & n

Quakers: barred from giving evidence in criminal prosecutions, 229 & n
quarter sessions, 29n

radical reform movement: and the English democratic tradition, 8; material culture, 10–11, 14, 37; political campaigns and debate, 3–7; radical press, 12–13 (*see also Black Dwarf*; *Manchester Observer*); reaction to Peterloo, 18–20; religious values, 7–8, 26; state repression of, 9–10, 11–13, 35–6; *see also* female reform societies
Read, Donald, 20n
Red Lion, Bullock Smithy, 61–2
revolution, fear of in upper and middle classes, 9
Richmond, Duke of, 158, 164, 193
Riding, Jacqueline, 28n
Riot Act, 178–9
Roberts, Rev. John Gough: evidence at trial, 280
Robinson, John: evidence at trial, 283–4
Rochdale, 138; contingent to St Peter's Field, 56, 72, 81, 82, 84, 197, 198, 202
Rockliffe, John: evidence at trial, 245–6
Rothwell. Thomas: evidence at trial, 264–5
Royton: contingent to St Peter's Field, 14, 25n109, 84, 86, 225, 251
Royton female reformers, 14, 225
rush-carts, 199
Russell, Mr (reformer), 8

Saddleworth: contingent to St Peter's Field, 14, 26, 84–5, 86, 118, 120, 137, 216, 230, 244, 251
Sanderson, Thomas William: evidence at trial, 276–8
Sandy Brow, Stockport, 63, 273
satirical prints, 7n, 8, 10, 20, 22, 59
*Saunders's News-Letter*, 266n
**SAXTON, JOHN**: involved with *Manchester Observer*, 28, 51; letter to *The Times*, 29; dines with John Hampshire, 209; prepares hustings, 57; on the hustings, 101, 107, 108–9, 112, 209; targeted by yeomanry, 29; trial (*see* trial, York Castle); not recognised by Samuel Morton, 68; speech in defence, 156–9; case abandoned by Crown, 303; acquitted, 29, 321; anniversary commemoration of Peterloo, 29; later life, 29
Saxton, Susanna, 15n, 28, 273
Scarlett, Mr: opening speech, 48–61; examinations (John Chadwick, 70–2; William Standring, 86–7; James Heath, 87; Roger Entwistle, 90–1; Jeremiah Smith, 98; Thomas Styan, 99; Matthew Cowper, 100–1; Henry Horton, 109–11; Jonathan Andrew, 119–20; William Hulton, 126–9; John Walker, 137–8; Michael Fitzpatrick, 148); re-examinations (John Chadwick, 74; Roger Entwistle, 93; Henry Horton, 117–18; John Walker, 142–3; Michael Fitzpatrick, 150); objects to request for delayed start, 285; objections, 65, 75, 122–3, 237; opening speech published in *The Times*, 151, 186, 194; cross-examinations (Edmund Grundy, 196; James Frankland, 202; Mary Yates, 203–4; William Elson, 205–6; John Smith, 212–13; John Hampshire, 215–16; John Tyas, 225–6; John Brettargh, 231; Edward Baines, 237–8; Robert Harrop, 240; Nancy Prestwich, 243–4; Robert Wright, 252–3; Robert Grundy, 258–60; James Scholefield, 270–1; Edmund Darley, 279; Rev. Mr Robert Hindmarsh, 281–2); objects to Commons speech as evidence, 261–3; reply for the prosecution, 284–304; claims of personal attacks by Hunt, 284–8; reads Smithfield resolutions to the jury, 293–5
Schofield, Joseph: evidence at trial, 265
Schofield, Thomas: evidence at trial, 238–9
Scholefield, James: newspaper articles and letters, 271–2; evidence at trial, 269–72; as witness, 298
Scottish Insurrectionists (1820), 35–6, 36n
secret societies, 9 & n
Seditious Meetings Act (1795), 11–12
Seditious Meetings Act (1817), 6, 12, 193
Septennial Act (1716), 164 & n
Shawcross, John: attacked at White Moss, 74–5; evidence at trial, 77–8, 147–8; as witness, 171, 298, 313; bankrupt, 147n
Sheppard, Elizabeth: evidence at trial, 203
Shuttleworth, John: evidence at trial, 216–21

# Index.

Sidmouth, Henry Addington, 1st Viscount, 6, 26, 193
Simpson, Edmond: evidence at trial, 100
Six Acts, 12–13
Skircoat Moor, near Halifax, 25
Slack, Samuel: evidence at trial, 265–6
Slater, Joseph: publican at Bay Horse, Manchester, 143, 144–5; evidence at trial, 145–7; as witness, 165, 302
Smedley Cottage, Manchester, 53, 76, 79, 83, 185, 189, 195, 208, 233, 257, 319
Smith, Rev. Dr Jeremiah: headmaster, 97n; evidence at trial, 97–8; as witness, 186-7, 190
Smith, John (cotton merchant): evidence at trial, 275–6
Smith, John (journalist): at Wigan meeting (1816), 212; at the Exchange, 213, 219; declines invitation to attend as speaker, 297; evidence at trial, 209–14
Smithfield meeting (21 July 1819), 7, 22, 52, 135, 148–9, 184, 193, 260, 290, 318
Smithfield resolutions, 52, 148, 149, 150, 253, 260, 313, 318; read in evidence to jury, 293–5, 313
songs and music, 14, 19n, 107–8, 155, 161, 198, 210, 275
Spa Fields meetings and riots (1816), 3–4, 6, 22, 35, 150, 157, 193, 218, 232–3, 290
Spence, Thomas, 4n
Spenceans and Spenceanism, 4
spies and informants, 4, 5n, 6, 9, 302
Spread Eagle (inn), Hanging Ditch, 77, 196, 267
St Peter's Field meeting, Manchester: chosen as site for meeting (August 16, 1819), 13–14
Standering, James: evidence at trial, 70
Standring, William: evidence at trial, 86–7
Star Inn, Deansgate, 56–7, 97–8, 126, 186–7, 222, 225, 227, 316
sticks and other 'weapons', 119, 120–1, 122, 141–2, 157, 171, 177, 190, 197, 211, 216, 234
Stockport: weaver strike (1818), 6; reform meetings, 5n, 62–3; Female Reform Society, 7; Hunt and Moorhouse at, 52, 62–3, 151–2, 154, 173, 233; contingent to St Peter's Field, 14, 28, 65, 66, 91, 93, 94, 95, 137, 154, 238, 239, 272; yeomanry troop, 64, 182

Stoddart, Dr John, 116, 150, 183, 193, 233
Stott, James: dines with Cobbett, 215; evidence at trial, 214–15
Styan, Thomas, 267; evidence at trial, 99–100; explosion at gun shop, 100n
suppression of radical thought and action (1810s), 9–10, 11–13, 36
**SWIFT, GEORGE:** shoemaker from Manchester, 51; prepares hustings, 57; on the hustings, 101, 109–10, 111; writes account of Peterloo event ('Swift Narrative'), 28; trial (*see* trial, York Castle); speech in defence, 162; judge's summary of evidence concerning, 320; acquitted, 321

Tambora: eruption (1815), 3n
Tandle Hill, near Oldham, 24n, 198, 199–200, 206, 298
Tate's grocers shop, Oldham Street, Manchester, 14n
Tatton, Thomas, 133, 135, 179
Taylor, James, 25n
Taylor, Michael, 9
textile industry, 5, 6
Thelwall, John, 12 & n, 35
Thelwall, William: evidence at trial, 256–7
Thistlewood, Arthur: acquitted on treason charges (1817), 35, 158n; challenges Lord Sidmouth to duel, 6; supposed association with Hunt, 194, 233; and Cato Street Conspiracy, 5n; executed, 35n, 158n
Thompson, E. P., 20n, 23–4
Thomson, James, *Edward and Eleonora*, 192 & n
*Times, The:* Tyas reports, 15, 28–9, 221, 226; publishes Scarlett's opening speech, 151, 186, 194; Saxton letter, 29
Tooke, John Horne, 35, 36, 267–8
trade unionism, 9, 25
transfer-print pottery, 18n
transportation (penal), 34n
Travis, Joseph: evidence at trial, 84–6; bankrupt, 84n
Treason Act (1795), 11–12
treason trials (1794), 35 & n, 267–8
trial, York Castle: venue altered, 29, 285–6; duration and number of witnesses, 29, 30n, 243, 277–8; public interest and attendance, 31, 47, 81, 105, 137; defendants arrive in court, 47–8,

339

# Index.

81; arraignments and pleas, 48; jury sworn, 48; seating arrangements, 48; legal teams, 48; opening speech for the prosecution, 48–61; case for the prosecution, 61–150; opening speeches for the defence, 150–95; case for the defence, 195–284; prosecutor's reply, 284–304; Judge's charge, 304–21; nature of indictment, 305–10; verdicts, 33, 37, 321–2; defendants bailed, 322–3; Hunt applies for new trial, 327–9; as theatre and performance space, 22, 31–3, 35, 38; class implications, 36–7; significance and contextual value, 1, 37–8
trial transcripts, 35, 37
Turner, John: evidence at trial, 202
Turner, William, 6
Two Acts, 11–12
Tyas, John: arrives with Hunt at St Peter's Field, 114, 222–3; witnesses massacre, 28–9; apprehended, 225; evidence at trial, 15, 221–7; as witness, 288, 298, 301; judge's summary of evidence, 316

universal (male) suffrage, 59, 271, 291–2
unlawful assembly *see* assembly, lawful and unlawful
Unlawful Drilling Act (1819), 12

vote by ballot, 59, 271, 292

Waddington, S. Ferrand, 8–9
Walker, John, 178; evidence at trial, 137–43
Walker, Sidney: evidence at trial, 254–6; death, 254n
Walmsley, Robert, 20n
Warren, Charles (Chief Justice of Chester), 194
Waterloo, battle of (1815), 2
Waterworth, Mary, 15 & n, 114, 214
Watson, James, 4, 35, 158 & n, 233
Watson, Joseph: evidence at trial, 248–9
weaver strikes (1818), 6
White Bear, Piccadilly, 90, 91, 93, 154, 272

White Lion, Stockport, 62–3
White Moss, near Manchester, 54, 71–5, 75n, 76, 78–9, 79n, 185, 297–8
Whitworth, John, 82
Whitworth, Nicholas, 145, 147
Williams, Charles, *The Smithfield Parliament ie Universal Suffrage*, 22
Willie, John: conversation with Johnson, 145, 146; evidence at trial, 143–5; testimony refuted by Johnson, 165–6; character impeached, 279–80; as witness, 302
Wilson, James, 35n, 36n
Windmill public house, Manchester, 218, 246, 247, 273
Wolseley, Sir Charles, 22–3, 52, 63, 65, 154, 295
women: among marchers, 69, 84, 154, 202–4, 222, 230, 238, 242, 264, 269; and female reformers' 'curse', 28 & n; present at Peterloo, 14, 15, 133, 199, 203–4, 214, 222, 225, 234, 242–3, 314; as trial spectators, 31, 47; *see also* female reform societies
women's rights, 8–9
Wood, Isaac: evidence at trial, 268–9
Wood, Robert: evidence at trial, 244–5
Wooler, Thomas, 241, 255, 256, 295
Worth, Thomas, 33n
Wright, Mr (magistrate), 247
Wright, Robert: evidence at trial, 251–4
Wroe, James, 8n, 25, 147, 266n
**WYLDE, ROBERT:** youthfulness, 27–8; little known about, 51; arrives at St Peter's Field, 106–7, 137–8; on the hustings, 108, 109, 241; trial (*see* trial, York Castle); part played in transaction, 303; judge's summary of evidence concerning, 320; acquitted, 321

Yates, Mary: evidence at trial, 203–4
'Year Without a Summer' (1816), 2–3
York, 20, 69
York Assize Court: description and setting, 11, 30–1; as venue for trial, 29, 31–2, 285–6; courtroom arrangements, 47

# NOTABLE BRITISH TRIALS SERIES.

| Trial | Date of Trial(s) | Editor(s) | Volume No. |
|---|---|---|---|
| Mary Queen of Scots | 1586 | A. Francis Steuart | 30 |
| Guy Fawkes | 1605-1606 | Donald Carswell | 61 |
| King Charles I | 1649 | J. G. Muddiman | 43 |
| The Bloody Assizes | 1685 | J. G. Muddiman | 48 |
| Captain Kidd | 1701 | Graham Brooks | 51 |
| Jack Sheppard | 1724 | Horace Bleackley | 59 |
| Captain Porteous | 1736 | William Roughead | 9 |
| The Annesley Case | 1743 | Andrew Lang | 16 |
| Lord Lovat | 1747 | David N. Mackay | 14 |
| Mary Blandy | 1752 | William Roughead | 22 |
| James Stewart | 1752 | David N. Mackay | 6 |
| Eugene Aram | 1759 | Eric R. Watson | 19 |
| Katharine Nairn | 1765 | William Roughead | 38 |
| The Douglas Cause | 1761-1769 | A. Francis Steuart | 8 |
| Duchess of Kingston | 1776 | Lewis Melville | 42 |
| Deacon Brodie | 1788 | William Roughead | 5 |
| The 'Bounty' Mutineers | 1792 | Owen Rutter | 55 |
| Eliza Fenning* | 1815 | Kate Clarke | 88 |
| Abraham Thornton | 1817 | Sir John Hall, Bt. | 37 |
| Henry Hunt and Others* | 1820 | Caitlin Kitchener | 89 |
| Henry Fauntleroy | 1824 | Horace Bleackley | 34 |
| Thurtell and Hunt | 1824 | Eric R. Watson | 26 |
| Burke and Hare | 1828 | William Roughead | 27 |
| James Blomfield Rush | 1849 | W. Teignmouth Shore | 45 |
| William Palmer | 1856 | Eric R. Watson | 15 |
| Madeleine Smith | 1857 | A. Duncan Smith (first edition) | |
| | | F. Tennyson Jesse (second edition) | 1 |
| Dr Smethurst | 1859 | L. A. Parry | 53 |
| Mrs M'Lachlan | 1862 | William Roughead | 12 |
| Franz Müller | 1864 | H. B. Irving | 13 |
| Dr Pritchard | 1865 | William Roughead | 3 |
| The Wainwrights | 1875 | H. B. Irving | 25 |
| The Stauntons | 1877 | J. B. Atlay | 11 |

# Notable British Trials Series.

| | | | |
|---|---|---|---|
| Kate Webster | 1879 | Elliott O'Donnell | 35 |
| City of Glasgow Bank Directors | 1879 | William Wallace | 2 |
| Charles Peace | 1879 | W. Teignmouth Shore | 39 |
| Percy Lefroy Mapleton* | 1881 | Adam Wood | 86 |
| Dr Lamson | 1882 | H. L. Adam | 18 |
| Adelaide Bartlett | 1886 | Sir John Hall, Bt. | 41 |
| Israel Lipski* | 1887 | M. W. Oldridge | 84 |
| Mrs Maybrick | 1889 | H. B. Irving | 17 |
| John Watson Laurie | 1889 | William Roughead | 57 |
| The Baccarat Case | 1891 | W. Teignmouth Shore | 56 |
| Thomas Neill Cream | 1892 | W. Teignmouth Shore | 31 |
| Alfred John Monson | 1893 | J. W. More | 7 |
| Oscar Wilde | 1895 | H. Montgomery Hyde | 70 |
| Louise Masset* | 1899 | Kate Clarke | 85 |
| William Gardiner | 1903 | William Henderson | 63 |
| George Chapman | 1903 | H. L. Adam | 50 |
| Samuel Herbert Dougal | 1903 | F. Tennyson Jesse | 44 |
| The 'Veronica' Mutineers | 1903 | Prof. G. W. Keeton and John Cameron | 76 |
| Adolf Beck | 1904 | Eric R. Watson | 33 |
| Robert Wood | 1907 | Basil Hogarth | 65 |
| Oscar Slater | 1909-1928 | William Roughead | 10 |
| Hawley Harvey Crippen | 1910 | Filson Young | 24 |
| John Alexander Dickman | 1910 | S. O. Rowan-Hamilton | 21 |
| Steinie Morrison | 1911 | H. Fletcher Moulton | 28 |
| The Seddons | 1912 | Filson Young | 20 |
| George Joseph Smith | 1915 | Eric R. Watson | 29 |
| Sir Roger Casement | 1916 | George H. Knott (first and second editions) | |
| | | H. Montgomery Hyde (third edition) | 23 |
| Ronald Light* | 1920 | Sally Smith | 87 |
| Harold Greenwood | 1920 | Winifred Duke | 52 |
| Field and Gray | 1920 | Winifred Duke | 67 |
| Bywaters and Thompson | 1922 | Filson Young | 32 |
| Ronald True | 1922 | Donald Carswell | 36 |
| Herbert Rowse Armstrong | 1922 | Filson Young | 40 |
| Jean Pierre Vaquier | 1924 | R. H. Blundell | 47 |
| John Donald Merrett | 1927 | William Roughead | 46 |
| Browne and Kennedy | 1927 | W. Teignmouth Shore | 49 |

# Notable British Trials Series.

| | | | |
|---|---|---|---|
| Benjamin Knowles | 1928 | Albert Lieck | 60 |
| Sidney Harry Fox | 1930 | F. Tennyson Jesse | 62 |
| Alfred Arthur Rouse | 1931 | Helena Normanton | 54 |
| The Royal Mail Case | 1931 | Collin Brooks | 58 |
| Jeannie Donald | 1934 | J. G. Wilson | 79 |
| Rattenbury and Stoner | 1935 | F. Tennyson Jesse | 64 |
| Buck Ruxton | 1936 | Prof. H. Wilson | 66 |
| Frederick Nodder | 1937 | Winifred Duke | 72 |
| Patrick Carraher | 1938-1946 | George Blake | 73 |
| Peter Barnes and Others | 1939 | Letitia Fairfield | 77 |
| August Sangret | 1943 | MacDonald Critchley | 83 |
| William Joyce | 1945 | J. W. Hall | 68 |
| Neville George Cleveley Heath | 1946 | MacDonald Critchley | 75 |
| Ley and Smith | 1947 | F. Tennyson Jesse | 69 |
| James Camb | 1948 | G. Clark | 71 |
| Peter Griffiths | 1948 | George Godwin | 74 |
| John George Haigh | 1949 | Lord Dunboyne | 78 |
| Evans and Christie | 1950 & 1953 | F. Tennyson Jesse | 82 |
| John Thomas Straffen | 1952 | Letitia Fairfield and Eric P. Fullbrook | 80 |
| Craig and Bentley | 1952 | H. Montgomery Hyde | 81 |

\* New series.

In preparation:
The Mannings (ed. Linda Stratmann)
Frederick Baker (ed. David Green)

www.ingramcontent.com/pod-product-compliance
Lightning Source LLC
Chambersburg PA
CBHW021830220426
43663CB00005B/190